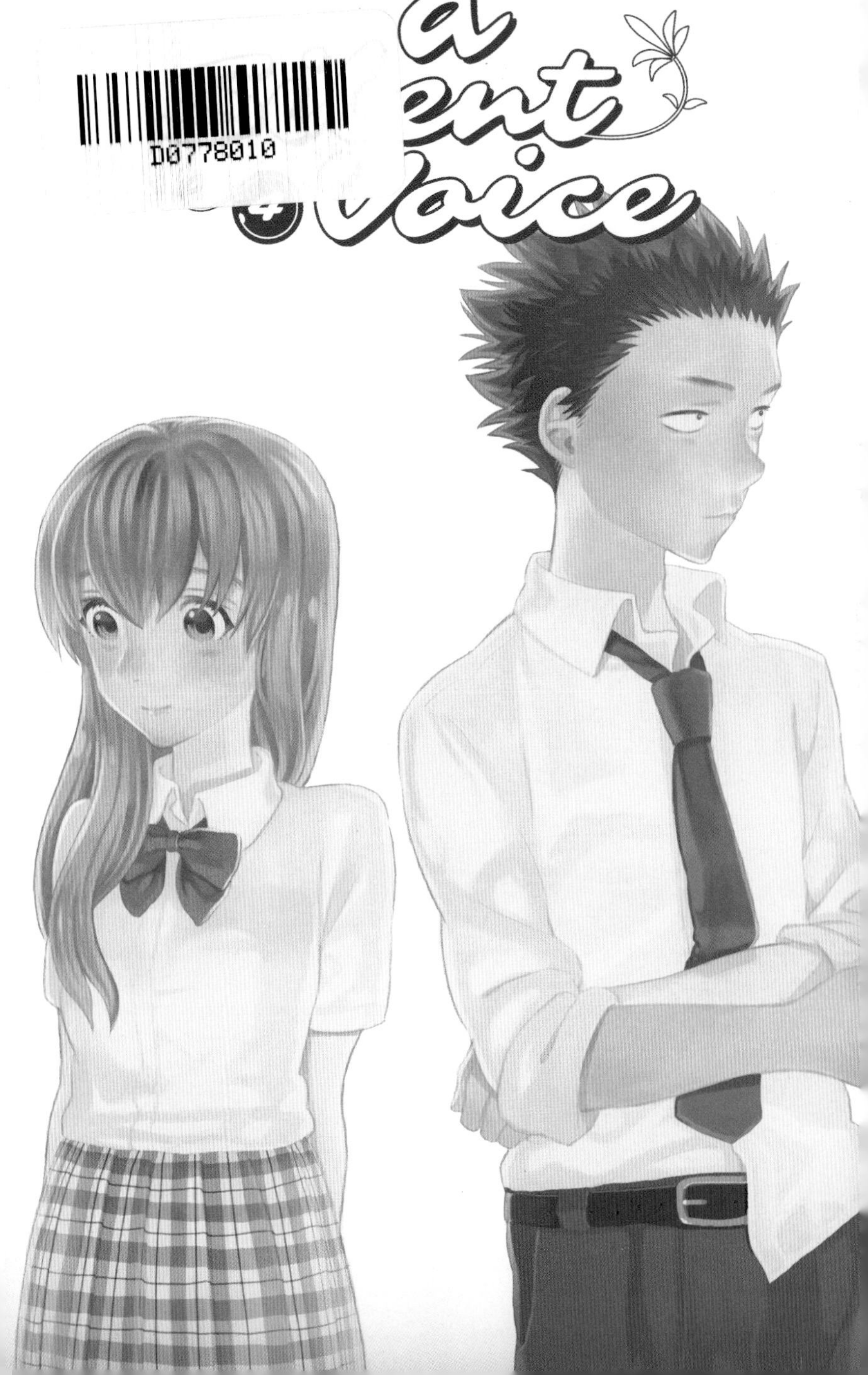
a
ent
Voice
4

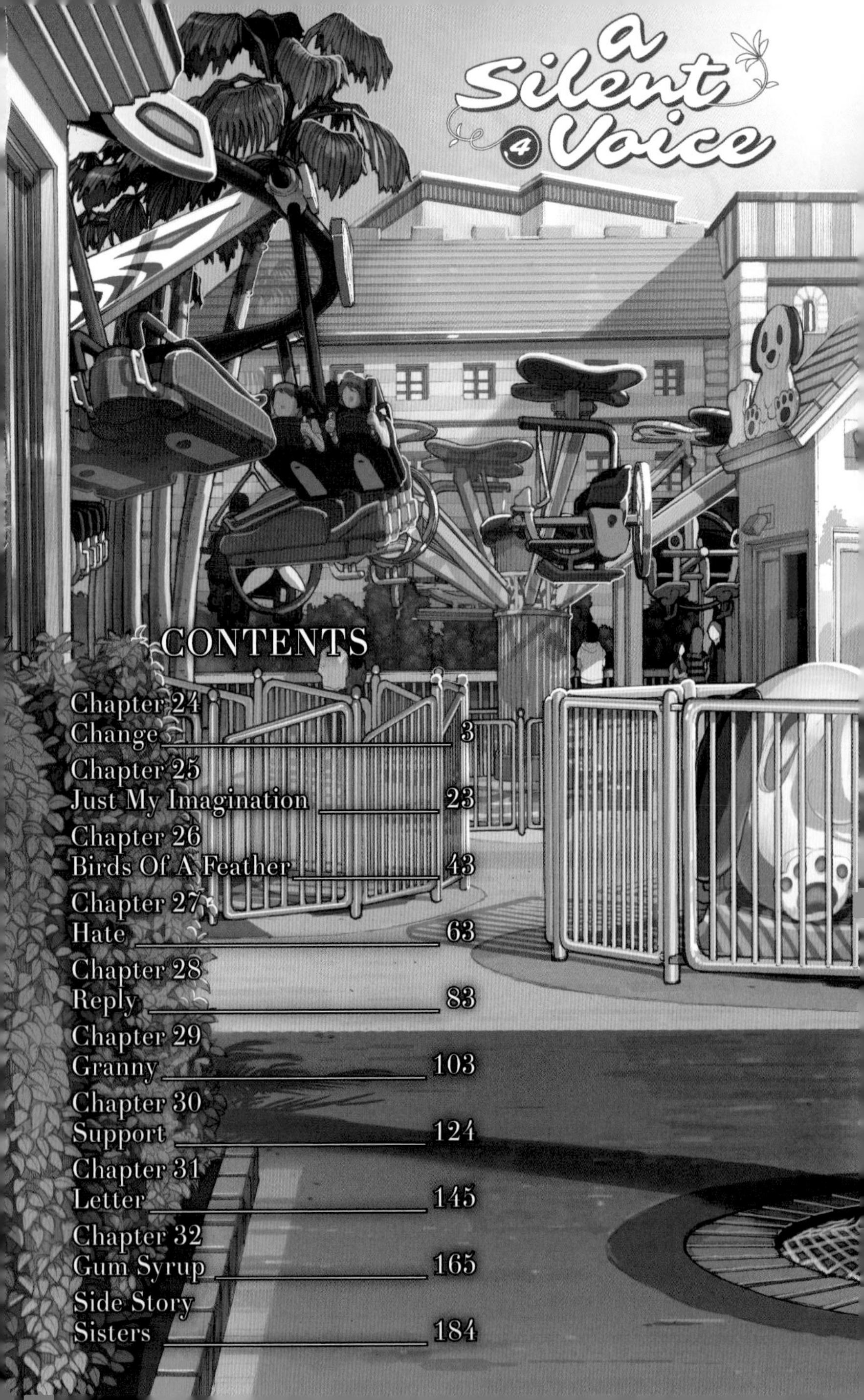

a Silent Voice 4

CONTENTS

CHAPTER 24: CHANGE

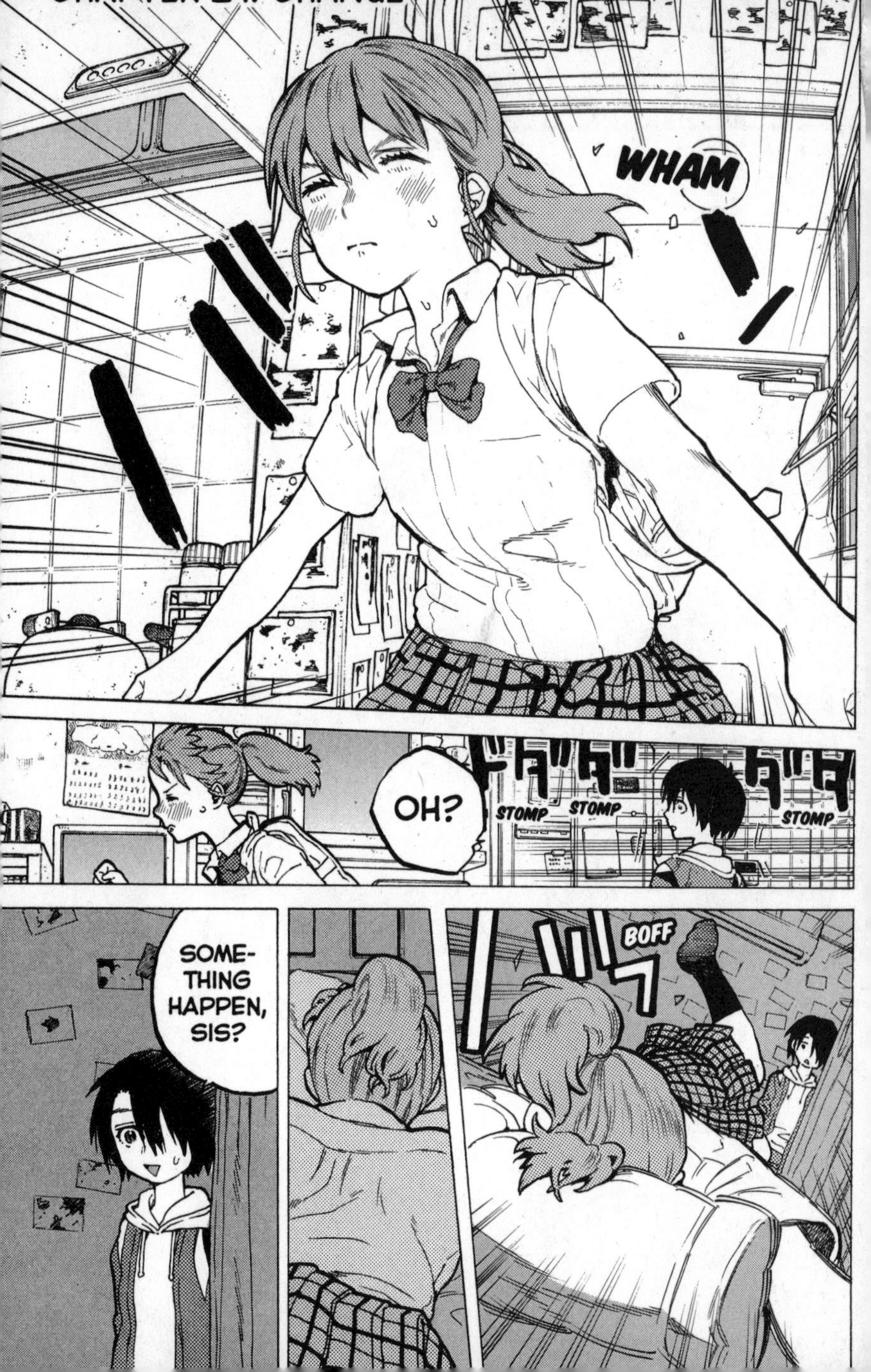
WHAM
STOMP
STOMP
STOMP
OH?
BOFF
SOME-THING HAPPEN, SIS?

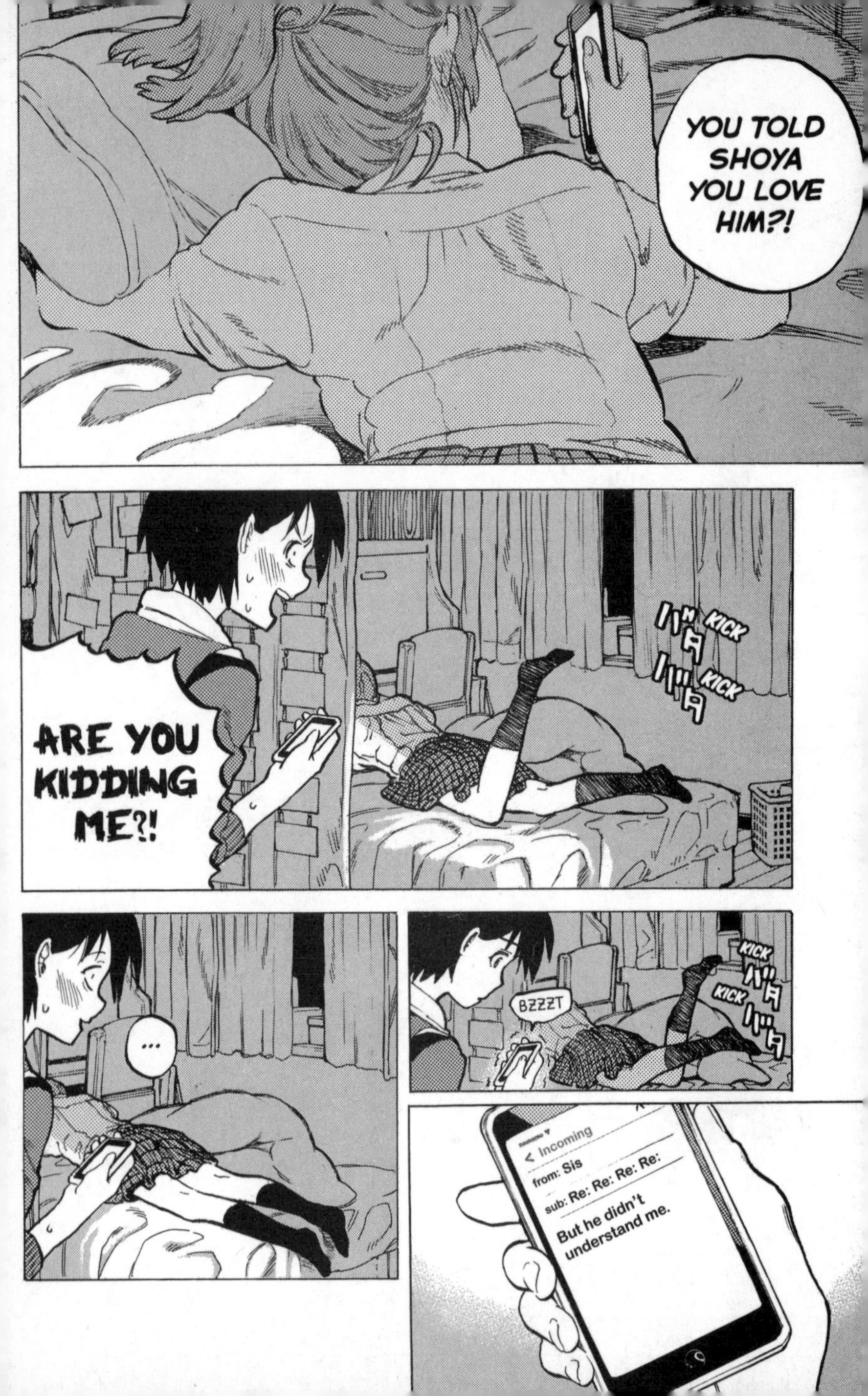
YOU TOLD SHOYA YOU LOVE HIM?!
ARE YOU KIDDING ME?!
バタ KICK
バタ KICK
BZZZT
KICK バタ
KICK バタ
< Incoming
from: Sis
sub: Re: Re: Re: Re:
But he didn't understand me.
...

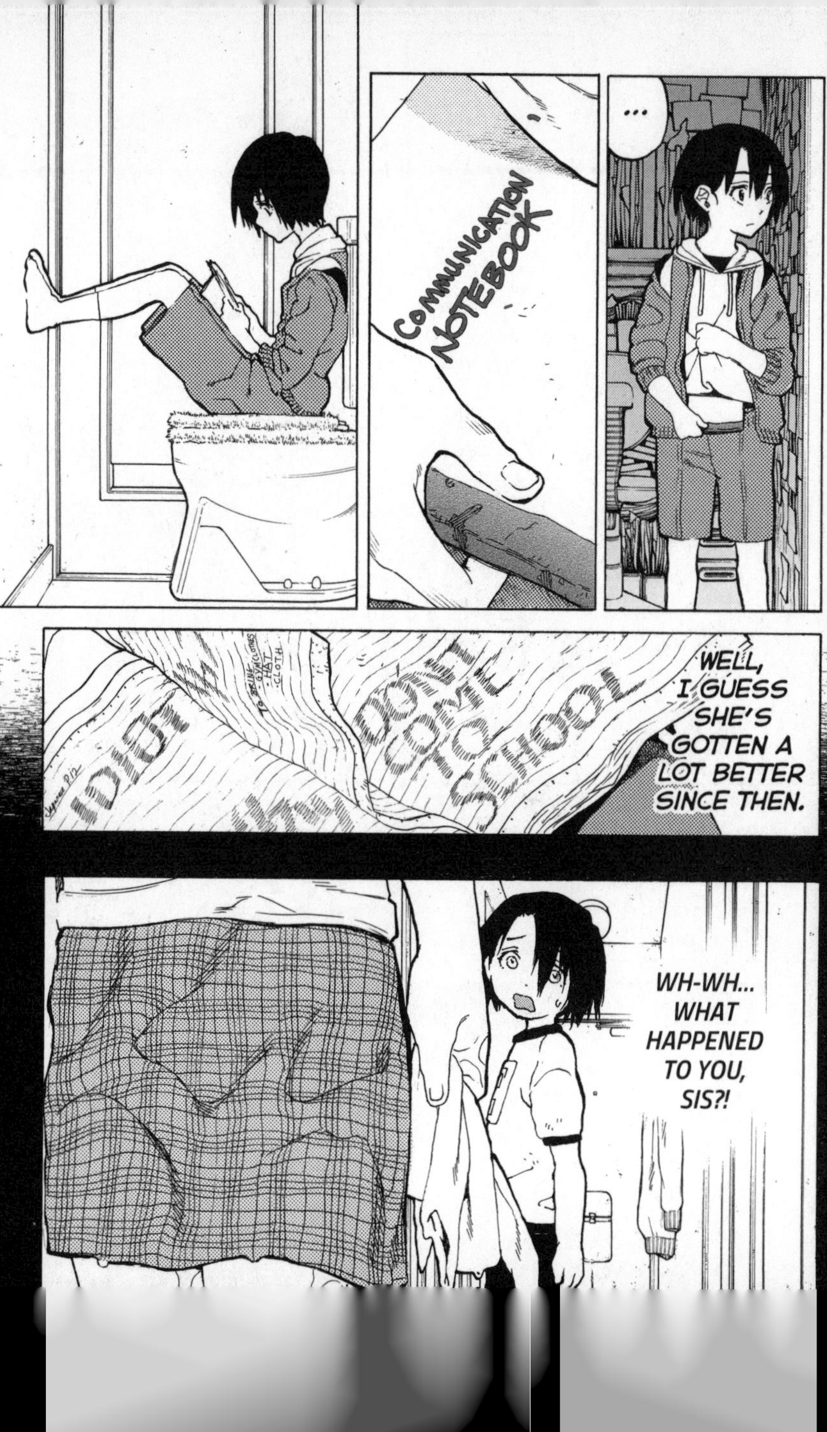
...
COMMUNICATION NOTEBOOK
WELL, I GUESS SHE'S GOTTEN A LOT BETTER SINCE THEN.
DON'T COME TO SCHOOL
TO BRING -GYM CLOTHES -HAT -CLOTH
IDIOT
WH-WH... WHAT HAPPENED TO YOU, SIS?!

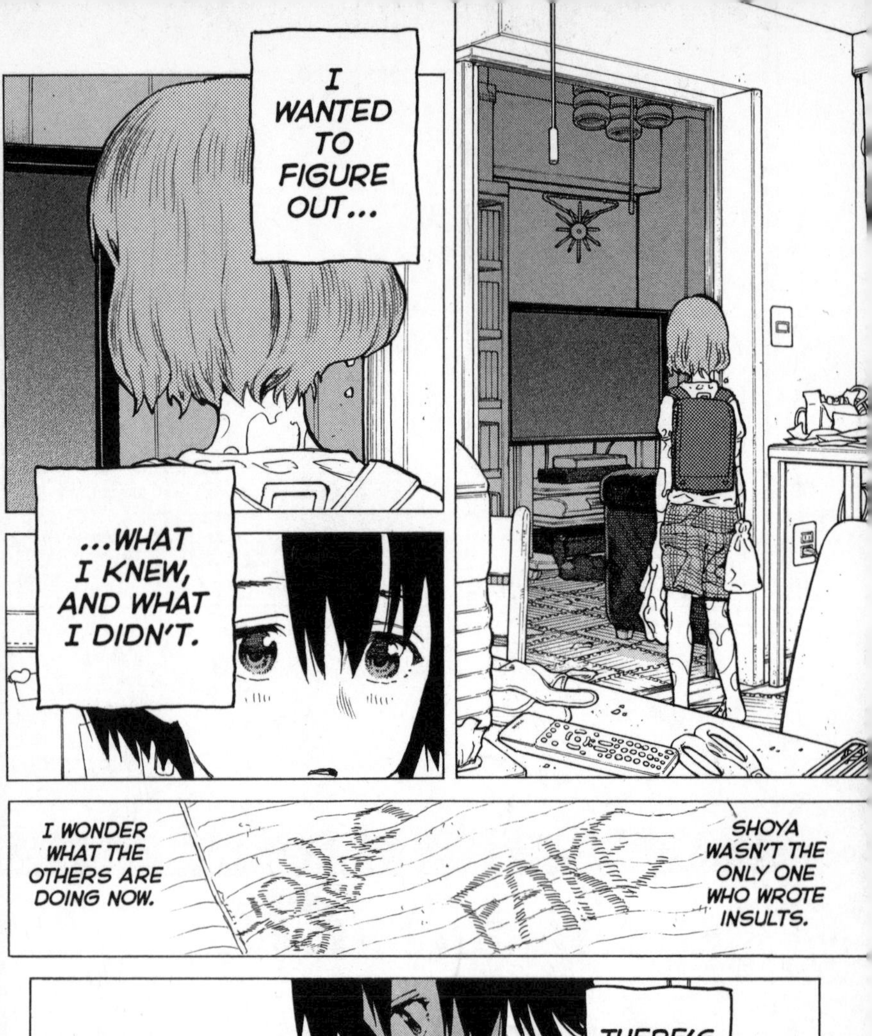
I WANTED TO FIGURE OUT...
...WHAT I KNEW, AND WHAT I DIDN'T.
SHOYA WASN'T THE ONLY ONE WHO WROTE INSULTS.
I WONDER WHAT THE OTHERS ARE DOING NOW.
THERE'S STILL A LOT...
...I DON'T KNOW.

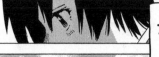

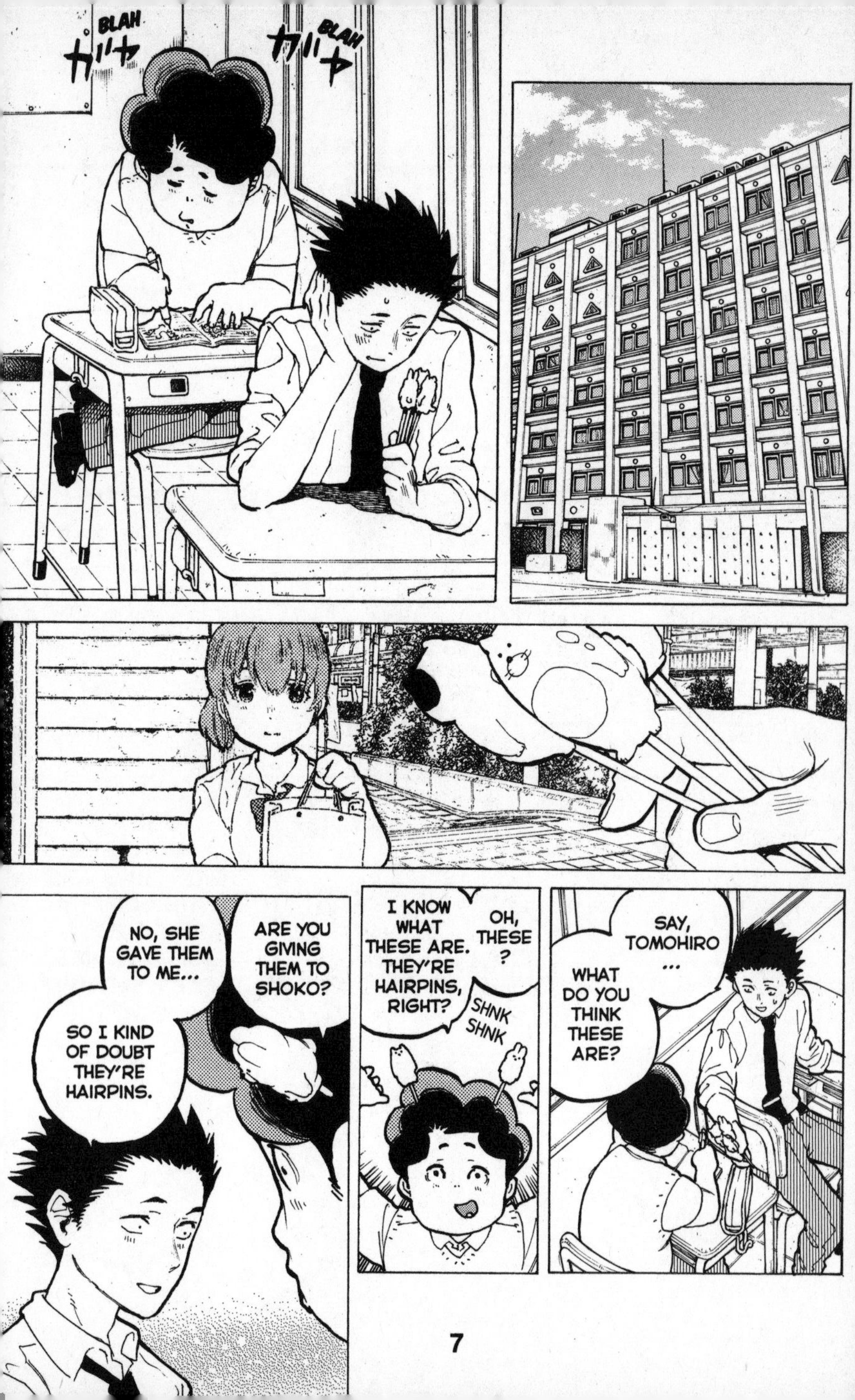
BLAH
BLAH
SAY, TOMOHIRO ...
WHAT DO YOU THINK THESE ARE?
OH, THESE?
I KNOW WHAT THESE ARE. THEY'RE HAIRPINS, RIGHT?
SHNK SHNK
ARE YOU GIVING THEM TO SHOKO?
NO, SHE GAVE THEM TO ME...
SO I KIND OF DOUBT THEY'RE HAIRPINS.

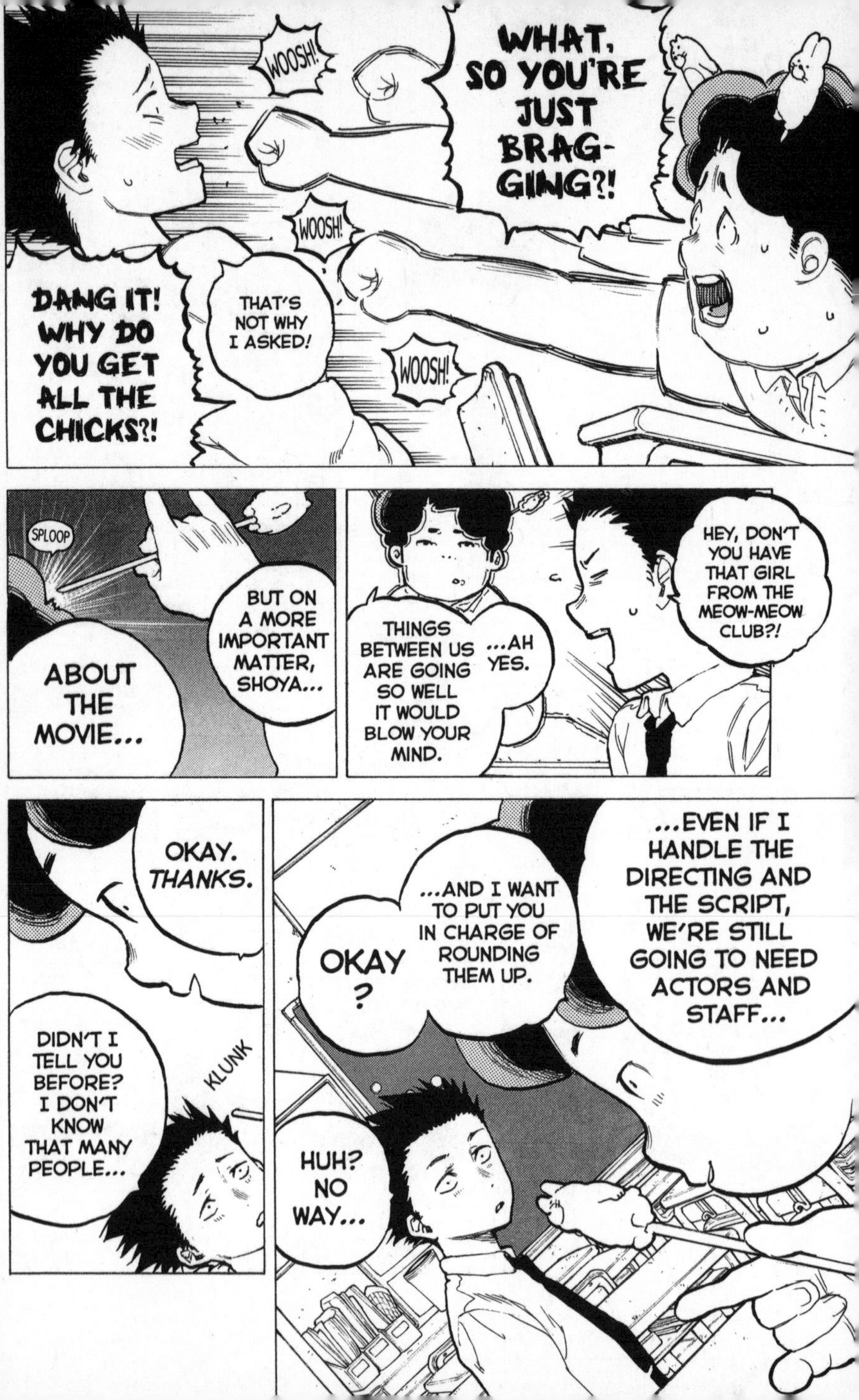
WHAT, SO YOU'RE JUST BRAG-GING?!
WOOSH!
WOOSH!
WOOSH!
THAT'S NOT WHY I ASKED!
DANG IT! WHY DO YOU GET ALL THE CHICKS?!
HEY, DON'T YOU HAVE THAT GIRL FROM THE MEOW-MEOW CLUB?!
...AH YES.
THINGS BETWEEN US ARE GOING SO WELL IT WOULD BLOW YOUR MIND.
SPLOOP
BUT ON A MORE IMPORTANT MATTER, SHOYA...
ABOUT THE MOVIE...
...EVEN IF I HANDLE THE DIRECTING AND THE SCRIPT, WE'RE STILL GOING TO NEED ACTORS AND STAFF...
...AND I WANT TO PUT YOU IN CHARGE OF ROUNDING THEM UP.
OKAY?
HUH? NO WAY...
OKAY. THANKS.
DIDN'T I TELL YOU BEFORE? I DON'T KNOW THAT MANY PEOPLE...
KLUNK

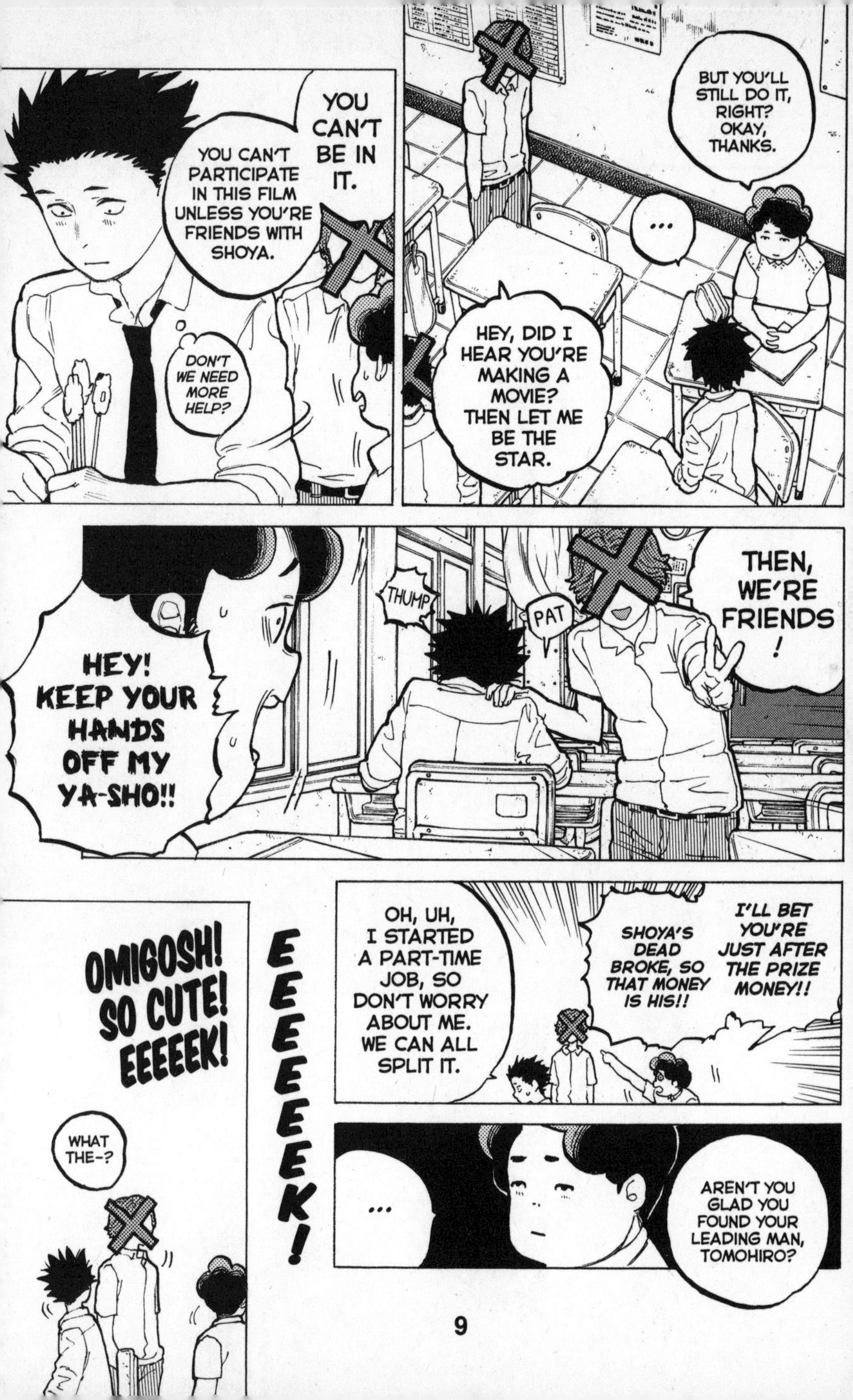

BUT YOU'LL STILL DO IT, RIGHT? OKAY, THANKS.
...
HEY, DID I HEAR YOU'RE MAKING A MOVIE? THEN LET ME BE THE STAR.
YOU CAN'T BE IN IT.
YOU CAN'T PARTICIPATE IN THIS FILM UNLESS YOU'RE FRIENDS WITH SHOYA.
DON'T WE NEED MORE HELP?
THEN, WE'RE FRIENDS!
PAT
THUMP
HEY! KEEP YOUR HANDS OFF MY YA-SHO!!
I'LL BET YOU'RE JUST AFTER THE PRIZE MONEY!!
SHOYA'S DEAD BROKE, SO THAT MONEY IS HIS!!
OH, UH, I STARTED A PART-TIME JOB, SO DON'T WORRY ABOUT ME. WE CAN ALL SPLIT IT.
AREN'T YOU GLAD YOU FOUND YOUR LEADING MAN, TOMOHIRO?
...
EEEEEEEK!
OMIGOSH! SO CUTE! EEEEEK!
WHAT THE-?

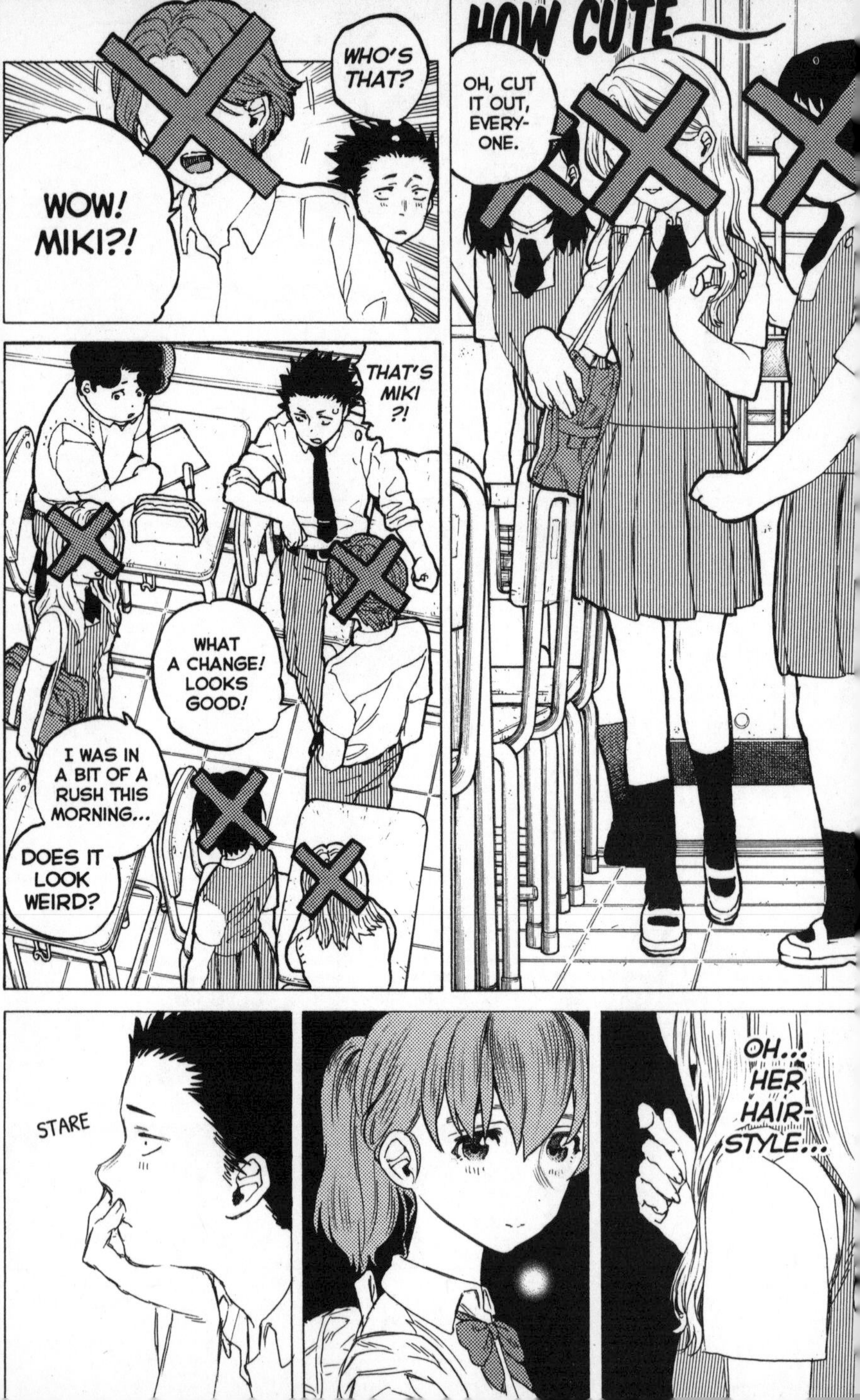
HOW CUTE~
OH, CUT IT OUT, EVERY-ONE.
WHO'S THAT?
WOW! MIKI?!
THAT'S MIKI ?!
WHAT A CHANGE! LOOKS GOOD!
I WAS IN A BIT OF A RUSH THIS MORNING...
DOES IT LOOK WEIRD?
OH... HER HAIR-STYLE...
STARE

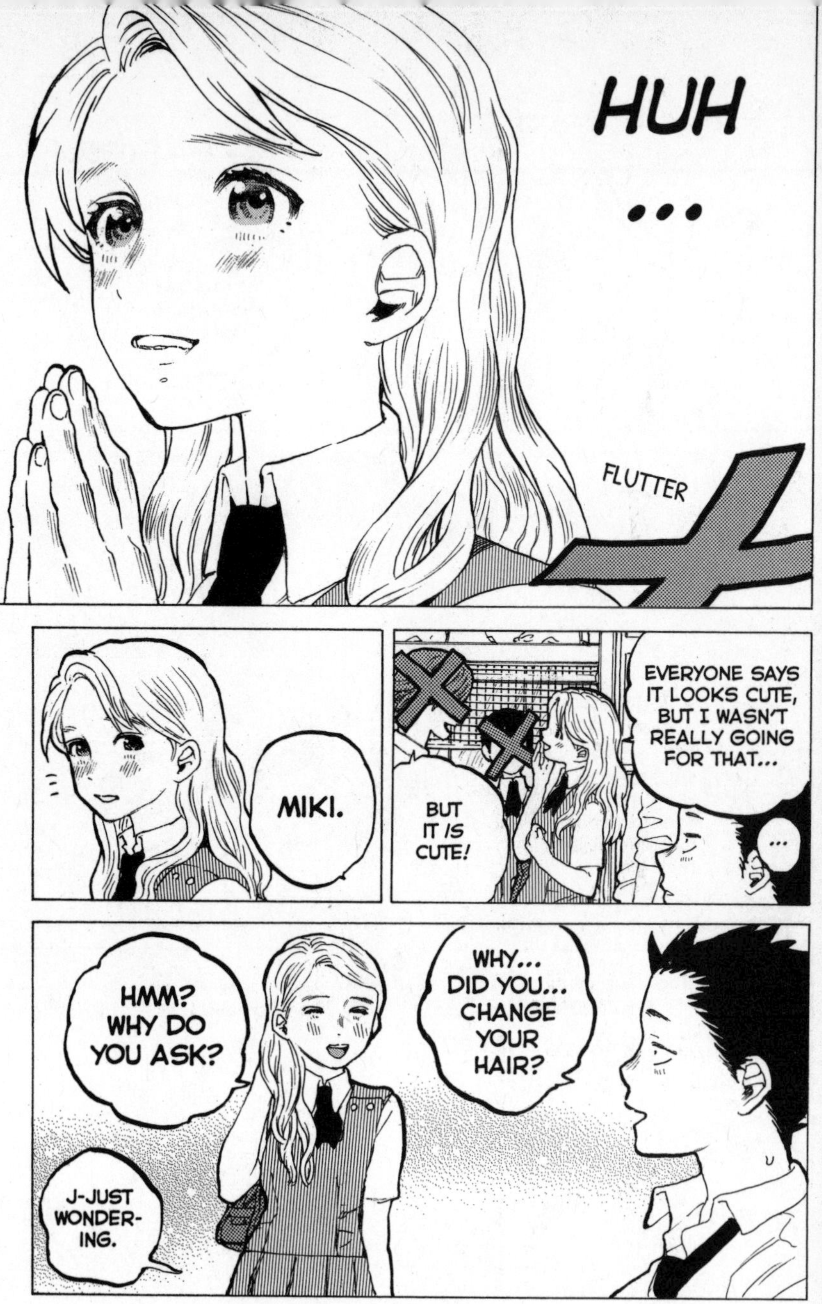
HUH
...
FLUTTER
EVERYONE SAYS IT LOOKS CUTE, BUT I WASN'T REALLY GOING FOR THAT...
BUT IT *IS* CUTE!
...
MIKI.
WHY... DID YOU... CHANGE YOUR HAIR?
HMM? WHY DO YOU ASK?
J-JUST WONDER-ING.

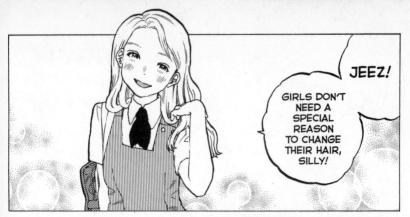

JEEZ!
GIRLS DON'T NEED A SPECIAL REASON TO CHANGE THEIR HAIR, SILLY!
...THEY DON'T?
WHISPER
SAY, SHOYA...
ARE YOU CLOSE WITH SATOSHI?
I DON'T THINK THEY'RE VERY CLOSE.
YEAH... NOT REALLY...
OH, SO YOU'RE NOT...
BUT DON'T YOU THINK HE'S HANDSOME ?
HUH? HE'S HAND-SOME ?
STARE
HE SAID HE WANTS TO BE FRIENDS WITH YOU.
HE THINKS YOU'RE COOL.
HUH?

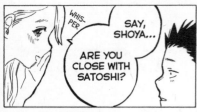

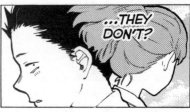

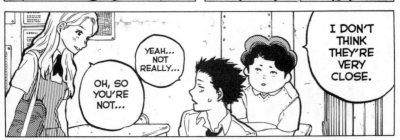

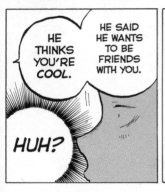

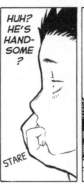

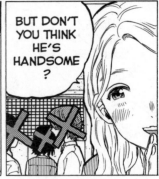

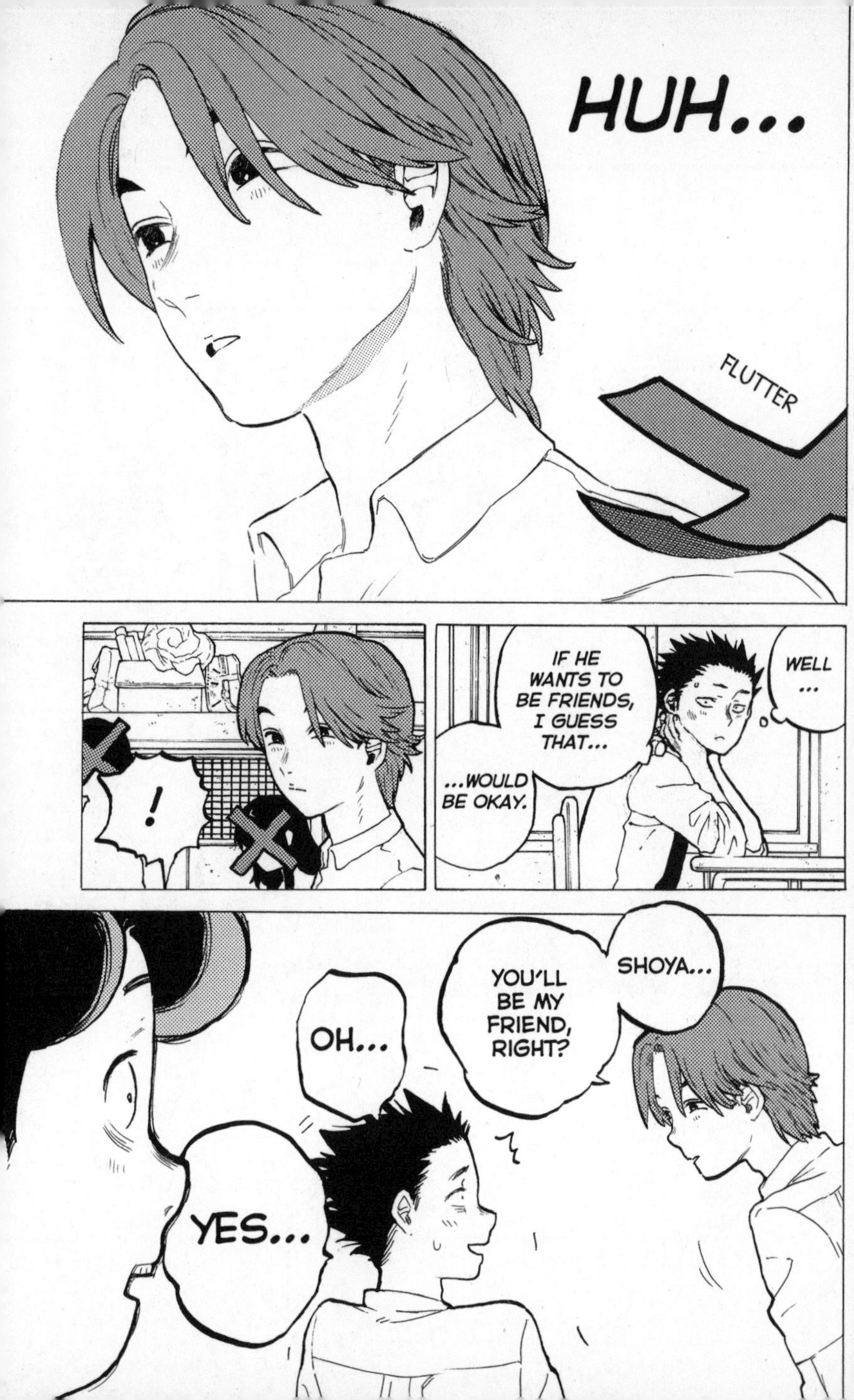
HUH...
FLUTTER
WELL ...
IF HE WANTS TO BE FRIENDS, I GUESS THAT...
...WOULD BE OKAY.
!
SHOYA...
YOU'LL BE MY FRIEND, RIGHT?
OH...
YES...

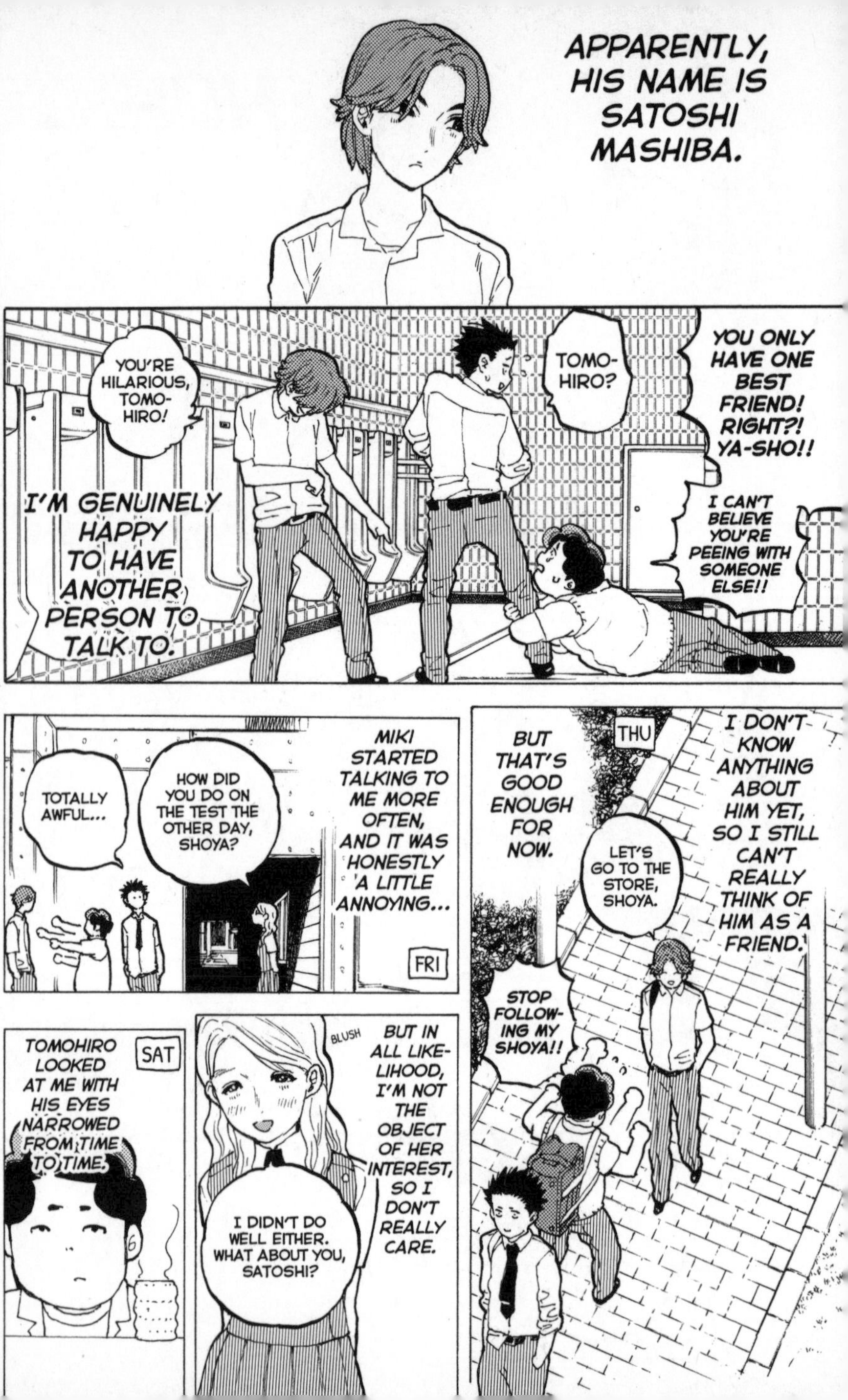
APPARENTLY, HIS NAME IS SATOSHI MASHIBA.
YOU ONLY HAVE ONE BEST FRIEND! RIGHT?! YA-SHO!!
I CAN'T BELIEVE YOU'RE PEEING WITH SOMEONE ELSE!!
TOMO-HIRO?
YOU'RE HILARIOUS, TOMO-HIRO!
I'M GENUINELY HAPPY TO HAVE ANOTHER PERSON TO TALK TO.
THU
I DON'T KNOW ANYTHING ABOUT HIM YET, SO I STILL CAN'T REALLY THINK OF HIM AS A FRIEND.
BUT THAT'S GOOD ENOUGH FOR NOW.
LET'S GO TO THE STORE, SHOYA.
STOP FOLLOW-ING MY SHOYA!!
MIKI STARTED TALKING TO ME MORE OFTEN, AND IT WAS HONESTLY A LITTLE ANNOYING...
FRI
HOW DID YOU DO ON THE TEST THE OTHER DAY, SHOYA?
TOTALLY AWFUL...
BLUSH
BUT IN ALL LIKE-LIHOOD, I'M NOT THE OBJECT OF HER INTEREST, SO I DON'T REALLY CARE.
I DIDN'T DO WELL EITHER. WHAT ABOUT YOU, SATOSHI?
SAT
TOMOHIRO LOOKED AT ME WITH HIS EYES NARROWED FROM TIME TO TIME.

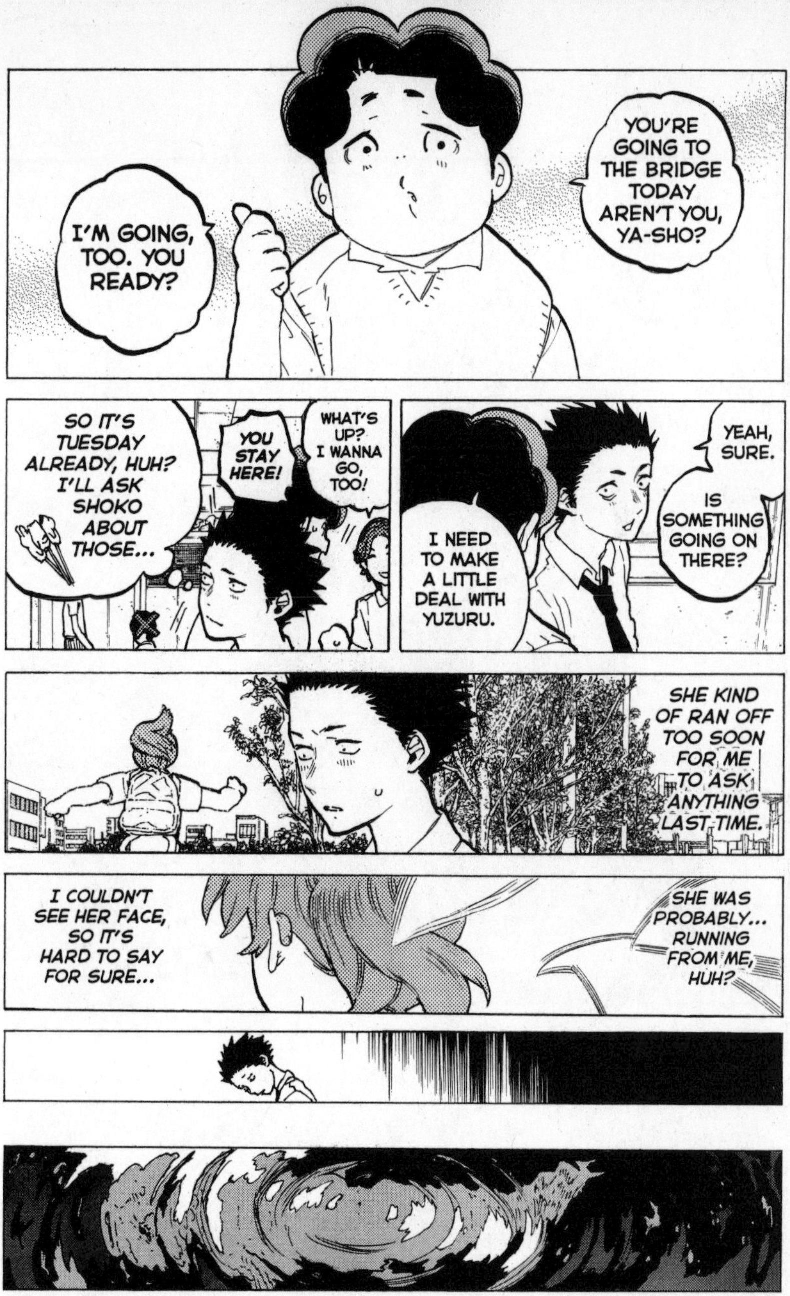
YOU'RE GOING TO THE BRIDGE TODAY AREN'T YOU, YA-SHO?
I'M GOING, TOO. YOU READY?
YEAH, SURE.
IS SOMETHING GOING ON THERE?
I NEED TO MAKE A LITTLE DEAL WITH YUZURU.
WHAT'S UP? I WANNA GO, TOO!
YOU STAY HERE!
SO IT'S TUESDAY ALREADY, HUH? I'LL ASK SHOKO ABOUT THOSE...
SHE KIND OF RAN OFF TOO SOON FOR ME TO ASK ANYTHING LAST TIME.
SHE WAS PROBABLY... RUNNING FROM ME, HUH?
I COULDN'T SEE HER FACE, SO IT'S HARD TO SAY FOR SURE...

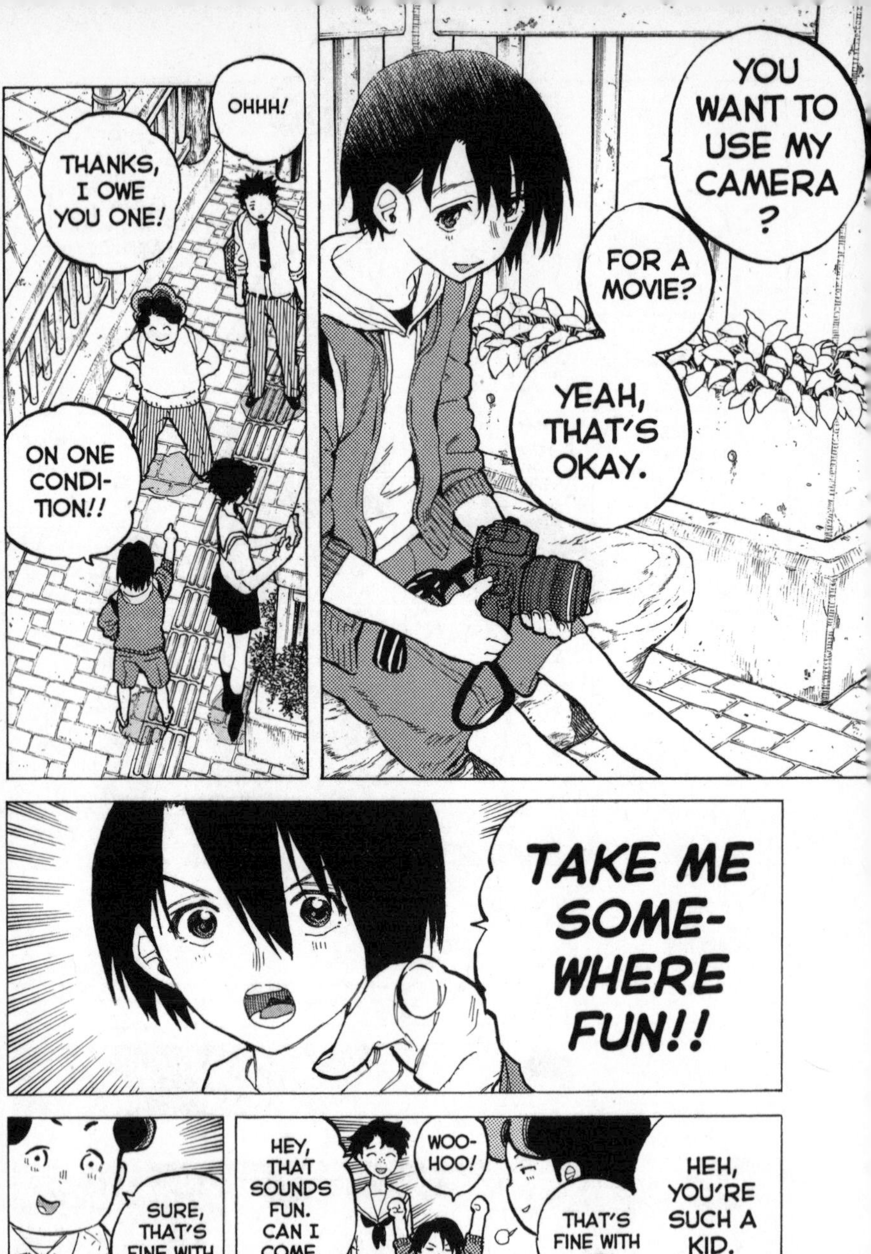

YOU WANT TO USE MY CAMERA?
FOR A MOVIE?
YEAH, THAT'S OKAY.
OHHH!
THANKS, I OWE YOU ONE!
ON ONE CONDITION!!
TAKE ME SOME-WHERE FUN!!
HEH, YOU'RE SUCH A KID.
THAT'S FINE WITH ME!
WOO-HOO!
HEY, THAT SOUNDS FUN. CAN I COME, TOO?
SURE, THAT'S FINE WITH ME.

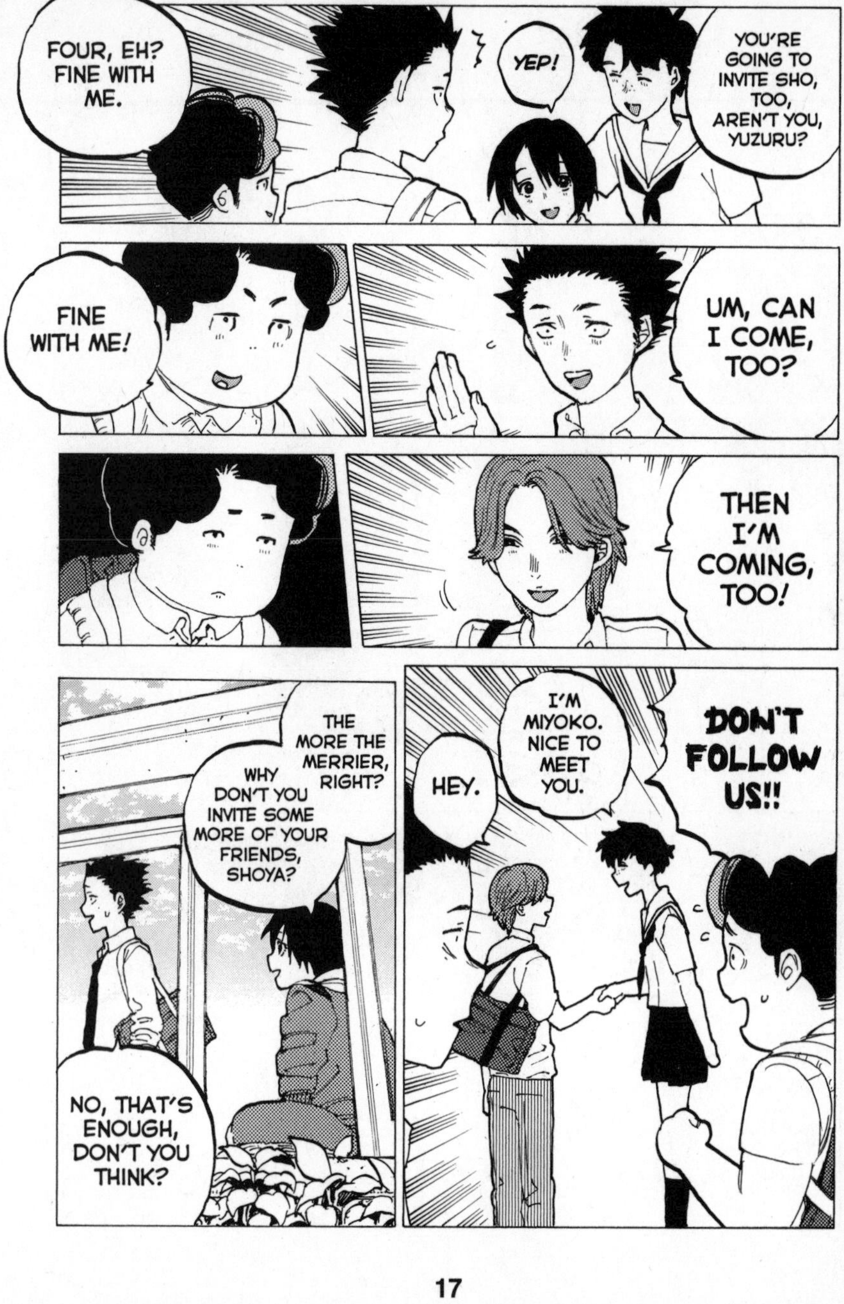
YOU'RE GOING TO INVITE SHO, TOO, AREN'T YOU, YUZURU?
YEP!
FOUR, EH? FINE WITH ME.
UM, CAN I COME, TOO?
FINE WITH ME!
THEN I'M COMING, TOO!
DON'T FOLLOW US!!
I'M MIYOKO. NICE TO MEET YOU.
HEY.
THE MORE THE MERRIER, RIGHT?
WHY DON'T YOU INVITE SOME MORE OF YOUR FRIENDS, SHOYA?
NO, THAT'S ENOUGH, DON'T YOU THINK?

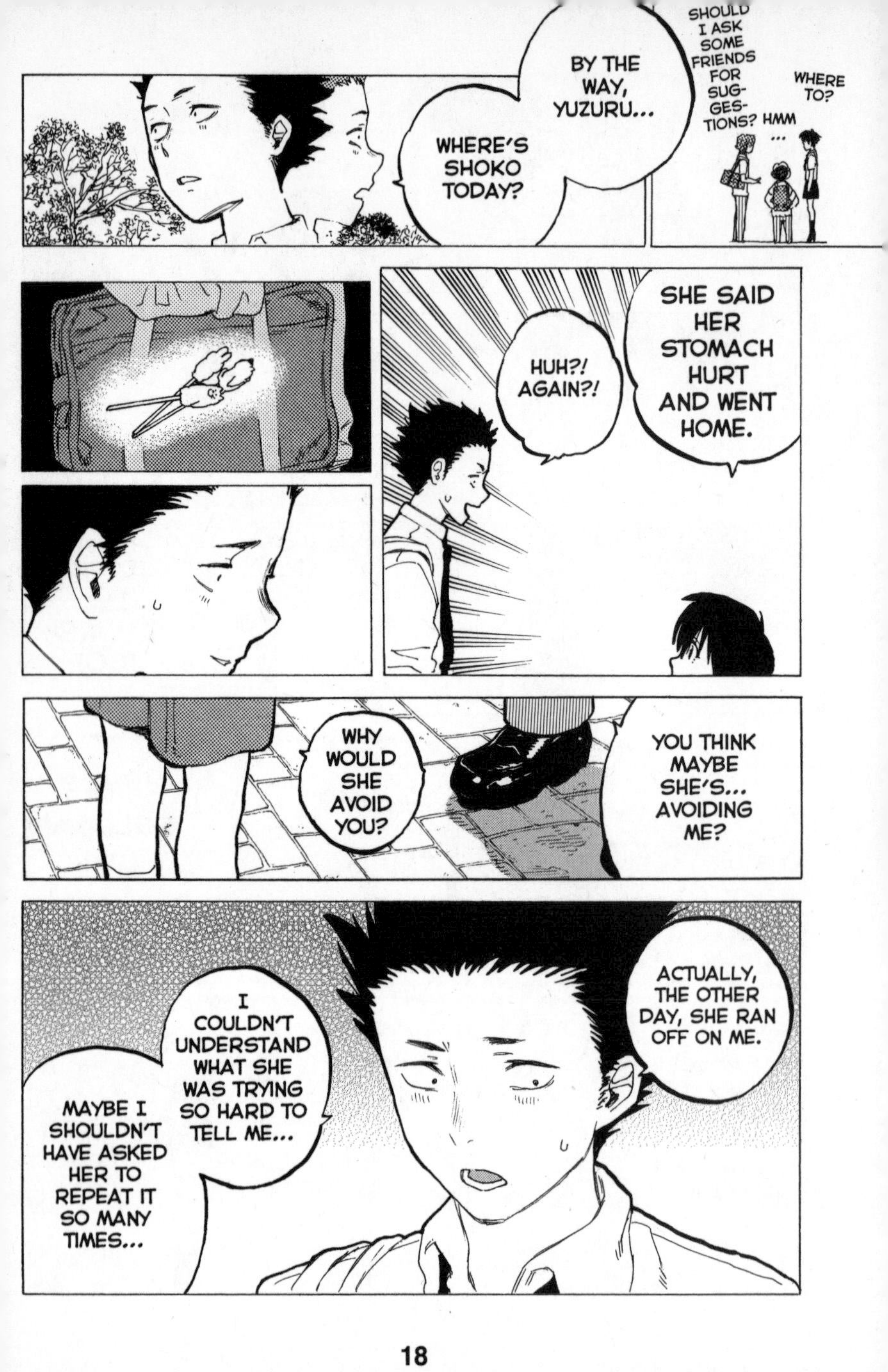
WHERE TO?
SHOULD I ASK SOME FRIENDS FOR SUGGESTIONS?
HMM...
BY THE WAY, YUZURU...
WHERE'S SHOKO TODAY?
SHE SAID HER STOMACH HURT AND WENT HOME.
HUH?! AGAIN?!
YOU THINK MAYBE SHE'S... AVOIDING ME?
WHY WOULD SHE AVOID YOU?
ACTUALLY, THE OTHER DAY, SHE RAN OFF ON ME.
I COULDN'T UNDERSTAND WHAT SHE WAS TRYING SO HARD TO TELL ME...
MAYBE I SHOULDN'T HAVE ASKED HER TO REPEAT IT SO MANY TIMES...

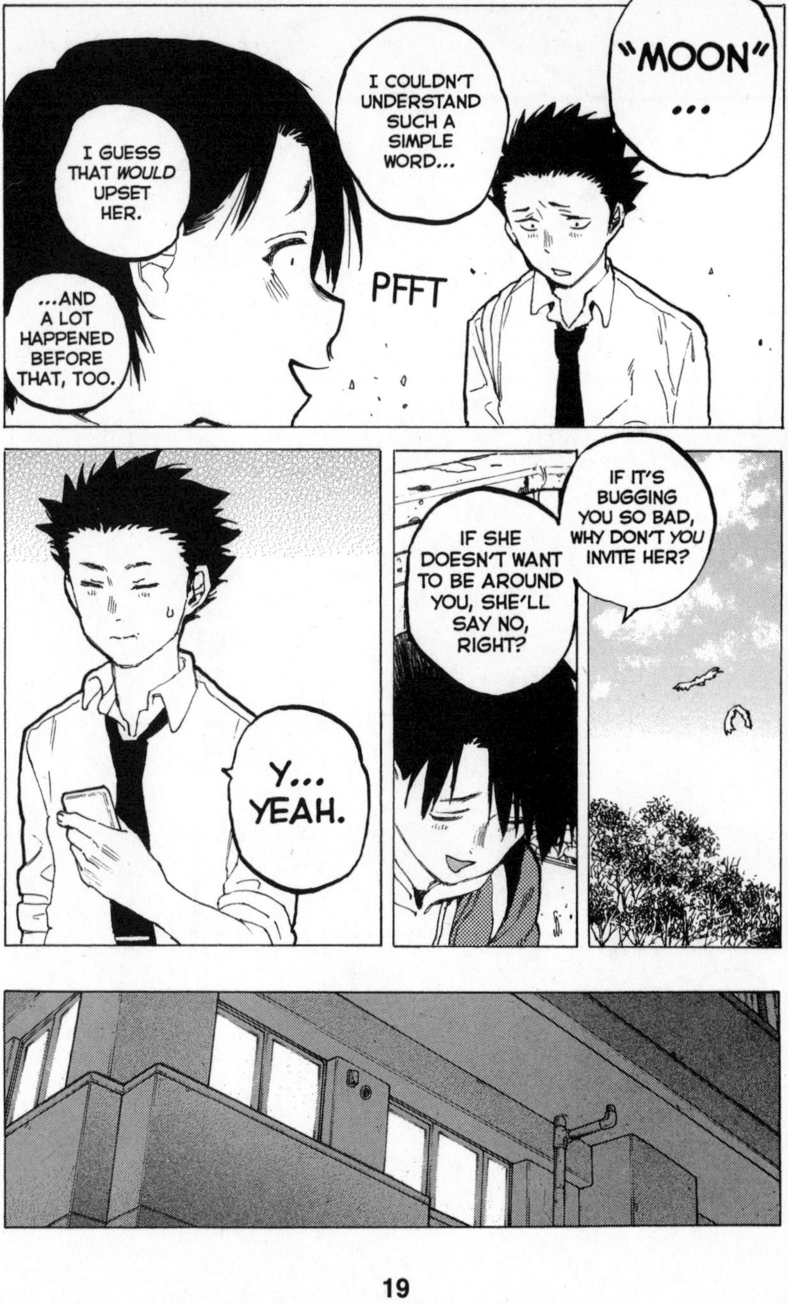
"MOON"...
I COULDN'T UNDERSTAND SUCH A SIMPLE WORD...
PFFT
I GUESS THAT WOULD UPSET HER.
...AND A LOT HAPPENED BEFORE THAT, TOO.
IF IT'S BUGGING YOU SO BAD, WHY DON'T YOU INVITE HER?
IF SHE DOESN'T WANT TO BE AROUND YOU, SHE'LL SAY NO, RIGHT?
Y... YEAH.

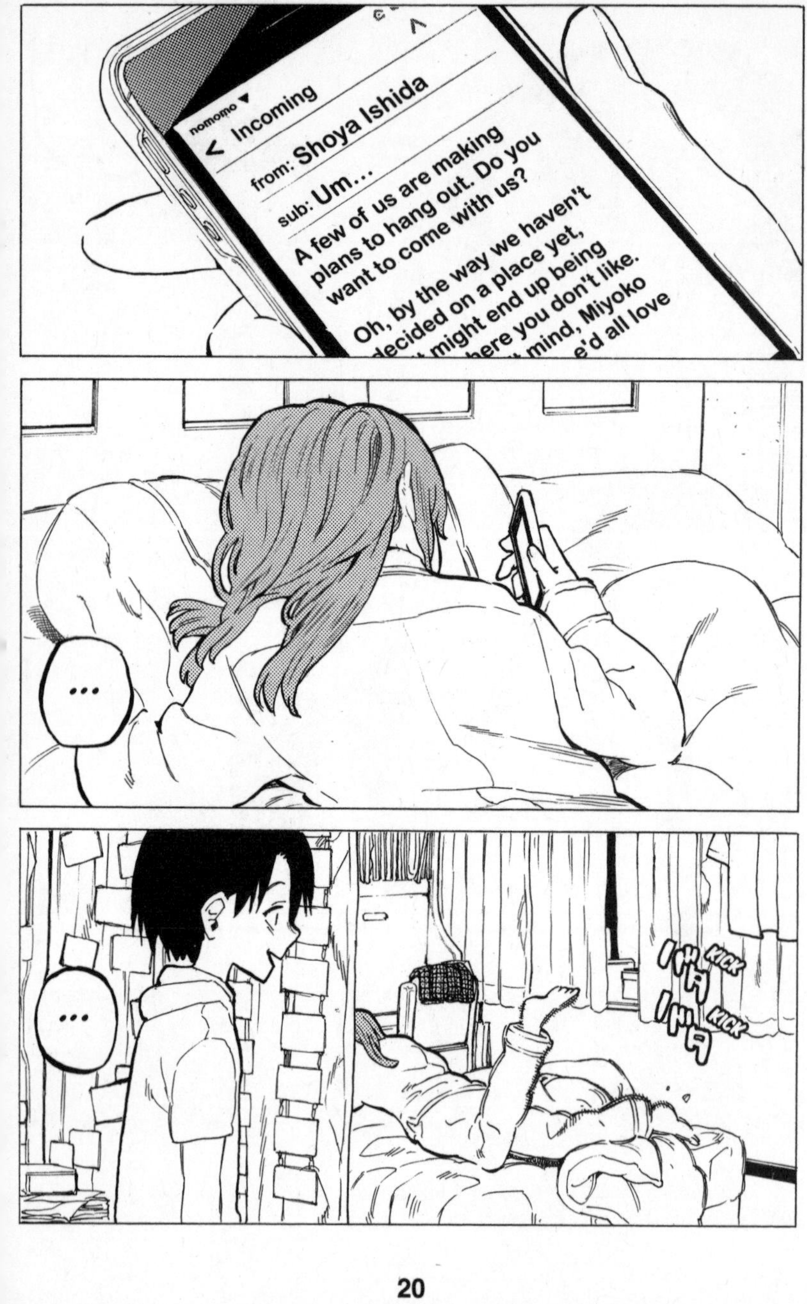
nomomo
Incoming
from: Shoya Ishida
sub: Um...
A few of us are making plans to hang out. Do you want to come with us?
Oh, by the way we haven't decided on a place yet,
might end up being
here you don't like.
mind, Miyoko
e'd all love
...
...
KICK
KICK

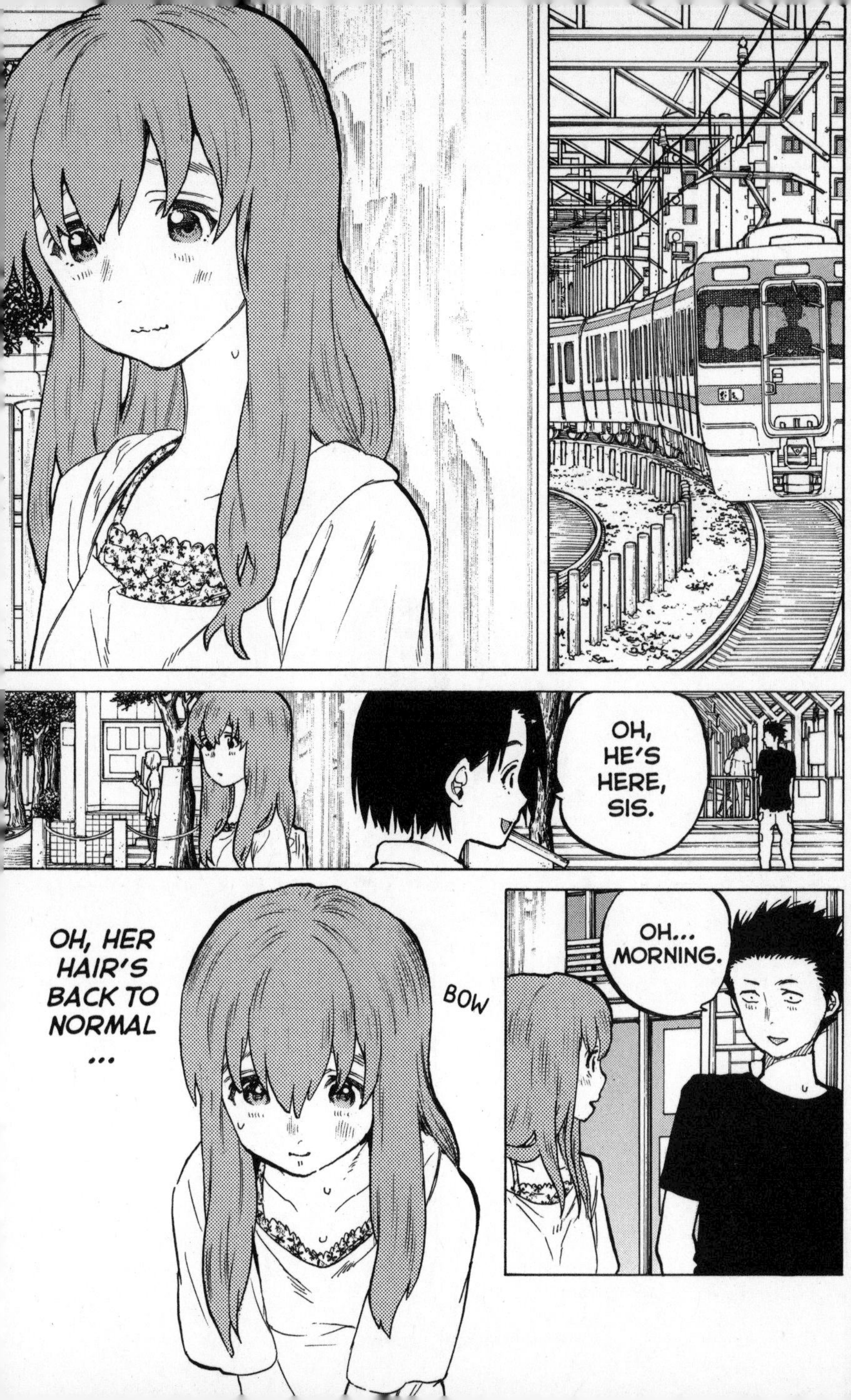
OH, HE'S HERE, SIS.
OH... MORNING.
OH, HER HAIR'S BACK TO NORMAL ...
BOW

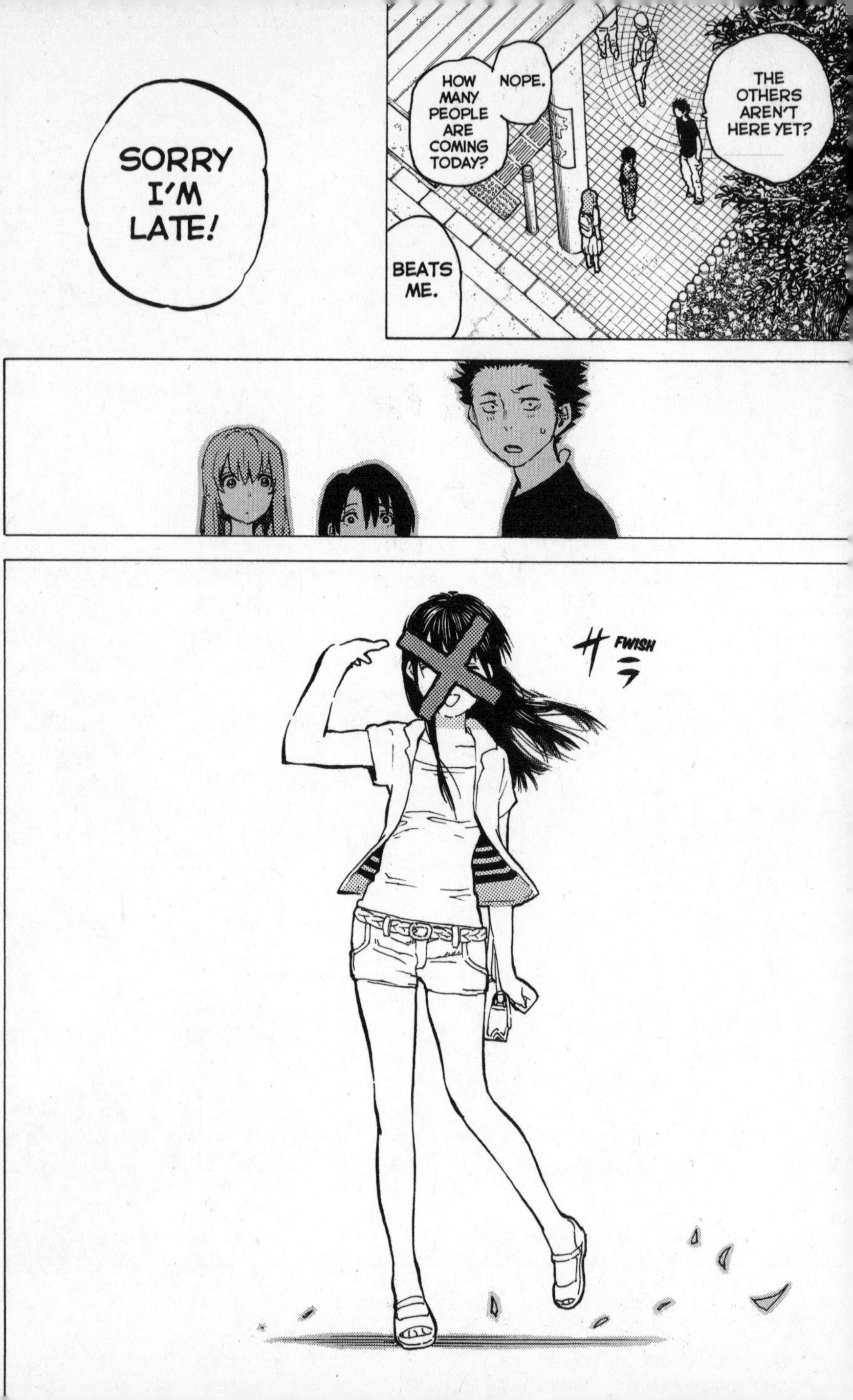
THE OTHERS AREN'T HERE YET?
NOPE.
HOW MANY PEOPLE ARE COMING TODAY?
BEATS ME.
SORRY I'M LATE!
FWISH

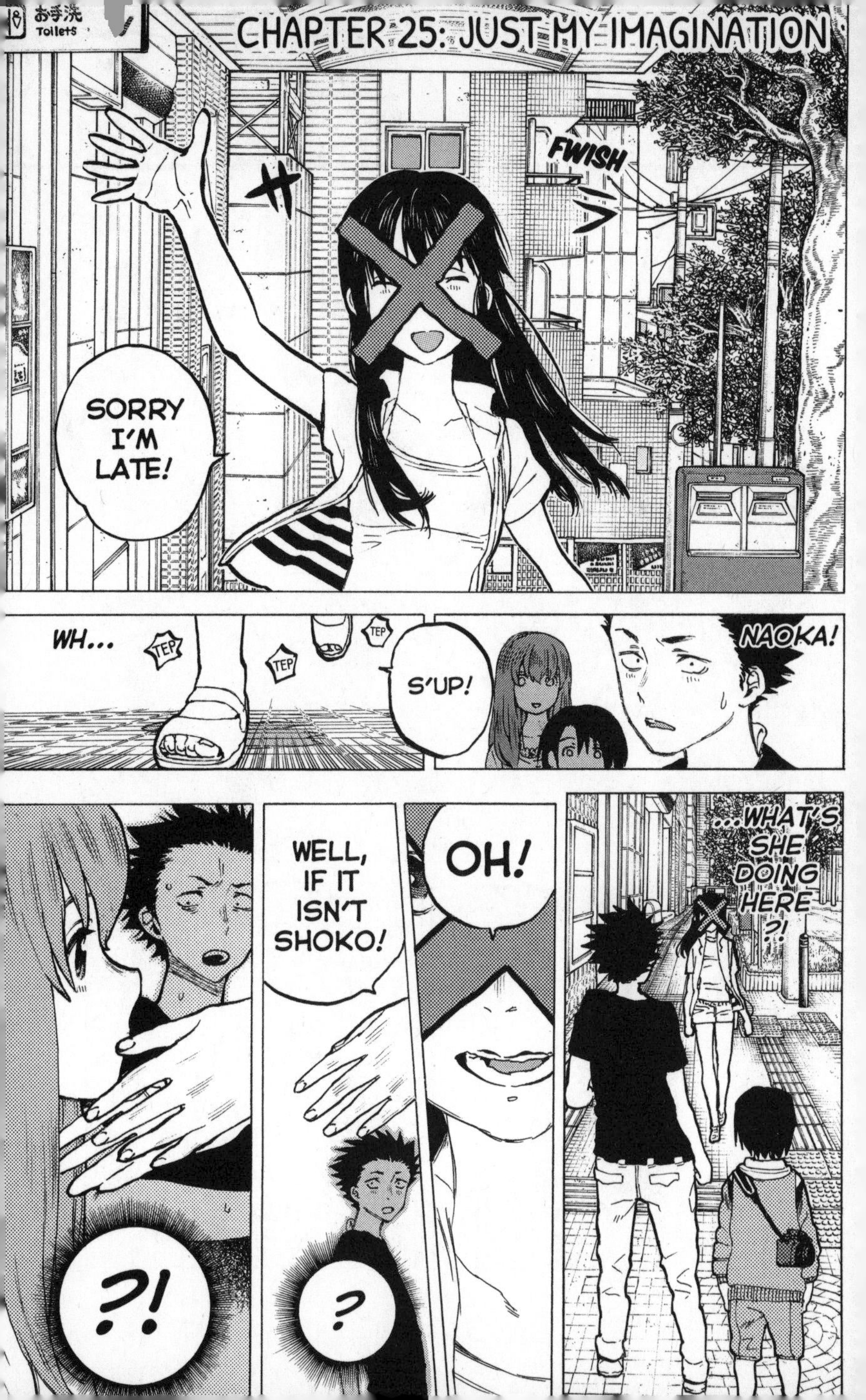
CHAPTER 25: JUST MY IMAGINATION
FWISH
お手洗
Toilets
SORRY I'M LATE!
NAOKA!
S'UP!
TEP
TEP
TEP
WH...
...WHAT'S SHE DOING HERE?!
OH!
WELL, IF IT ISN'T SHOKO!
?
?!

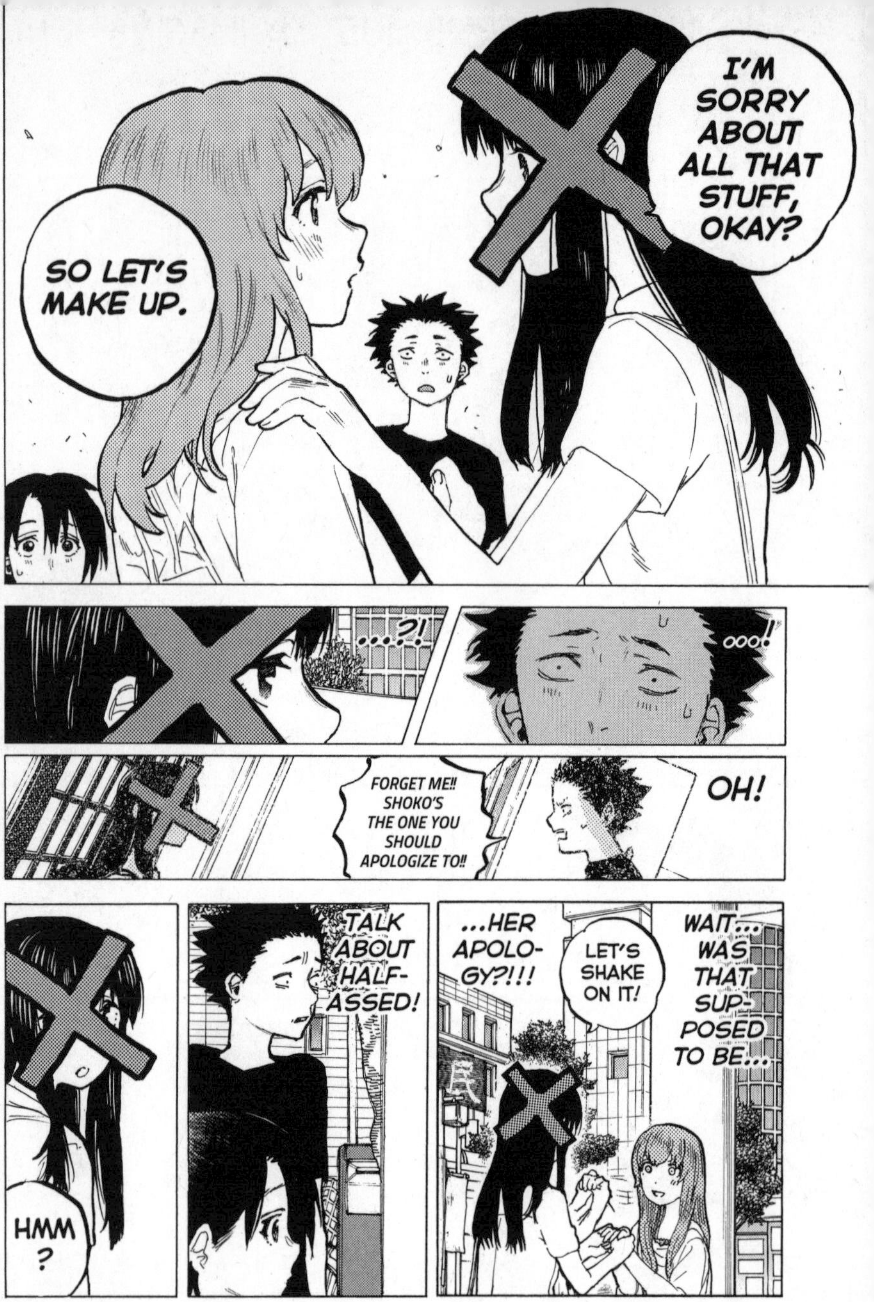
I'M SORRY ABOUT ALL THAT STUFF, OKAY?
SO LET'S MAKE UP.
ooo!
...?!
OH!
FORGET ME!! SHOKO'S THE ONE YOU SHOULD APOLOGIZE TO!!
WAIT... WAS THAT SUP-POSED TO BE...
LET'S SHAKE ON IT!
...HER APOLO-GY?!!!
TALK ABOUT HALF-ASSED!
HMM ?

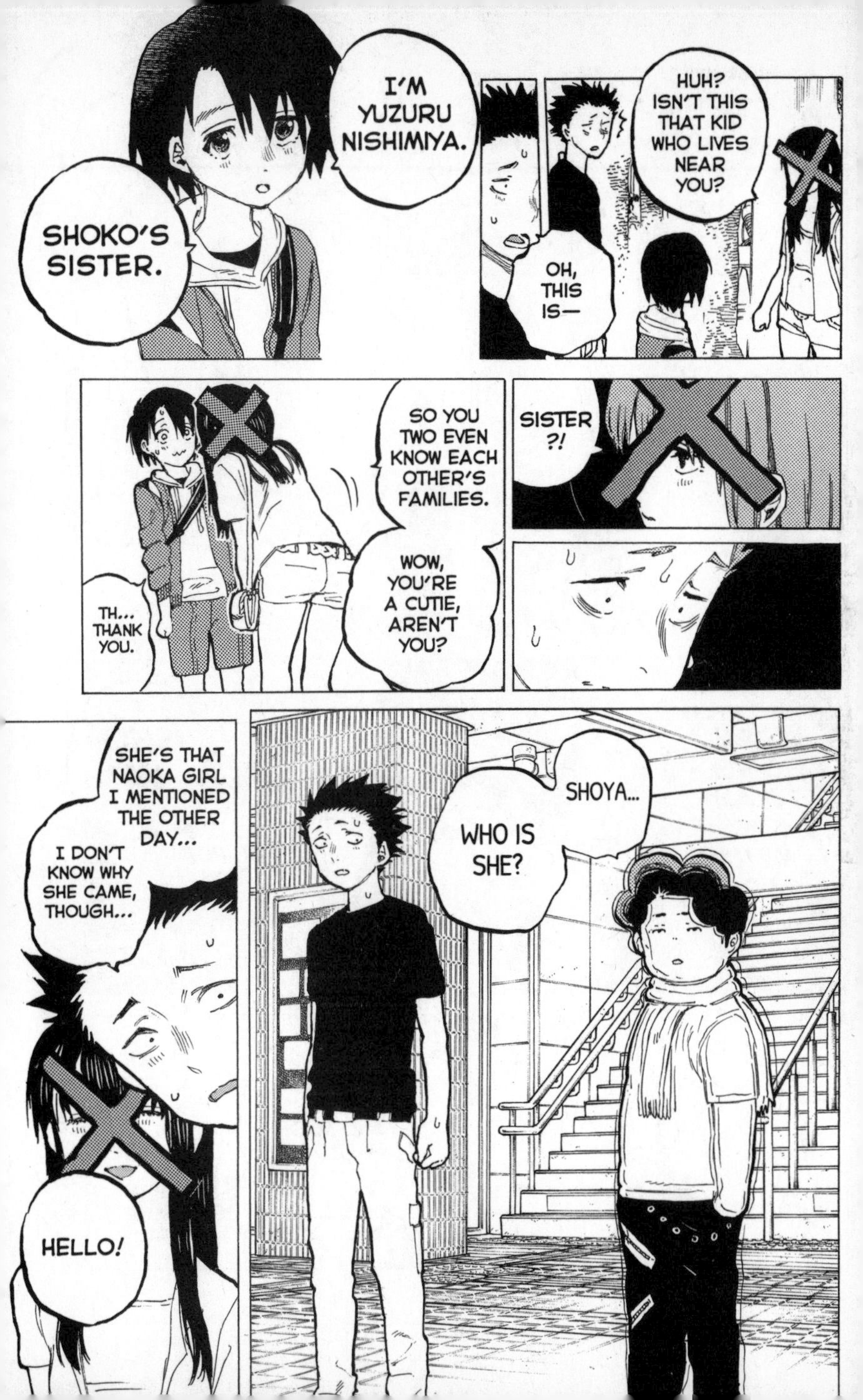
HUH? ISN'T THIS THAT KID WHO LIVES NEAR YOU?
OH, THIS IS—
I'M YUZURU NISHIMIYA.
SHOKO'S SISTER.
SISTER ?!
SO YOU TWO EVEN KNOW EACH OTHER'S FAMILIES.
WOW, YOU'RE A CUTIE, AREN'T YOU?
TH... THANK YOU.
SHOYA...
WHO IS SHE?
SHE'S THAT NAOKA GIRL I MENTIONED THE OTHER DAY...
I DON'T KNOW WHY SHE CAME, THOUGH...
HELLO!

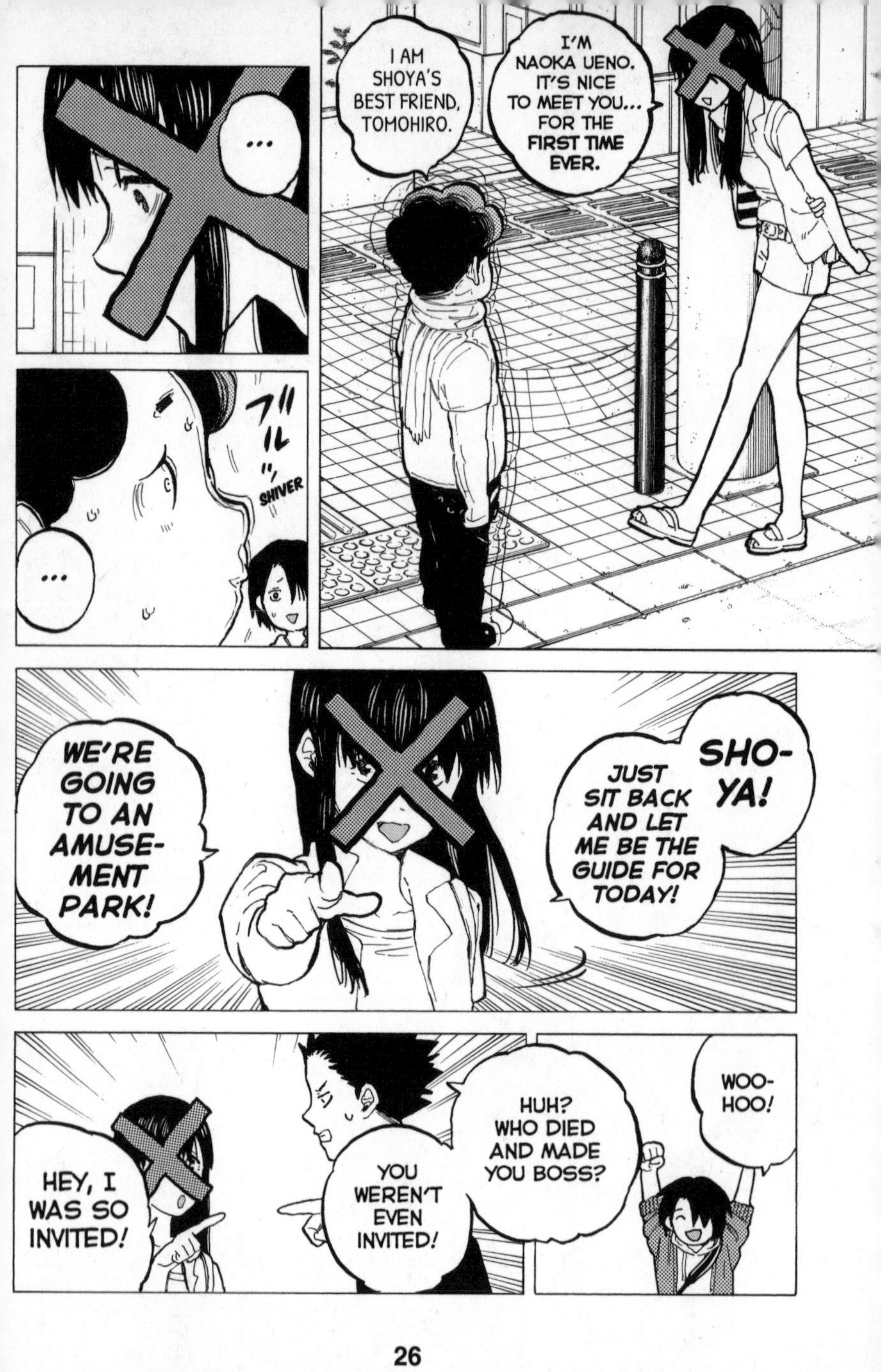
I'M NAOKA UENO. IT'S NICE TO MEET YOU... FOR THE FIRST TIME EVER.
I AM SHOYA'S BEST FRIEND, TOMOHIRO.
...
ブル
SHIVER
...
SHO-YA! JUST SIT BACK AND LET ME BE THE GUIDE FOR TODAY!
WE'RE GOING TO AN AMUSEMENT PARK!
WOO-HOO!
HUH? WHO DIED AND MADE YOU BOSS?
YOU WEREN'T EVEN INVITED!
HEY, I WAS SO INVITED!

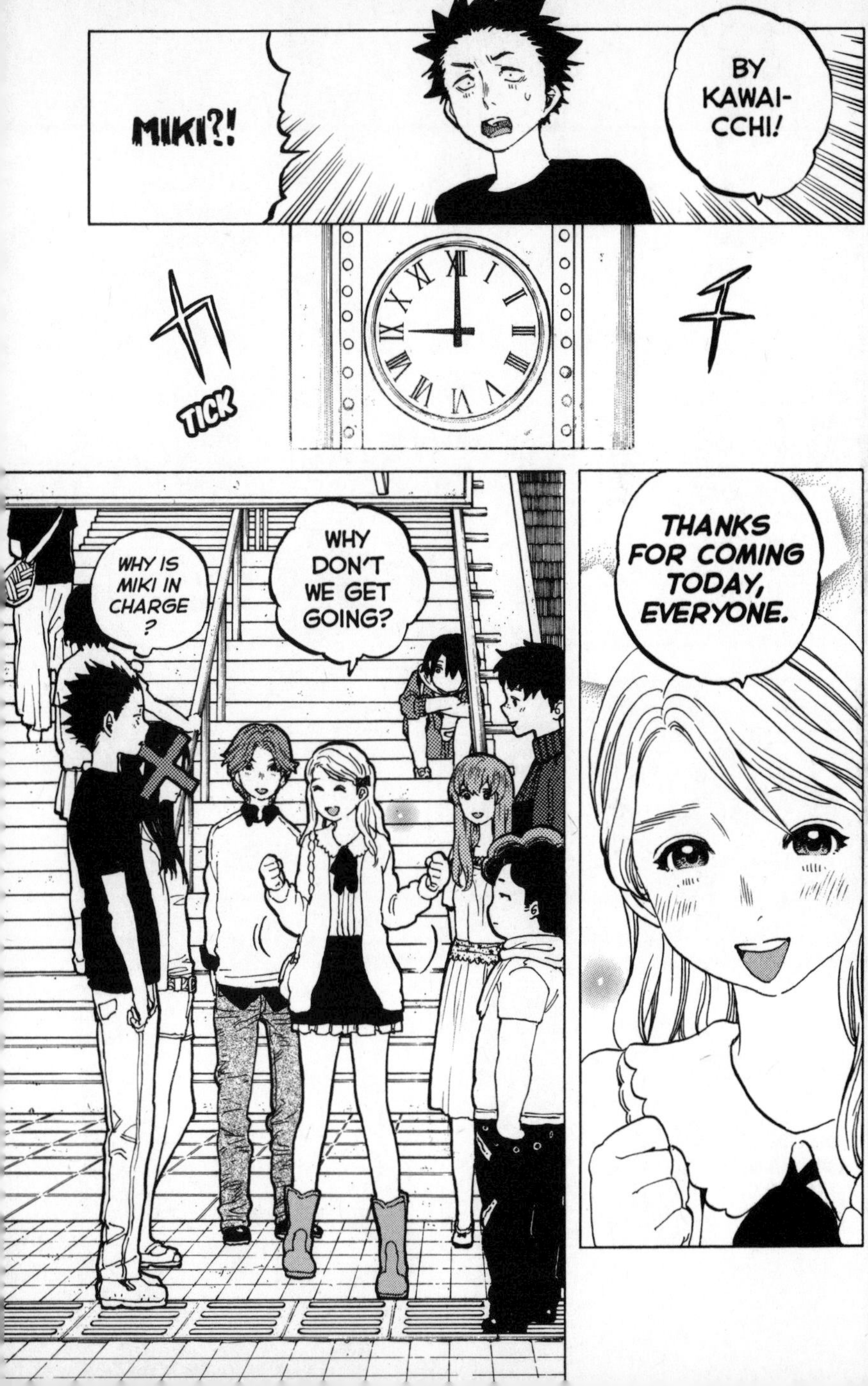
BY KAWAI-CCHI!
MIKI?!
TICK
THANKS FOR COMING TODAY, EVERYONE.
WHY DON'T WE GET GOING?
WHY IS MIKI IN CHARGE?

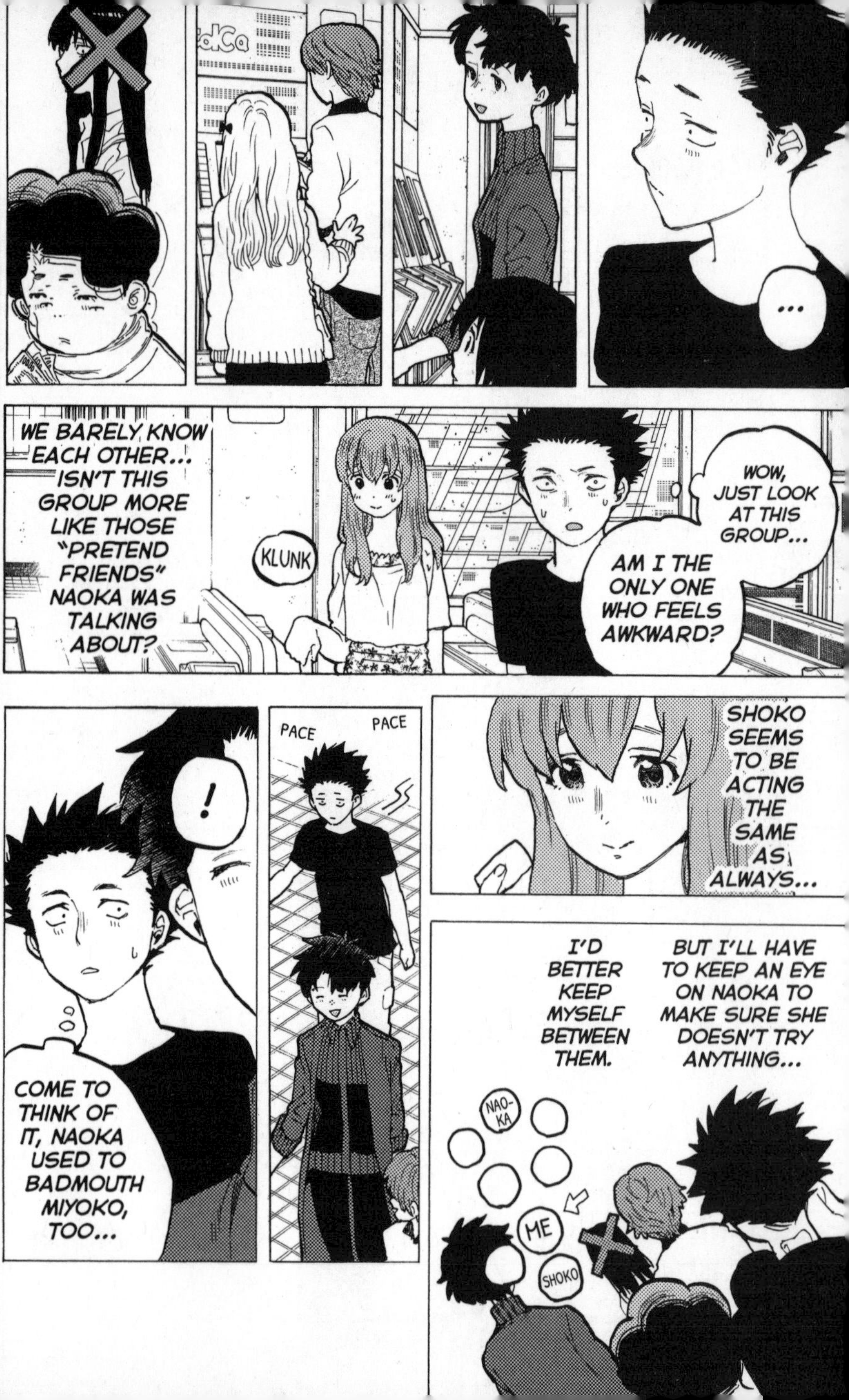
...
WOW, JUST LOOK AT THIS GROUP...
AM I THE ONLY ONE WHO FEELS AWKWARD?
KLUNK
WE BARELY KNOW EACH OTHER... ISN'T THIS GROUP MORE LIKE THOSE "PRETEND FRIENDS" NAOKA WAS TALKING ABOUT?
SHOKO SEEMS TO BE ACTING THE SAME AS ALWAYS...
BUT I'LL HAVE TO KEEP AN EYE ON NAOKA TO MAKE SURE SHE DOESN'T TRY ANYTHING...
I'D BETTER KEEP MYSELF BETWEEN THEM.
NAO-KA
ME
SHOKO
PACE
PACE
!
COME TO THINK OF IT, NAOKA USED TO BADMOUTH MIYOKO, TOO...

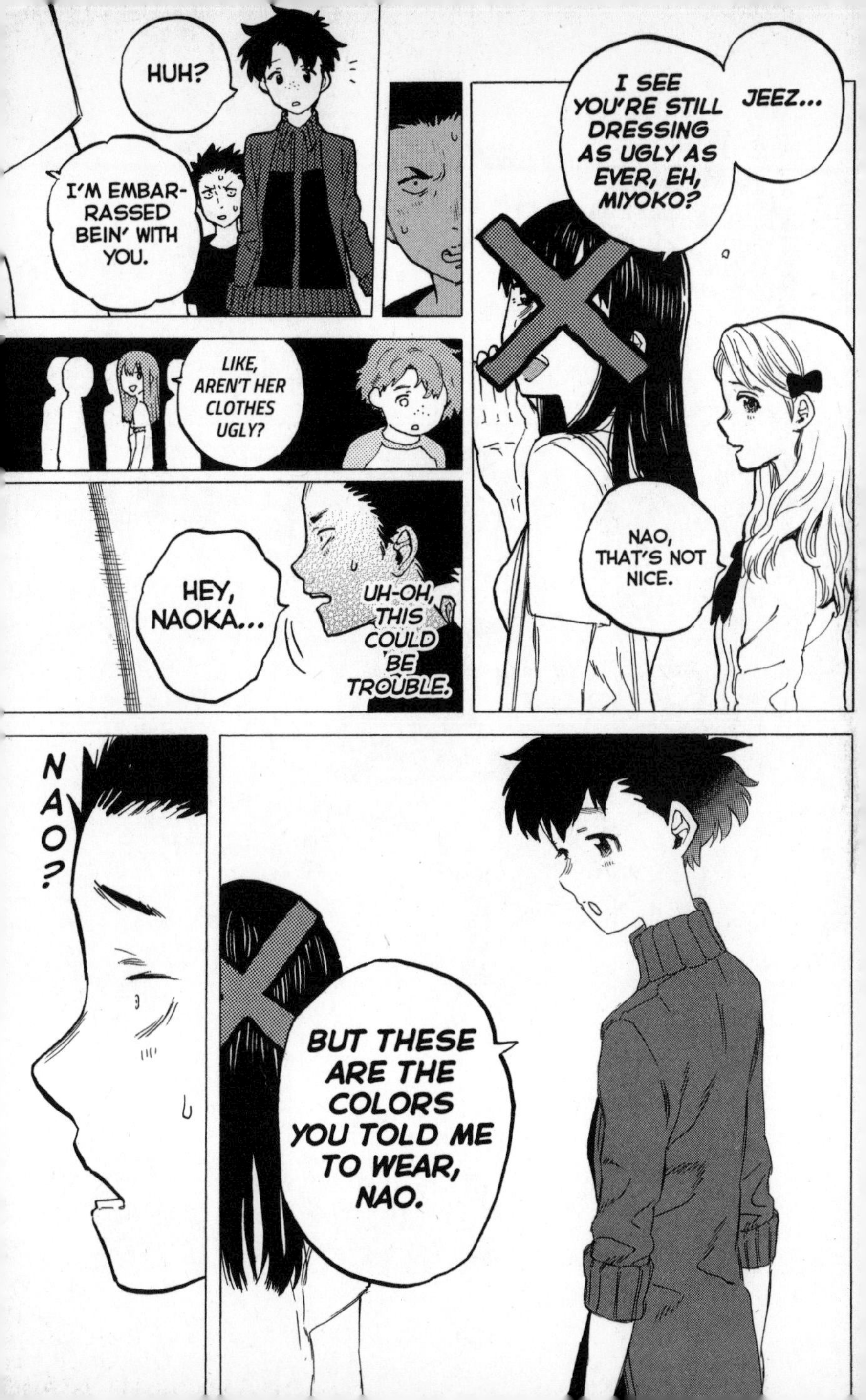
JEEZ...
I SEE YOU'RE STILL DRESSING AS UGLY AS EVER, EH, MIYOKO?
NAO, THAT'S NOT NICE.
HUH?
I'M EMBAR-RASSED BEIN' WITH YOU.
LIKE, AREN'T HER CLOTHES UGLY?
HEY, NAOKA...
UH-OH, THIS COULD BE TROUBLE.
BUT THESE ARE THE COLORS YOU TOLD ME TO WEAR, NAO.
NAO?

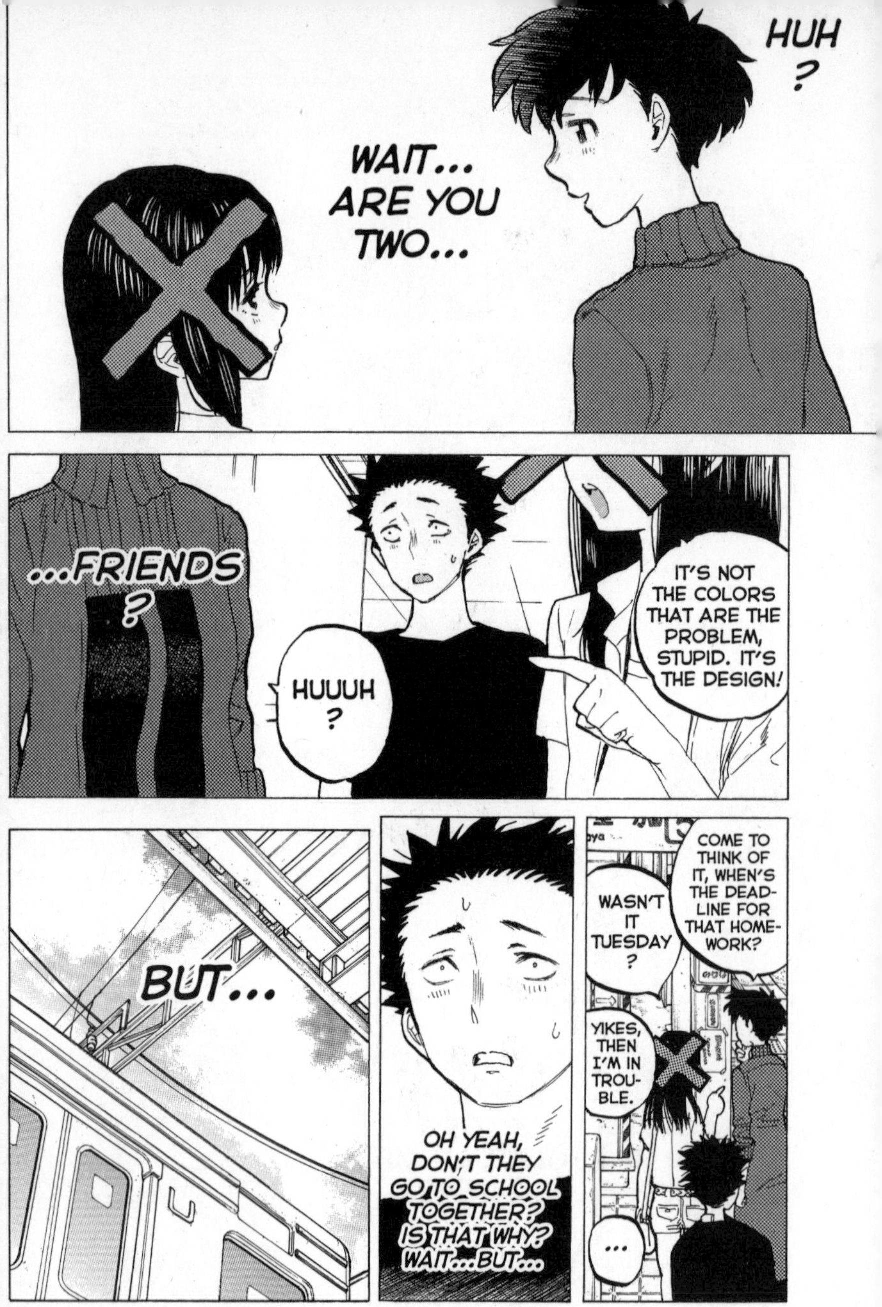
HUH?
WAIT... ARE YOU TWO...
...FRIENDS?
IT'S NOT THE COLORS THAT ARE THE PROBLEM, STUPID. IT'S THE DESIGN!
HUUUH?
COME TO THINK OF IT, WHEN'S THE DEAD-LINE FOR THAT HOME-WORK?
WASN'T IT TUESDAY?
YIKES, THEN I'M IN TROU-BLE.
...
OH YEAH, DON'T THEY GO TO SCHOOL TOGETHER? IS THAT WHY? WAIT...BUT...
BUT...

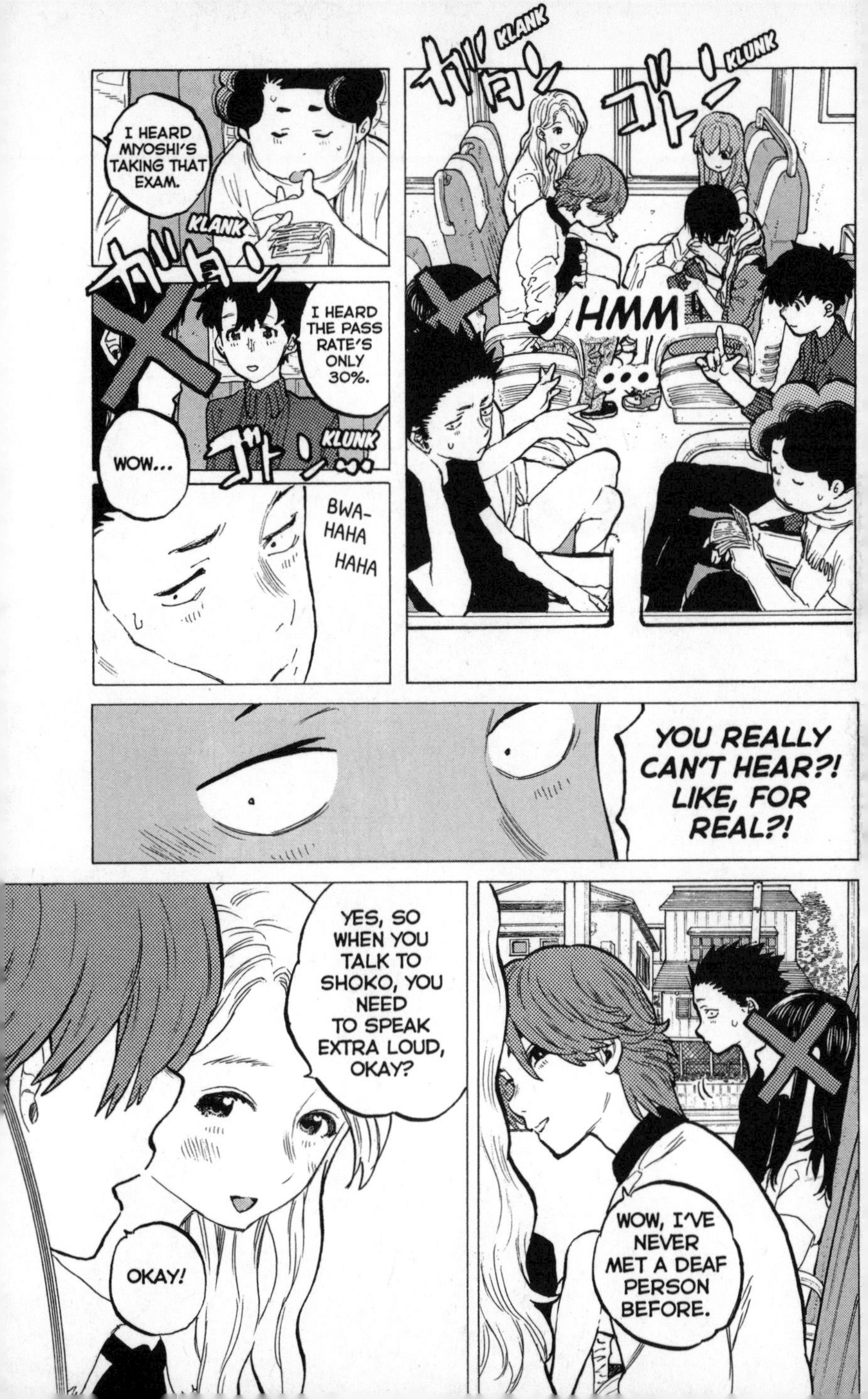
KLANK
KLUNK
HMM
...
I HEARD MIYOSHI'S TAKING THAT EXAM.
KLANK
I HEARD THE PASS RATE'S ONLY 30%.
WOW...
KLUNK
BWA-HAHA HAHA
YOU REALLY CAN'T HEAR?! LIKE, FOR REAL?!
WOW, I'VE NEVER MET A DEAF PERSON BEFORE.
YES, SO WHEN YOU TALK TO SHOKO, YOU NEED TO SPEAK EXTRA LOUD, OKAY?
OKAY!

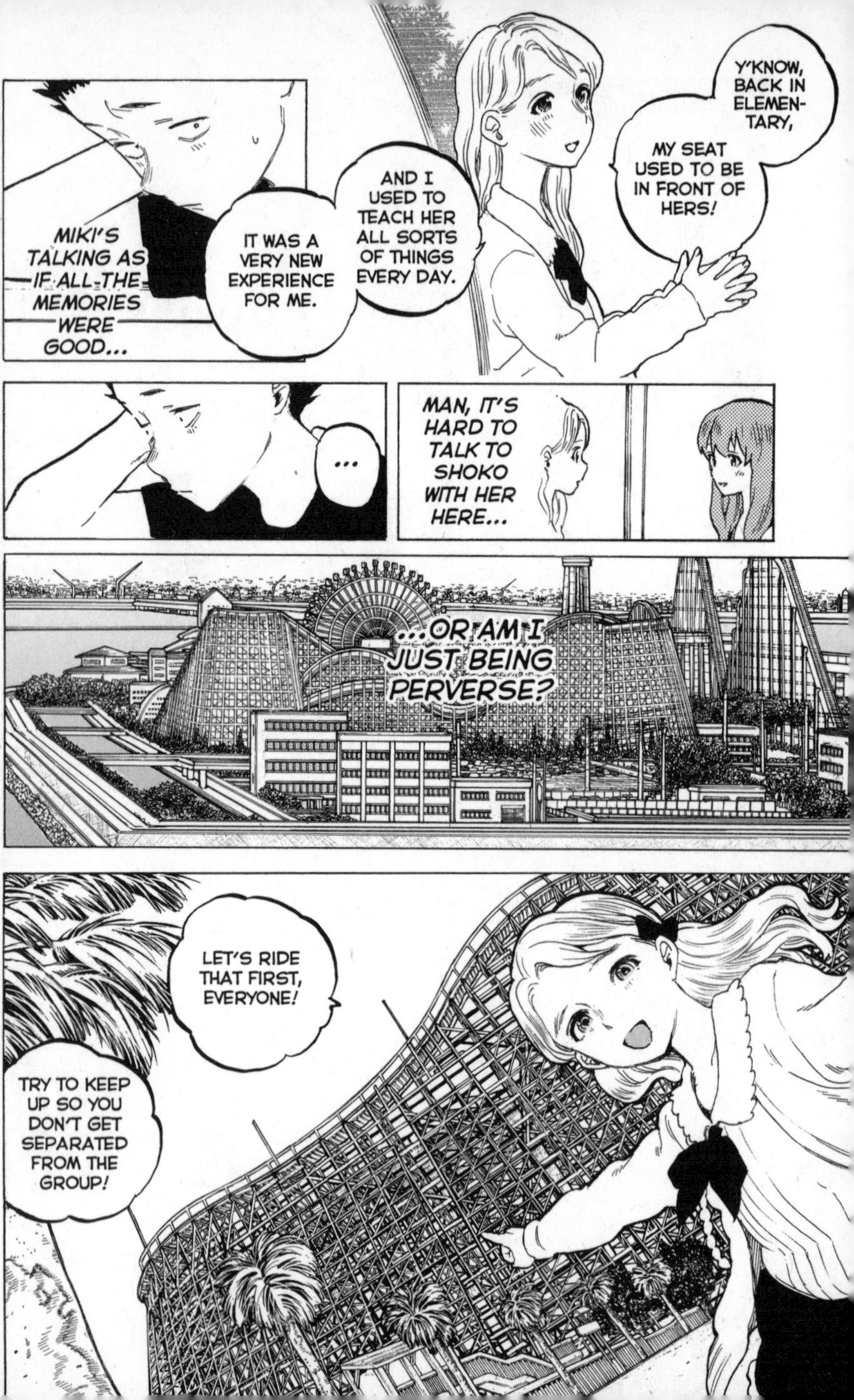
Y'KNOW, BACK IN ELEMENTARY,
MY SEAT USED TO BE IN FRONT OF HERS!
AND I USED TO TEACH HER ALL SORTS OF THINGS EVERY DAY.
IT WAS A VERY NEW EXPERIENCE FOR ME.
MIKI'S TALKING AS IF ALL THE MEMORIES WERE GOOD...
MAN, IT'S HARD TO TALK TO SHOKO WITH HER HERE...
...
...OR AM I JUST BEING PERVERSE?
LET'S RIDE THAT FIRST, EVERYONE!
TRY TO KEEP UP SO YOU DON'T GET SEPARATED FROM THE GROUP!

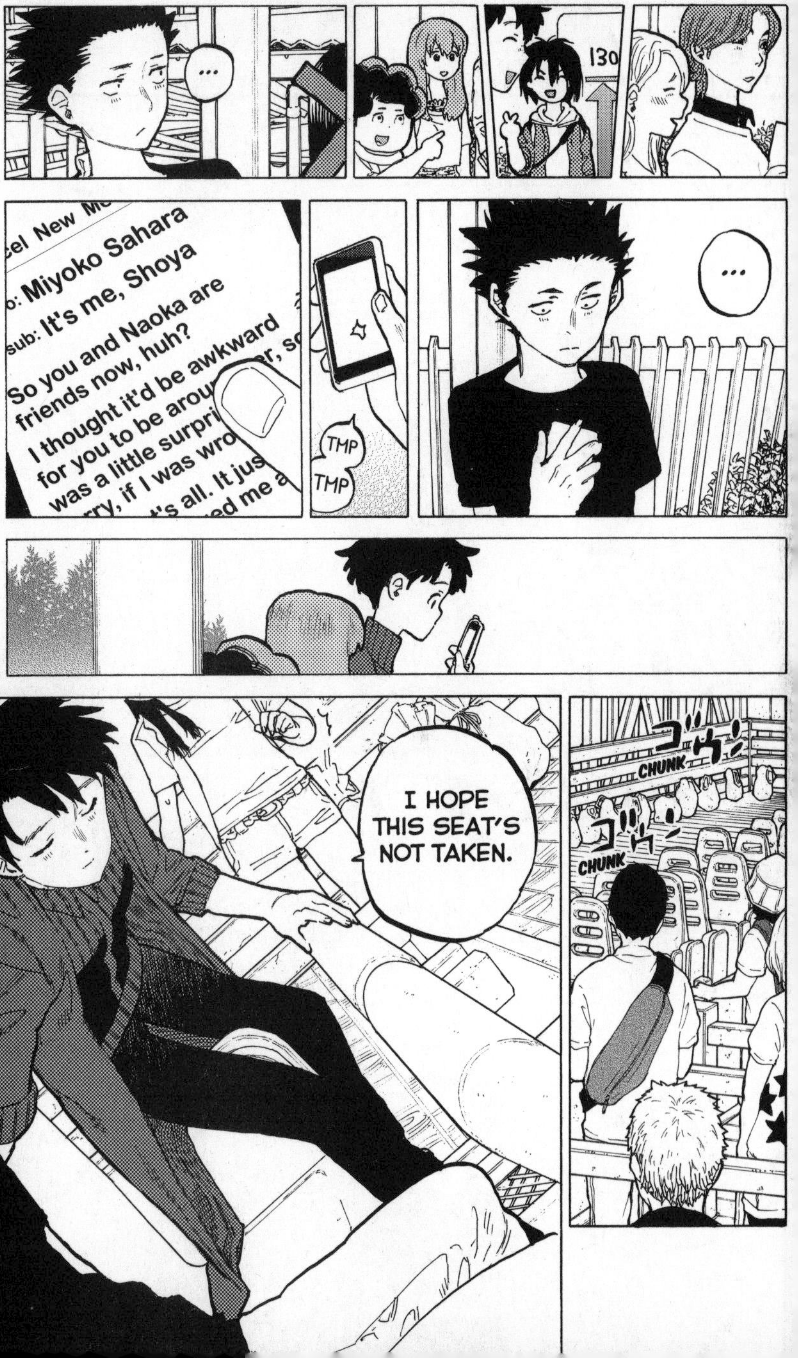
130
...
...
TMP
TMP
cel New Me
o: Miyoko Sahara
sub: It's me, Shoya
So you and Naoka are
friends now, huh?
I thought it'd be awkward
for you to be arou
was a little surpri
rry, if I was wro
t's all. It jus
ed me a
CHUNK
CHUNK
I HOPE THIS SEAT'S NOT TAKEN.

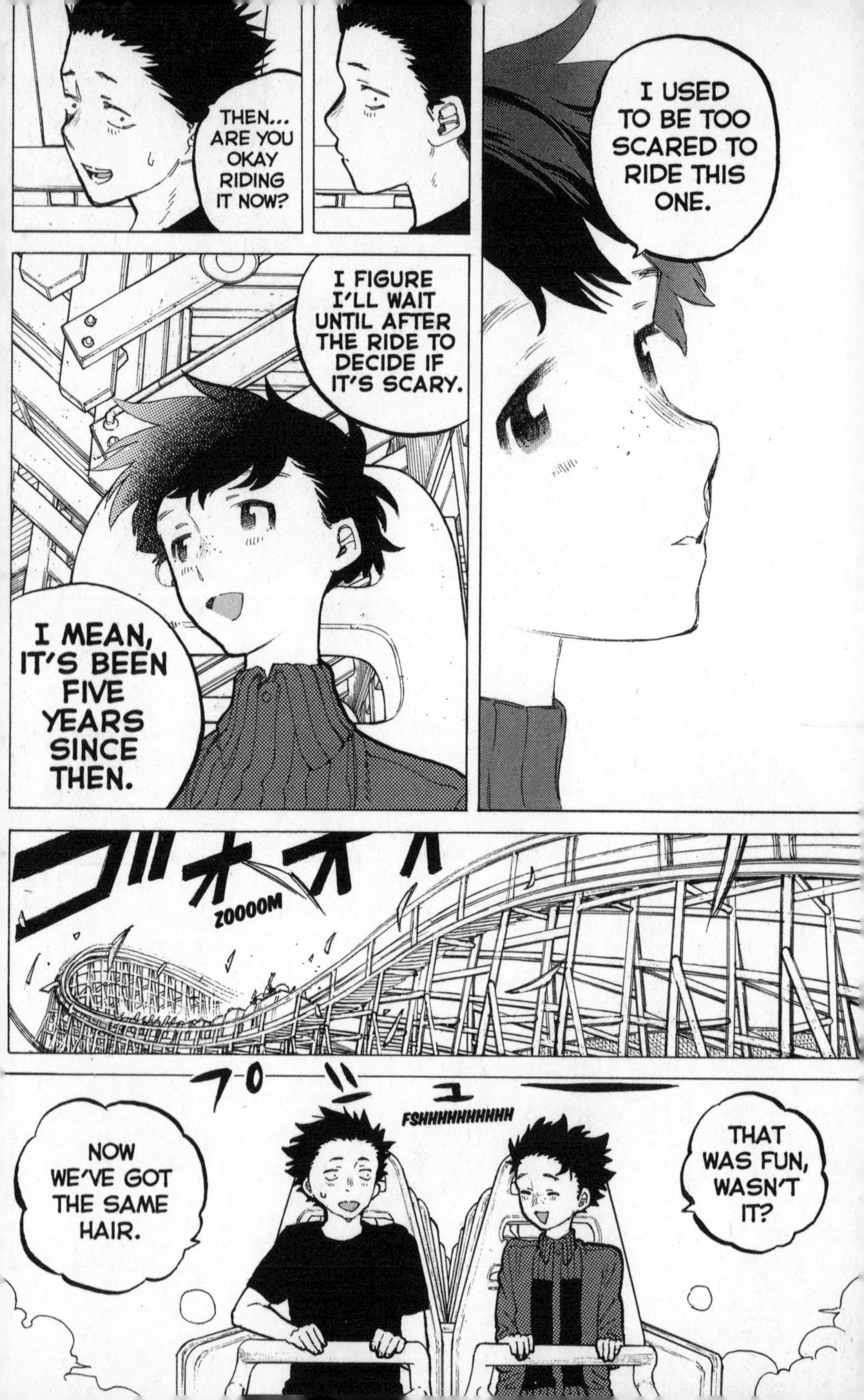
I USED TO BE TOO SCARED TO RIDE THIS ONE.
THEN... ARE YOU OKAY RIDING IT NOW?
I FIGURE I'LL WAIT UNTIL AFTER THE RIDE TO DECIDE IF IT'S SCARY.
I MEAN, IT'S BEEN FIVE YEARS SINCE THEN.
ZOOOOM
FSHHHHHHHHHH
THAT WAS FUN, WASN'T IT?
NOW WE'VE GOT THE SAME HAIR.

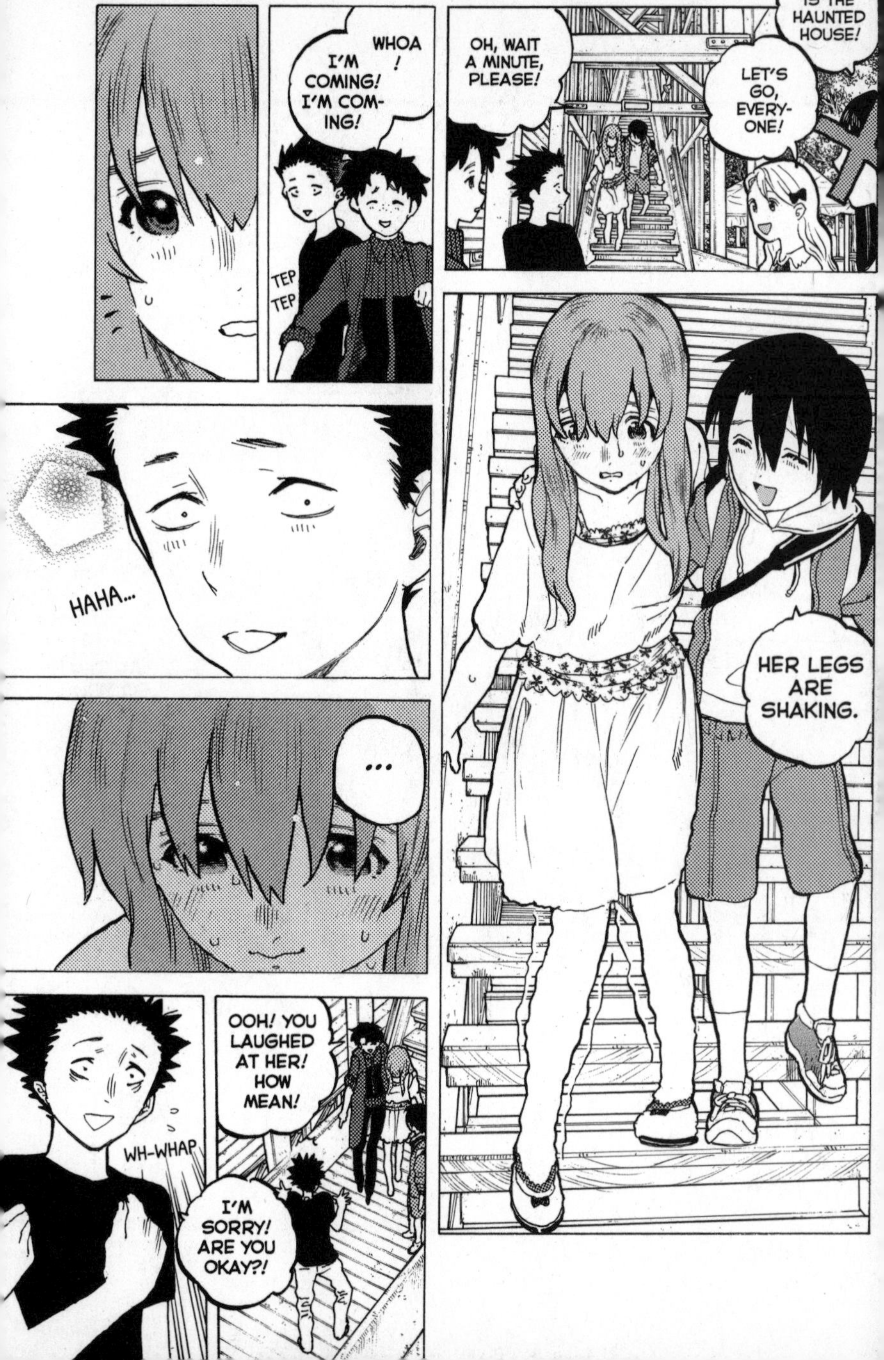
NEXT UP IS THE HAUNTED HOUSE!
LET'S GO, EVERYONE!
OH, WAIT A MINUTE, PLEASE!
WHOA!
I'M COMING! I'M COMING!
TEP TEP
HER LEGS ARE SHAKING.
HAHA...
...
OOH! YOU LAUGHED AT HER! HOW MEAN!
I'M SORRY! ARE YOU OKAY?!
WH-WHAP

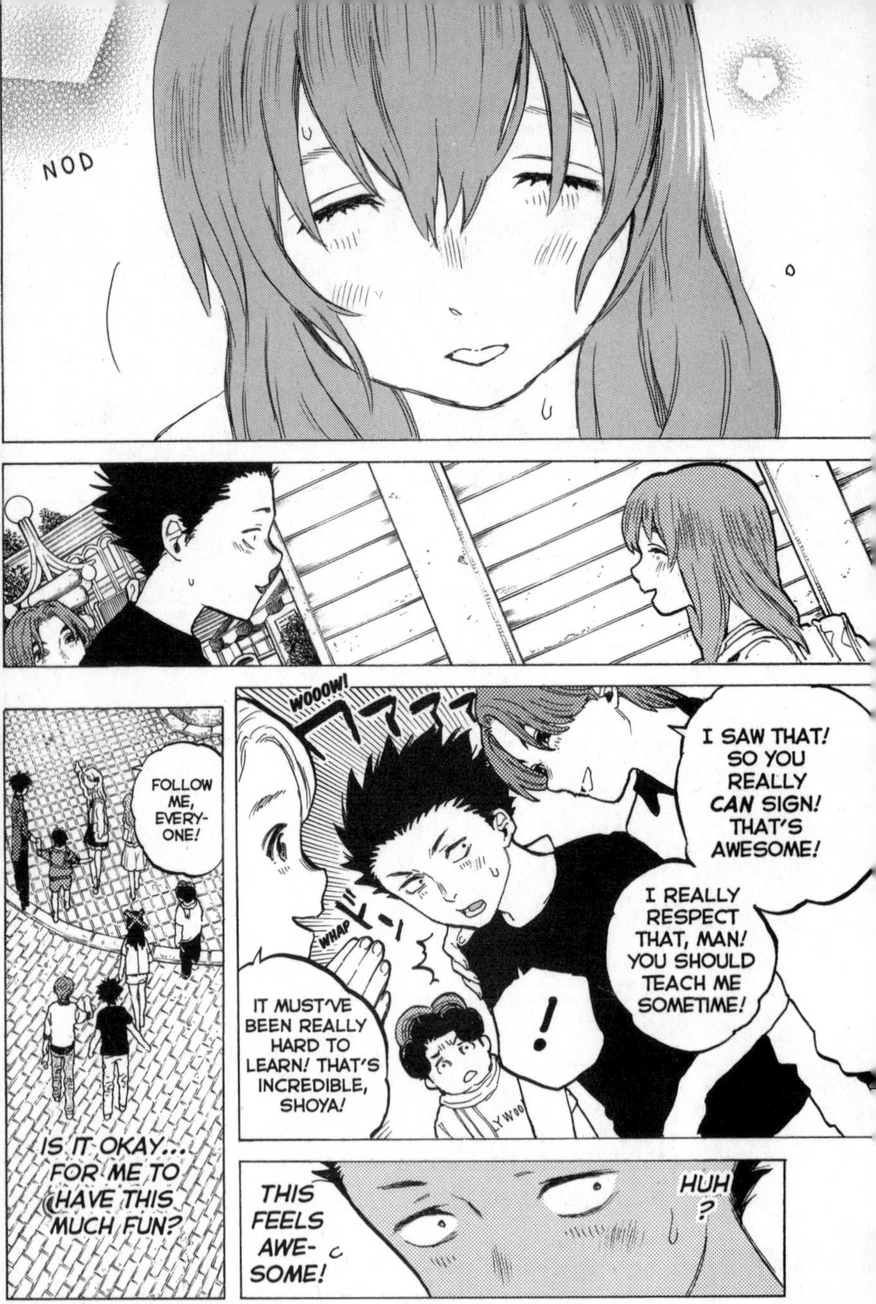
NOD
WOOOW!
I SAW THAT! SO YOU REALLY *CAN* SIGN! THAT'S AWESOME!
I REALLY RESPECT THAT, MAN! YOU SHOULD TEACH ME SOMETIME!
WHAP
IT MUST'VE BEEN REALLY HARD TO LEARN! THAT'S INCREDIBLE, SHOYA!
!
HUH?
THIS FEELS AWE-SOME!
FOLLOW ME, EVERY-ONE!
IS IT OKAY... FOR ME TO HAVE THIS MUCH FUN?

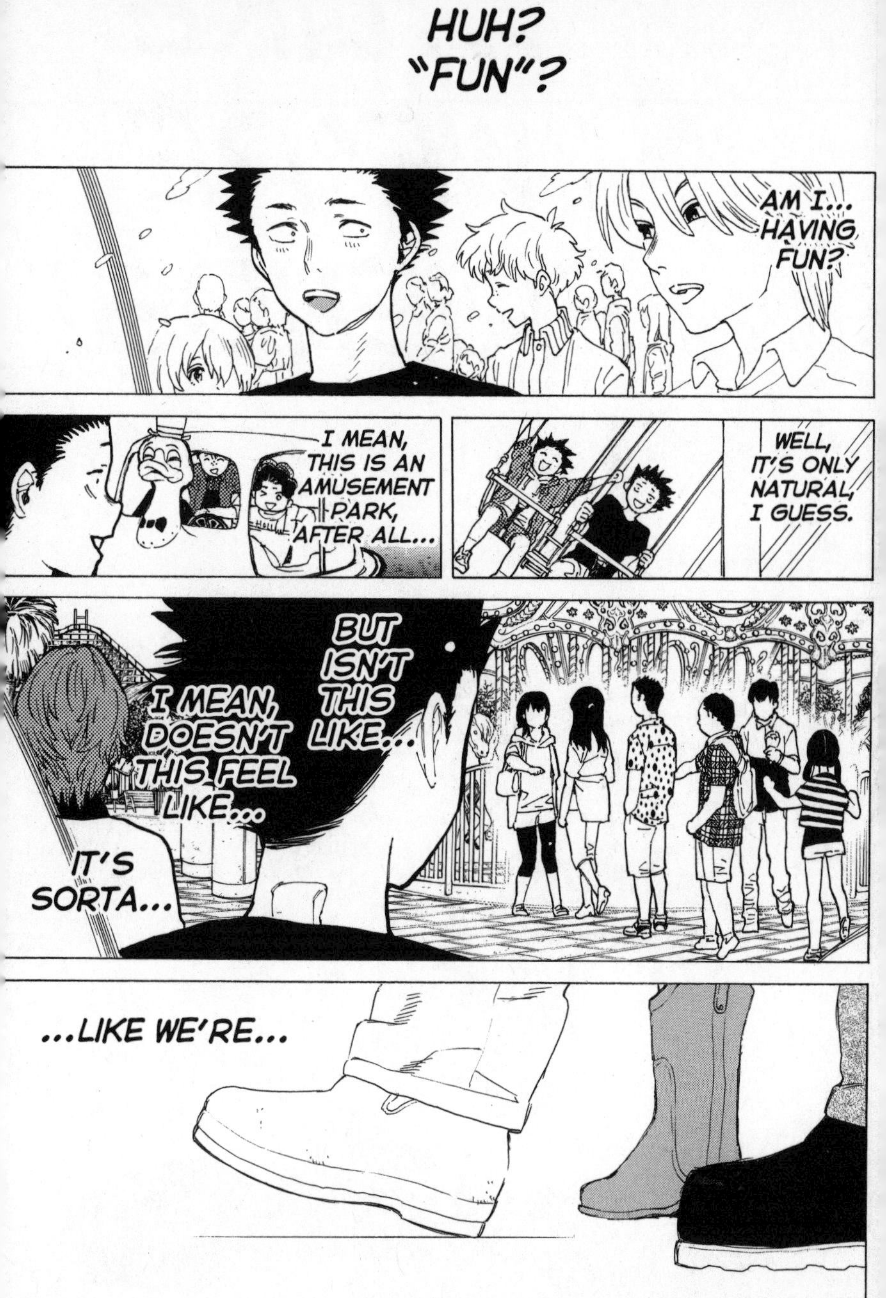
HUH? "FUN"?
AM I... HAVING FUN?
WELL, IT'S ONLY NATURAL, I GUESS.
I MEAN, THIS IS AN AMUSEMENT PARK, AFTER ALL...
BUT ISN'T THIS LIKE...
I MEAN, DOESN'T THIS FEEL LIKE...
IT'S SORTA...
...LIKE WE'RE...

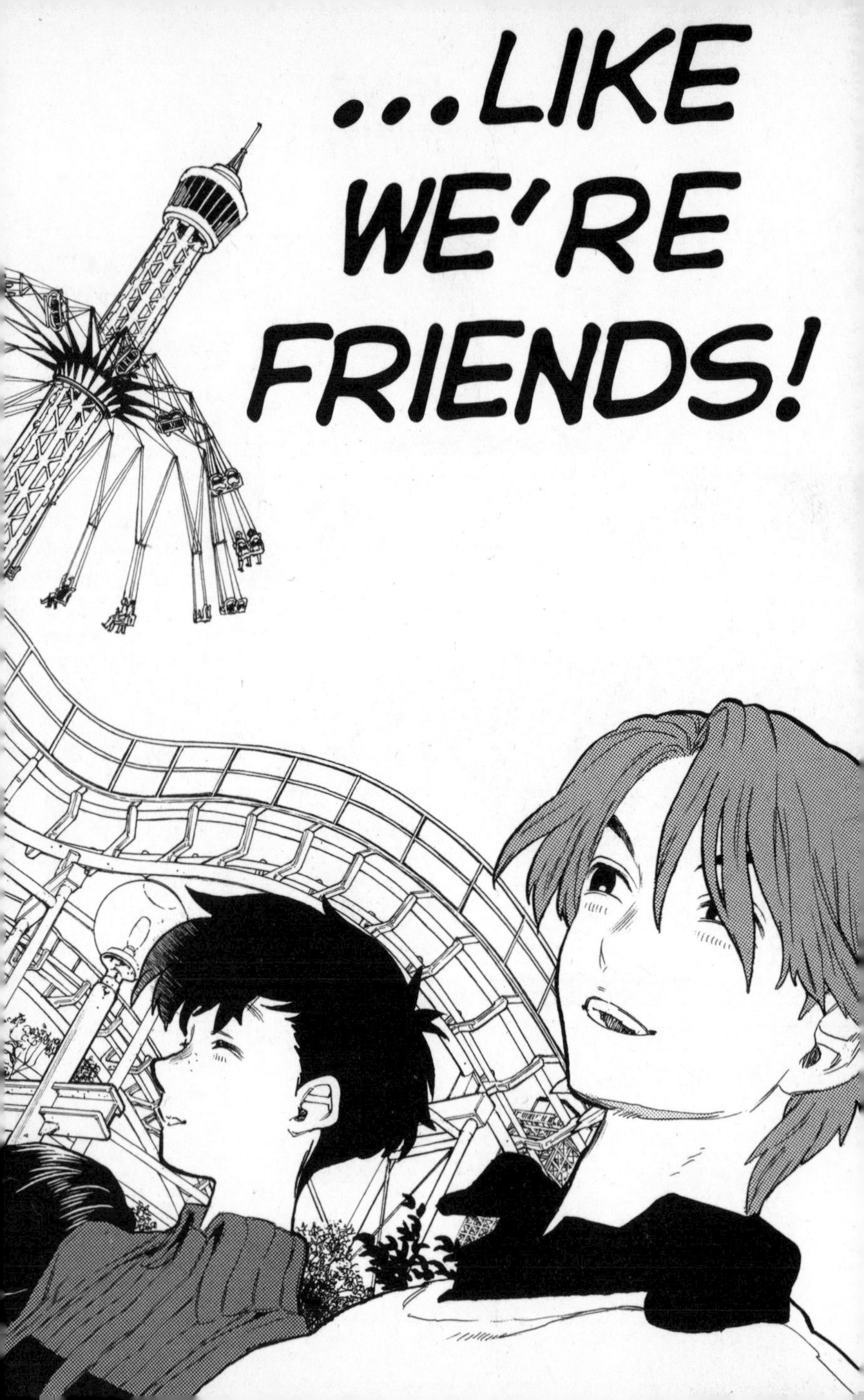
...LIKE WE'RE FRIENDS!

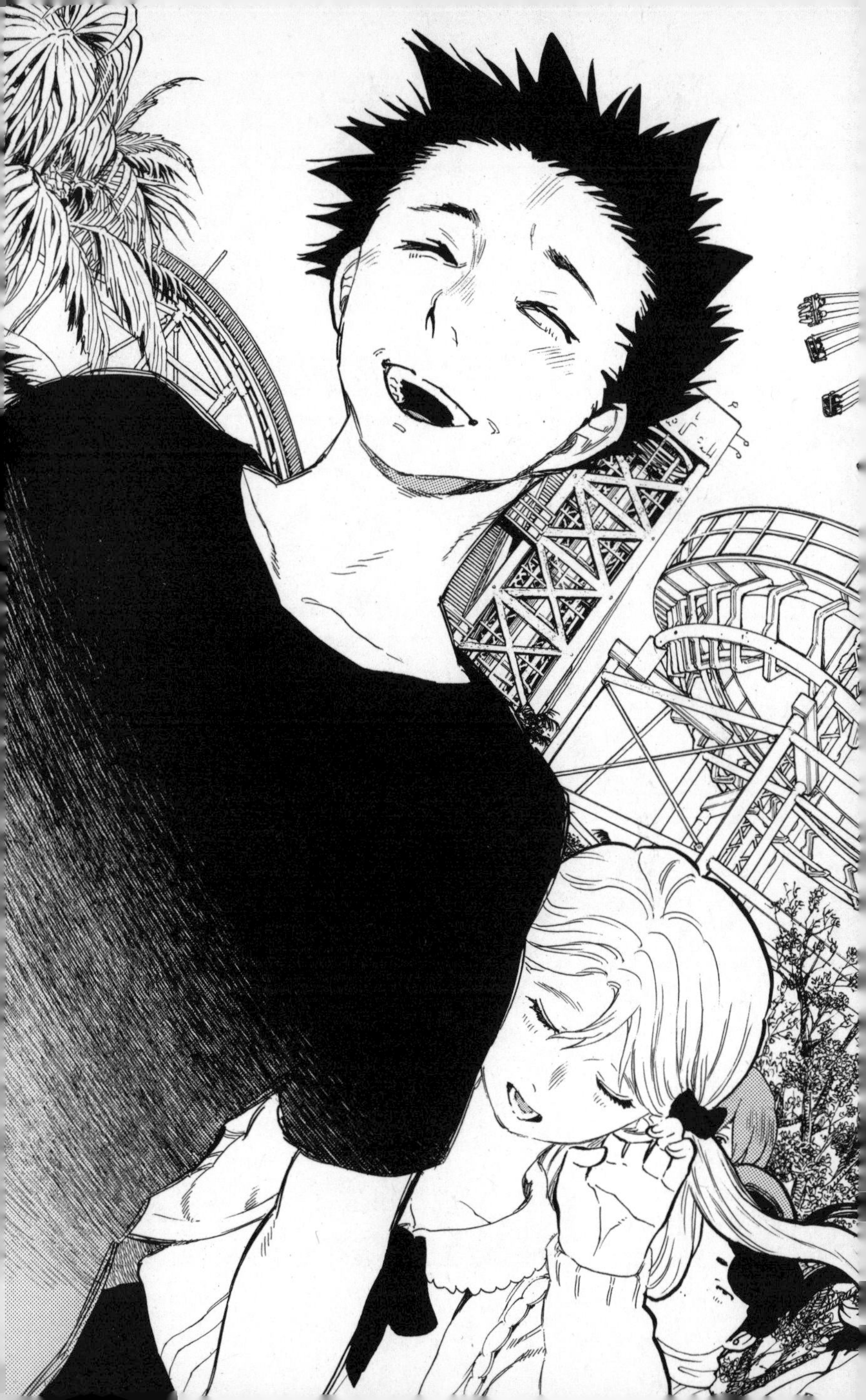

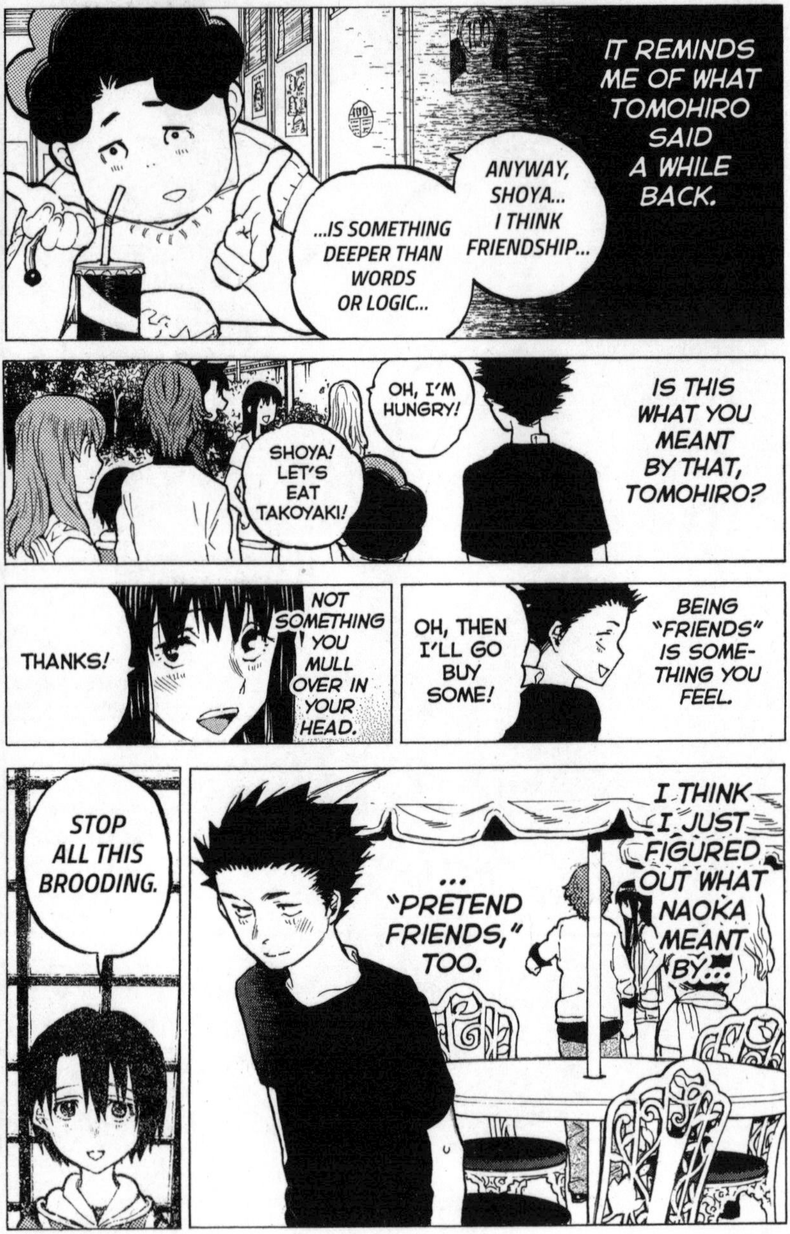
IT REMINDS ME OF WHAT TOMOHIRO SAID A WHILE BACK.
ANYWAY, SHOYA... I THINK FRIENDSHIP...
...IS SOMETHING DEEPER THAN WORDS OR LOGIC...
IS THIS WHAT YOU MEANT BY THAT, TOMOHIRO?
OH, I'M HUNGRY!
SHOYA! LET'S EAT TAKOYAKI!
BEING "FRIENDS" IS SOME-THING YOU FEEL.
OH, THEN I'LL GO BUY SOME!
NOT SOMETHING YOU MULL OVER IN YOUR HEAD.
THANKS!
I THINK I JUST FIGURED OUT WHAT NAOKA MEANT BY...
... "PRETEND FRIENDS," TOO.
STOP ALL THIS BROODING.

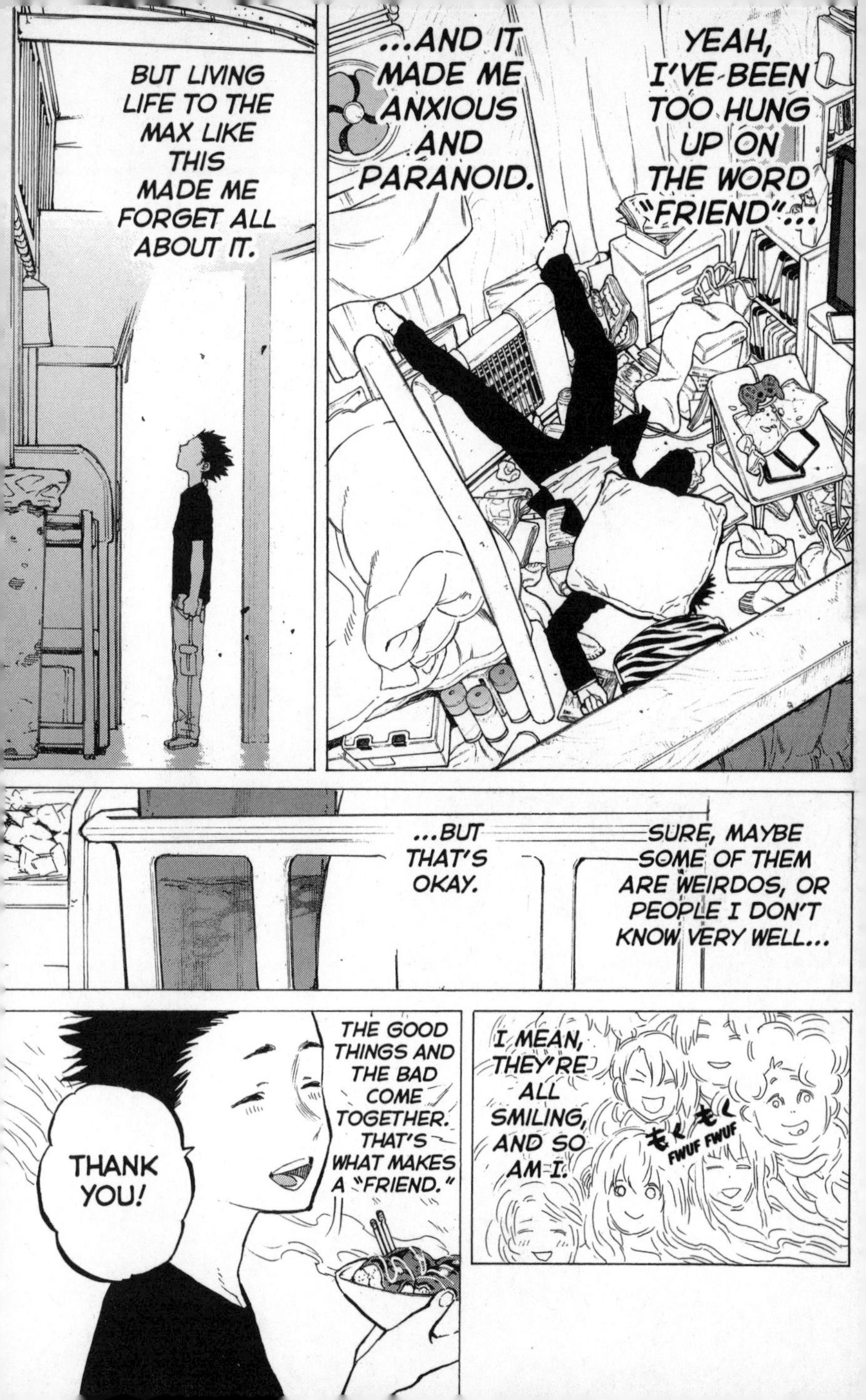
YEAH, I'VE BEEN TOO HUNG UP ON THE WORD "FRIEND"...
...AND IT MADE ME ANXIOUS AND PARANOID.
BUT LIVING LIFE TO THE MAX LIKE THIS MADE ME FORGET ALL ABOUT IT.
SURE, MAYBE SOME OF THEM ARE WEIRDOS, OR PEOPLE I DON'T KNOW VERY WELL...
...BUT THAT'S OKAY.
I MEAN, THEY'RE ALL SMILING, AND SO AM I.
もく もく
FWUF FWUF
THE GOOD THINGS AND THE BAD COME TOGETHER. THAT'S WHAT MAKES A "FRIEND."
THANK YOU!

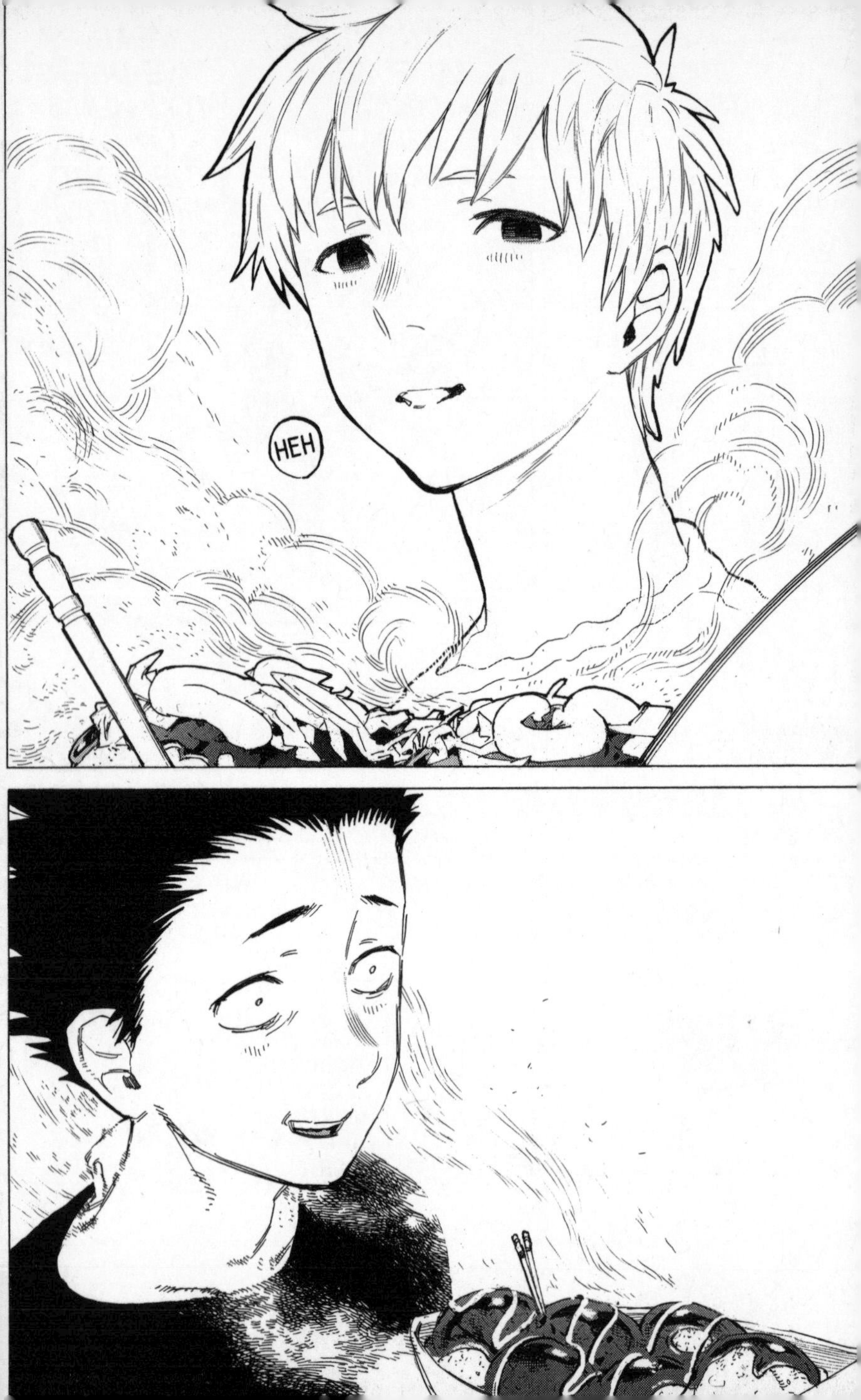
HEH

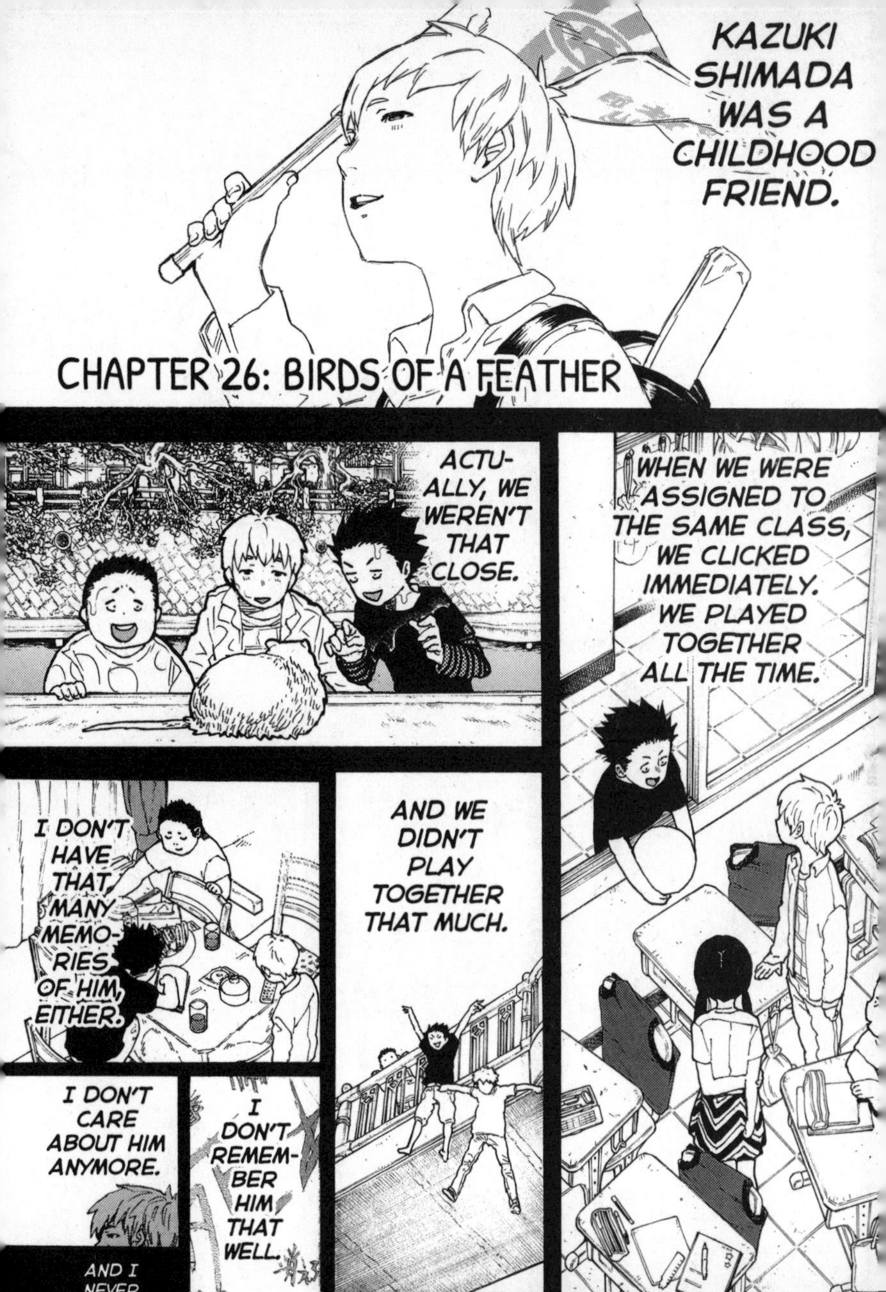
KAZUKI SHIMADA WAS A CHILDHOOD FRIEND.
CHAPTER 26: BIRDS OF A FEATHER
WHEN WE WERE ASSIGNED TO THE SAME CLASS, WE CLICKED IMMEDIATELY. WE PLAYED TOGETHER ALL THE TIME.
ACTU-ALLY, WE WEREN'T THAT CLOSE.
AND WE DIDN'T PLAY TOGETHER THAT MUCH.
I DON'T HAVE THAT MANY MEMO-RIES OF HIM, EITHER.
I DON'T REMEM-BER HIM THAT WELL.
I DON'T CARE ABOUT HIM ANYMORE.
AND I NEVER

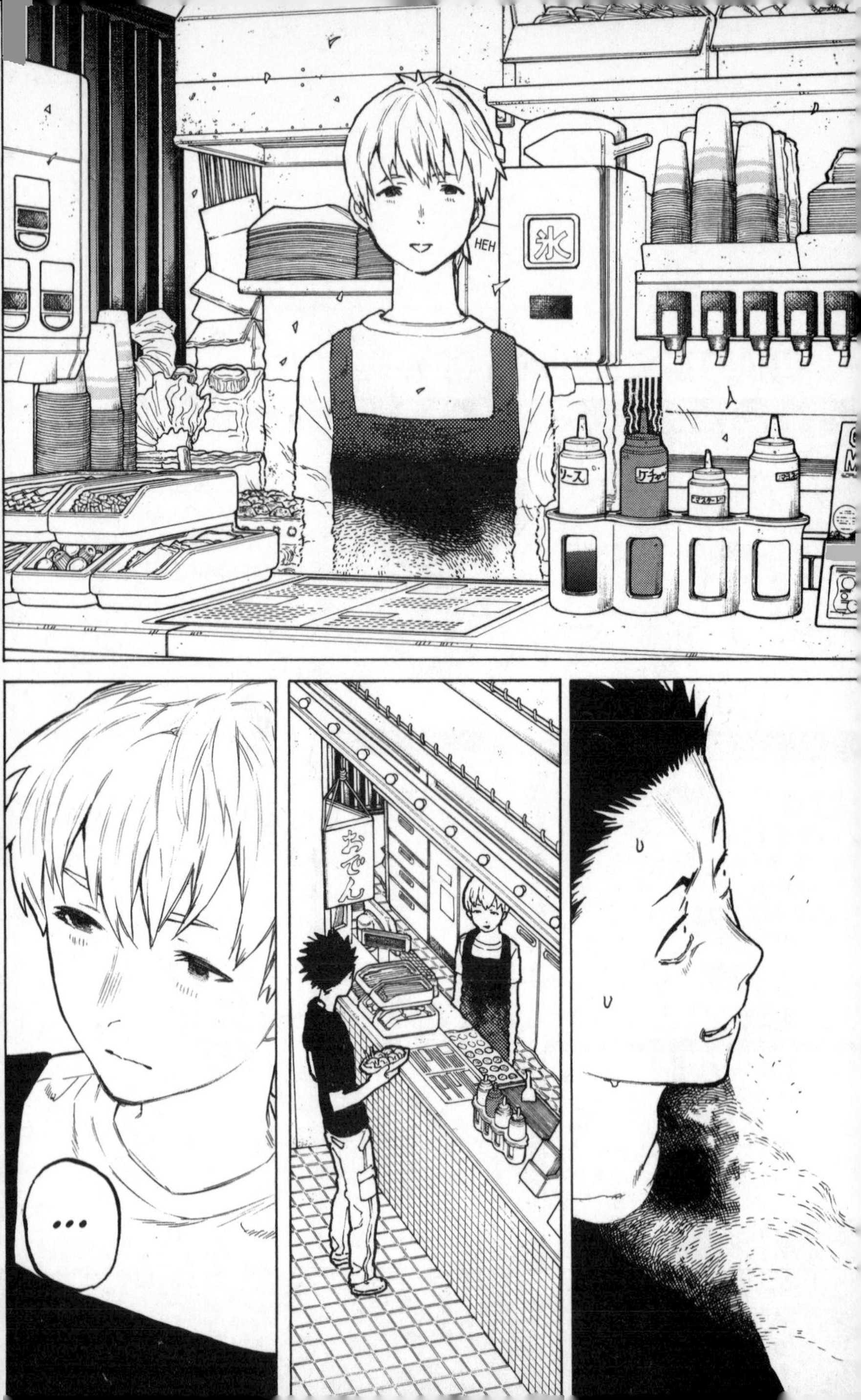
HEH
氷
ソース
おでん
...

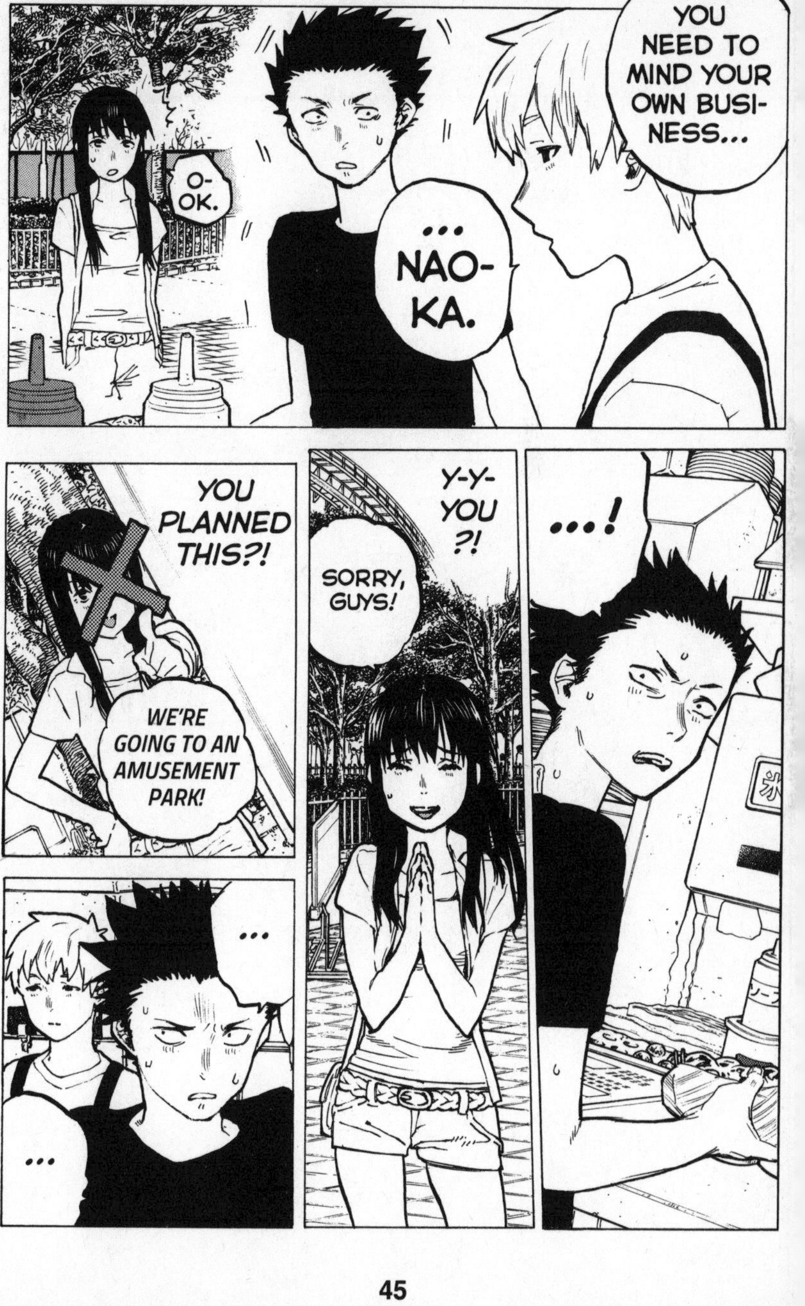
YOU NEED TO MIND YOUR OWN BUSI-NESS...
...NAO-KA.
O-OK.
...!
Y-Y-YOU ?!
SORRY, GUYS!
YOU PLANNED THIS?!
WE'RE GOING TO AN AMUSEMENT PARK!
...
...

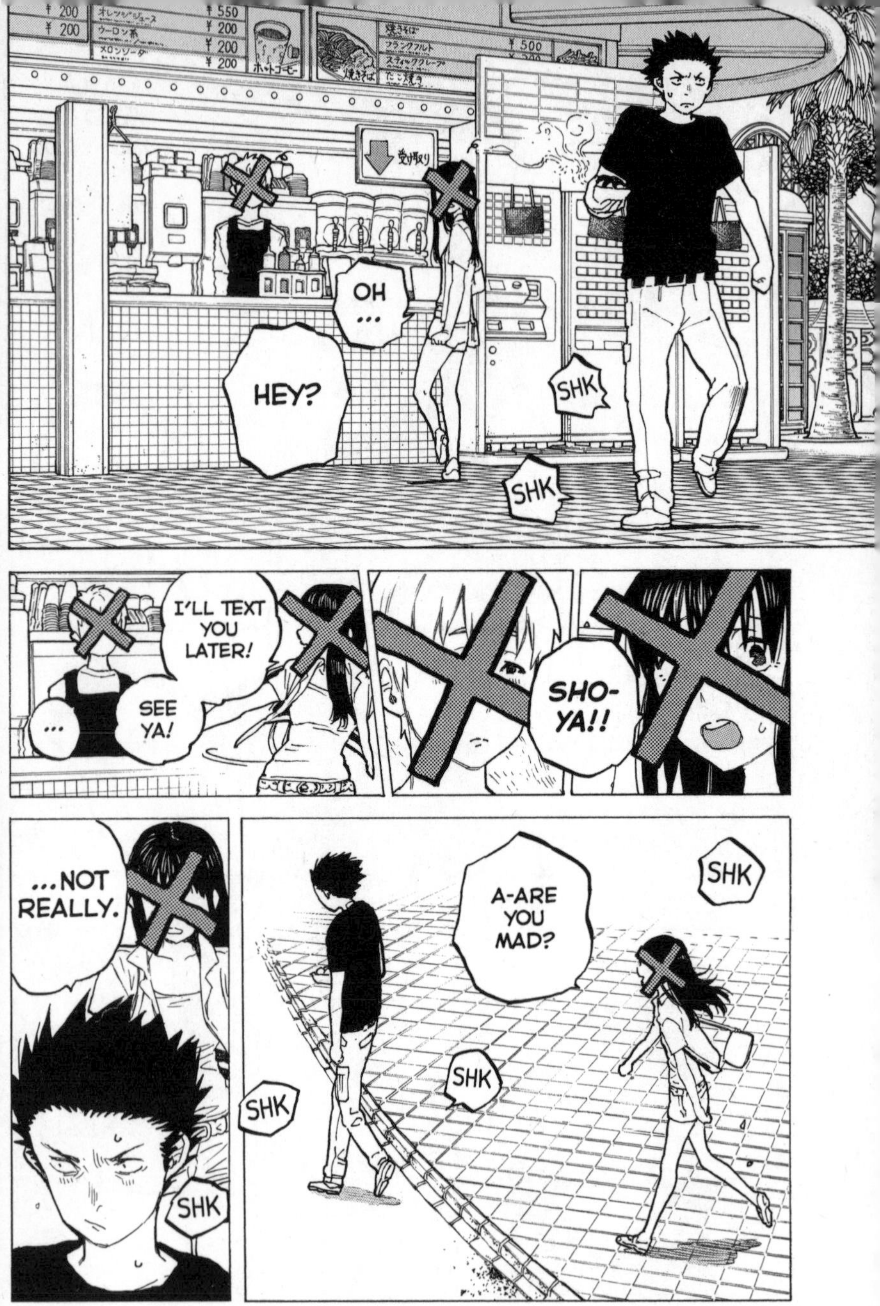

OH ...
SHK
HEY?
SHK
SHO-YA!!
I'LL TEXT YOU LATER!
SEE YA!
...
SHK
A-ARE YOU MAD?
SHK
SHK
...NOT REALLY.
SHK

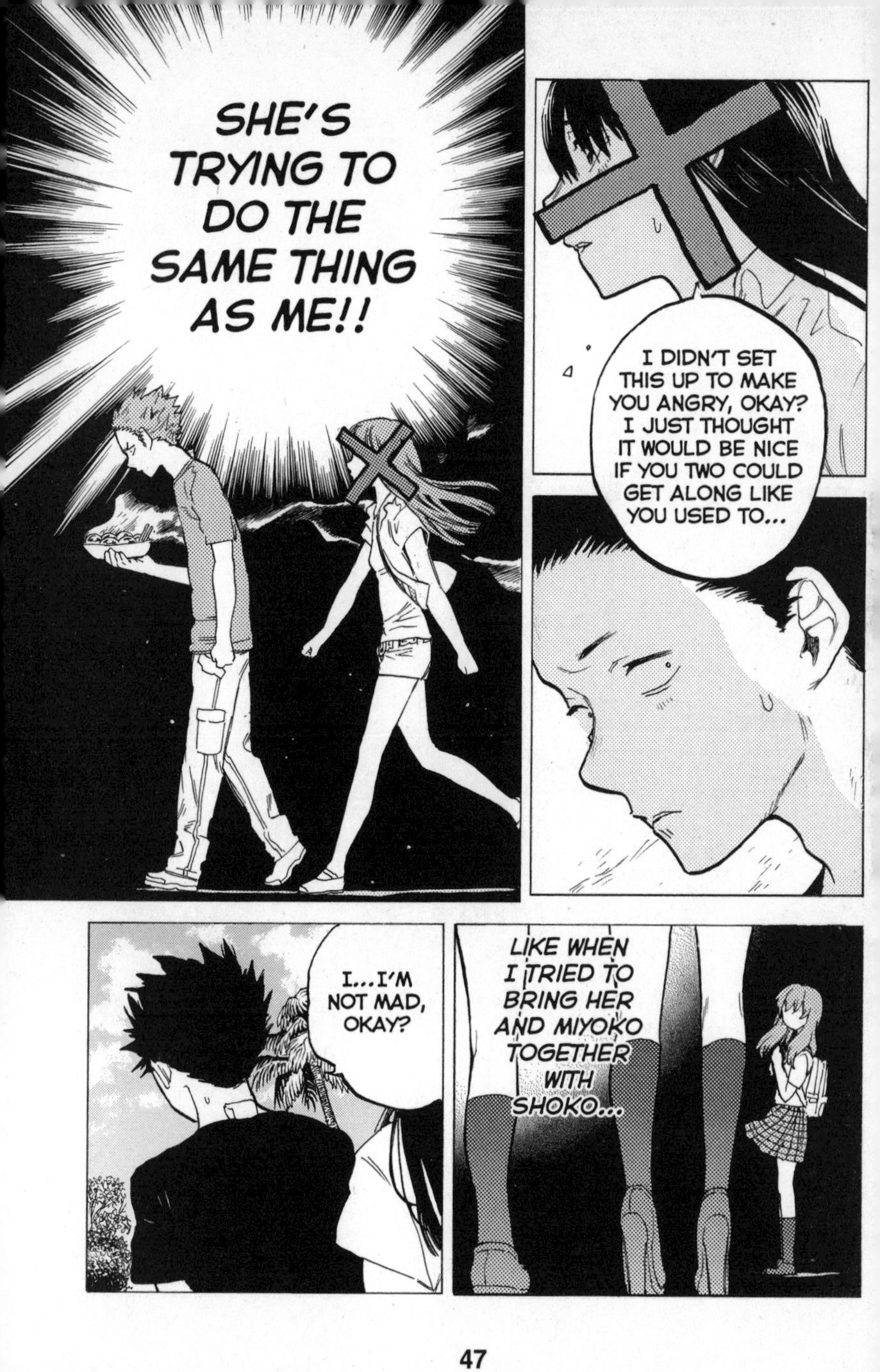
I DIDN'T SET THIS UP TO MAKE YOU ANGRY, OKAY? I JUST THOUGHT IT WOULD BE NICE IF YOU TWO COULD GET ALONG LIKE YOU USED TO...
SHE'S TRYING TO DO THE SAME THING AS ME!!
LIKE WHEN I TRIED TO BRING HER AND MIYOKO TOGETHER WITH SHOKO...
I...I'M NOT MAD, OKAY?

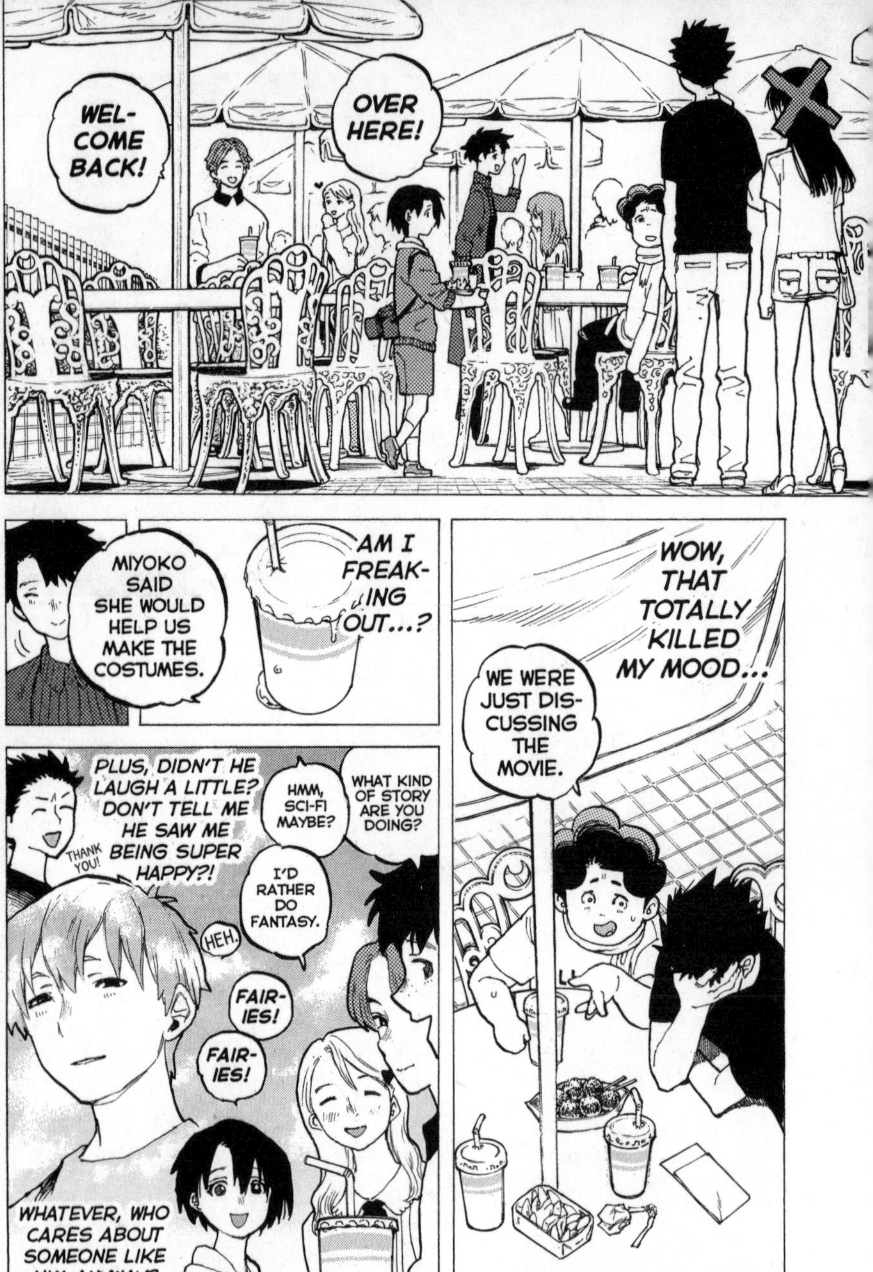
OVER HERE!
WELCOME BACK!
WOW, THAT TOTALLY KILLED MY MOOD...
WE WERE JUST DISCUSSING THE MOVIE.
AM I FREAKING OUT...?
MIYOKO SAID SHE WOULD HELP US MAKE THE COSTUMES.
WHAT KIND OF STORY ARE YOU DOING?
HMM, SCI-FI MAYBE?
PLUS, DIDN'T HE LAUGH A LITTLE? DON'T TELL ME HE SAW ME BEING SUPER HAPPY?!
I'D RATHER DO FANTASY.
THANK YOU!
HEH.
FAIRIES!
FAIRIES!
WHATEVER, WHO CARES ABOUT SOMEONE LIKE HIM ANYWAY?

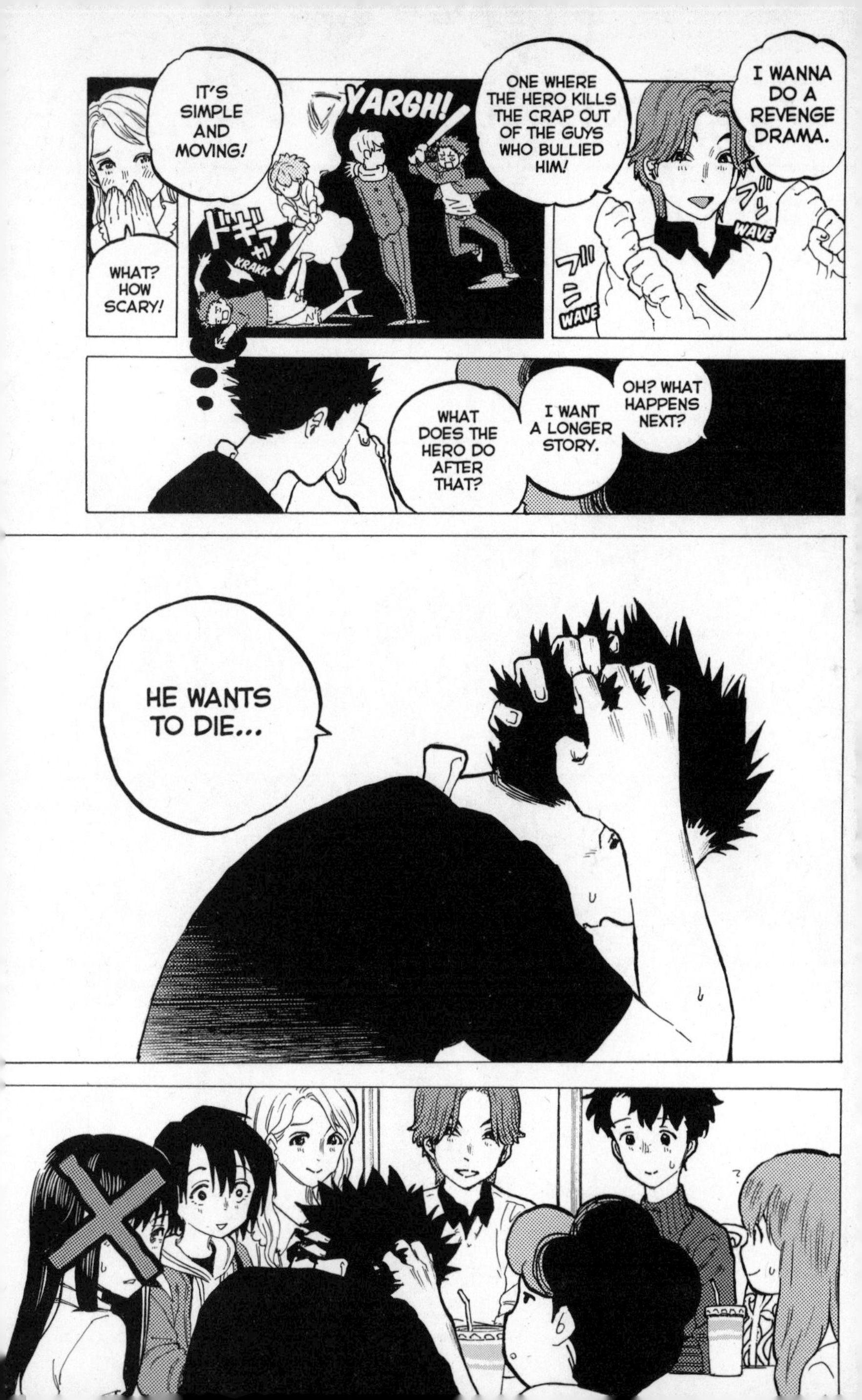
I WANNA DO A REVENGE DRAMA.
WAVE
WAVE
ONE WHERE THE HERO KILLS THE CRAP OUT OF THE GUYS WHO BULLIED HIM!
YARGH!
ドギャッ
KRAKK
IT'S SIMPLE AND MOVING!
WHAT? HOW SCARY!
OH? WHAT HAPPENS NEXT?
I WANT A LONGER STORY.
WHAT DOES THE HERO DO AFTER THAT?
HE WANTS TO DIE...

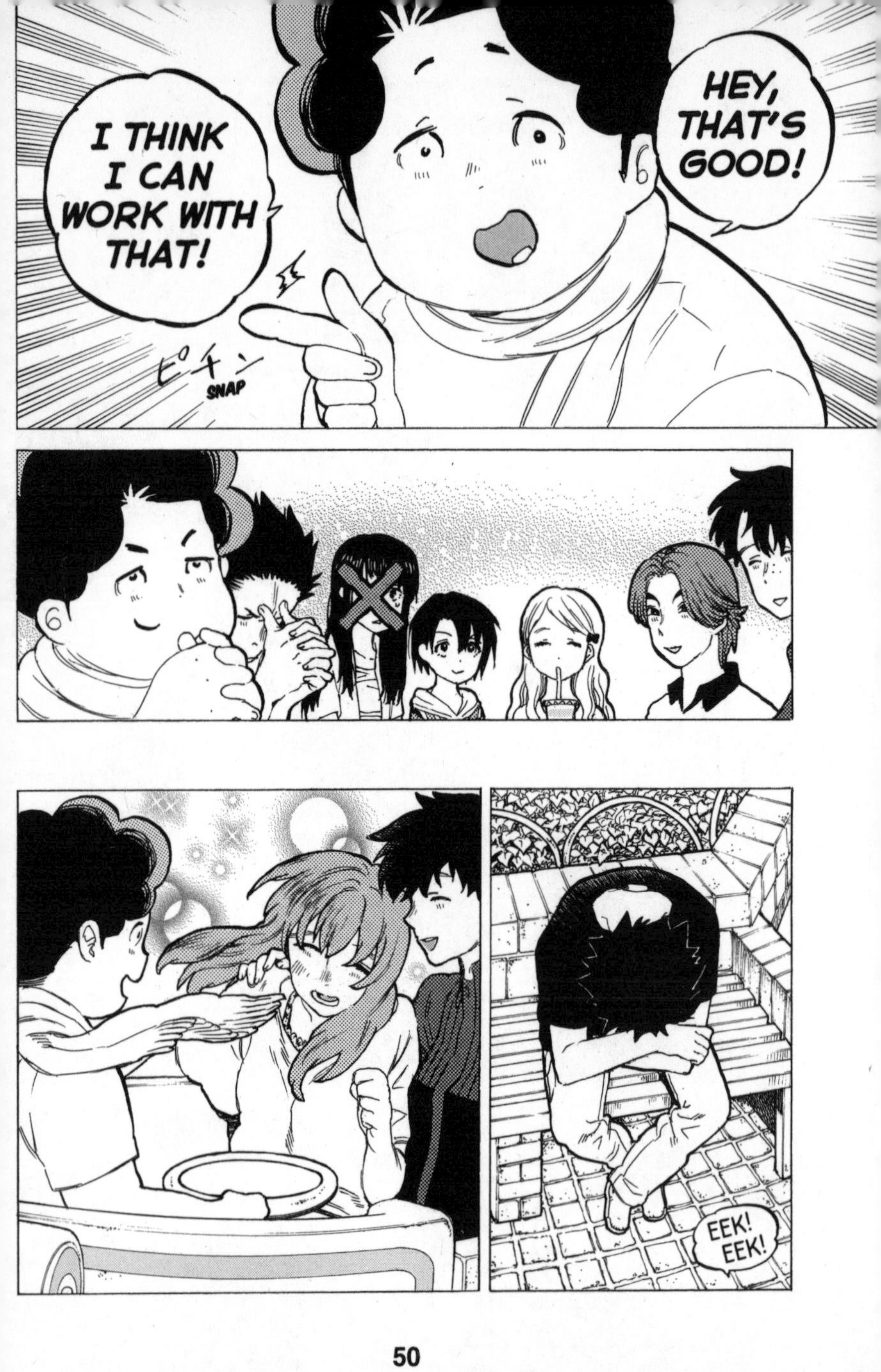
HEY, THAT'S GOOD!
I THINK I CAN WORK WITH THAT!
ピキン
SNAP
EEK! EEK!

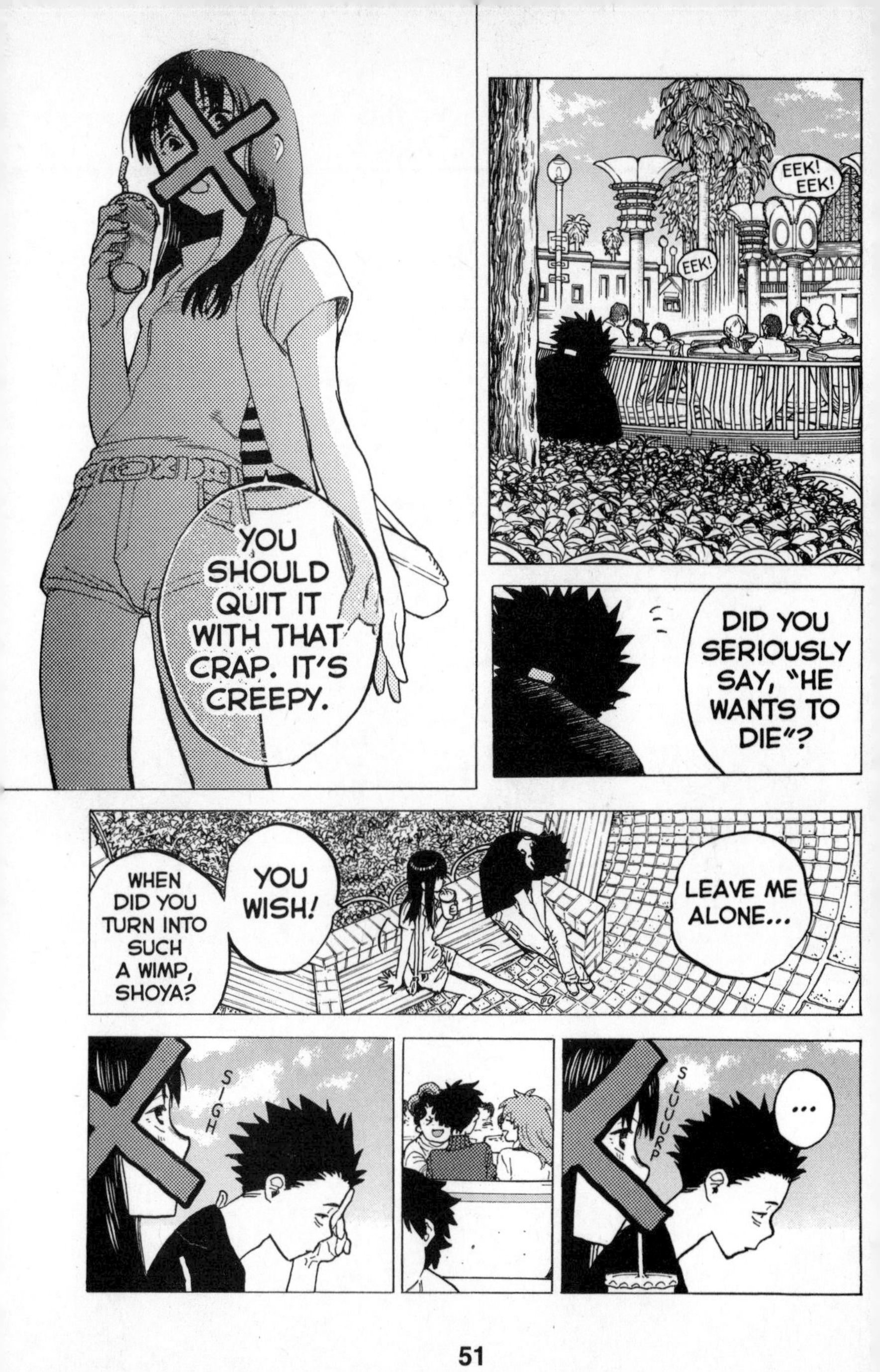
EEK! EEK!
EEK!
DID YOU SERIOUSLY SAY, "HE WANTS TO DIE"?
YOU SHOULD QUIT IT WITH THAT CRAP. IT'S CREEPY.
LEAVE ME ALONE...
YOU WISH!
WHEN DID YOU TURN INTO SUCH A WIMP, SHOYA?
SLUUURP
...
SIGH

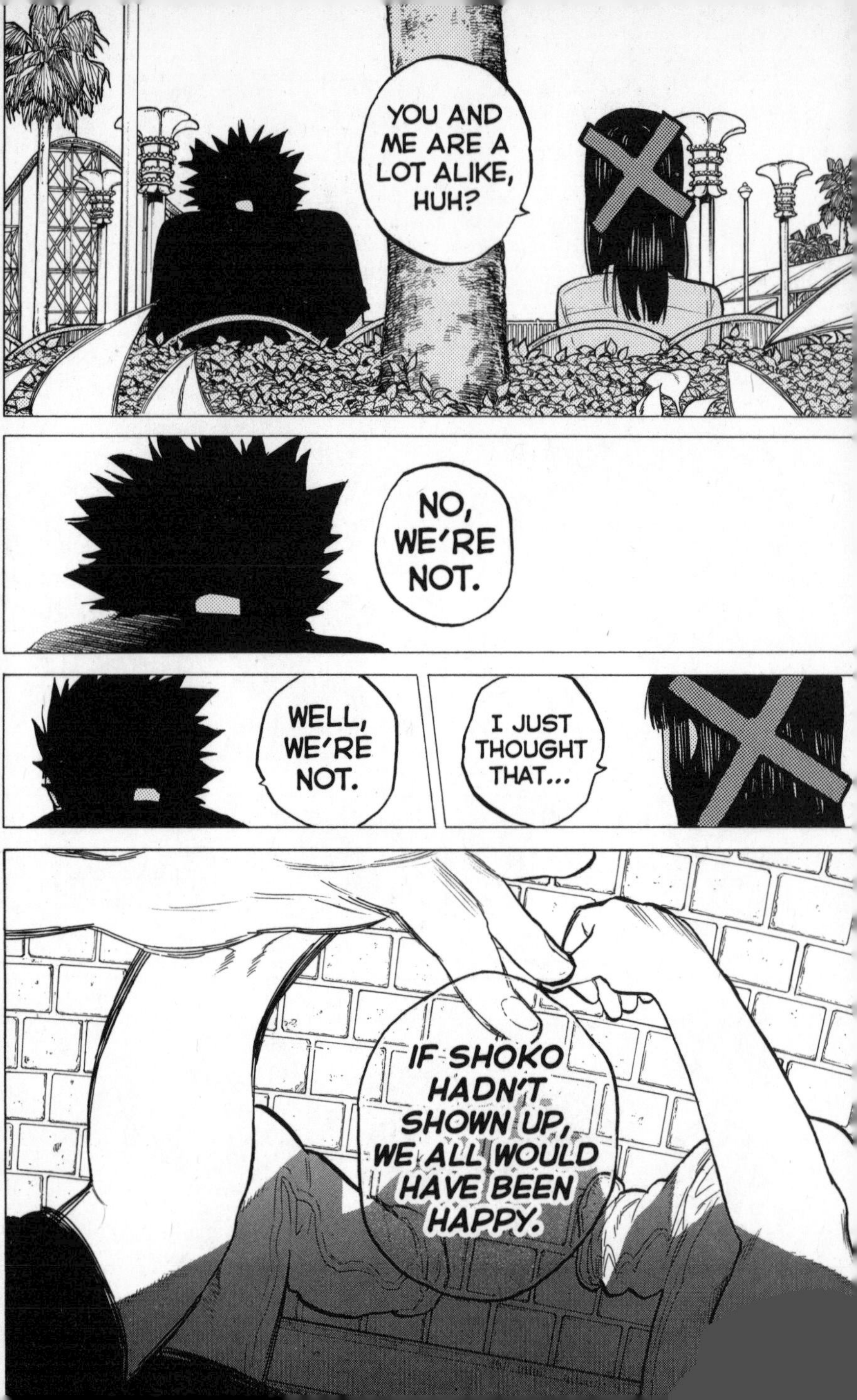
YOU AND ME ARE A LOT ALIKE, HUH?
NO, WE'RE NOT.
I JUST THOUGHT THAT...
WELL, WE'RE NOT.
IF SHOKO HADN'T SHOWN UP, WE ALL WOULD HAVE BEEN HAPPY.

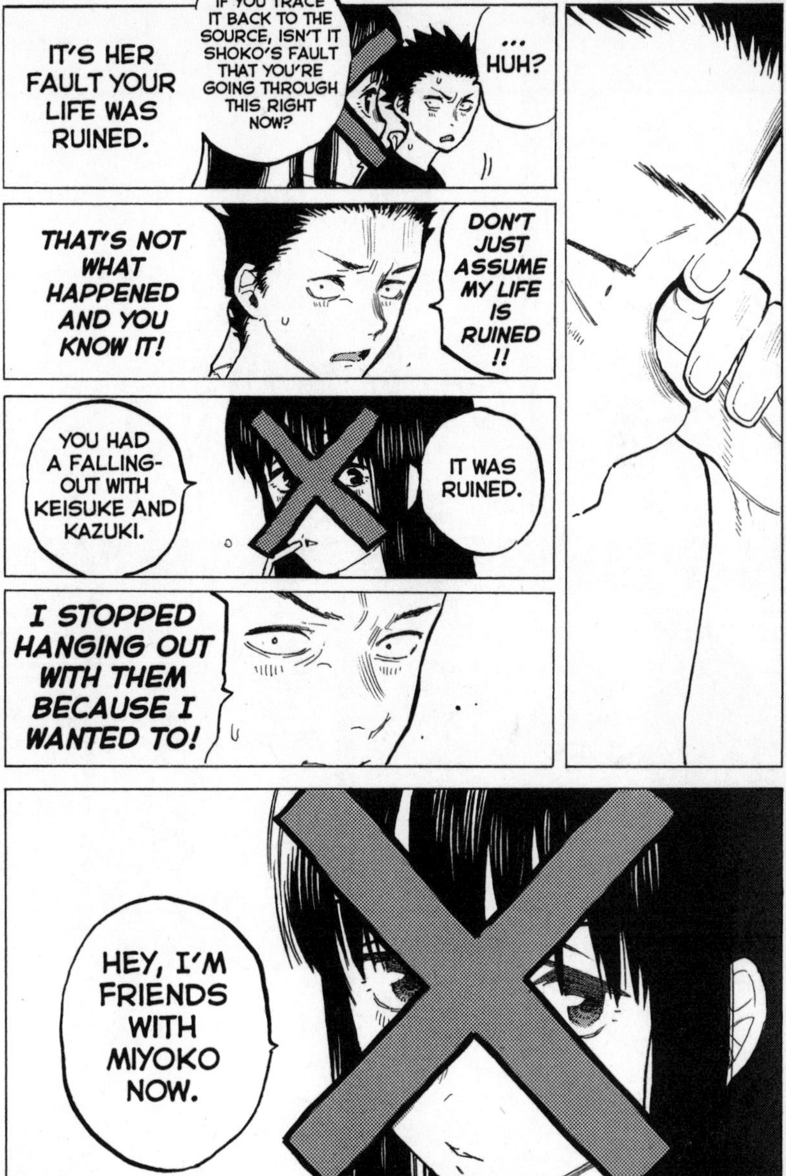
... HUH?
IF YOU TRACE IT BACK TO THE SOURCE, ISN'T IT SHOKO'S FAULT THAT YOU'RE GOING THROUGH THIS RIGHT NOW?
IT'S HER FAULT YOUR LIFE WAS RUINED.
DON'T JUST ASSUME MY LIFE IS RUINED !!
THAT'S NOT WHAT HAPPENED AND YOU KNOW IT!
IT WAS RUINED.
YOU HAD A FALLING-OUT WITH KEISUKE AND KAZUKI.
I STOPPED HANGING OUT WITH THEM BECAUSE I WANTED TO!
HEY, I'M FRIENDS WITH MIYOKO NOW.

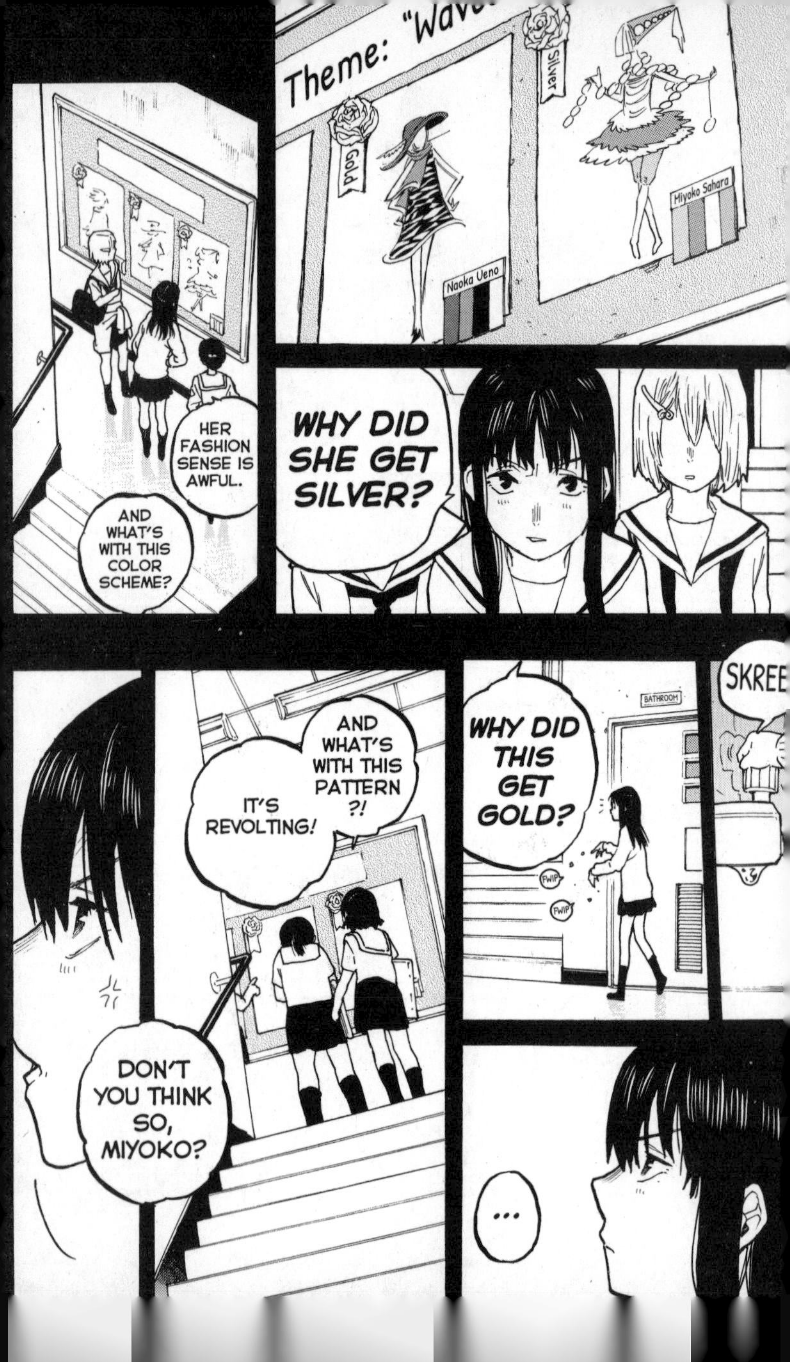
Theme: "Wav
Silver
Gold
Miyoko Sahara
Naoka Ueno
WHY DID SHE GET SILVER?
HER FASHION SENSE IS AWFUL.
AND WHAT'S WITH THIS COLOR SCHEME?
SKREE
BATHROOM
WHY DID THIS GET GOLD?
FWIP
FWIP
...
AND WHAT'S WITH THIS PATTERN ?!
IT'S REVOLTING!
DON'T YOU THINK SO, MIYOKO?

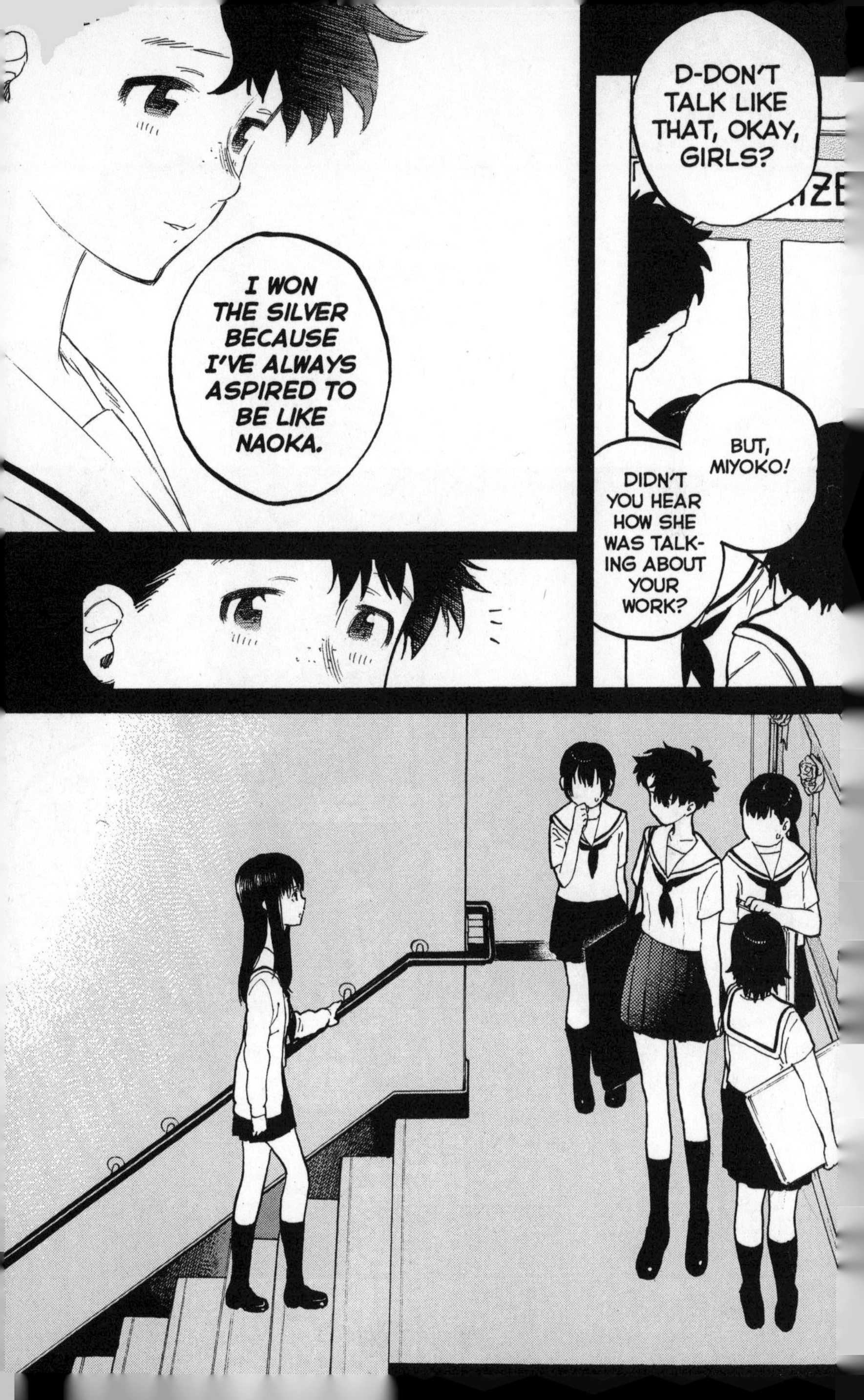
D-DON'T TALK LIKE THAT, OKAY, GIRLS?
BUT, MIYOKO!
DIDN'T YOU HEAR HOW SHE WAS TALK-ING ABOUT YOUR WORK?
I WON THE SILVER BECAUSE I'VE ALWAYS ASPIRED TO BE LIKE NAOKA.

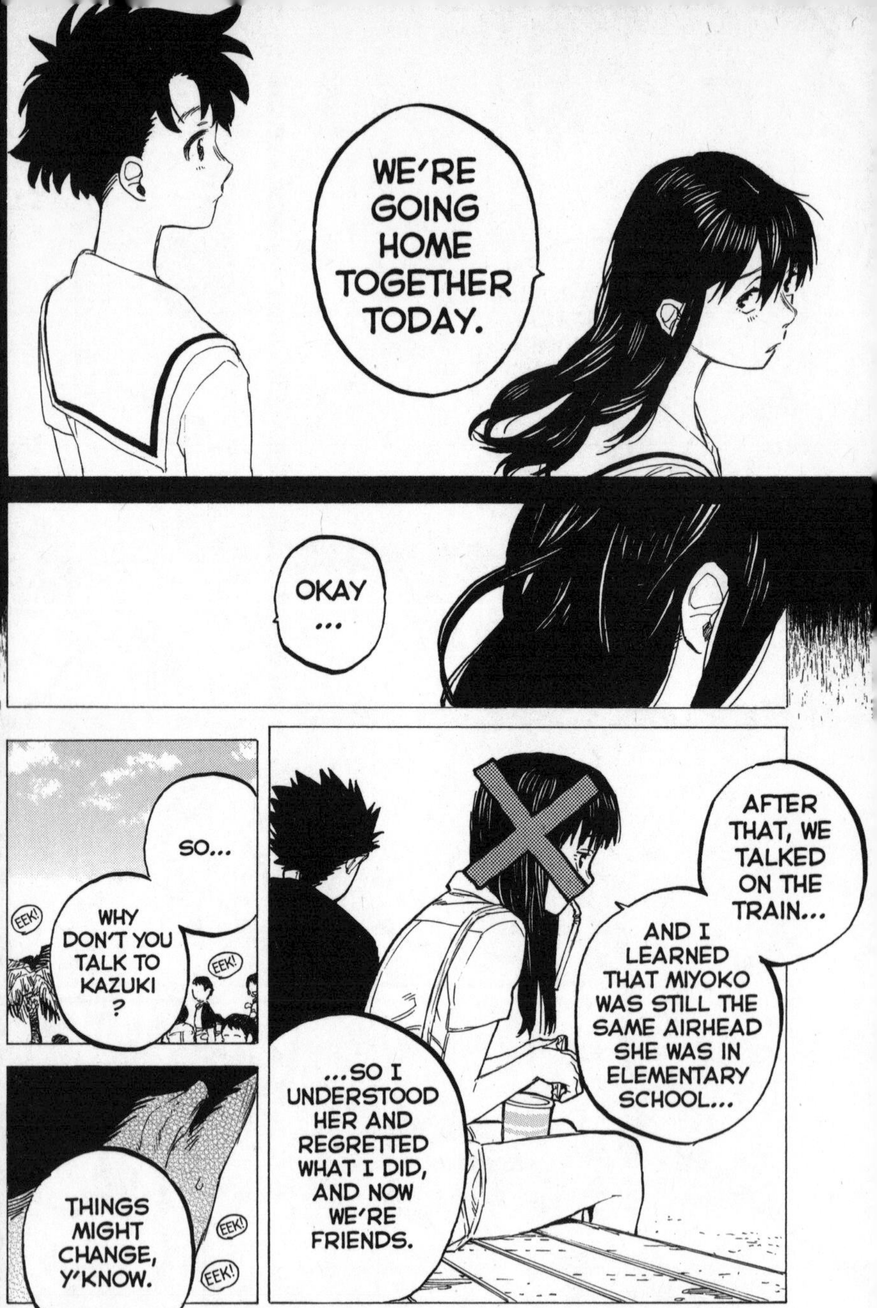
WE'RE GOING HOME TOGETHER TODAY.
OKAY ...
AFTER THAT, WE TALKED ON THE TRAIN...
AND I LEARNED THAT MIYOKO WAS STILL THE SAME AIRHEAD SHE WAS IN ELEMENTARY SCHOOL...
...SO I UNDERSTOOD HER AND REGRETTED WHAT I DID, AND NOW WE'RE FRIENDS.
SO...
WHY DON'T YOU TALK TO KAZUKI ?
EEK!
EEK!
THINGS MIGHT CHANGE, Y'KNOW.
EEK!
EEK!

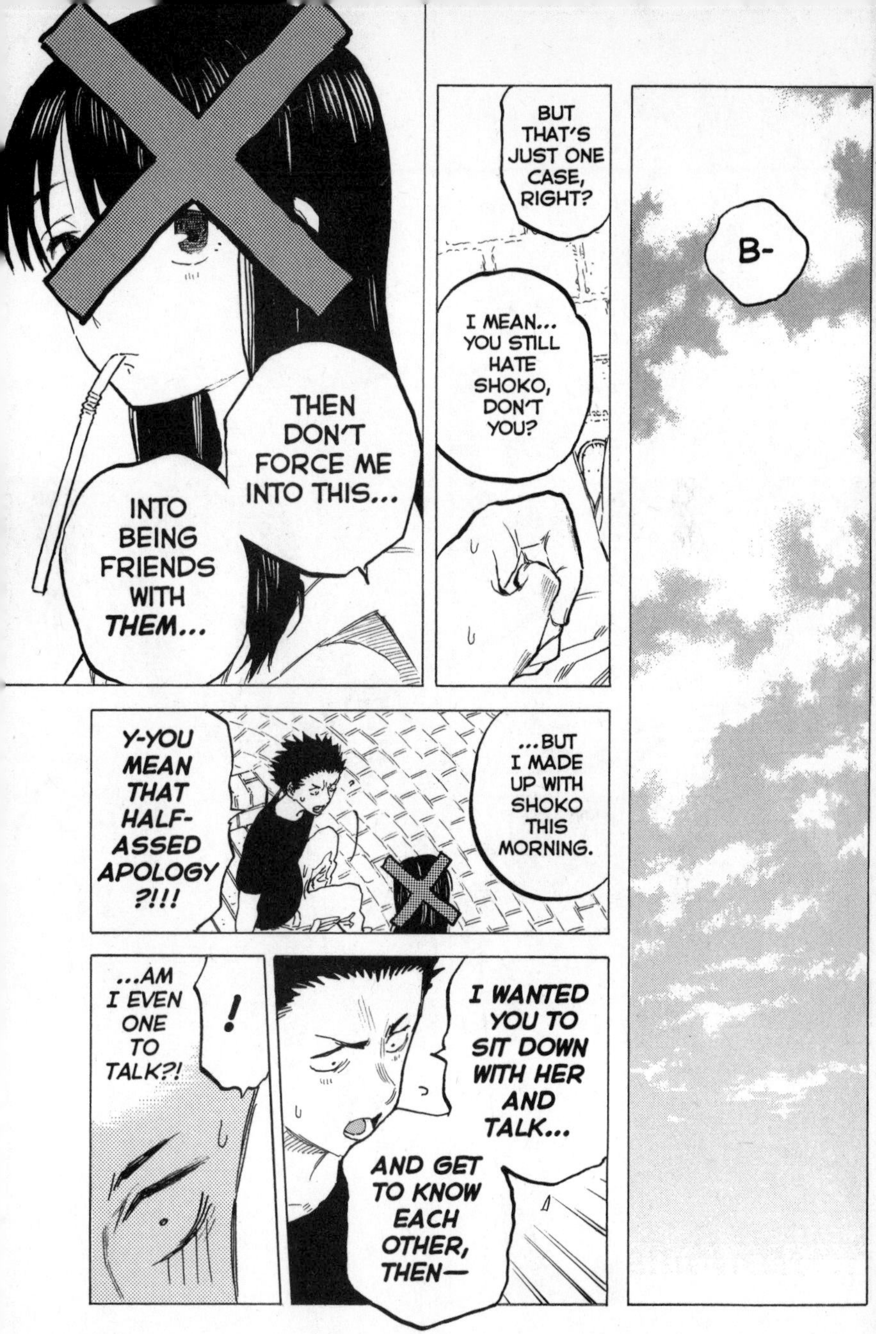
B-
BUT THAT'S JUST ONE CASE, RIGHT?
I MEAN... YOU STILL HATE SHOKO, DON'T YOU?
THEN DON'T FORCE ME INTO THIS...
INTO BEING FRIENDS WITH *THEM*...
...BUT I MADE UP WITH SHOKO THIS MORNING.
Y-YOU MEAN THAT HALF-ASSED APOLOGY ?!!!
I WANTED YOU TO SIT DOWN WITH HER AND TALK...
AND GET TO KNOW EACH OTHER, THEN—
!
...AM I EVEN ONE TO TALK?!

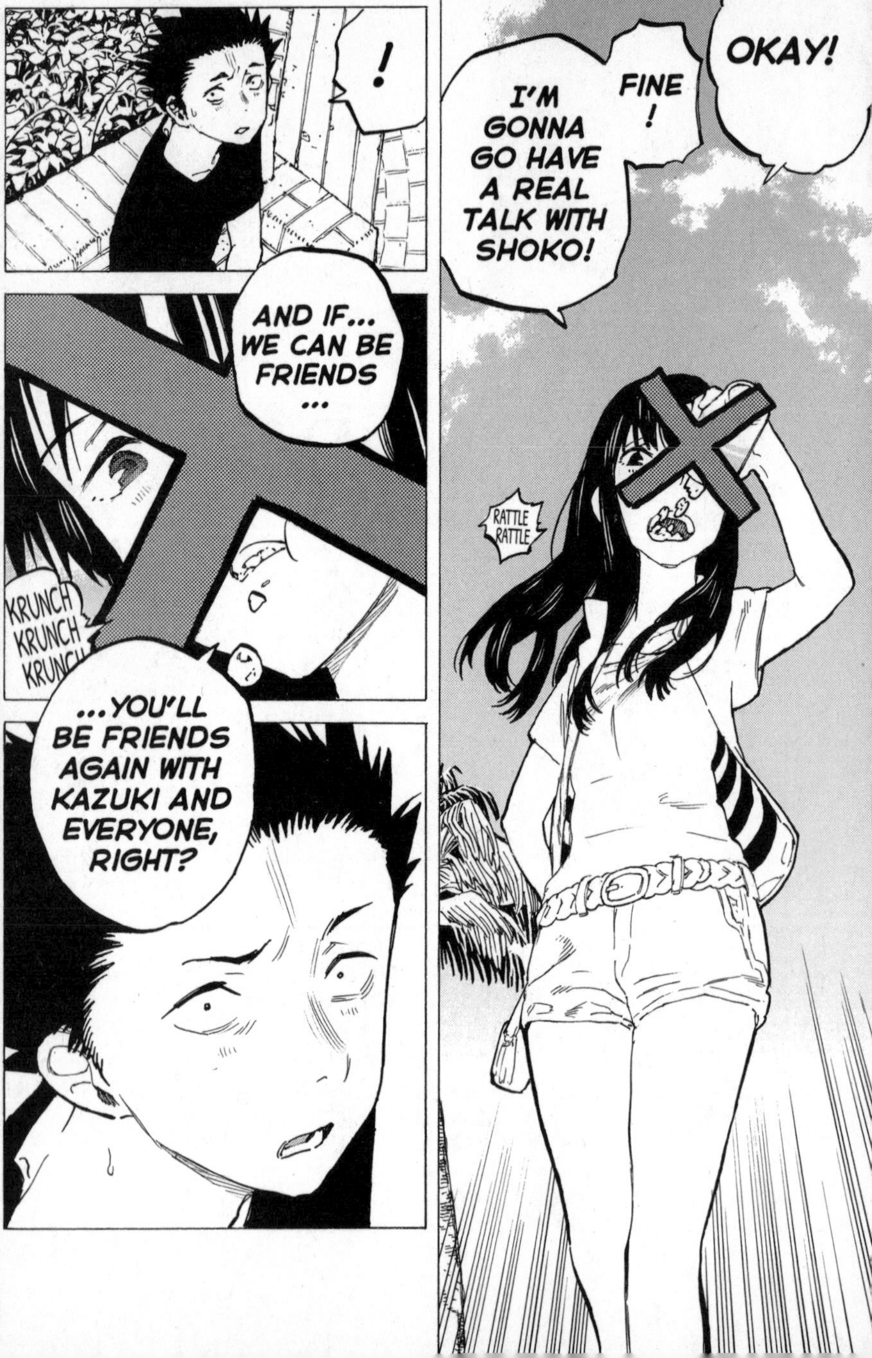
OKAY!
FINE!
I'M GONNA GO HAVE A REAL TALK WITH SHOKO!
RATTLE RATTLE
!
AND IF... WE CAN BE FRIENDS ...
KRUNCH KRUNCH
...YOU'LL BE FRIENDS AGAIN WITH KAZUKI AND EVERYONE, RIGHT?

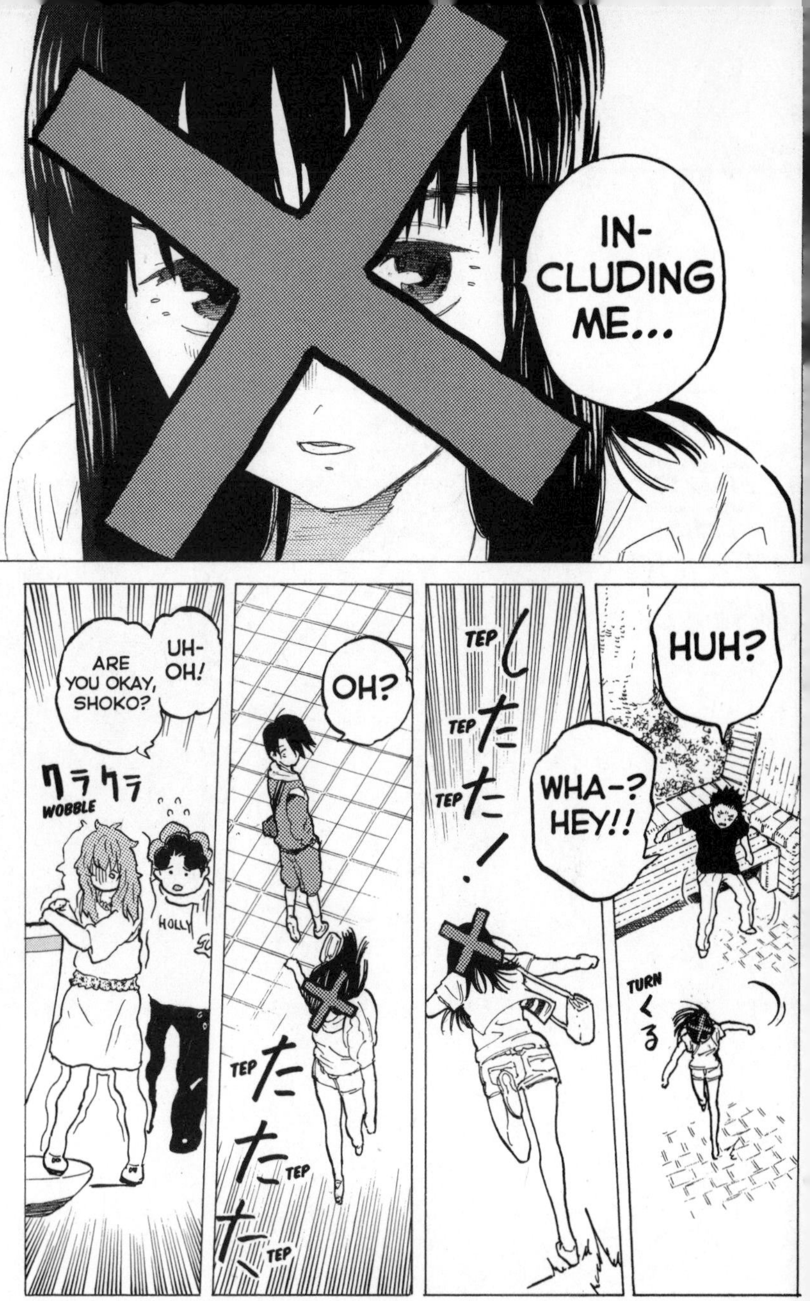
IN-CLUDING ME...
HUH?
WHA-? HEY!!
TURN くる
TEP し TEP た TEP た!
OH?
TEP たた TEP た、 TEP
UH-OH!
ARE YOU OKAY, SHOKO?
クラクラ WOBBLE
HOLLY

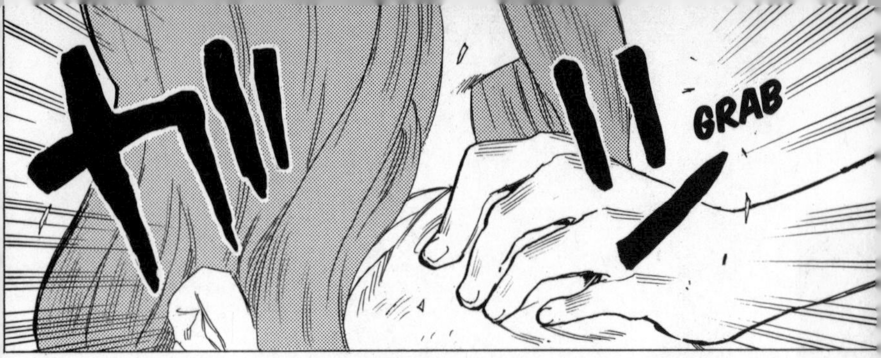
GRAB

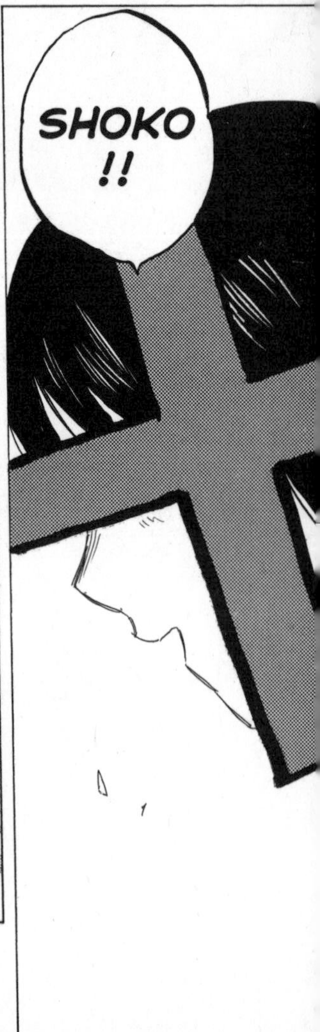
SHOKO !!

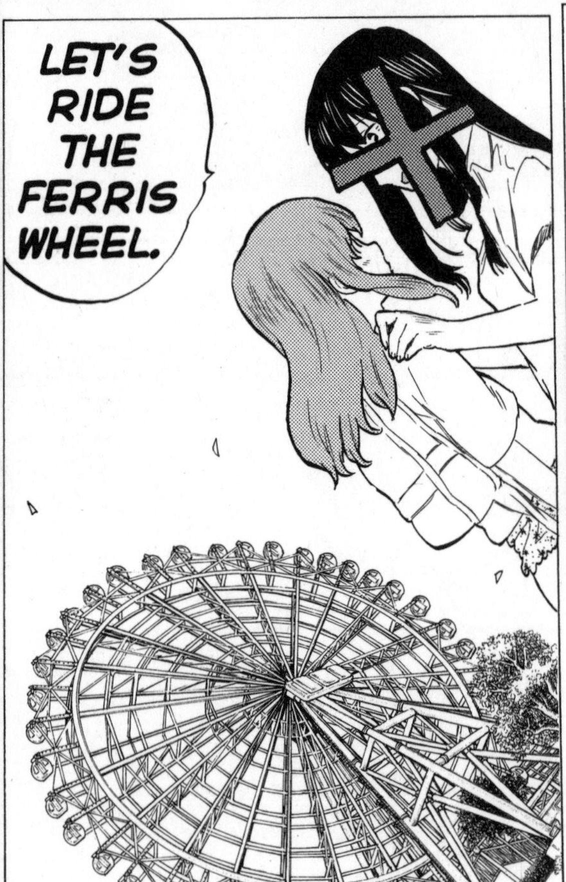
LET'S RIDE THE FERRIS WHEEL.

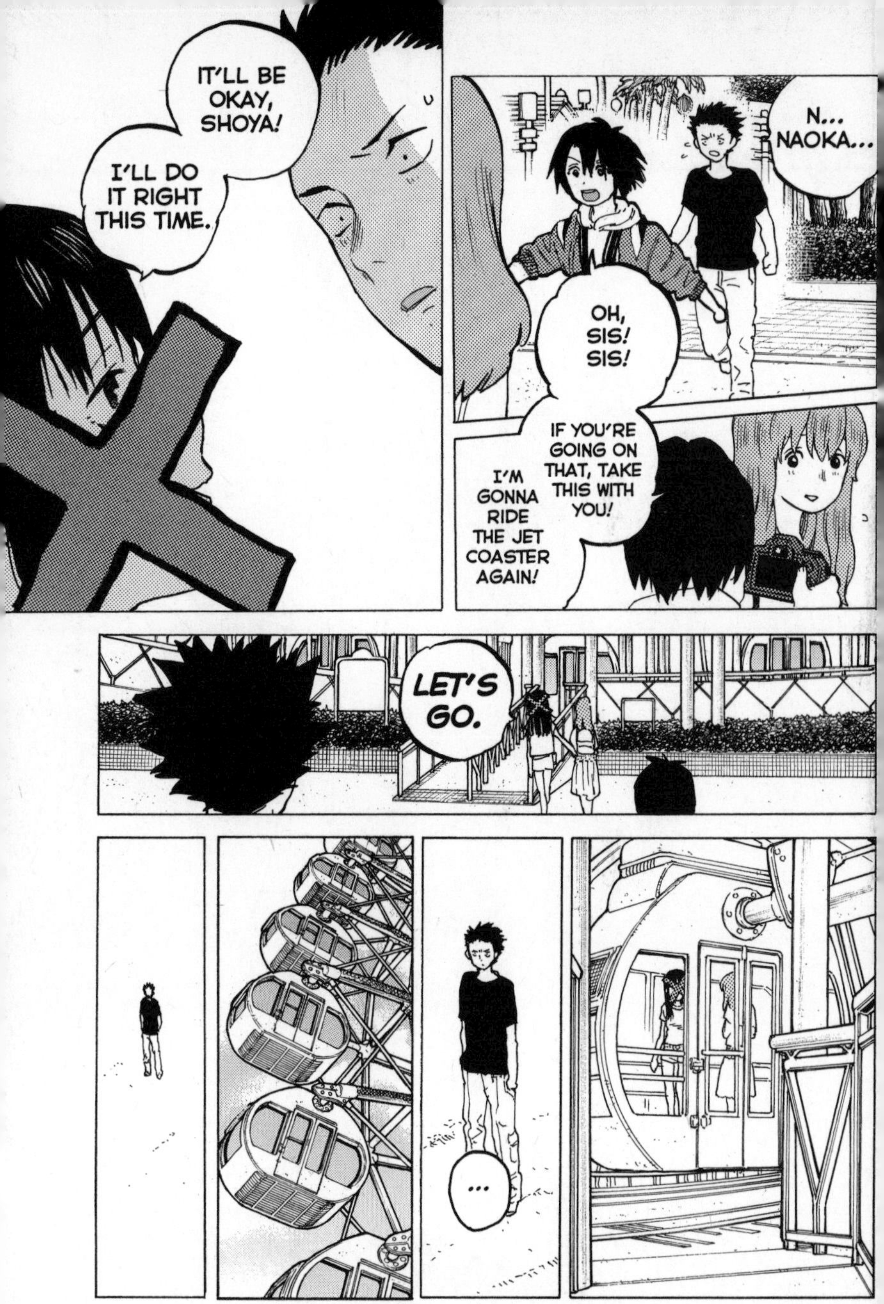
N... NAOKA...
OH, SIS! SIS!
IF YOU'RE GOING ON THAT, TAKE THIS WITH YOU!
I'M GONNA RIDE THE JET COASTER AGAIN!
IT'LL BE OKAY, SHOYA!
I'LL DO IT RIGHT THIS TIME.
LET'S GO.
...

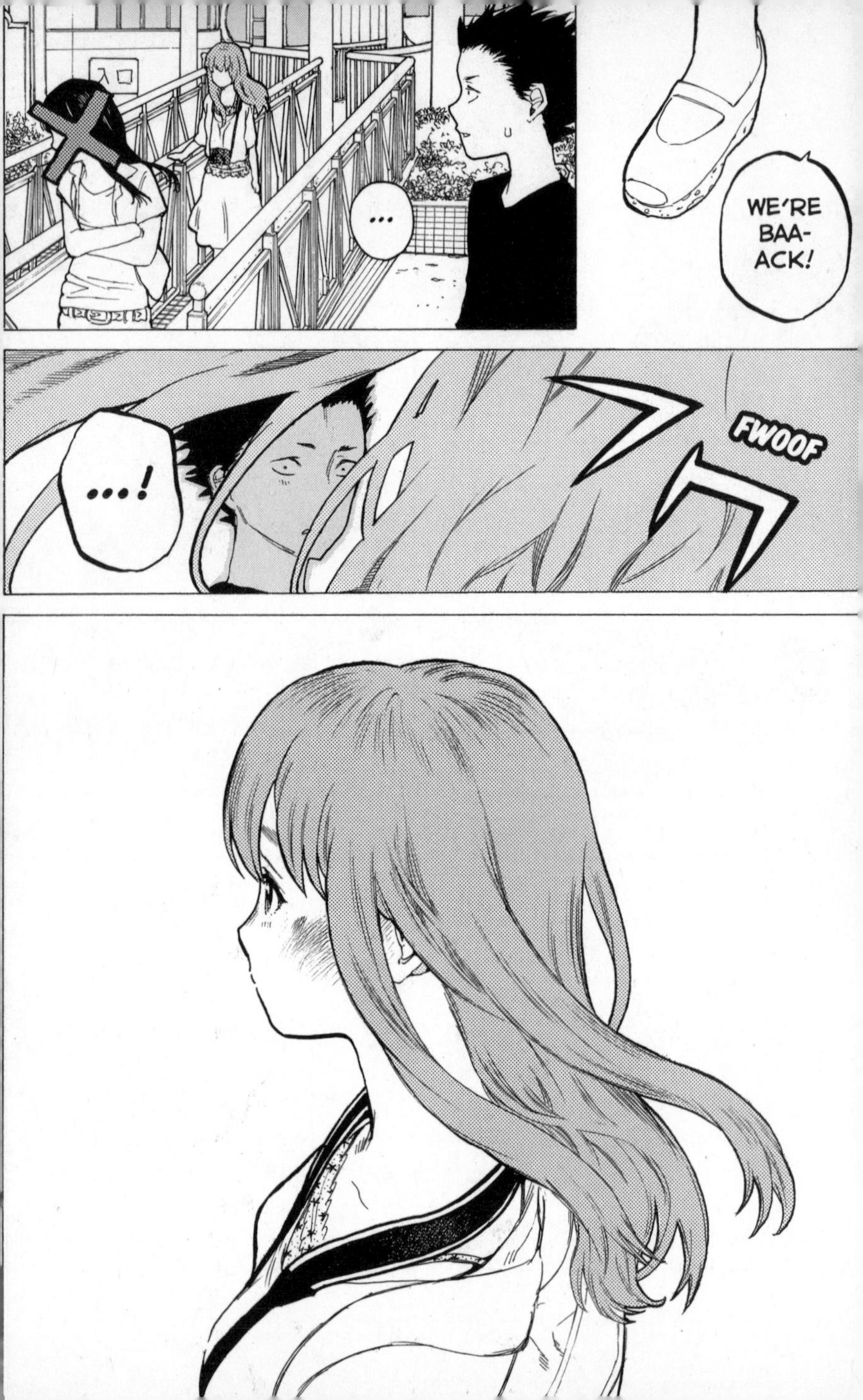
WE'RE BAAA- ACK!
...
入口
FWOOF
...!

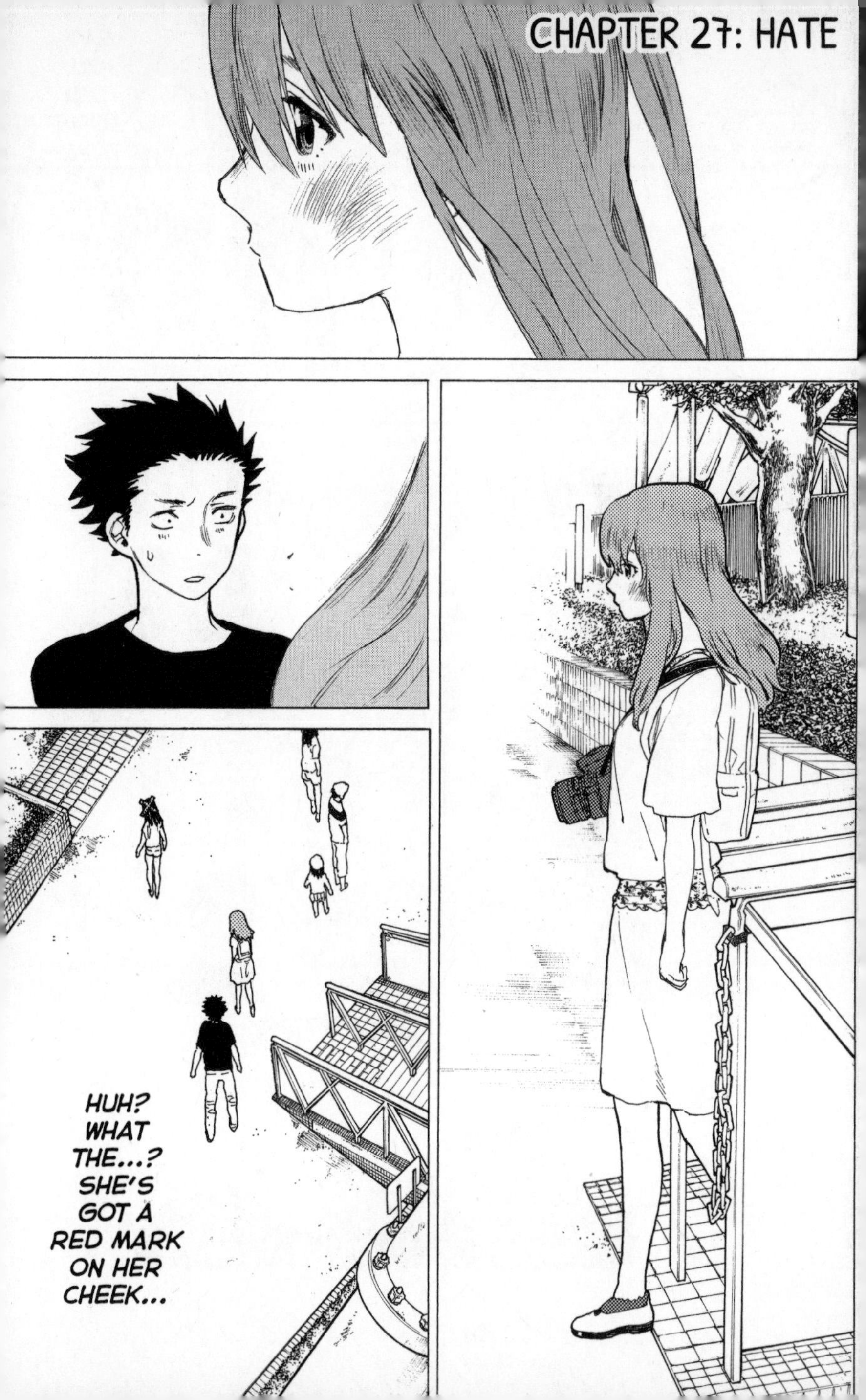
CHAPTER 27: HATE
HUH? WHAT THE...? SHE'S GOT A RED MARK ON HER CHEEK...

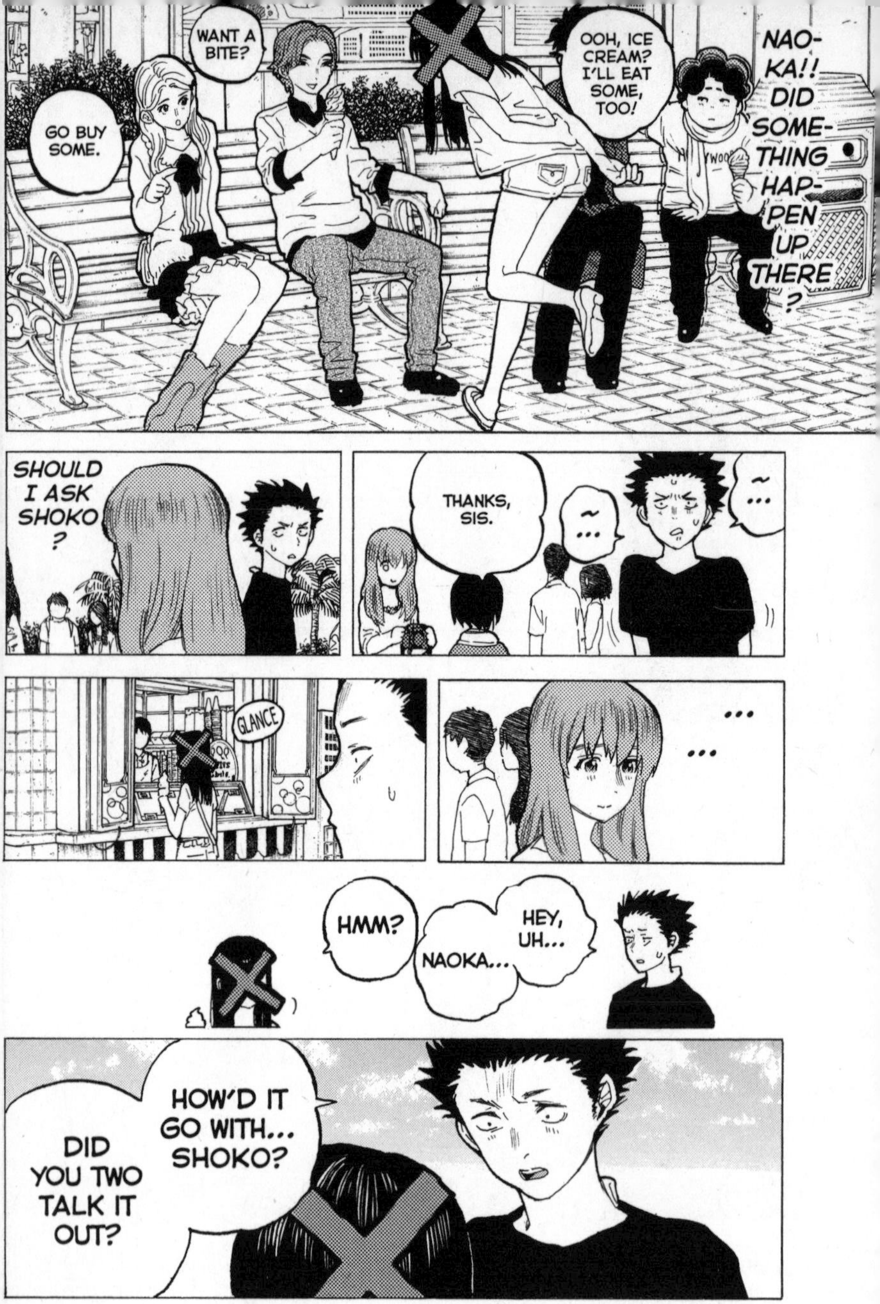
NAOKA!! DID SOMETHING HAPPEN UP THERE?
OOH, ICE CREAM? I'LL EAT SOME, TOO!
WANT A BITE?
GO BUY SOME.
~...
THANKS, SIS.
~...
SHOULD I ASK SHOKO?
...
...
GLANCE
HEY, UH... NAOKA...
HMM?
HOW'D IT GO WITH... SHOKO?
DID YOU TWO TALK IT OUT?

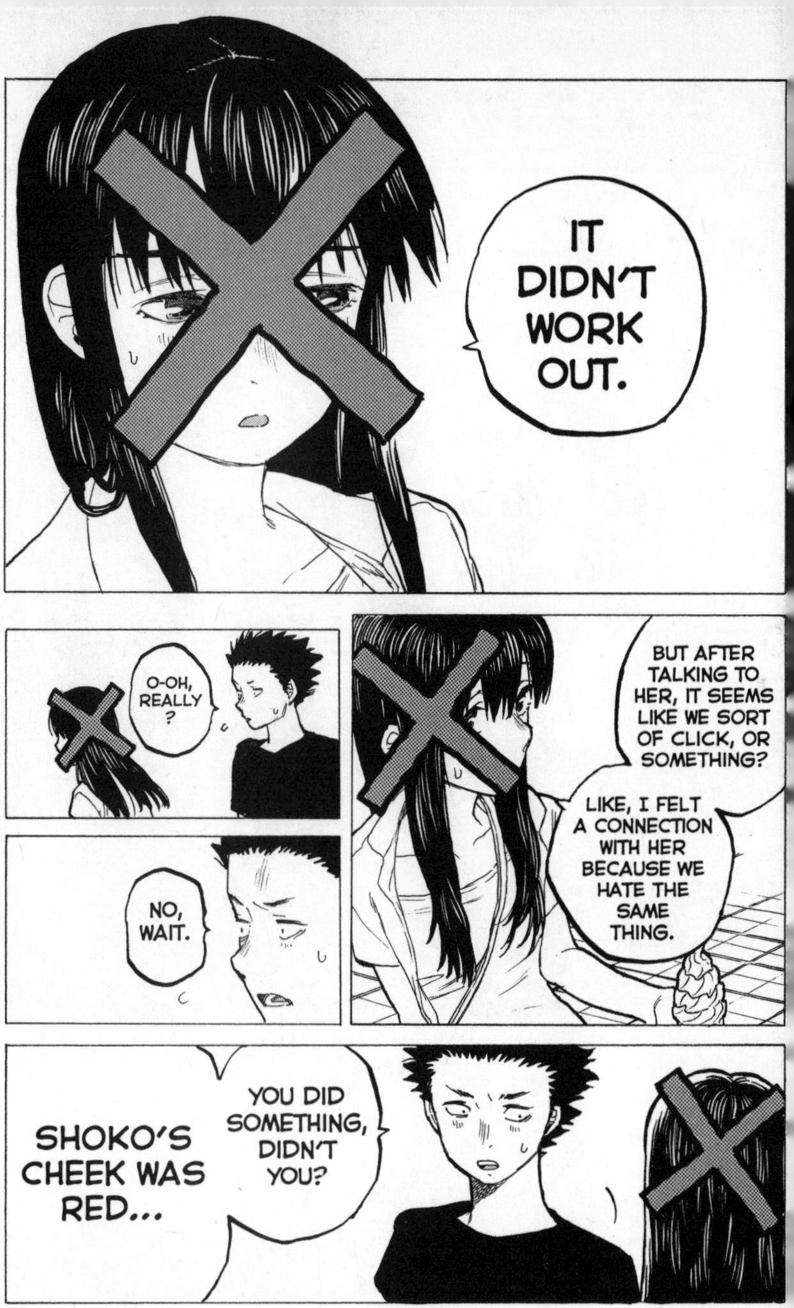
IT DIDN'T WORK OUT.
BUT AFTER TALKING TO HER, IT SEEMS LIKE WE SORT OF CLICK, OR SOMETHING?
LIKE, I FELT A CONNECTION WITH HER BECAUSE WE HATE THE SAME THING.
O-OH, REALLY?
NO, WAIT.
YOU DID SOMETHING, DIDN'T YOU?
SHOKO'S CHEEK WAS RED...

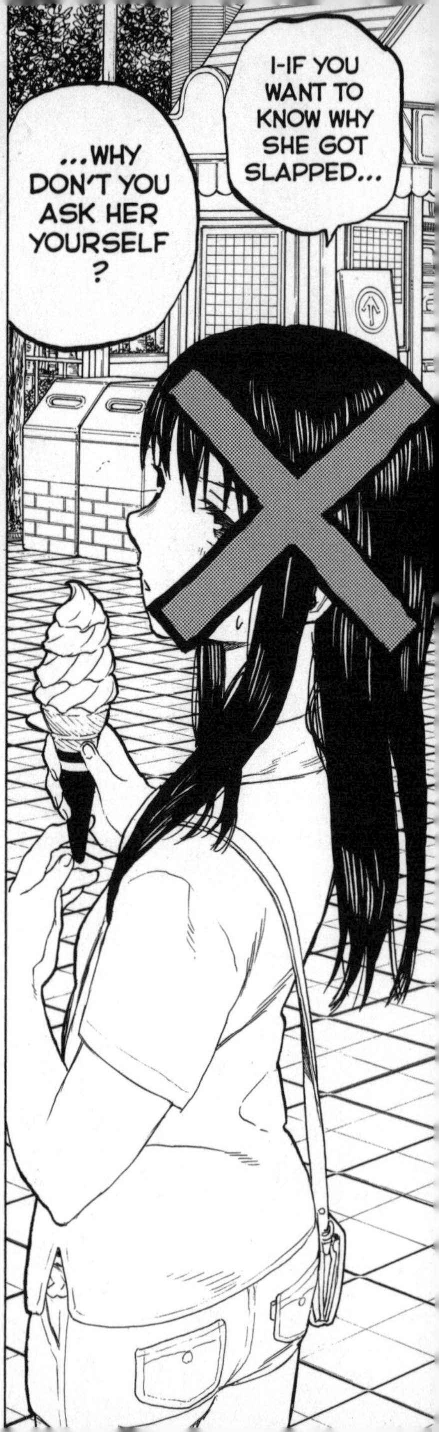
I-IF YOU WANT TO KNOW WHY SHE GOT SLAPPED...
...WHY DON'T YOU ASK HER YOURSELF?

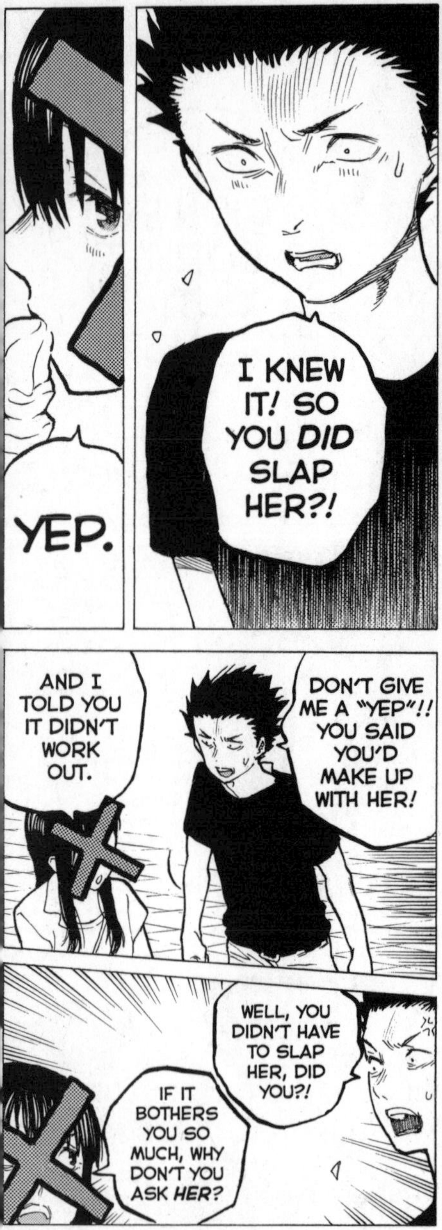
I KNEW IT! SO YOU *DID* SLAP HER?!
YEP.
DON'T GIVE ME A "YEP"!! YOU SAID YOU'D MAKE UP WITH HER!
AND I TOLD YOU IT DIDN'T WORK OUT.
WELL, YOU DIDN'T HAVE TO SLAP HER, DID YOU?!
IF IT BOTHERS YOU SO MUCH, WHY DON'T YOU ASK *HER*?

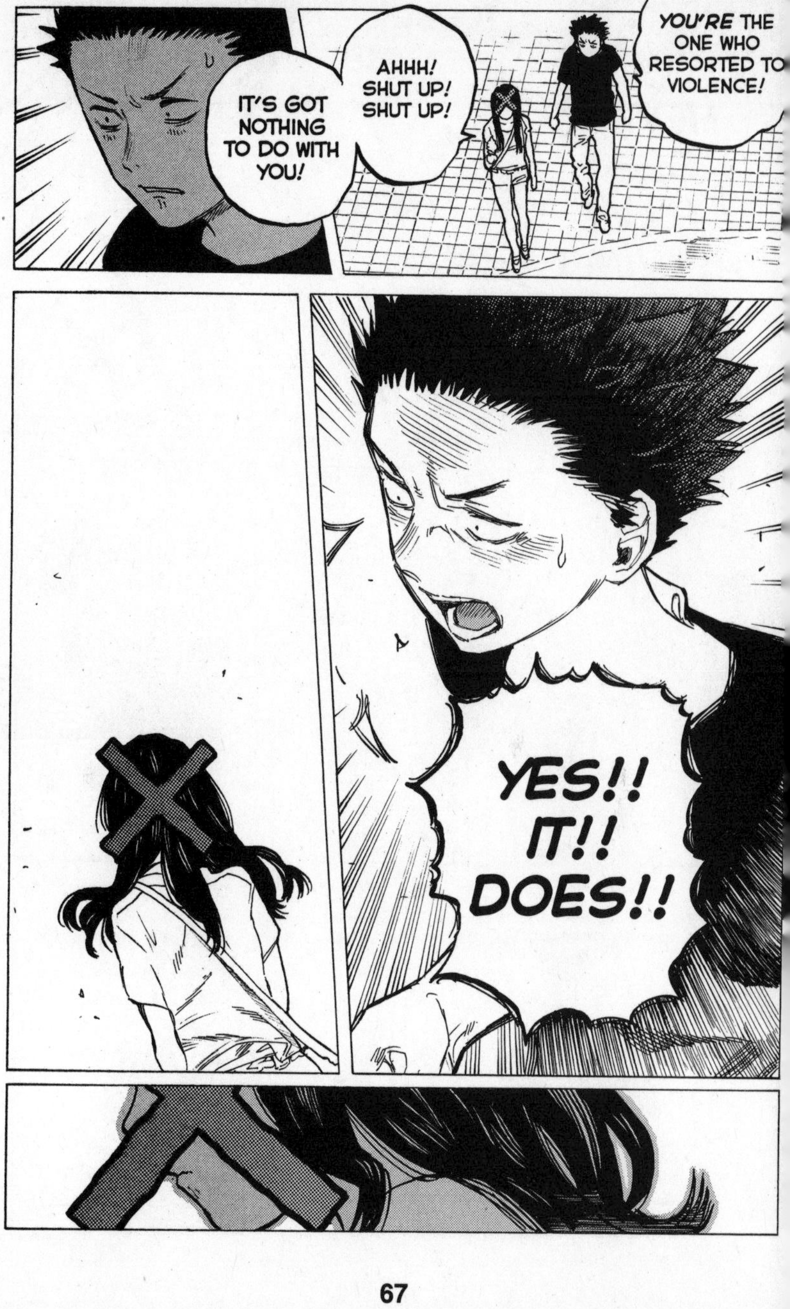
YOU'RE THE ONE WHO RESORTED TO VIOLENCE!
AHHH! SHUT UP! SHUT UP!
IT'S GOT NOTHING TO DO WITH YOU!
YES!! IT!! DOES!!

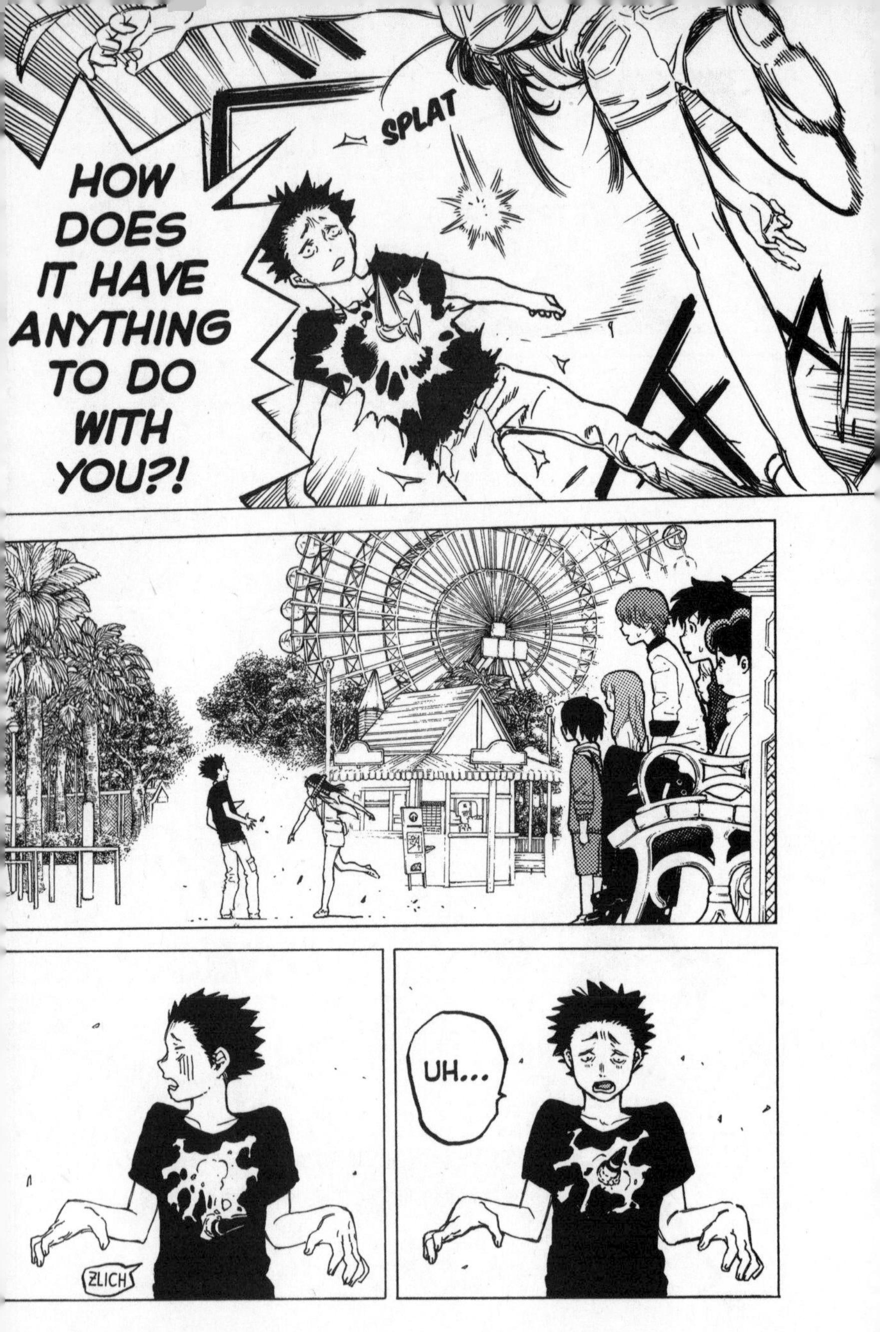
SPLAT
HOW DOES IT HAVE ANYTHING TO DO WITH YOU?!
UH...
ZLICH

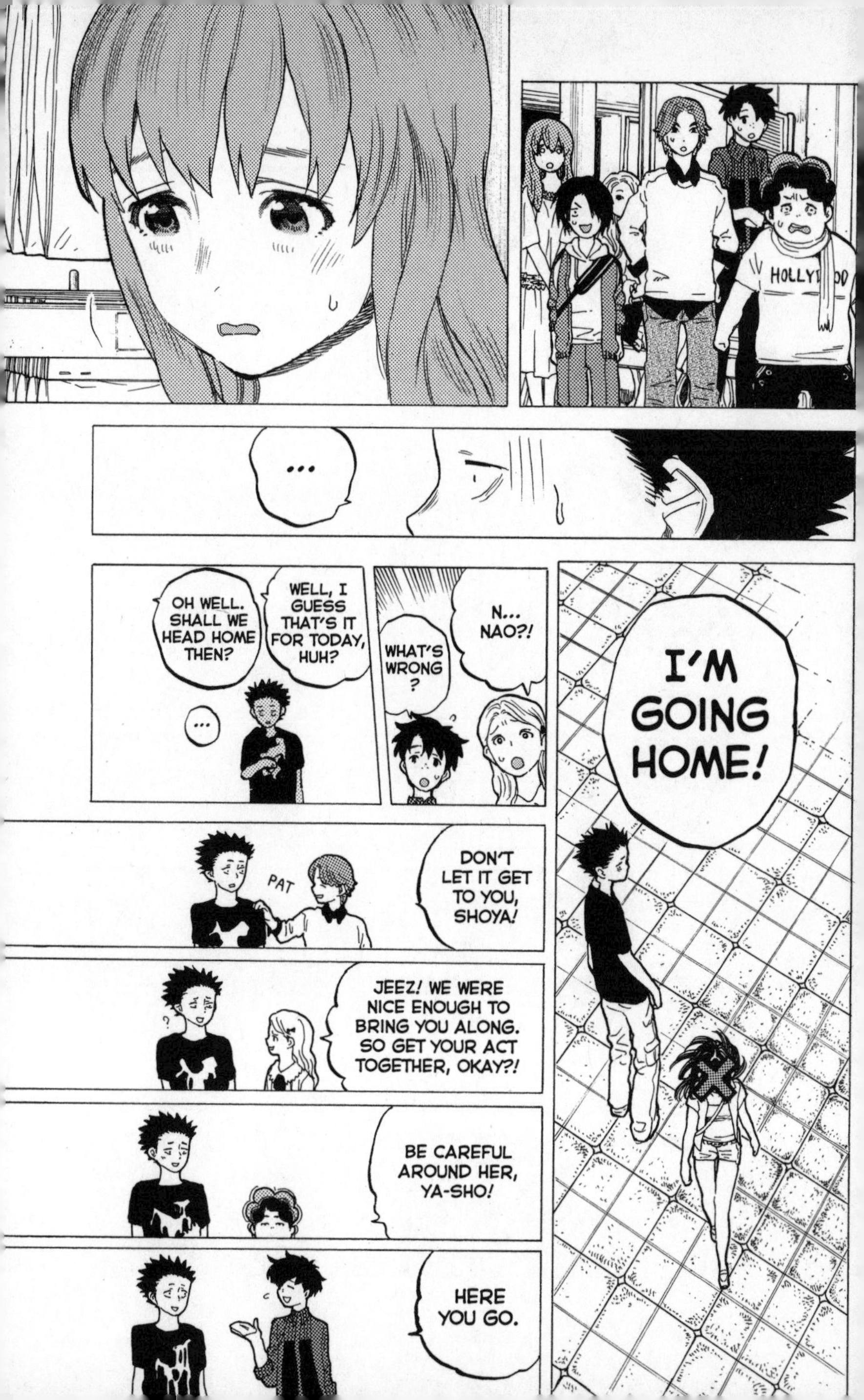
...
I'M GOING HOME!
N... NAO?!
WHAT'S WRONG?
WELL, I GUESS THAT'S IT FOR TODAY, HUH?
OH WELL. SHALL WE HEAD HOME THEN?
...
DON'T LET IT GET TO YOU, SHOYA!
PAT
JEEZ! WE WERE NICE ENOUGH TO BRING YOU ALONG. SO GET YOUR ACT TOGETHER, OKAY?!
BE CAREFUL AROUND HER, YA-SHO!
HERE YOU GO.

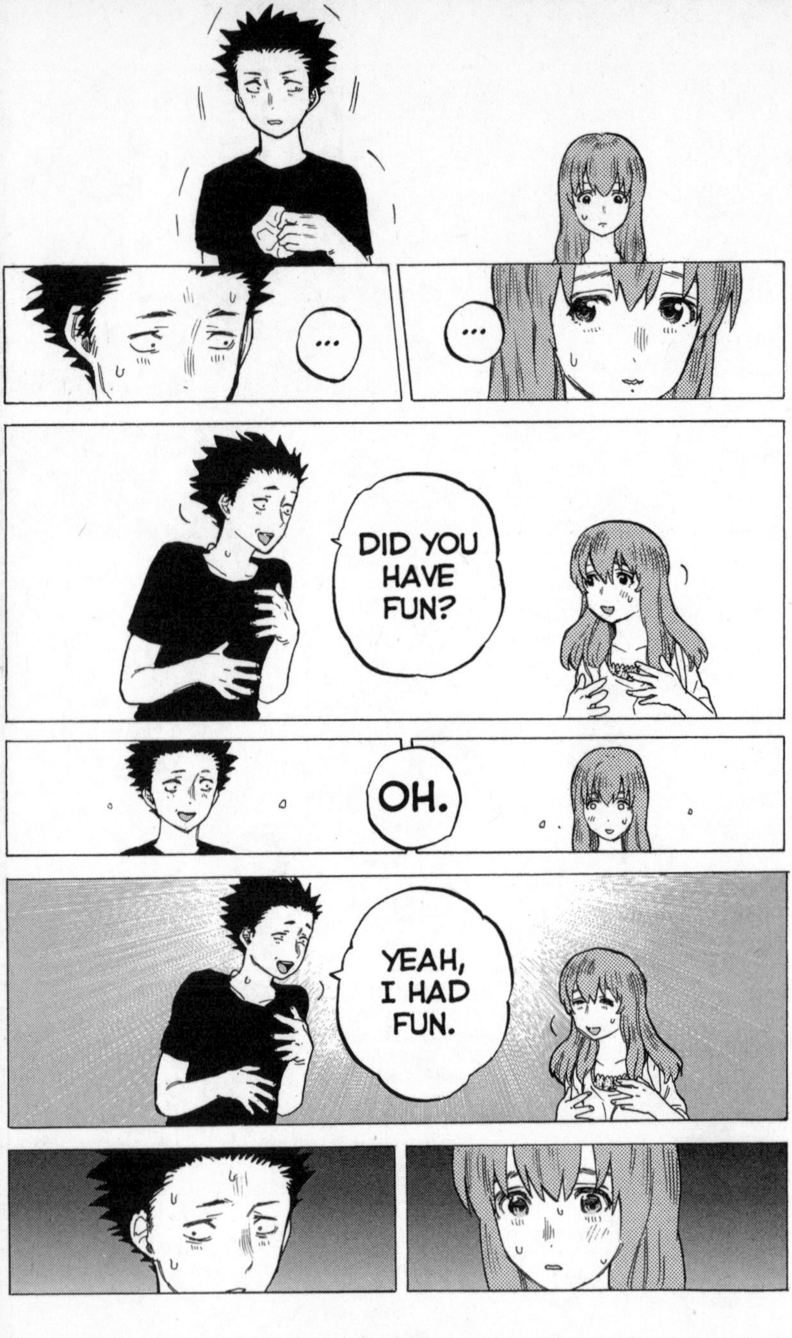
...
...
DID YOU HAVE FUN?
OH.
YEAH, I HAD FUN.

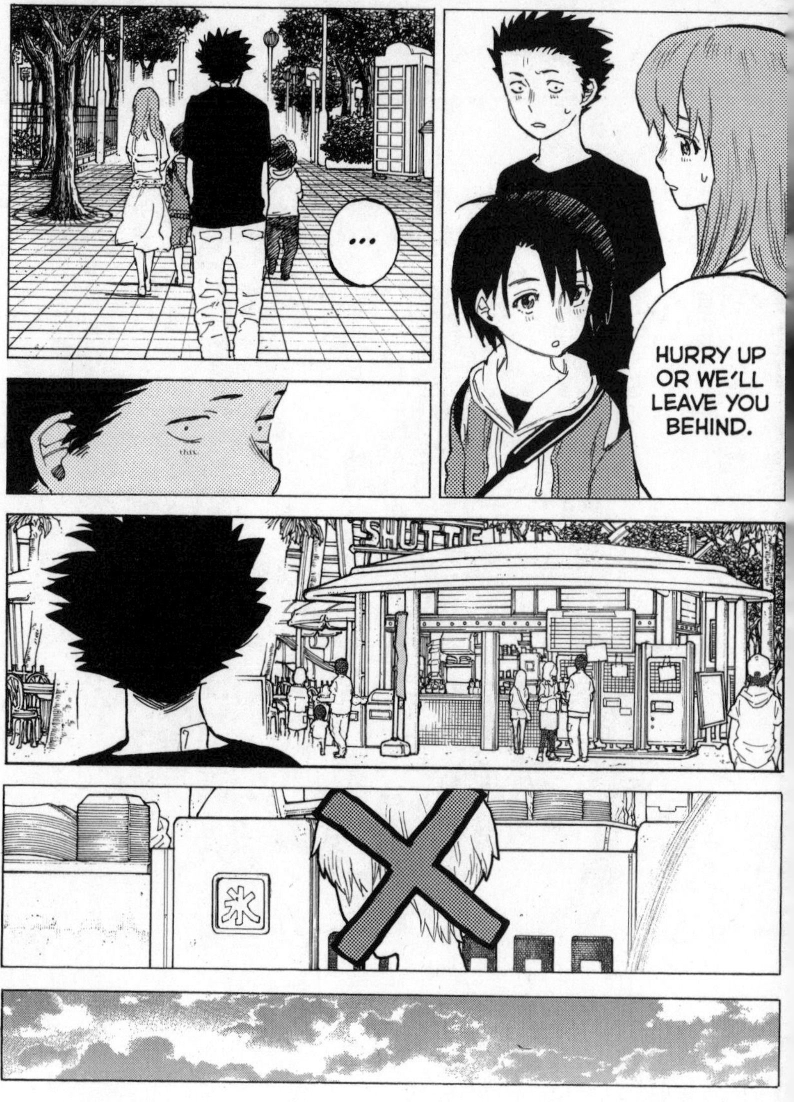
HURRY UP OR WE'LL LEAVE YOU BEHIND.
...
氷
WHAT WAS I SUPPOSED TO DO...?

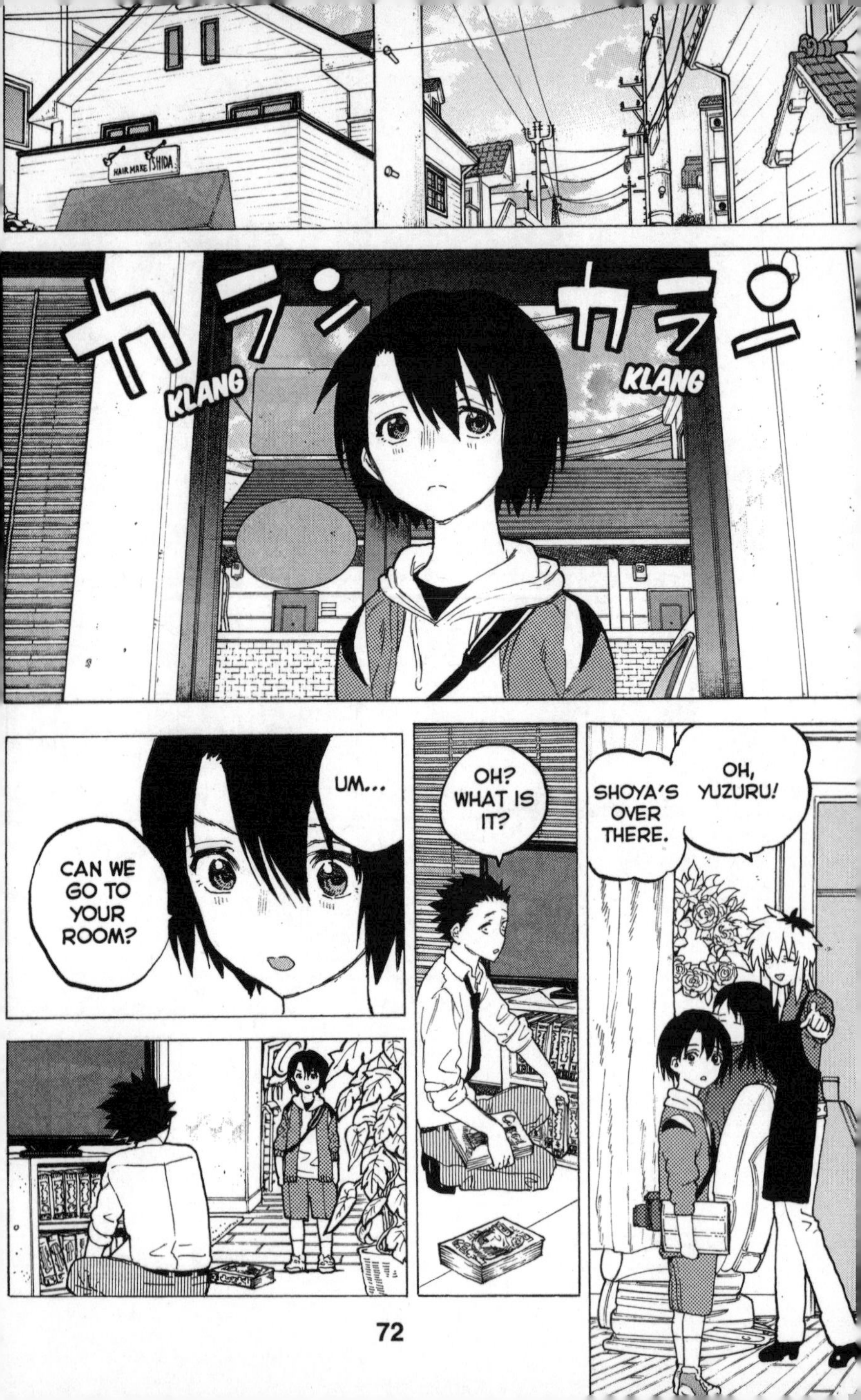
HAIR MAKE ISHIDA
カラン KLANG
カラン KLANG
OH, YUZURU!
SHOYA'S OVER THERE.
OH? WHAT IS IT?
UM...
CAN WE GO TO YOUR ROOM?

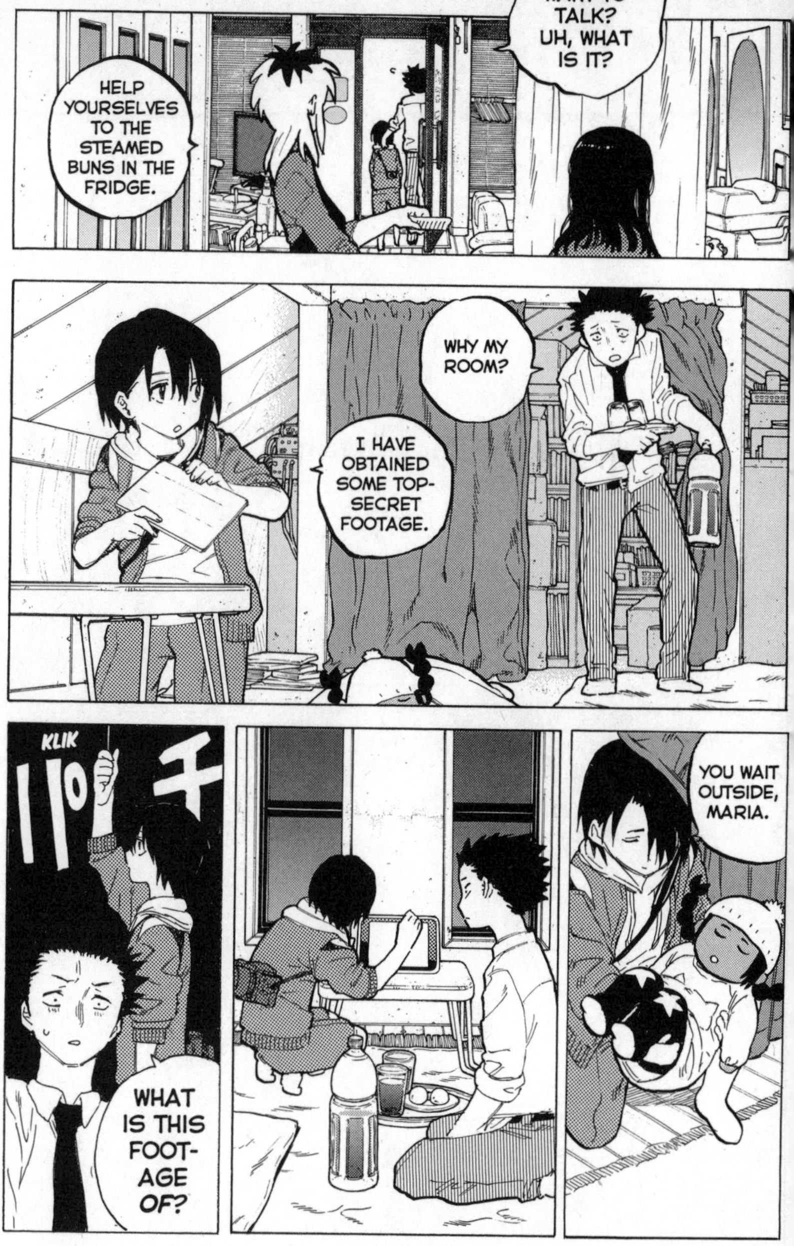
YOU WANT TO TALK? UH, WHAT IS IT?
HELP YOURSELVES TO THE STEAMED BUNS IN THE FRIDGE.
WHY MY ROOM?
I HAVE OBTAINED SOME TOP-SECRET FOOTAGE.
YOU WAIT OUTSIDE, MARIA.
KLIK
パチ
WHAT IS THIS FOOTAGE OF?

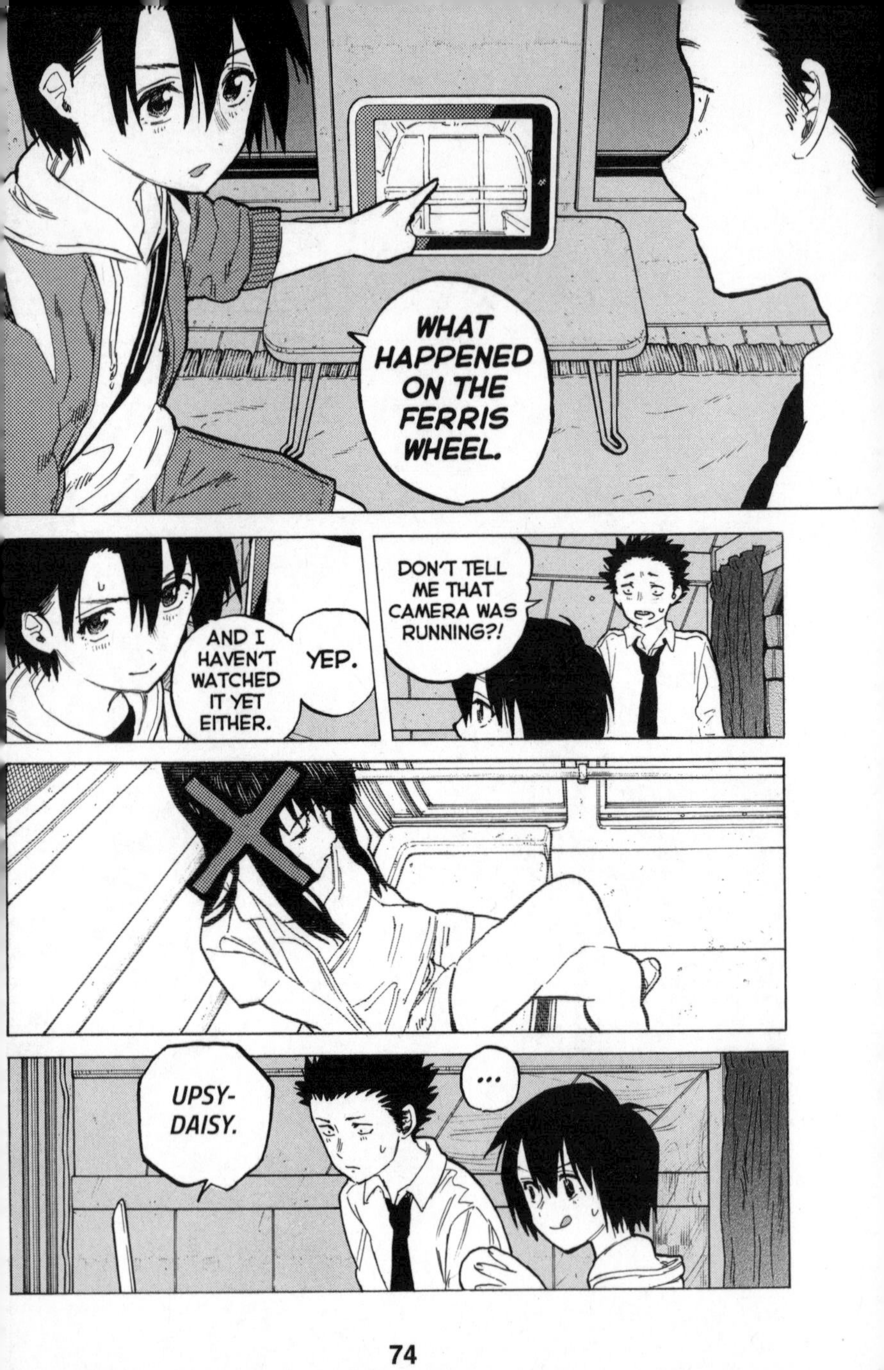
WHAT HAPPENED ON THE FERRIS WHEEL.
DON'T TELL ME THAT CAMERA WAS RUNNING?!
YEP.
AND I HAVEN'T WATCHED IT YET EITHER.
...
UPSY-DAISY.

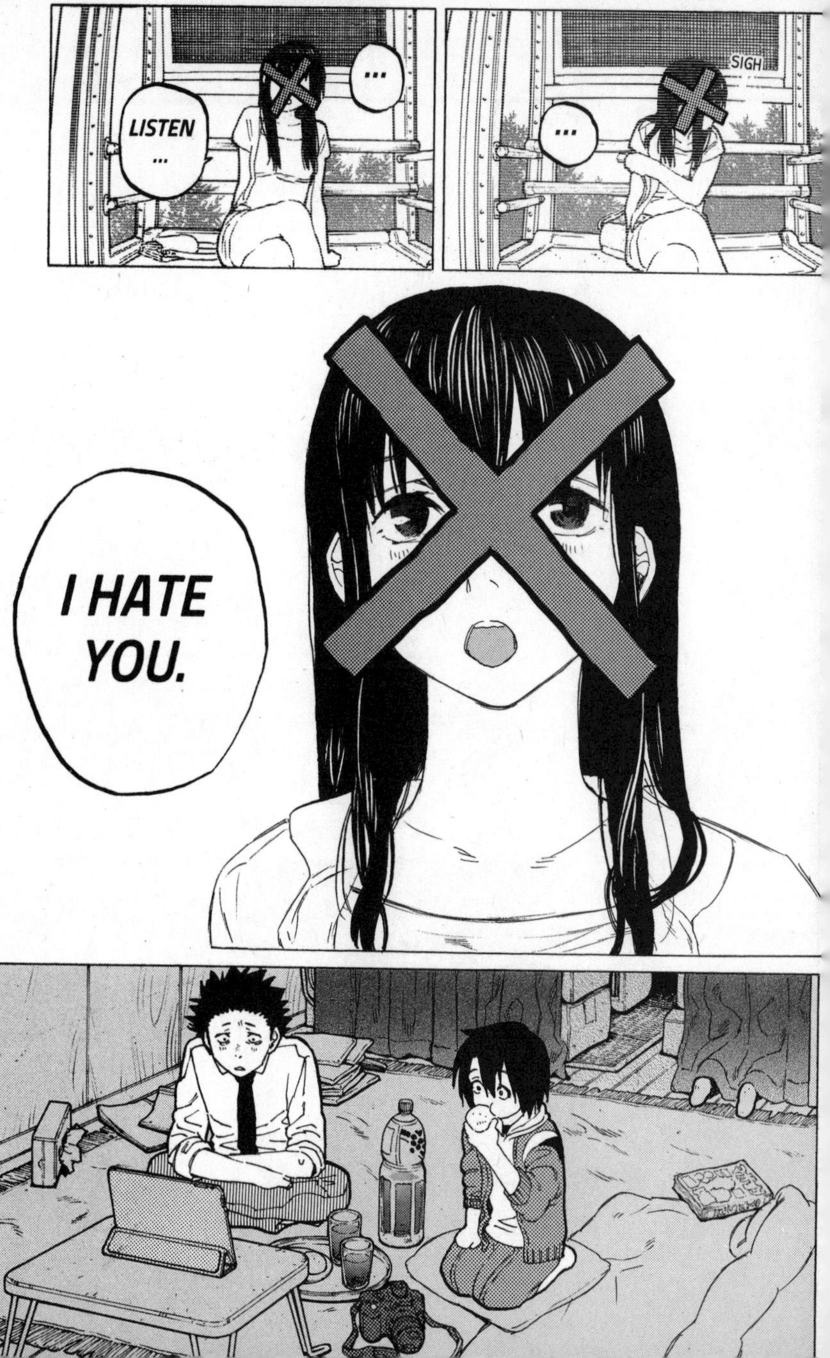
SIGH
...
...
LISTEN ...
I HATE YOU.

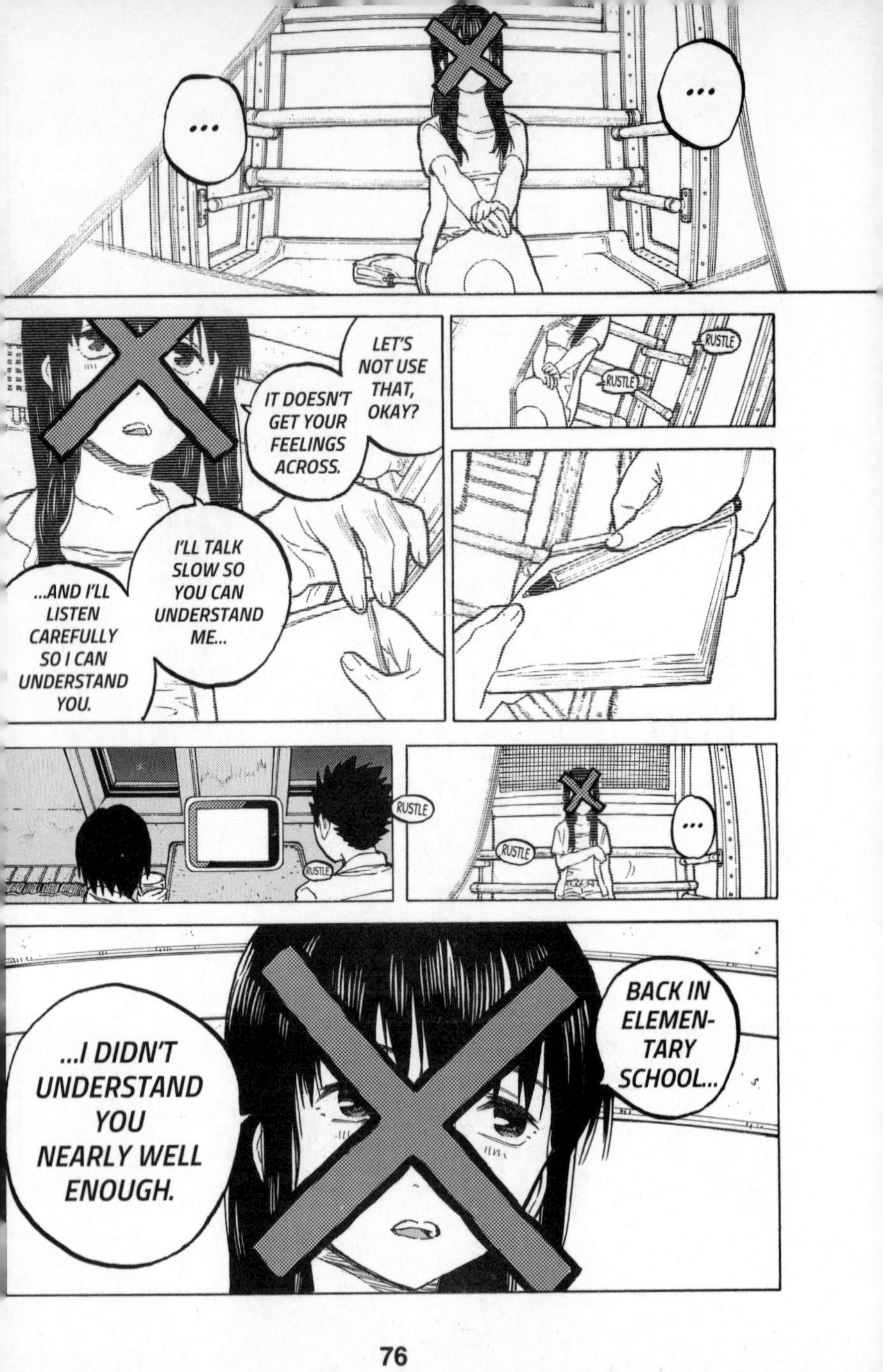
...
...
RUSTLE
RUSTLE
LET'S NOT USE THAT, OKAY?
IT DOESN'T GET YOUR FEELINGS ACROSS.
I'LL TALK SLOW SO YOU CAN UNDERSTAND ME...
...AND I'LL LISTEN CAREFULLY SO I CAN UNDERSTAND YOU.
...
RUSTLE
RUSTLE
RUSTLE
BACK IN ELEMEN-TARY SCHOOL...
...I DIDN'T UNDERSTAND YOU NEARLY WELL ENOUGH.

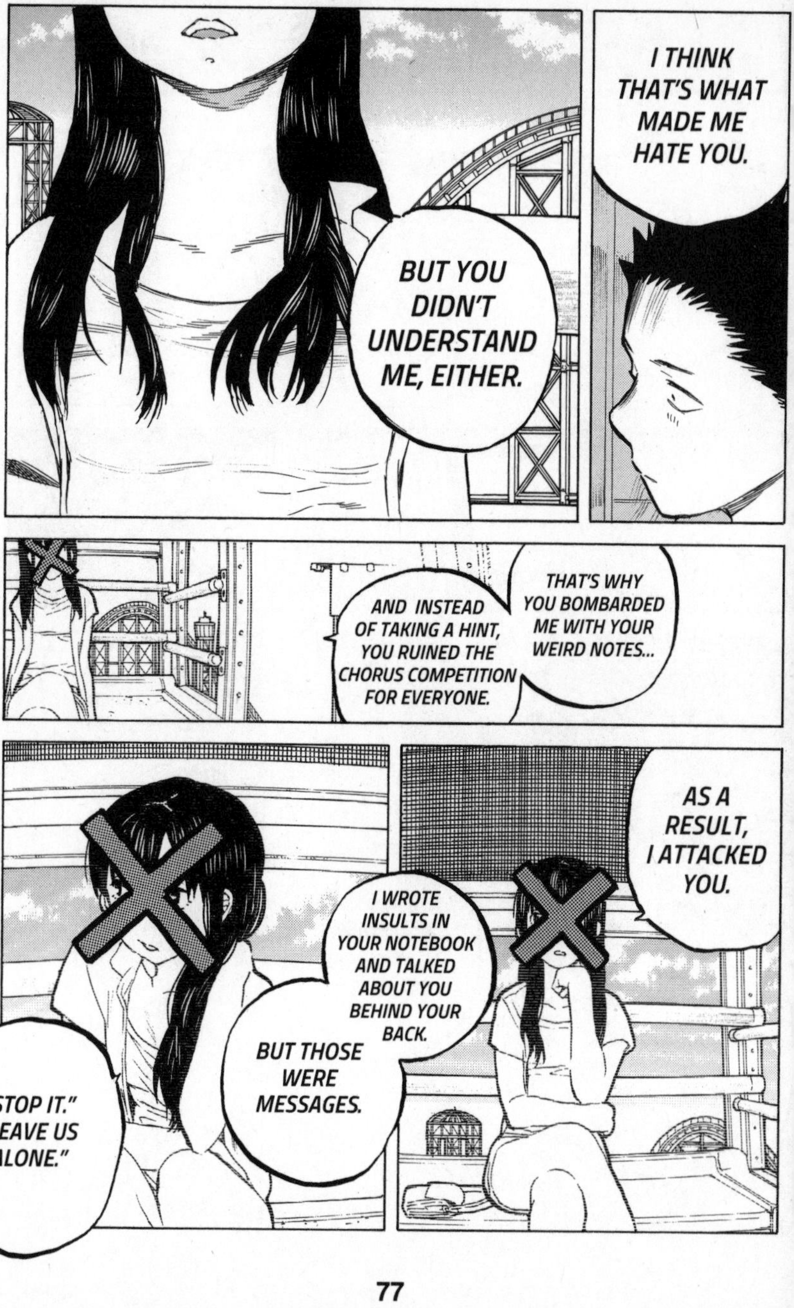
I THINK THAT'S WHAT MADE ME HATE YOU.
BUT YOU DIDN'T UNDERSTAND ME, EITHER.
THAT'S WHY YOU BOMBARDED ME WITH YOUR WEIRD NOTES...
AND INSTEAD OF TAKING A HINT, YOU RUINED THE CHORUS COMPETITION FOR EVERYONE.
AS A RESULT, I ATTACKED YOU.
I WROTE INSULTS IN YOUR NOTEBOOK AND TALKED ABOUT YOU BEHIND YOUR BACK.
BUT THOSE WERE MESSAGES.
"STOP IT." "LEAVE US ALONE."

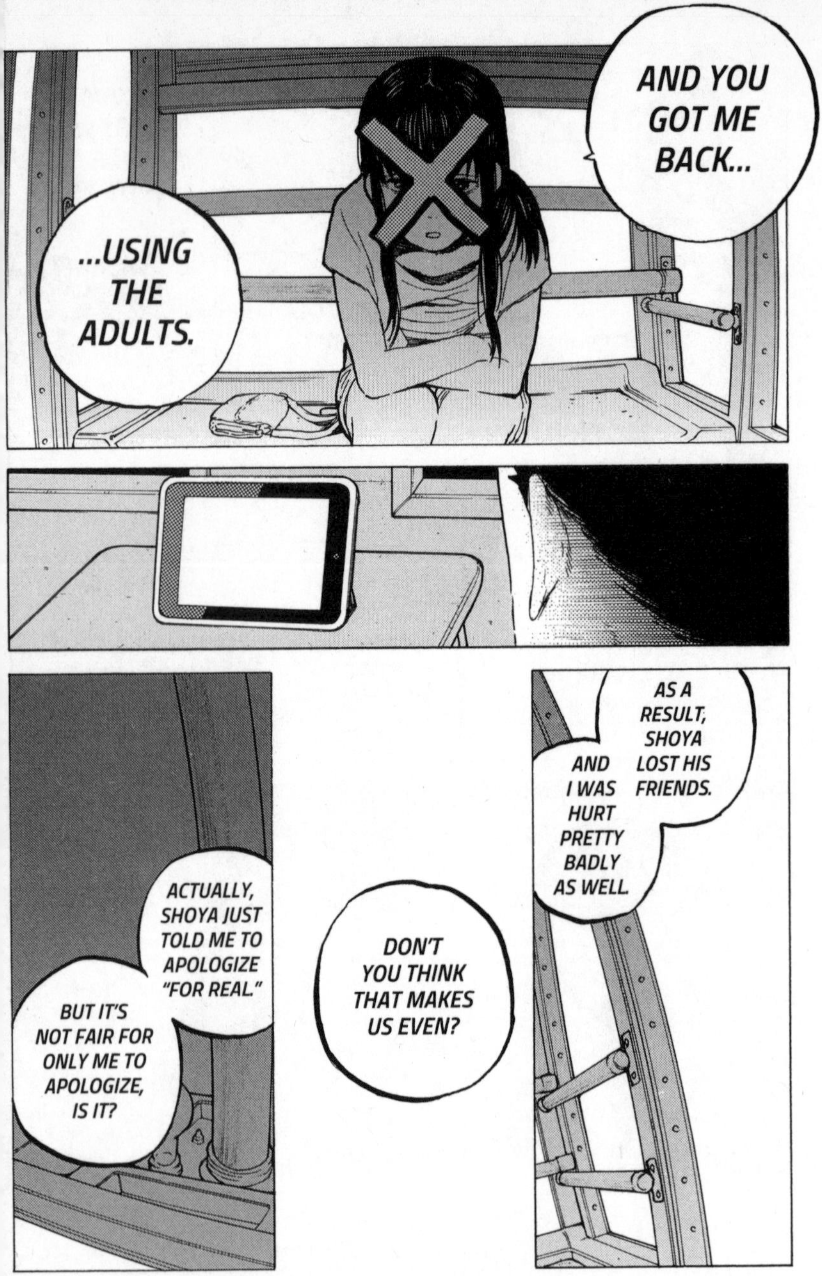
AND YOU GOT ME BACK...
...USING THE ADULTS.
AS A RESULT, SHOYA LOST HIS FRIENDS.
AND I WAS HURT PRETTY BADLY AS WELL.
DON'T YOU THINK THAT MAKES US EVEN?
ACTUALLY, SHOYA JUST TOLD ME TO APOLOGIZE "FOR REAL."
BUT IT'S NOT FAIR FOR ONLY ME TO APOLOGIZE, IS IT?

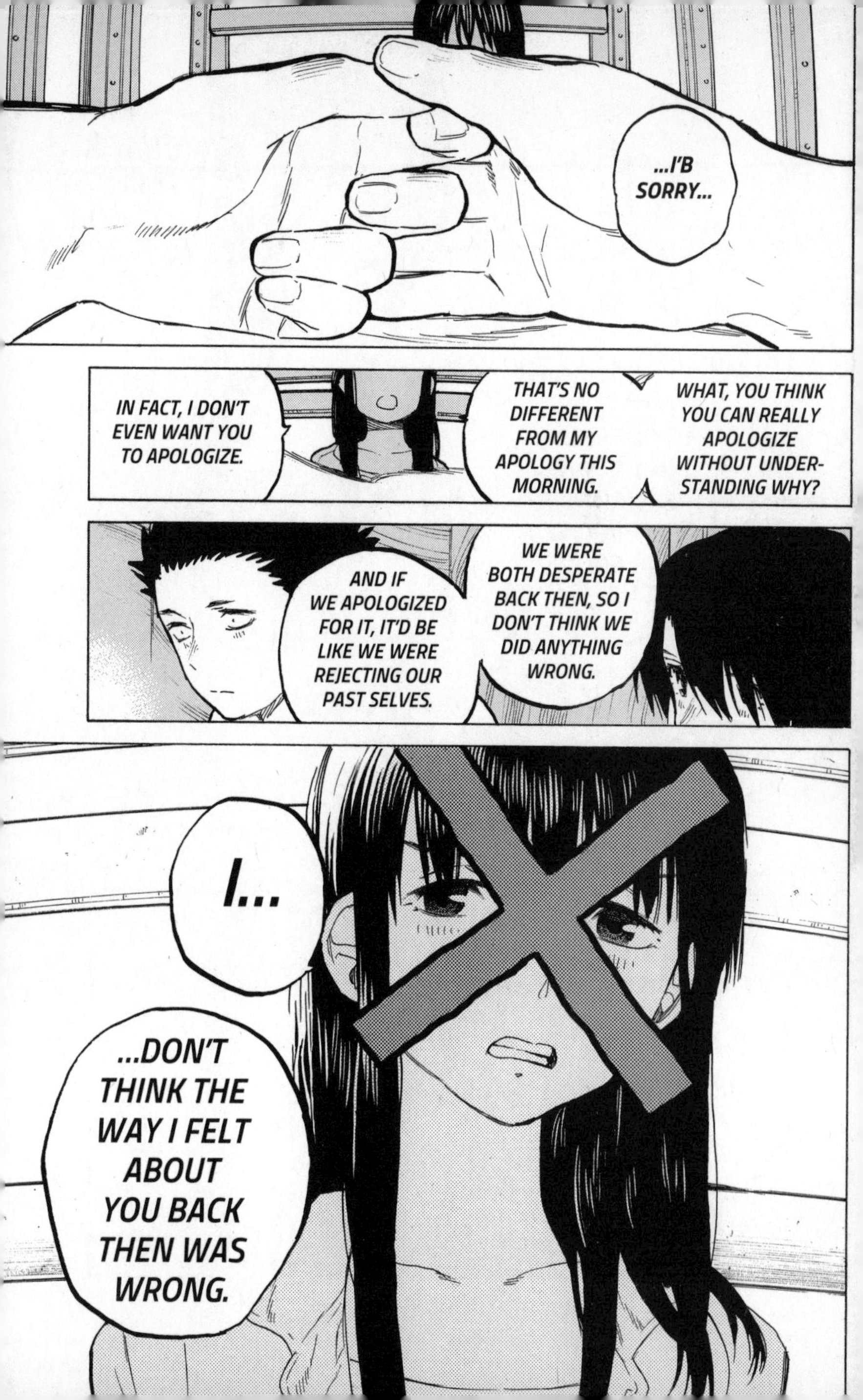
...I'B SORRY...
WHAT, YOU THINK YOU CAN REALLY APOLOGIZE WITHOUT UNDER-STANDING WHY?
THAT'S NO DIFFERENT FROM MY APOLOGY THIS MORNING.
IN FACT, I DON'T EVEN WANT YOU TO APOLOGIZE.
WE WERE BOTH DESPERATE BACK THEN, SO I DON'T THINK WE DID ANYTHING WRONG.
AND IF WE APOLOGIZED FOR IT, IT'D BE LIKE WE WERE REJECTING OUR PAST SELVES.
I...
...DON'T THINK THE WAY I FELT ABOUT YOU BACK THEN WAS WRONG.

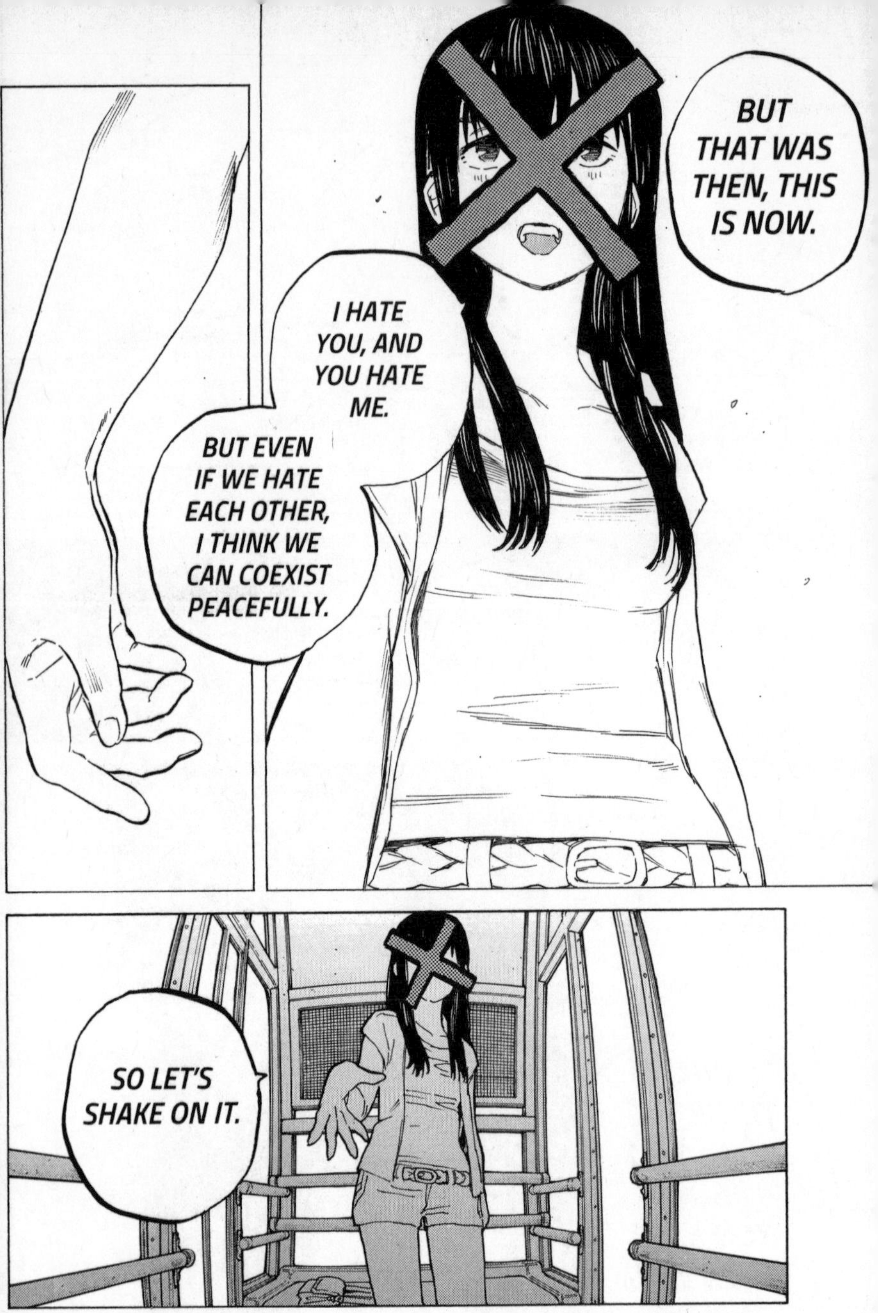
BUT THAT WAS THEN, THIS IS NOW.
I HATE YOU, AND YOU HATE ME.
BUT EVEN IF WE HATE EACH OTHER, I THINK WE CAN COEXIST PEACEFULLY.
SO LET'S SHAKE ON IT.

I DON'D HADE YOU...

...I...

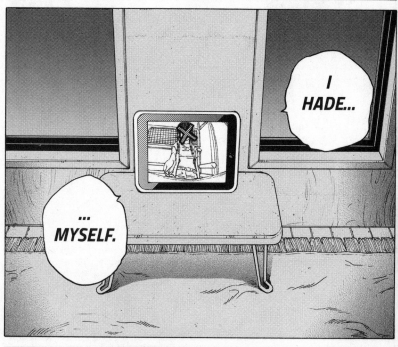

I HADE...

...MYSELF.

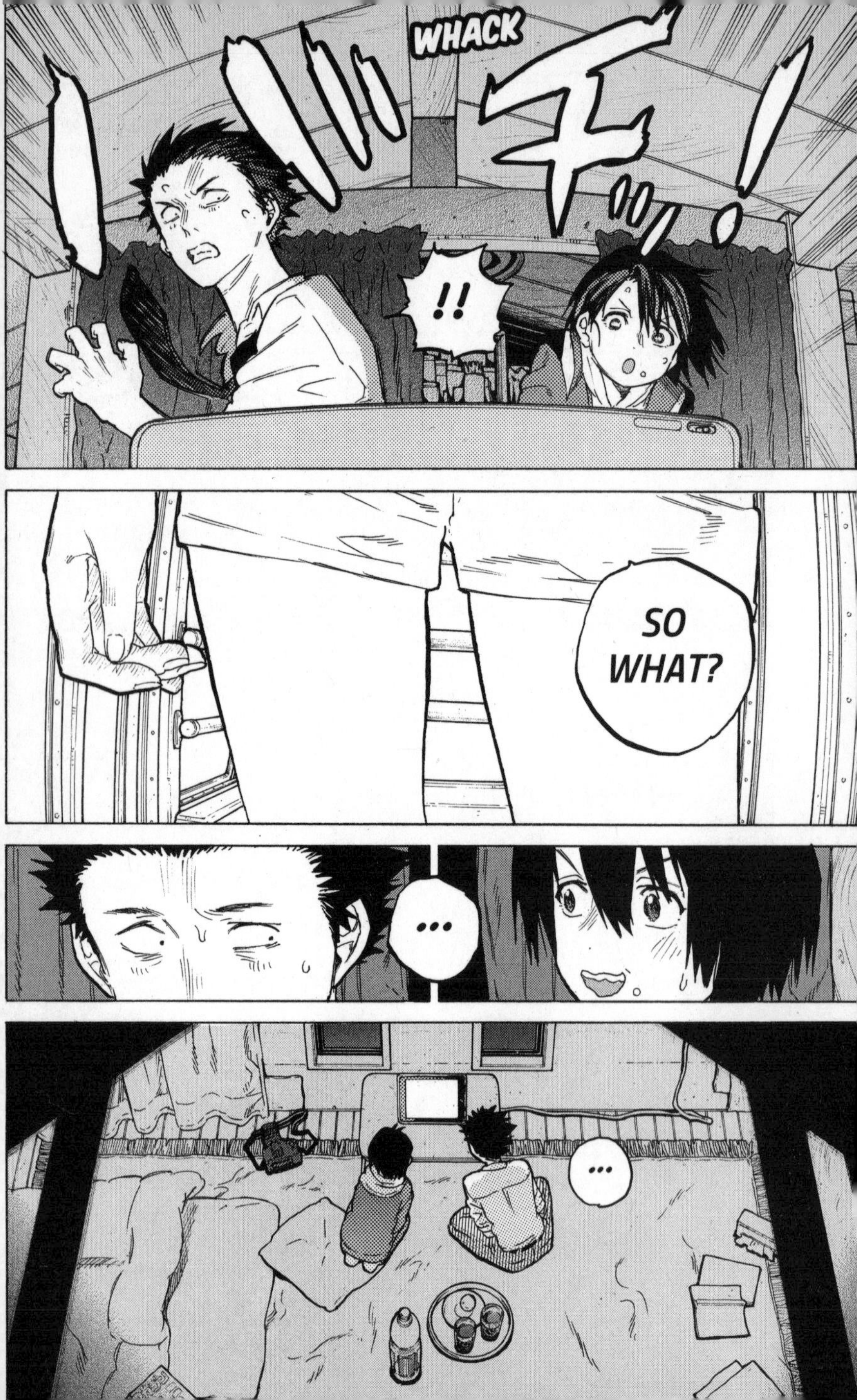
WHACK
!!
SO WHAT?
...
...

I HATE MYSELF.

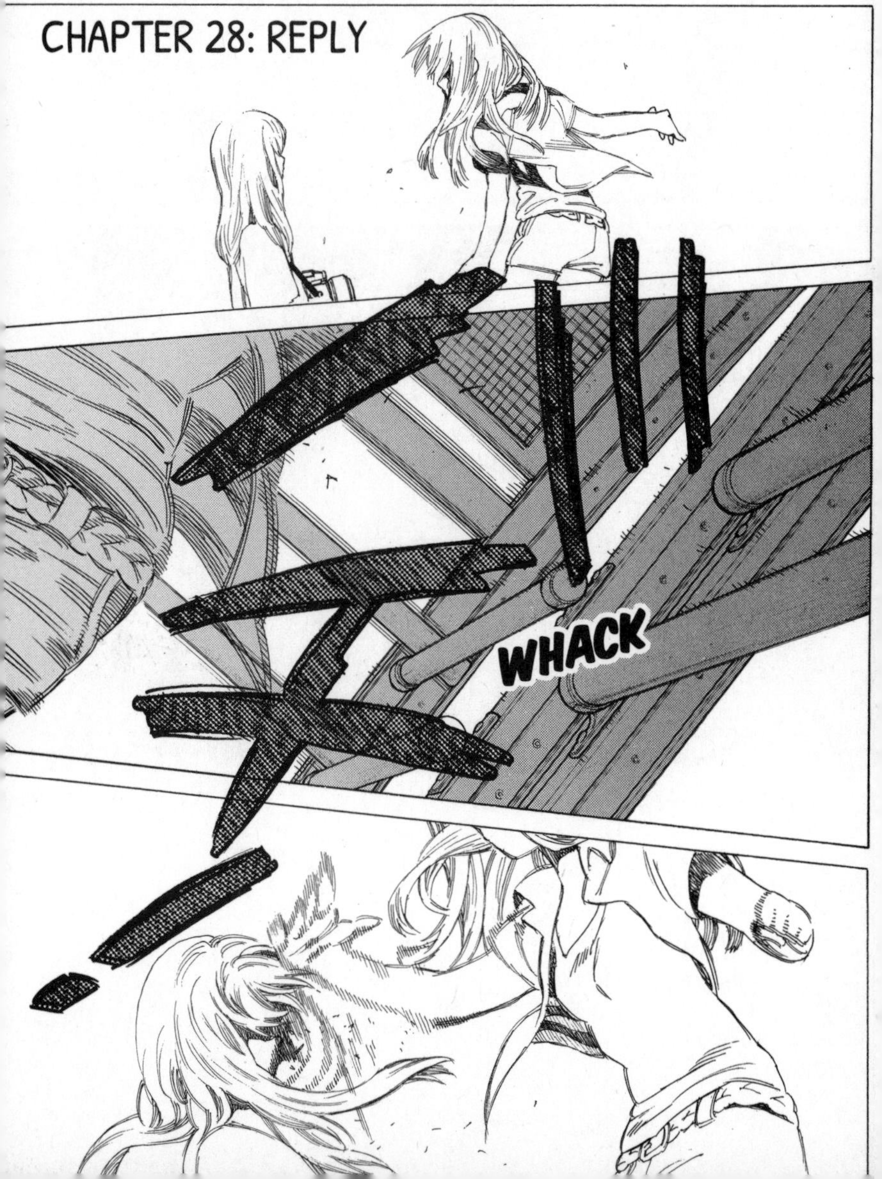
CHAPTER 28: REPLY
WHACK

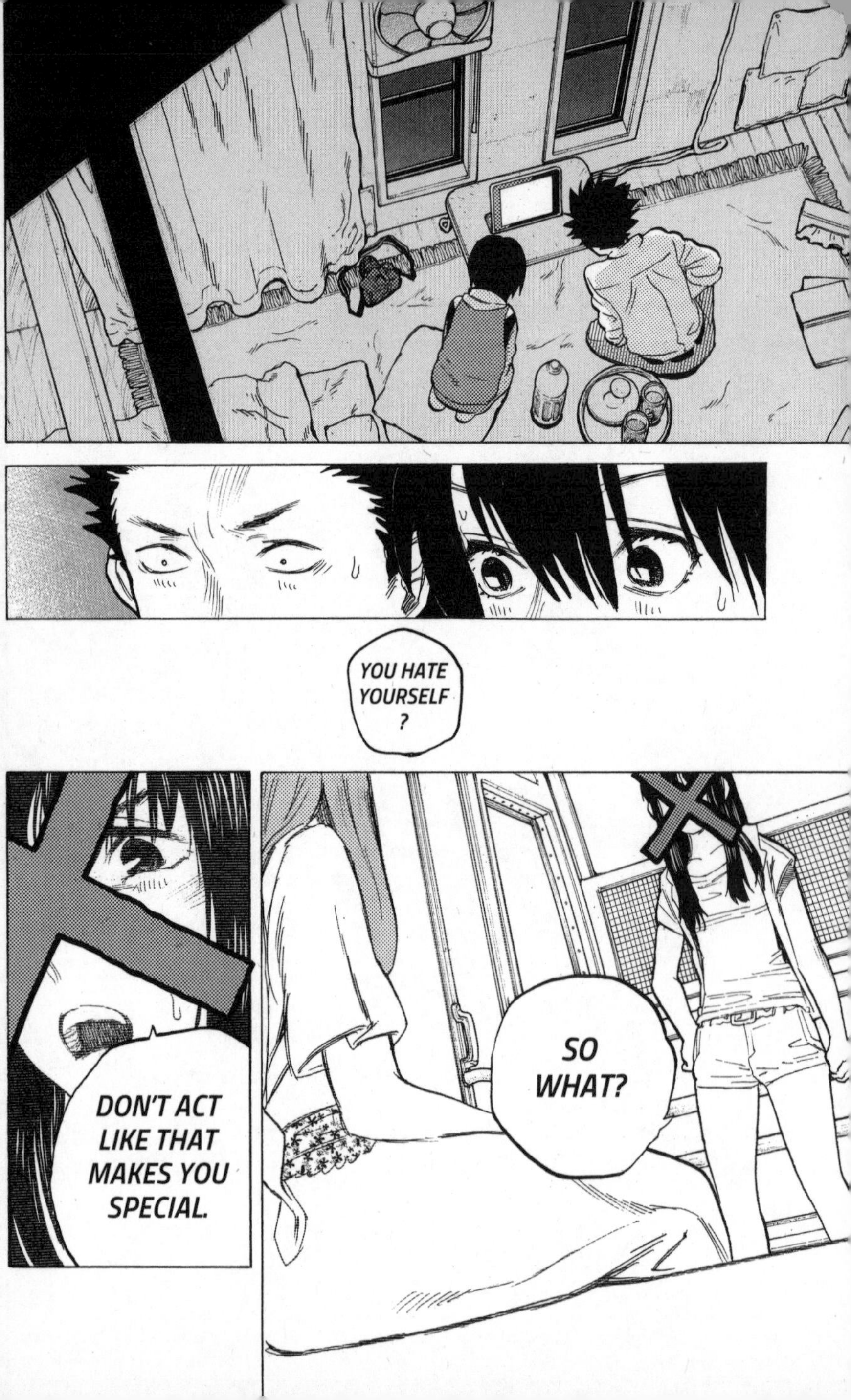
YOU HATE YOURSELF ?
SO WHAT?
DON'T ACT LIKE THAT MAKES YOU SPECIAL.

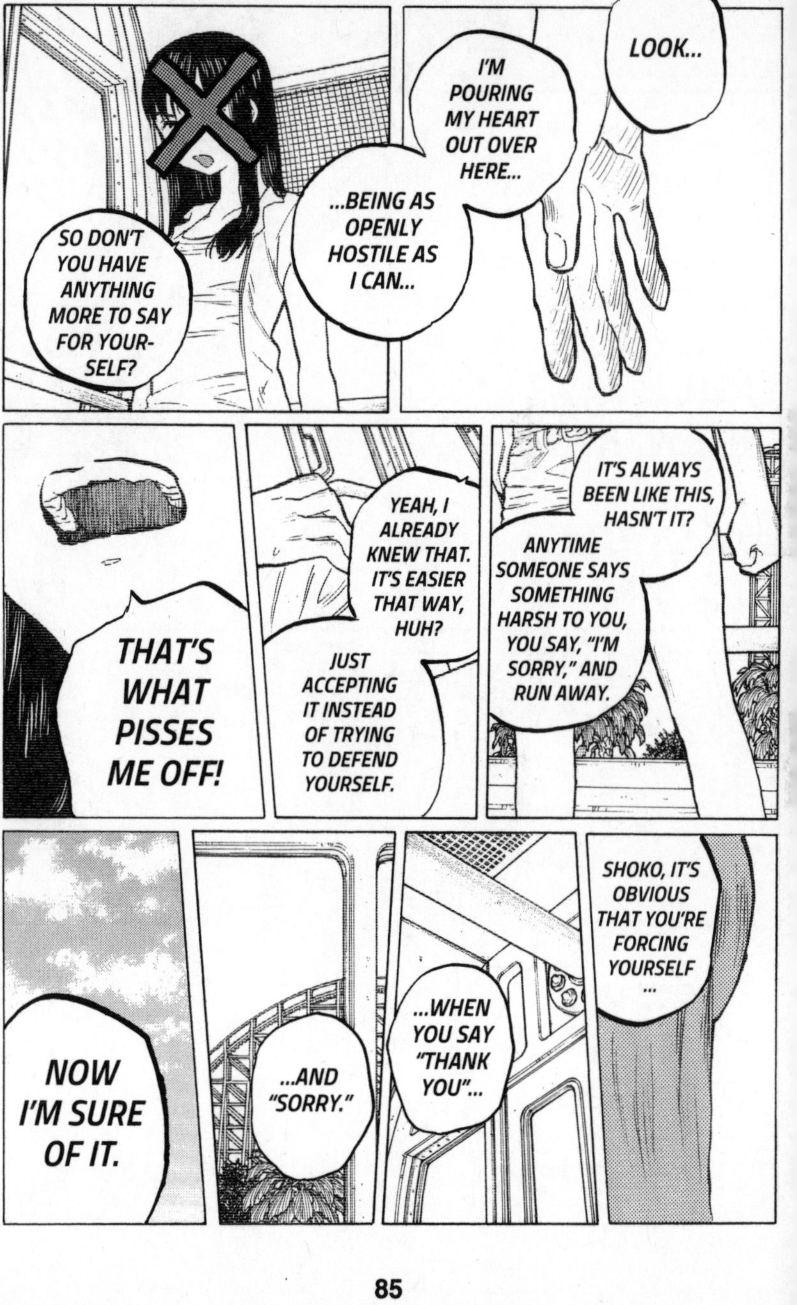
LOOK...
I'M POURING MY HEART OUT OVER HERE...
...BEING AS OPENLY HOSTILE AS I CAN...
SO DON'T YOU HAVE ANYTHING MORE TO SAY FOR YOUR-SELF?
IT'S ALWAYS BEEN LIKE THIS, HASN'T IT?
ANYTIME SOMEONE SAYS SOMETHING HARSH TO YOU, YOU SAY, "I'M SORRY," AND RUN AWAY.
YEAH, I ALREADY KNEW THAT. IT'S EASIER THAT WAY, HUH?
JUST ACCEPTING IT INSTEAD OF TRYING TO DEFEND YOURSELF.
THAT'S WHAT PISSES ME OFF!
SHOKO, IT'S OBVIOUS THAT YOU'RE FORCING YOURSELF...
...WHEN YOU SAY "THANK YOU"...
...AND "SORRY."
NOW I'M SURE OF IT.

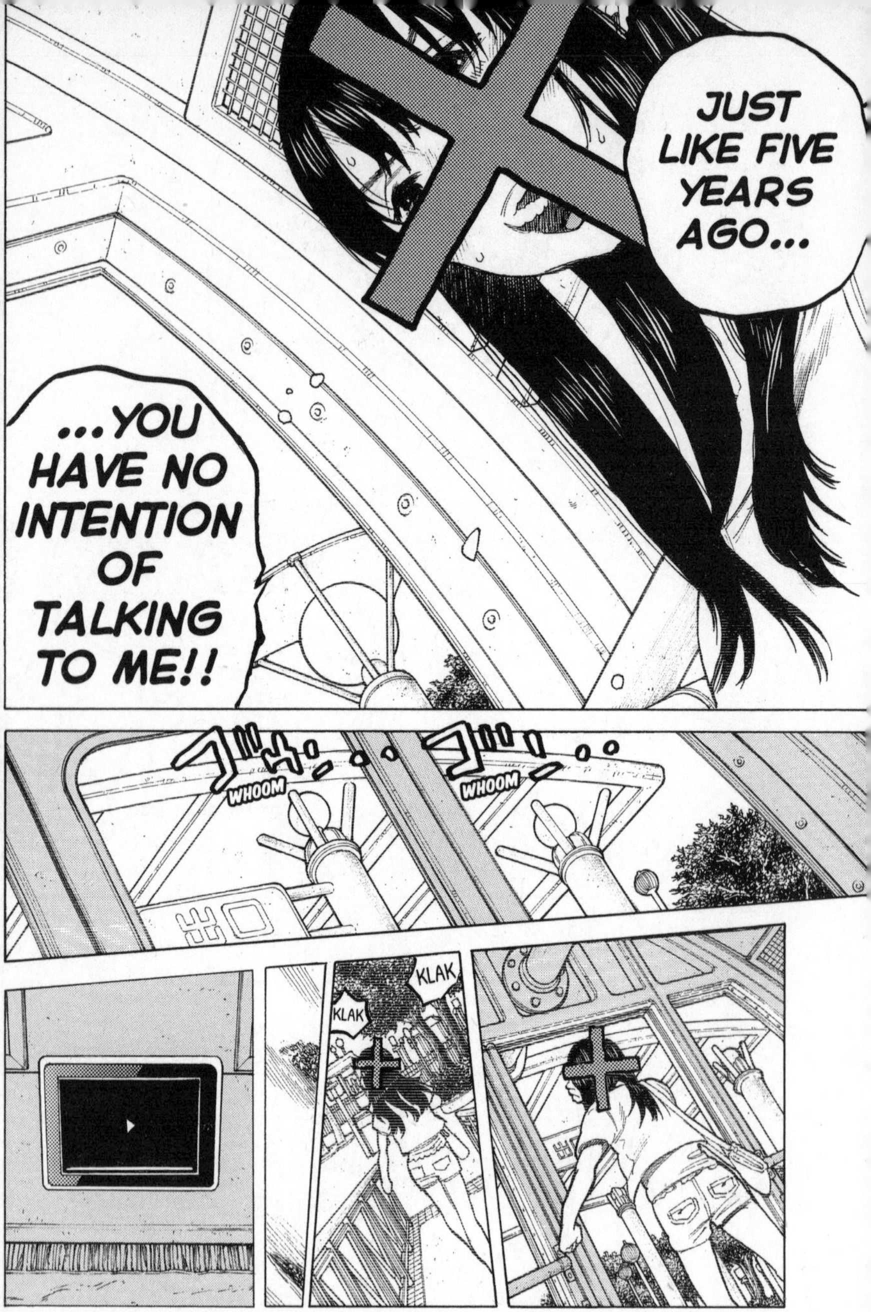
JUST LIKE FIVE YEARS AGO...
...YOU HAVE NO INTENTION OF TALKING TO ME!!
WHOOM
WHOOM
KLAK
KLAK

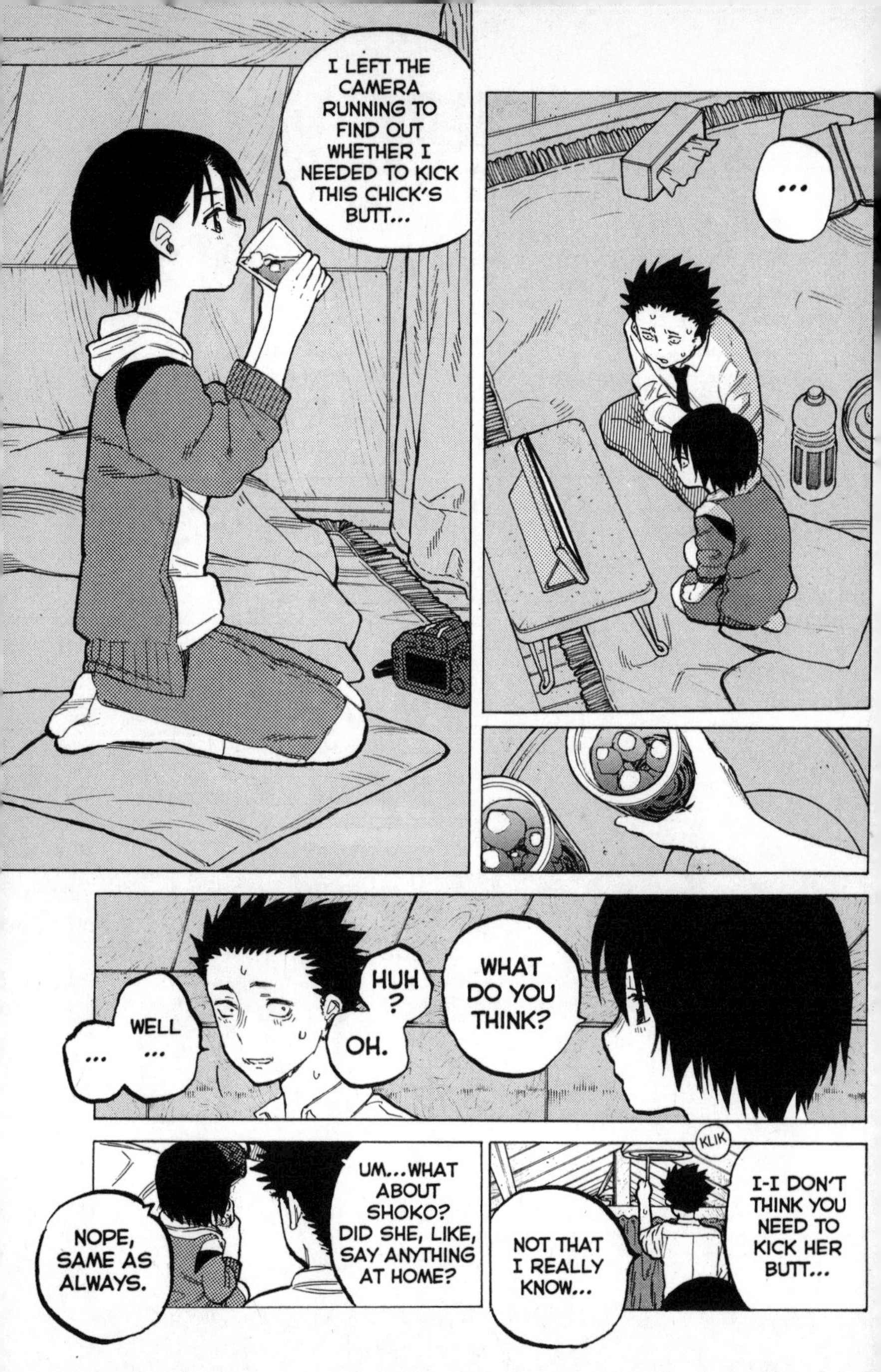
...
I LEFT THE CAMERA RUNNING TO FIND OUT WHETHER I NEEDED TO KICK THIS CHICK'S BUTT...
WHAT DO YOU THINK?
HUH?
OH.
WELL... ...
KLIK
I-I DON'T THINK YOU NEED TO KICK HER BUTT...
NOT THAT I REALLY KNOW...
UM...WHAT ABOUT SHOKO? DID SHE, LIKE, SAY ANYTHING AT HOME?
NOPE, SAME AS ALWAYS.

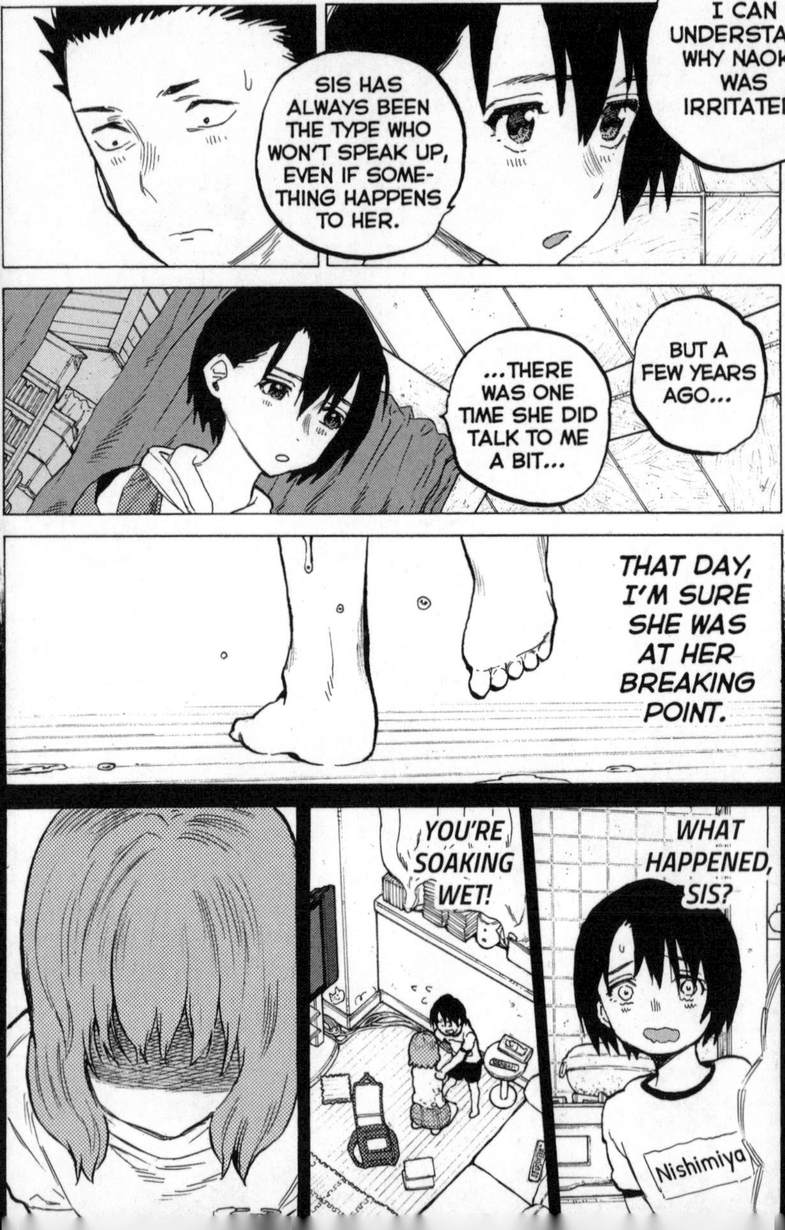
I CAN UNDERSTAND WHY NAOKA WAS IRRITATED.
SIS HAS ALWAYS BEEN THE TYPE WHO WON'T SPEAK UP, EVEN IF SOME-THING HAPPENS TO HER.
BUT A FEW YEARS AGO...
...THERE WAS ONE TIME SHE DID TALK TO ME A BIT...
THAT DAY, I'M SURE SHE WAS AT HER BREAKING POINT.
WHAT HAPPENED, SIS?
Nishimiya
YOU'RE SOAKING WET!

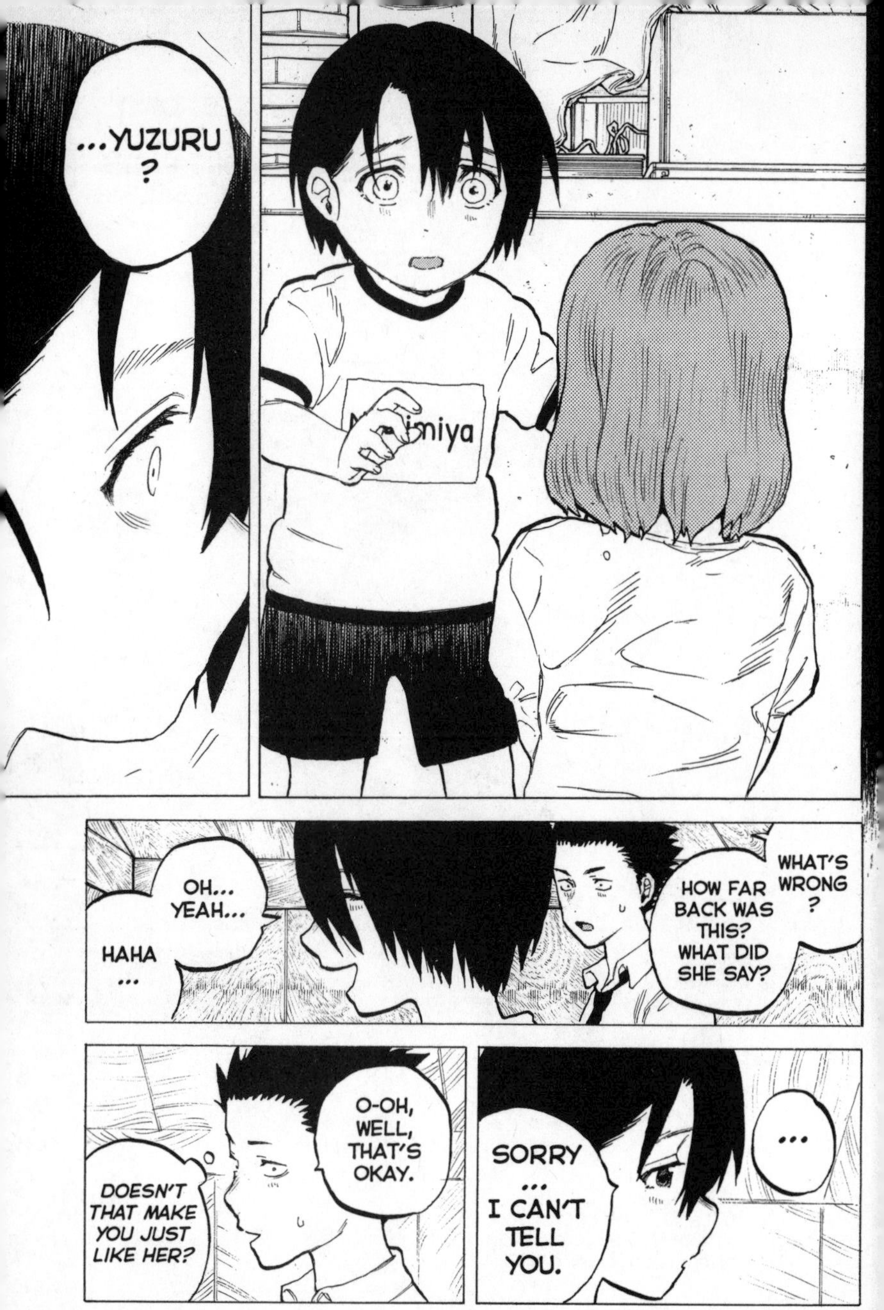
...YUZURU ?
WHAT'S WRONG ?
HOW FAR BACK WAS THIS? WHAT DID SHE SAY?
OH... YEAH...
HAHA ...
...
SORRY ... I CAN'T TELL YOU.
O-OH, WELL, THAT'S OKAY.
DOESN'T THAT MAKE YOU JUST LIKE HER?

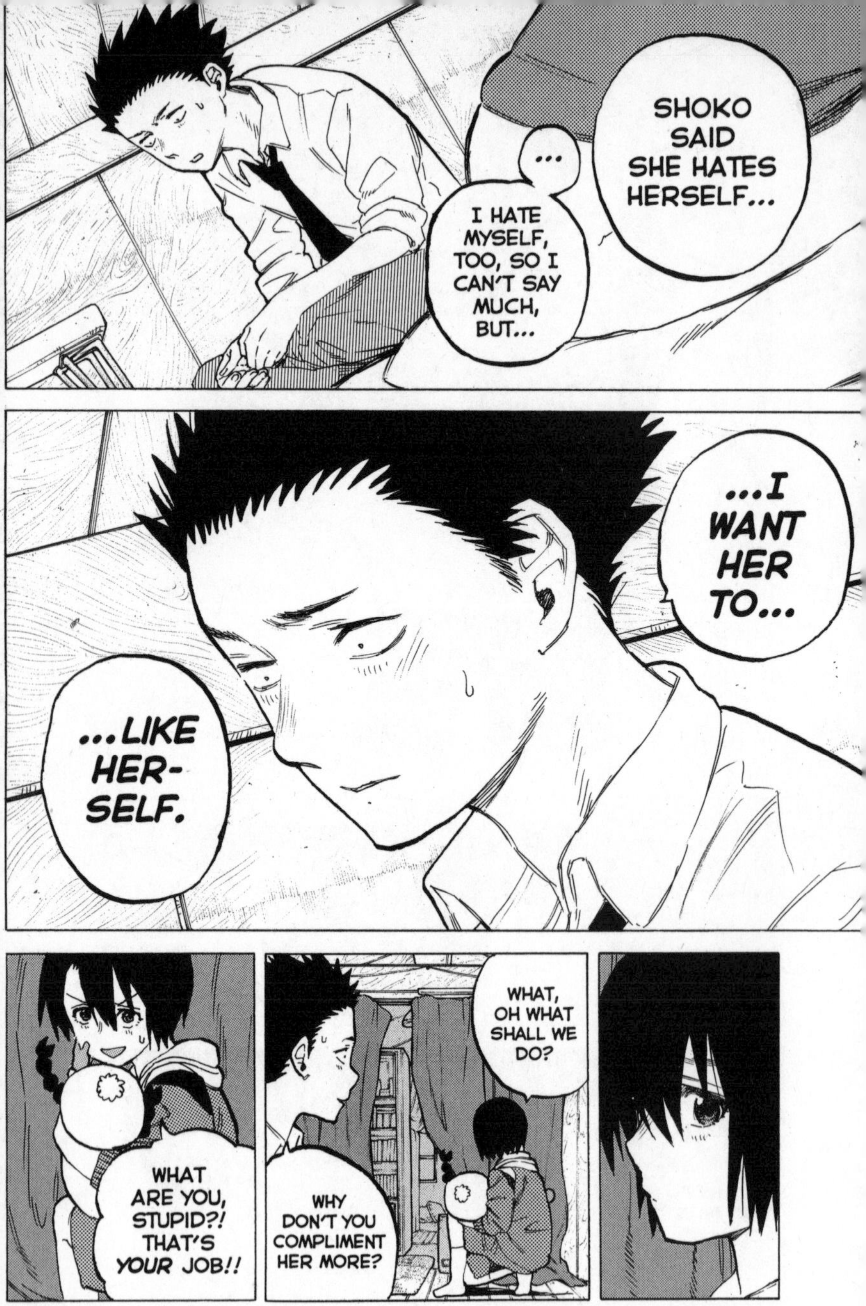
SHOKO SAID SHE HATES HERSELF...
...
I HATE MYSELF, TOO, SO I CAN'T SAY MUCH, BUT...
...I WANT HER TO...
...LIKE HER-SELF.
WHAT, OH WHAT SHALL WE DO?
WHY DON'T YOU COMPLIMENT HER MORE?
WHAT ARE YOU, STUPID?! THAT'S *YOUR* JOB!!

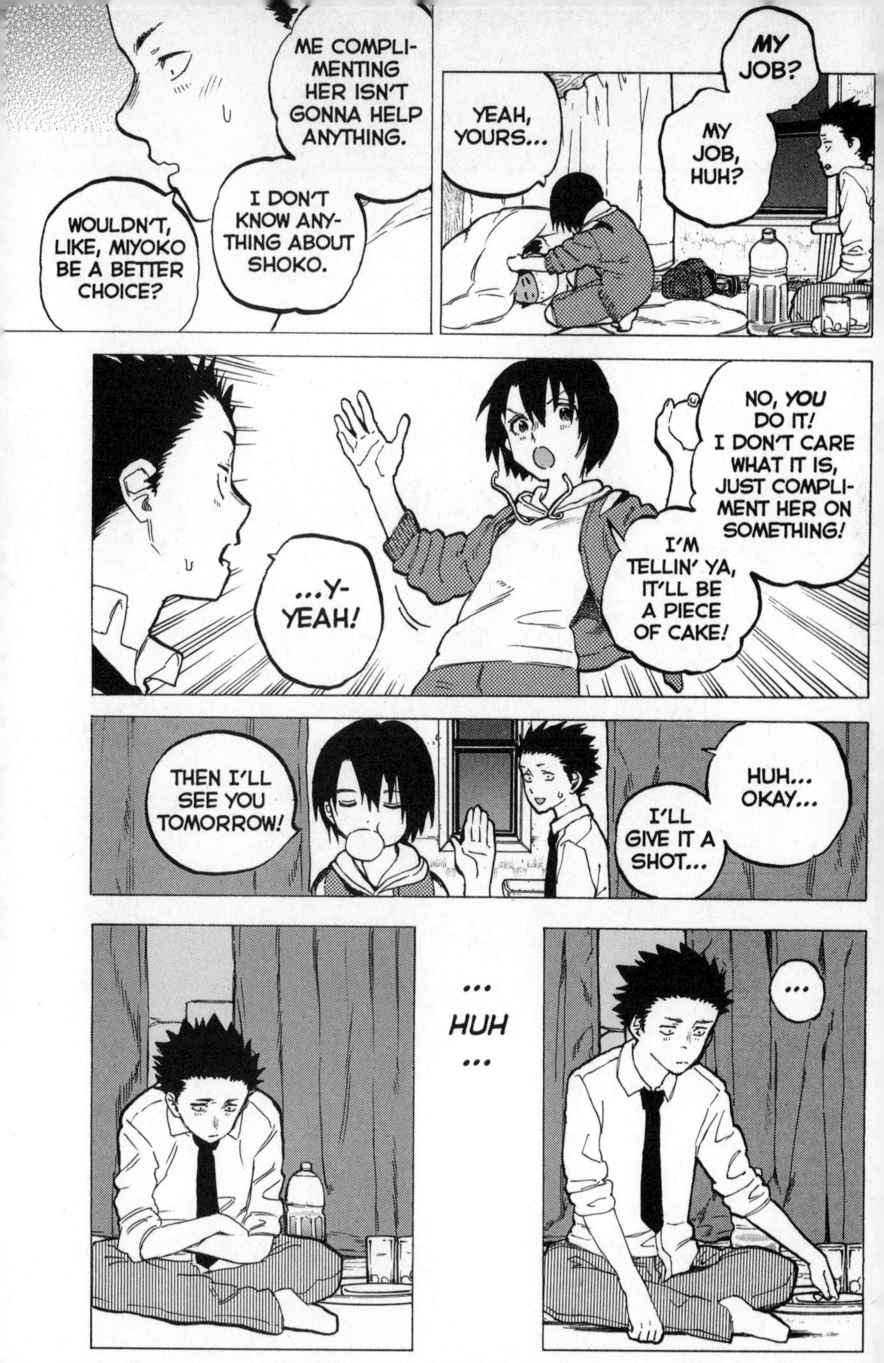
MY JOB?
YEAH, YOURS...
MY JOB, HUH?
ME COMPLIMENTING HER ISN'T GONNA HELP ANYTHING.
I DON'T KNOW ANYTHING ABOUT SHOKO.
WOULDN'T, LIKE, MIYOKO BE A BETTER CHOICE?
NO, *YOU* DO IT! I DON'T CARE WHAT IT IS, JUST COMPLIMENT HER ON SOMETHING!
I'M TELLIN' YA, IT'LL BE A PIECE OF CAKE!
...Y-YEAH!
HUH... OKAY...
I'LL GIVE IT A SHOT...
THEN I'LL SEE YOU TOMORROW!
...
...HUH...

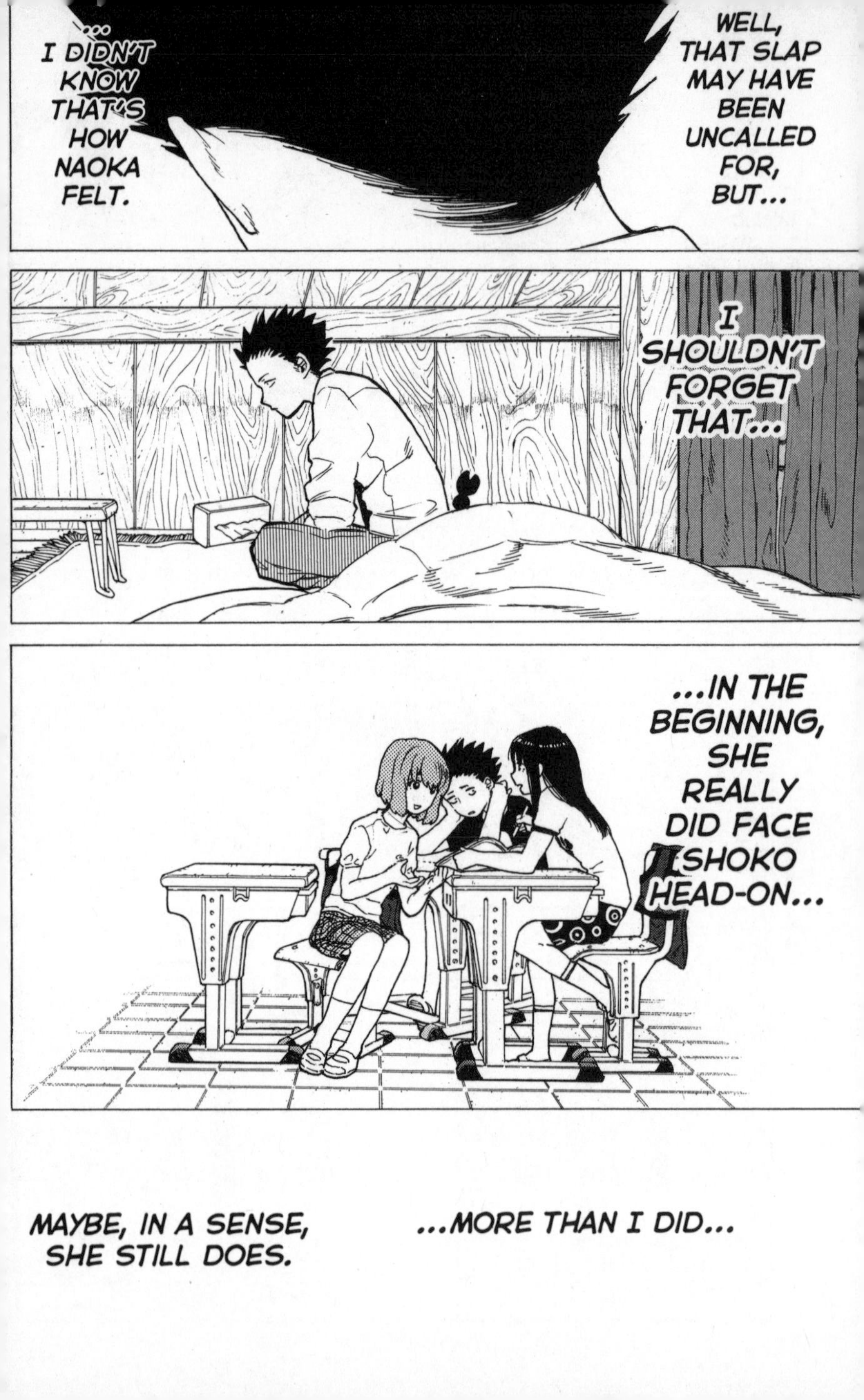
WELL, THAT SLAP MAY HAVE BEEN UNCALLED FOR, BUT...
...I DIDN'T KNOW THAT'S HOW NAOKA FELT.
I SHOULDN'T FORGET THAT...
...IN THE BEGINNING, SHE REALLY DID FACE SHOKO HEAD-ON...
...MORE THAN I DID...
MAYBE, IN A SENSE, SHE STILL DOES.

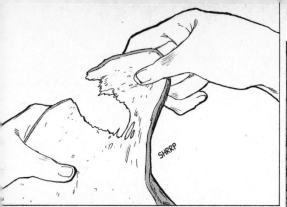

SHRRP

I NEED TO MEET SHOKO HEAD-ON, TOO...

YO...

HEY THERE.

YO...

SHOKO...

BOW

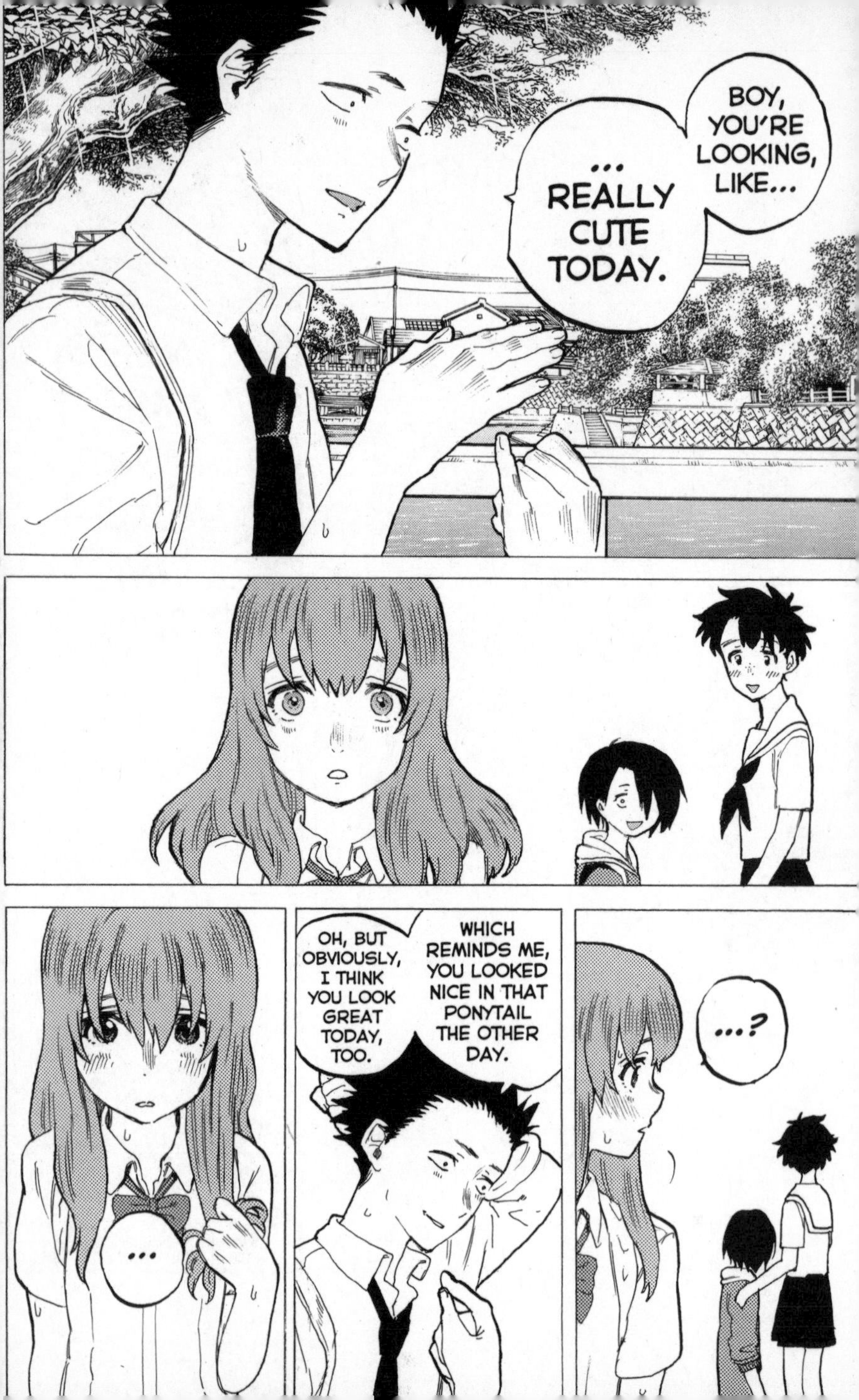
BOY, YOU'RE LOOKING, LIKE...
...REALLY CUTE TODAY.
...?
WHICH REMINDS ME, YOU LOOKED NICE IN THAT PONYTAIL THE OTHER DAY.
OH, BUT OBVIOUSLY, I THINK YOU LOOK GREAT TODAY, TOO.
...

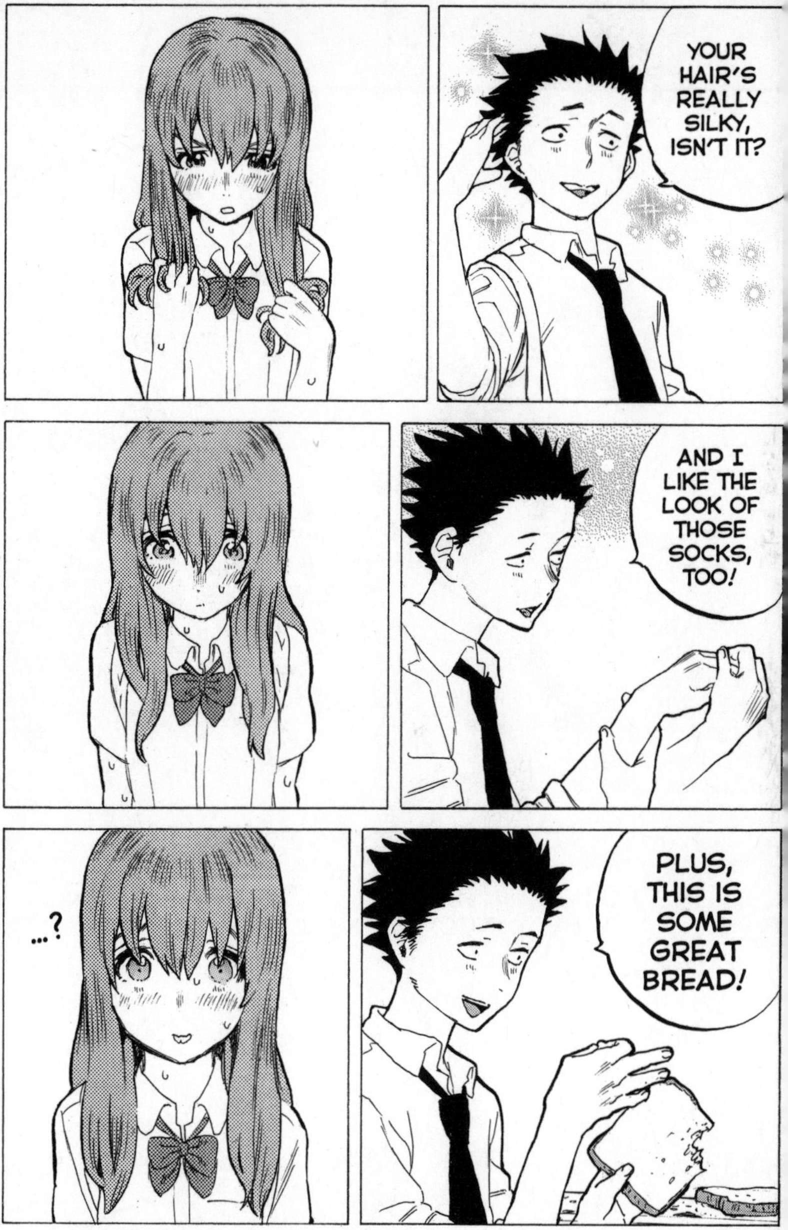
YOUR HAIR'S REALLY SILKY, ISN'T IT?
AND I LIKE THE LOOK OF THOSE SOCKS, TOO!
PLUS, THIS IS SOME GREAT BREAD!
...?

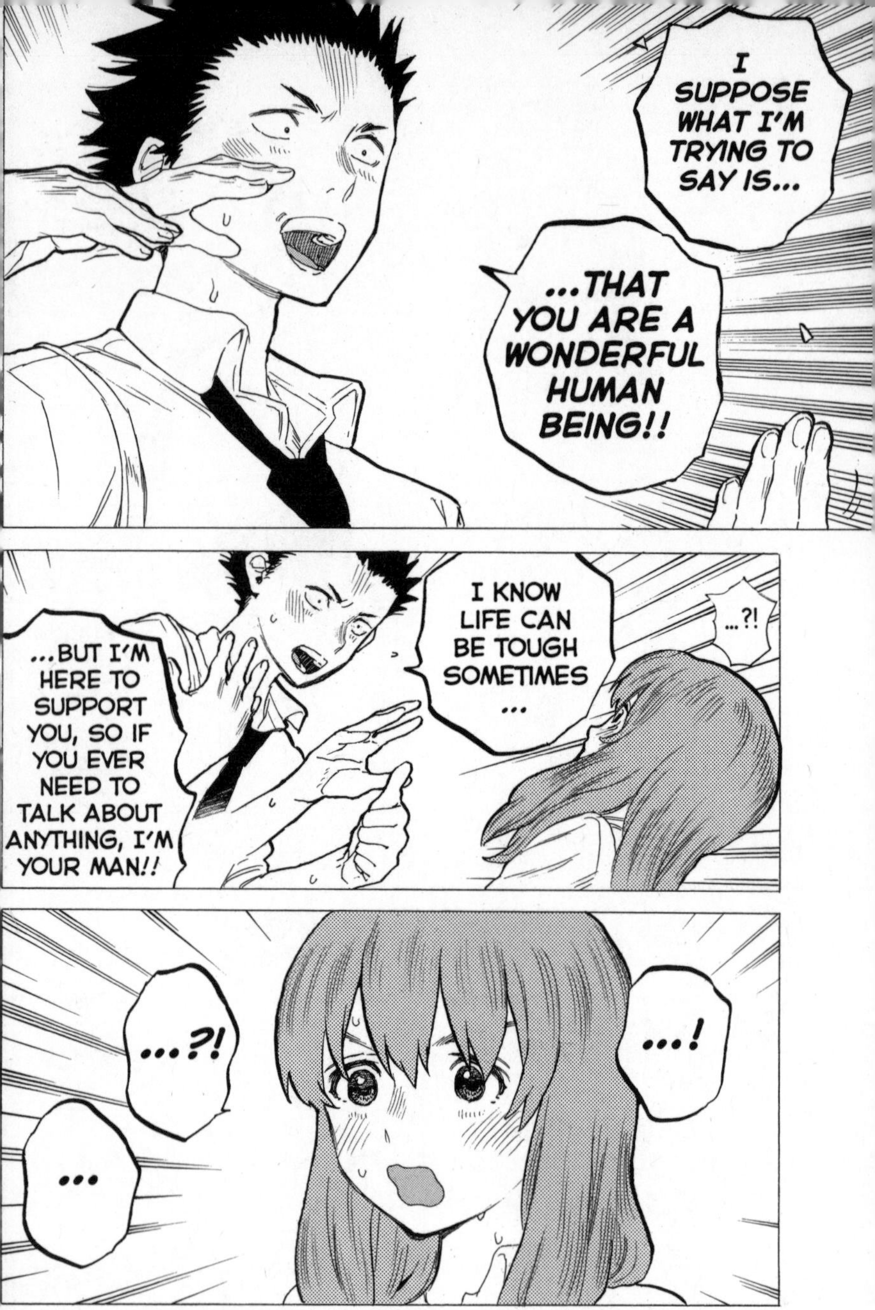
I SUPPOSE WHAT I'M TRYING TO SAY IS...
...THAT YOU ARE A WONDERFUL HUMAN BEING!!
...?!
I KNOW LIFE CAN BE TOUGH SOMETIMES...
...BUT I'M HERE TO SUPPORT YOU, SO IF YOU EVER NEED TO TALK ABOUT ANYTHING, I'M YOUR MAN!!
...!
...?!
...

I WONDER WHAT'S GOTTEN INTO SHOYA TODAY...

BOW!

JUST LEAVE HIM BE.

TEE HEE!

?! SO THAT WASN'T SO SMOOTH, HUH?

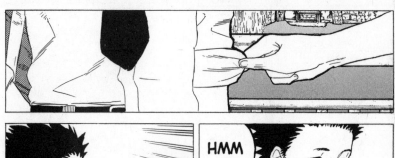

HMM ?

YOU WANT TO ASK ME SOMETHING? SURE, ASK AWAY!!

...

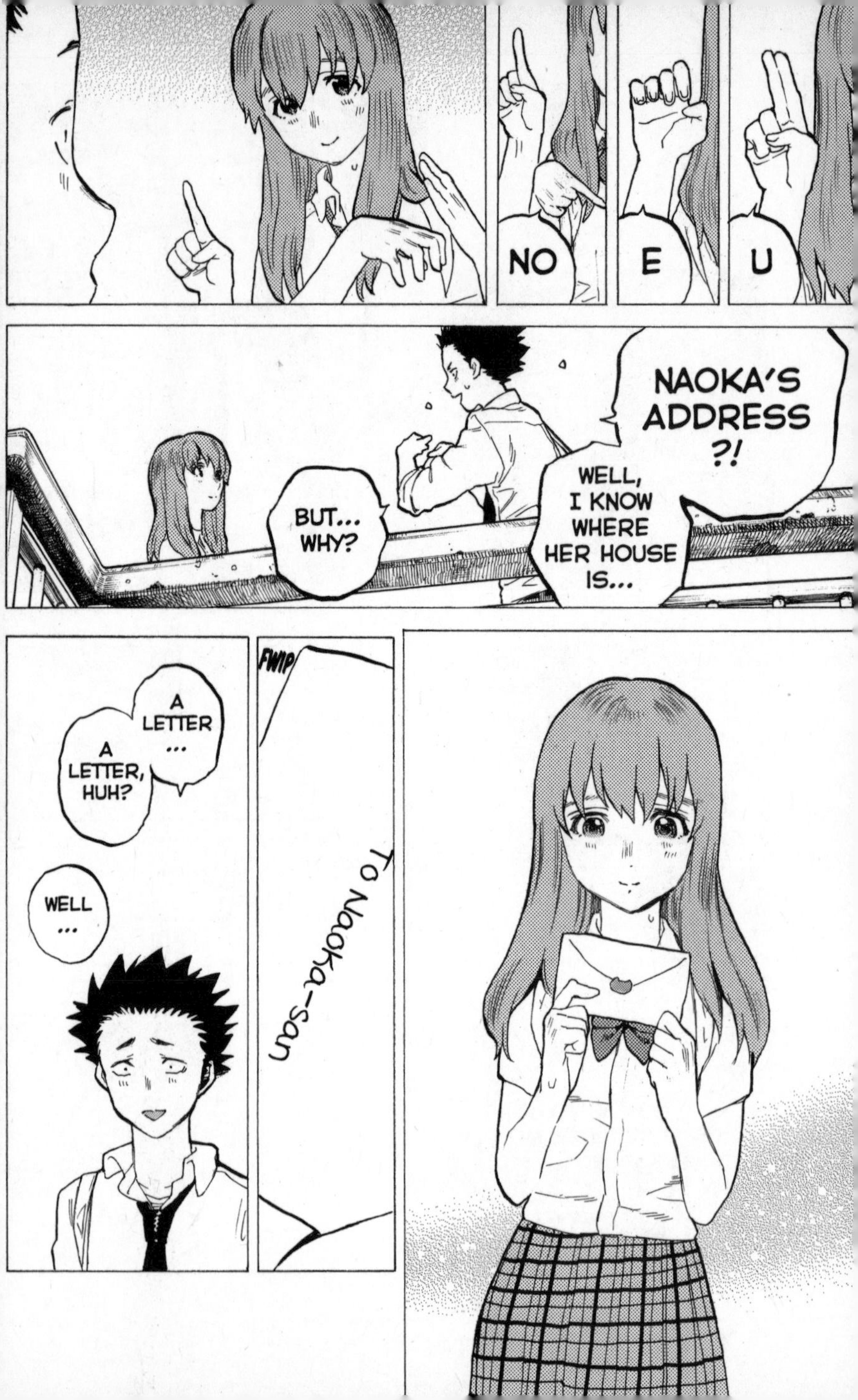
U
E
NO
NAOKA'S ADDRESS ?!
WELL, I KNOW WHERE HER HOUSE IS...
BUT... WHY?
FWIP
To Naoka-san
A LETTER ...
A LETTER, HUH?
WELL ...

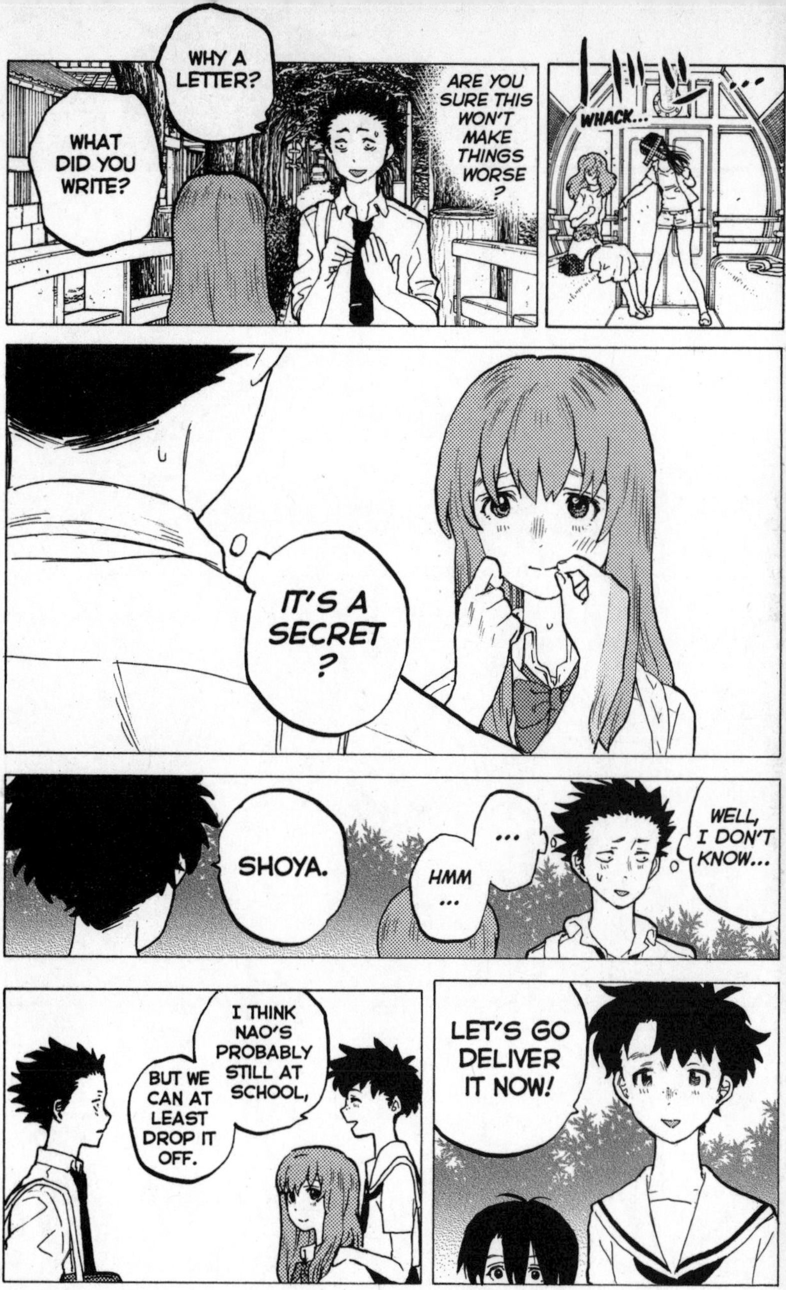
WHACK...
ARE YOU SURE THIS WON'T MAKE THINGS WORSE?
WHY A LETTER?
WHAT DID YOU WRITE?
IT'S A SECRET?
WELL, I DON'T KNOW...
...
HMM...
SHOYA.
LET'S GO DELIVER IT NOW!
I THINK NAO'S PROBABLY STILL AT SCHOOL,
BUT WE CAN AT LEAST DROP IT OFF.

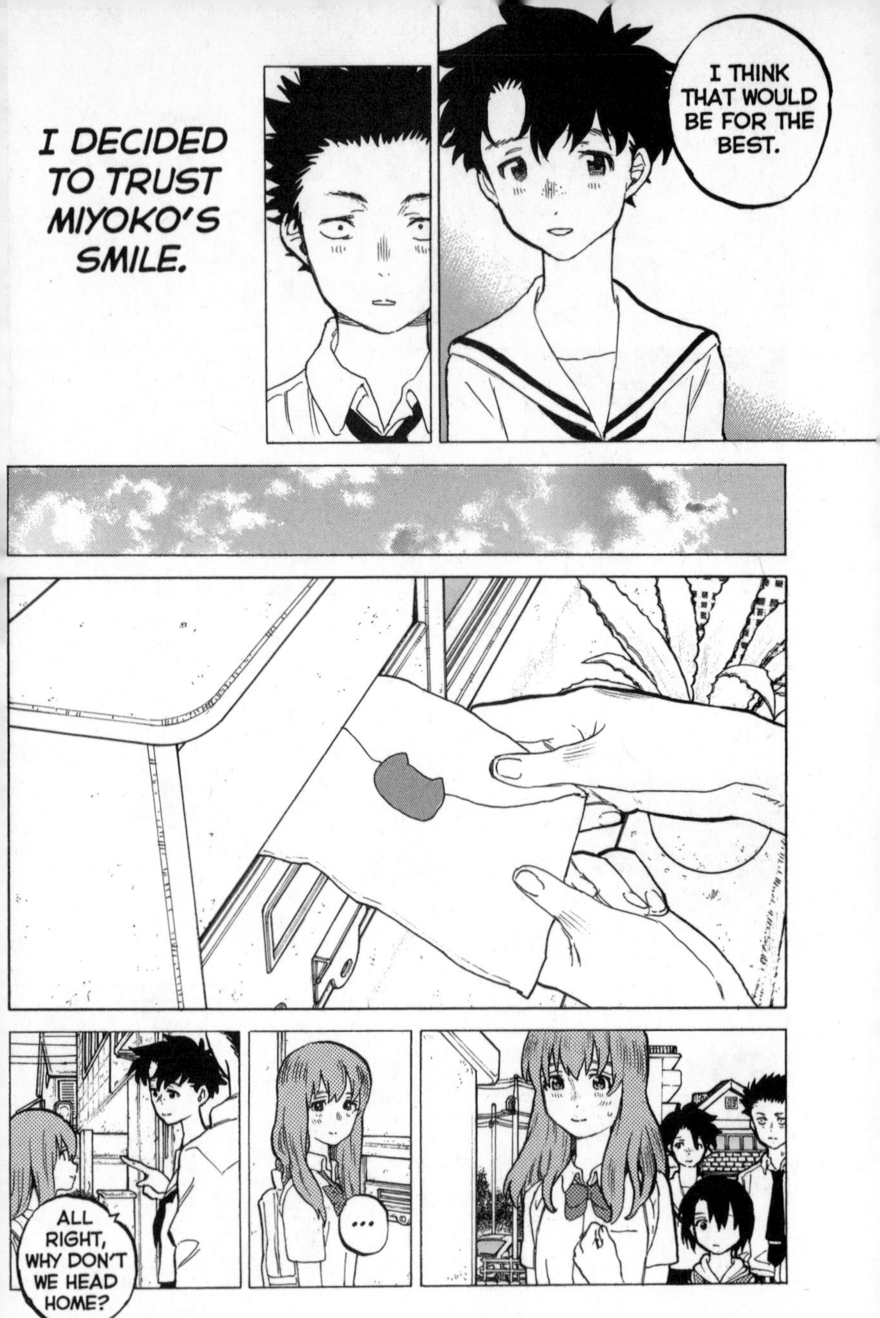
I THINK THAT WOULD BE FOR THE BEST.
I DECIDED TO TRUST MIYOKO'S SMILE.
...
ALL RIGHT, WHY DON'T WE HEAD HOME?

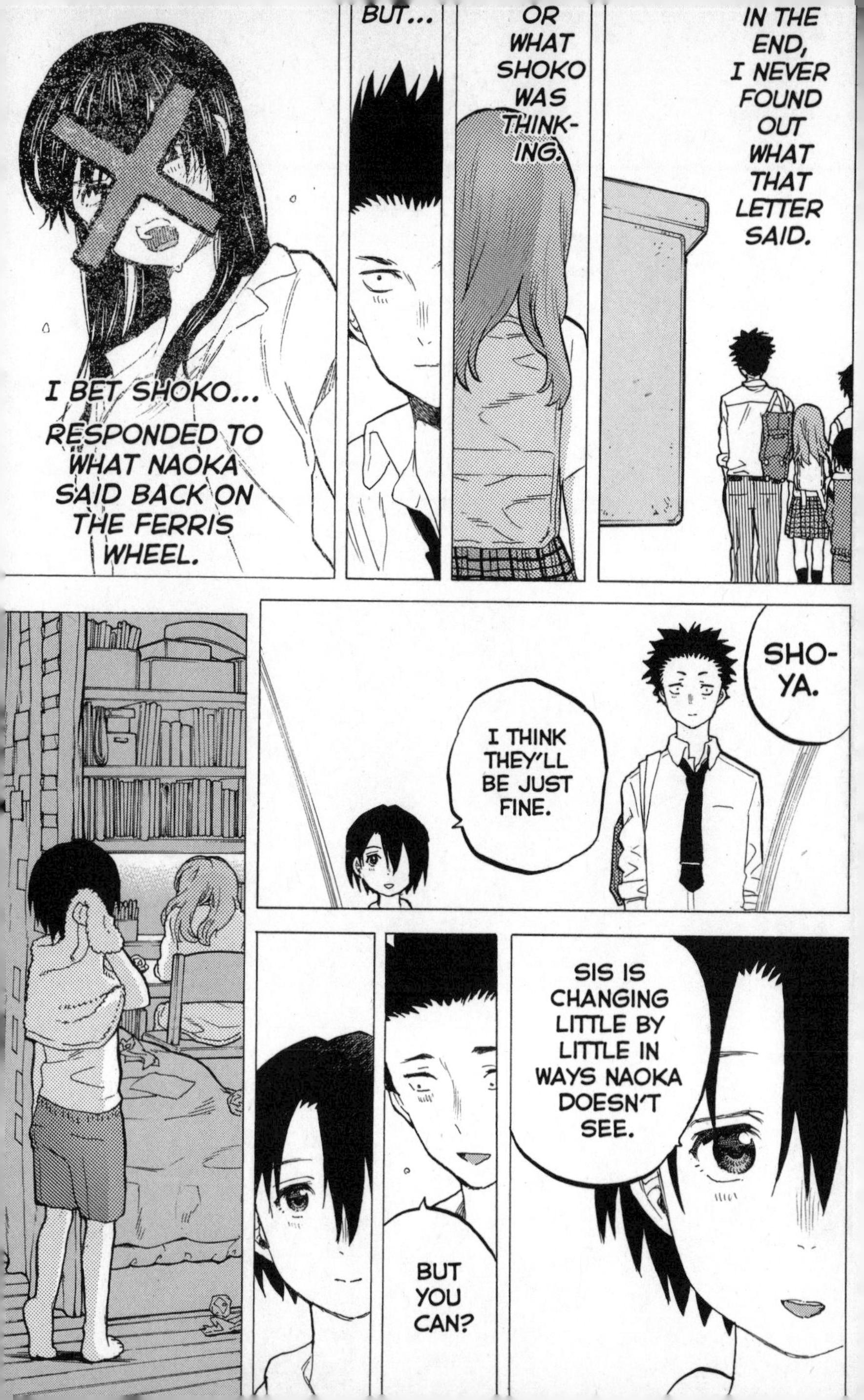
IN THE END, I NEVER FOUND OUT WHAT THAT LETTER SAID.
OR WHAT SHOKO WAS THINKING.
BUT...
I BET SHOKO...
RESPONDED TO WHAT NAOKA SAID BACK ON THE FERRIS WHEEL.
SHO-YA.
I THINK THEY'LL BE JUST FINE.
SIS IS CHANGING LITTLE BY LITTLE IN WAYS NAOKA DOESN'T SEE.
BUT YOU CAN?

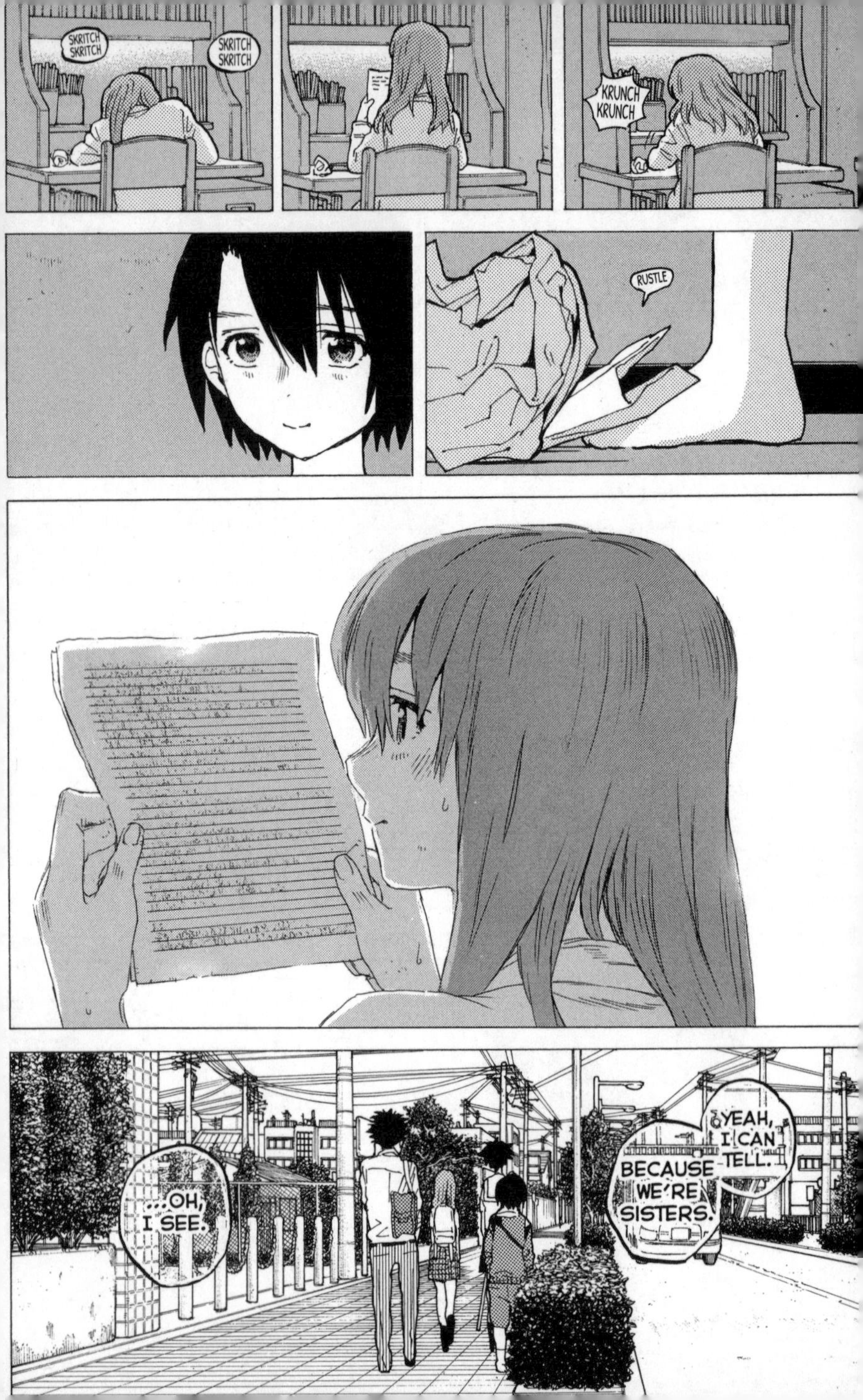
KRUNCH KRUNCH
SKRITCH SKRITCH
SKRITCH SKRITCH
RUSTLE
YEAH, I CAN TELL.
BECAUSE WE'RE SISTERS.
...OH, I SEE.

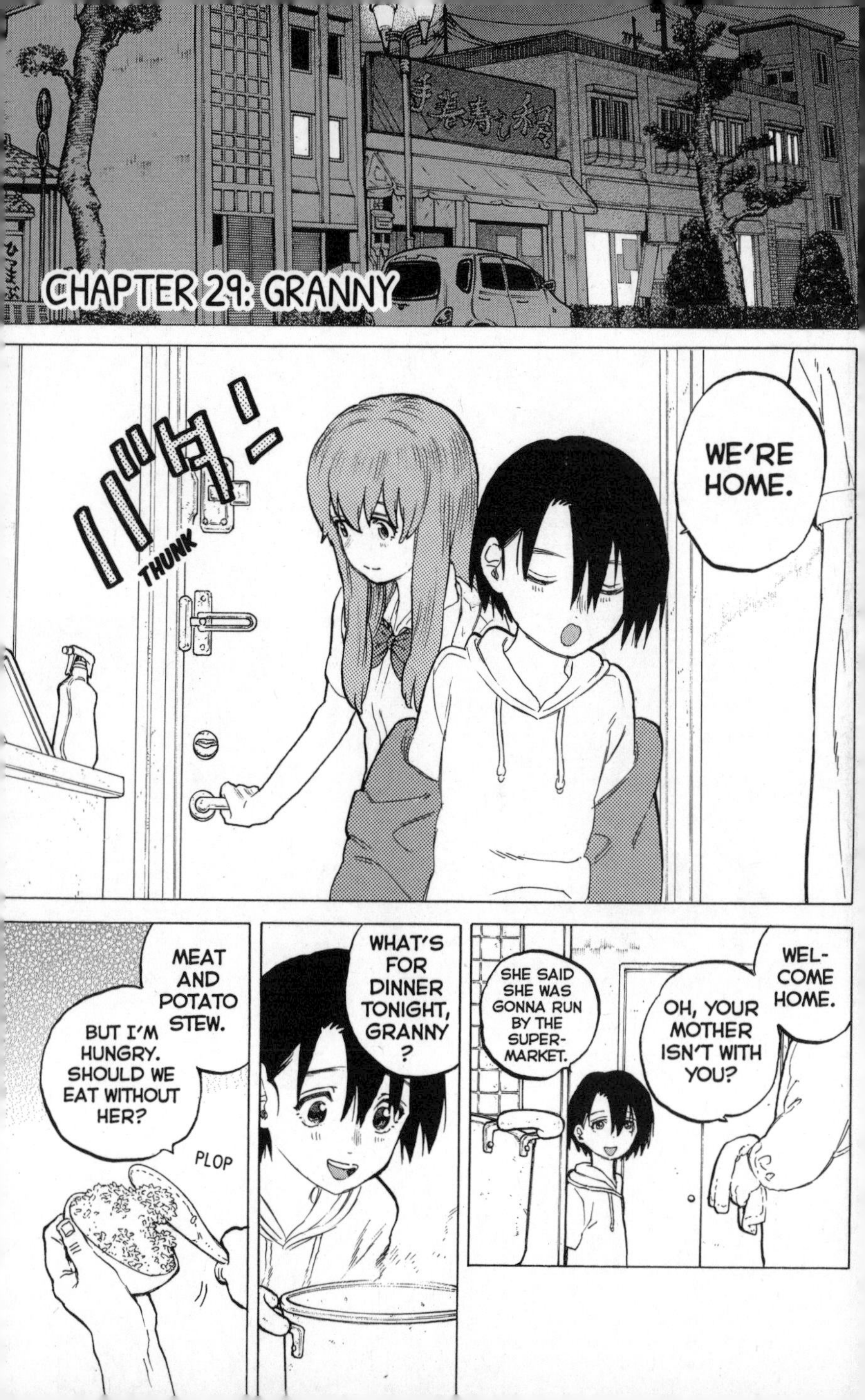
CHAPTER 29: GRANNY
THUNK
WE'RE HOME.
WEL-COME HOME.
OH, YOUR MOTHER ISN'T WITH YOU?
SHE SAID SHE WAS GONNA RUN BY THE SUPER-MARKET.
WHAT'S FOR DINNER TONIGHT, GRANNY?
MEAT AND POTATO STEW.
BUT I'M HUNGRY. SHOULD WE EAT WITHOUT HER?
PLOP

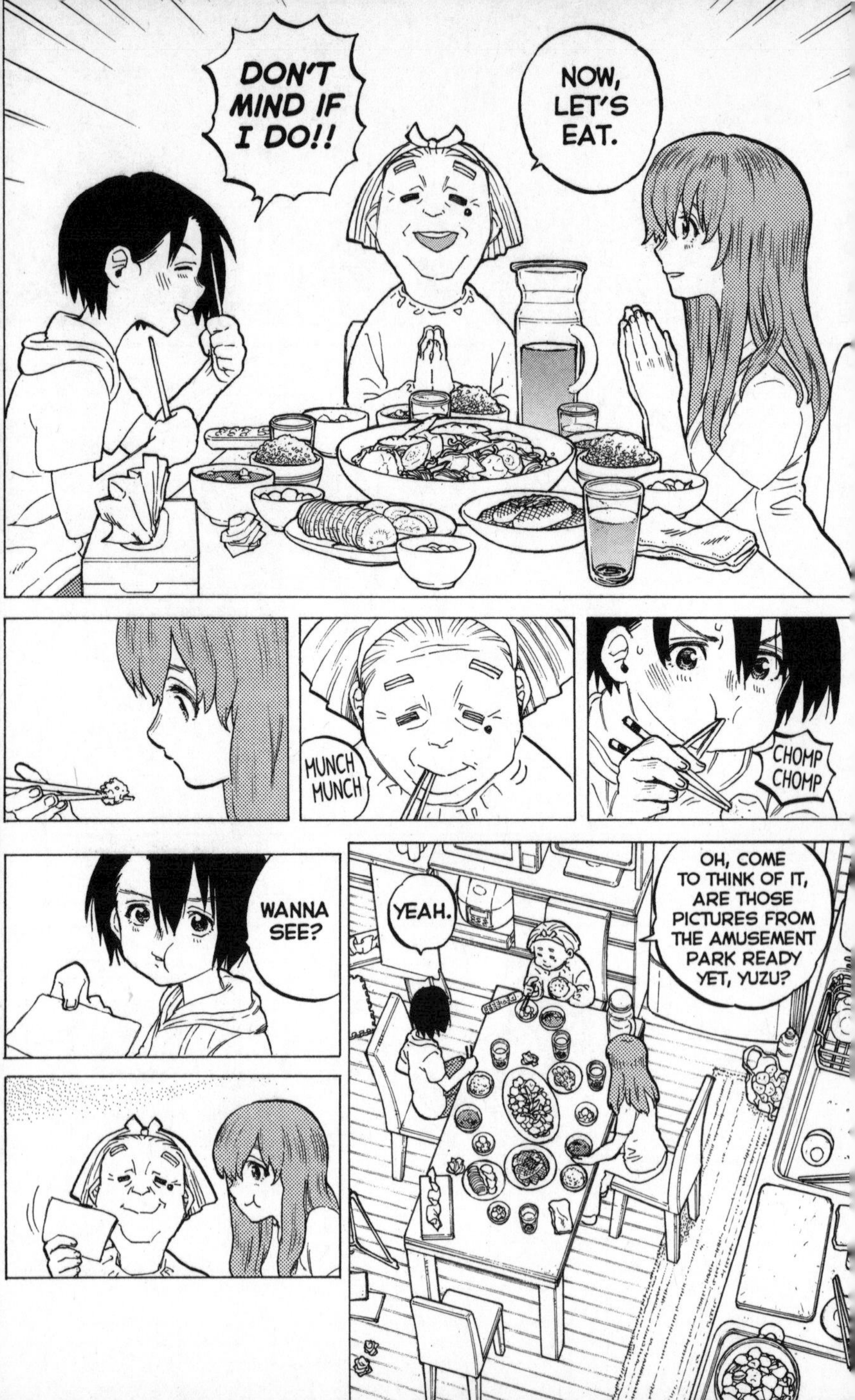
NOW, LET'S EAT.
DON'T MIND IF I DO!!
CHOMP CHOMP
MUNCH MUNCH
OH, COME TO THINK OF IT, ARE THOSE PICTURES FROM THE AMUSEMENT PARK READY YET, YUZU?
YEAH.
WANNA SEE?

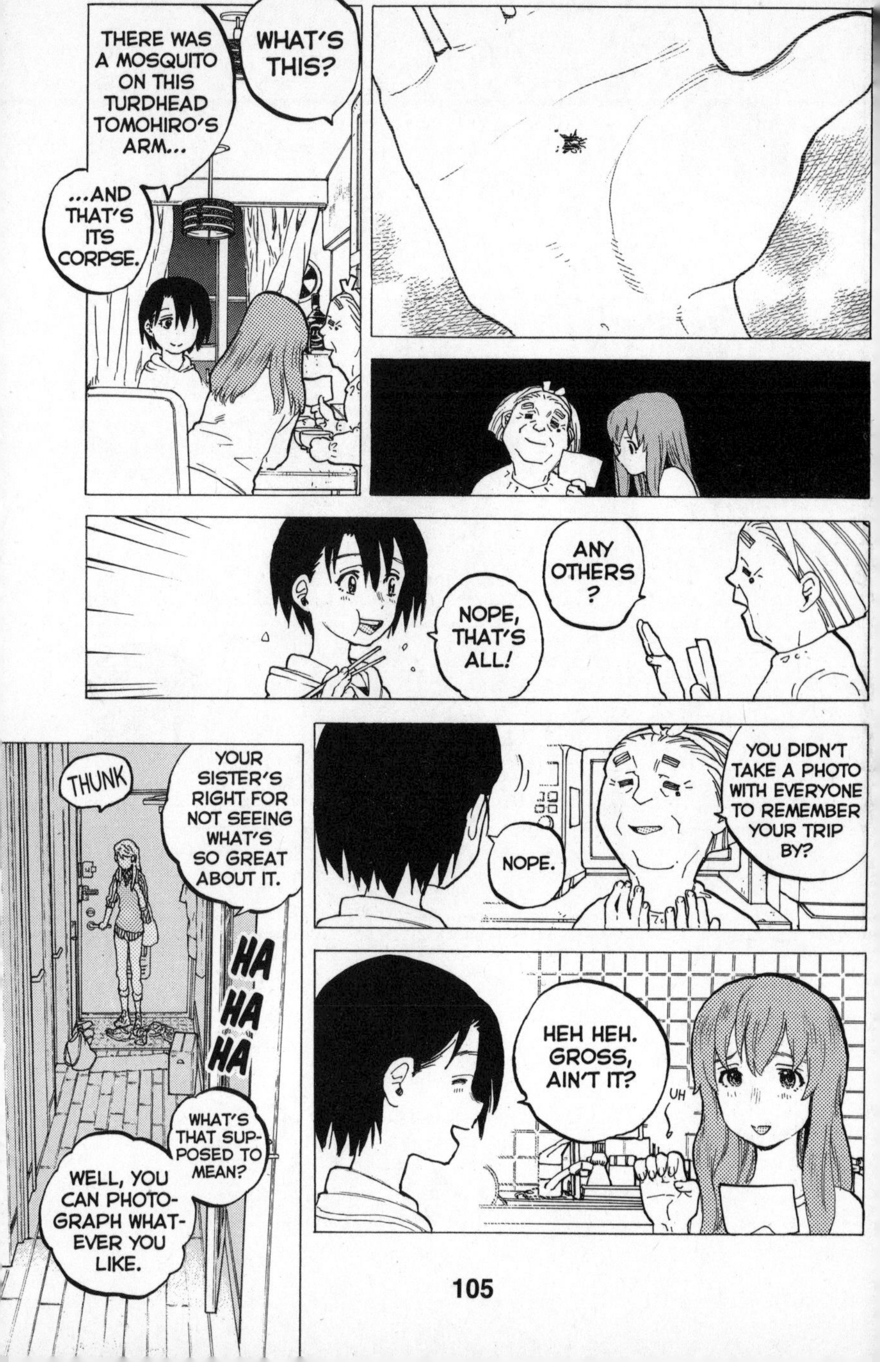
WHAT'S THIS?
THERE WAS A MOSQUITO ON THIS TURDHEAD TOMOHIRO'S ARM...
...AND THAT'S ITS CORPSE.
ANY OTHERS?
NOPE, THAT'S ALL!
YOU DIDN'T TAKE A PHOTO WITH EVERYONE TO REMEMBER YOUR TRIP BY?
NOPE.
HEH HEH. GROSS, AIN'T IT?
UH
THUNK
YOUR SISTER'S RIGHT FOR NOT SEEING WHAT'S SO GREAT ABOUT IT.
HA HA HA
WHAT'S THAT SUPPOSED TO MEAN?
WELL, YOU CAN PHOTOGRAPH WHATEVER YOU LIKE.

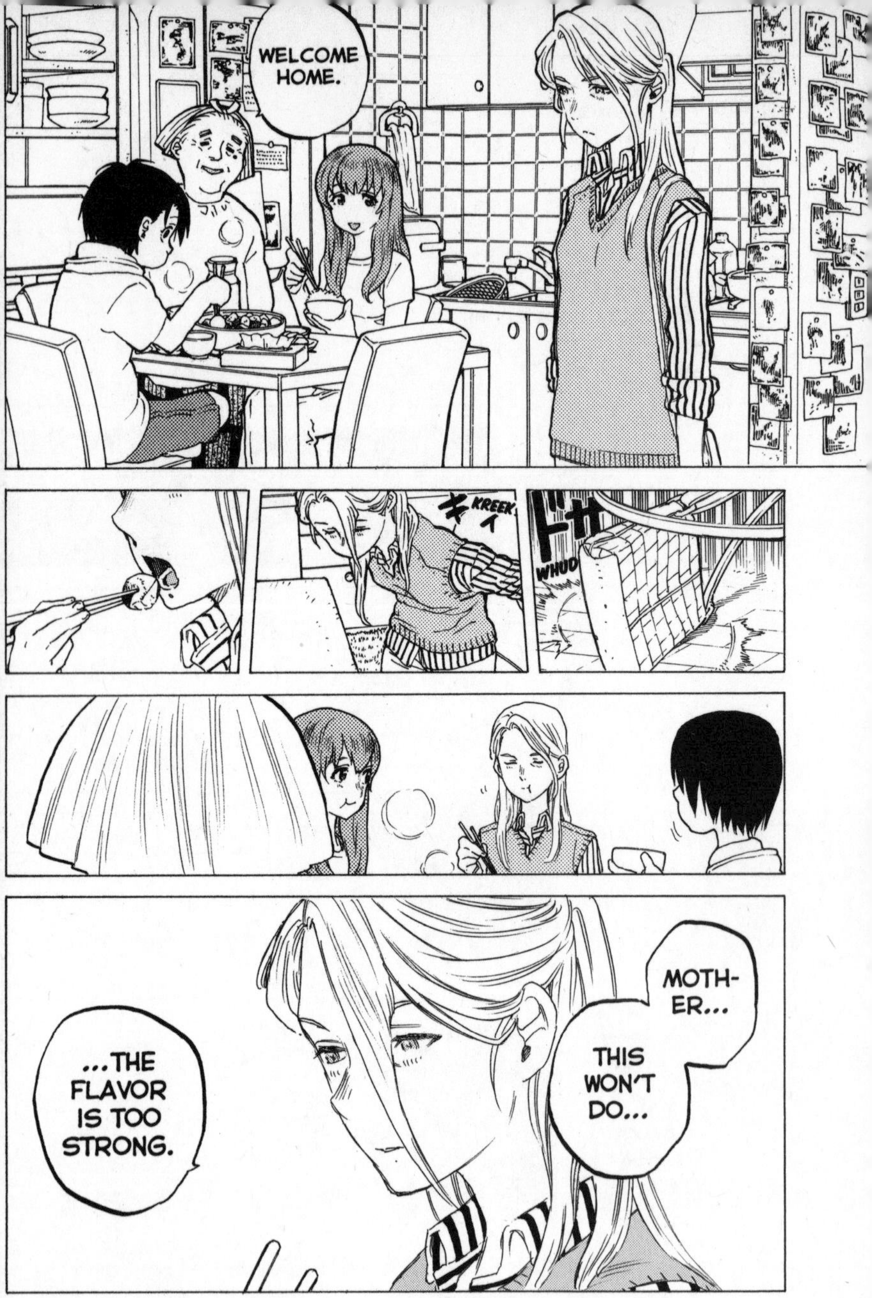
WELCOME HOME.
ドサ
WHUD
キィ
KREEK
MOTH-ER...
THIS WON'T DO...
...THE FLAVOR IS TOO STRONG.

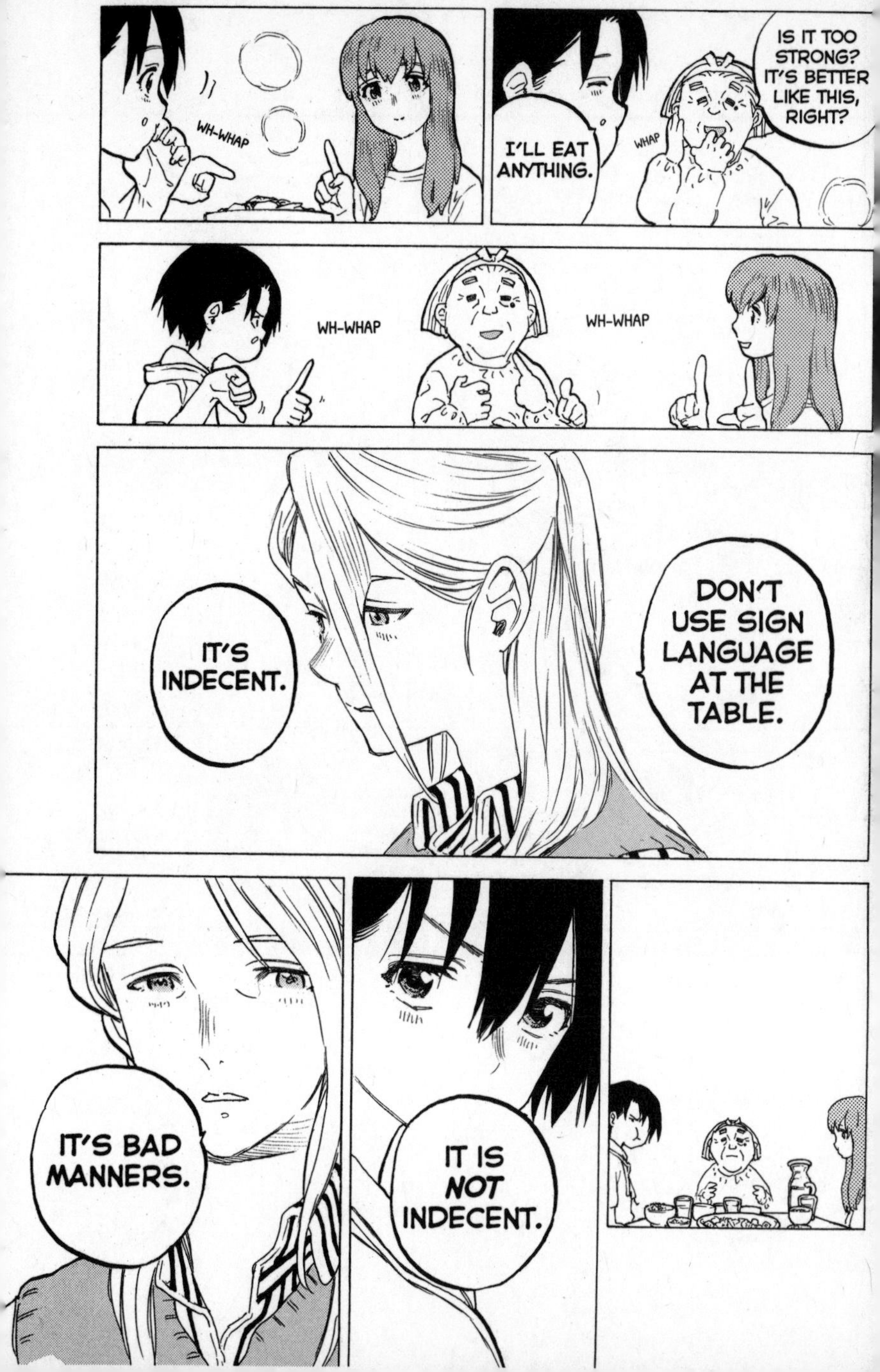
IS IT TOO STRONG? IT'S BETTER LIKE THIS, RIGHT?
WHAP
I'LL EAT ANYTHING.
WH-WHAP
WH-WHAP
WH-WHAP
DON'T USE SIGN LANGUAGE AT THE TABLE.
IT'S INDECENT.
IT IS *NOT* INDECENT.
IT'S BAD MANNERS.

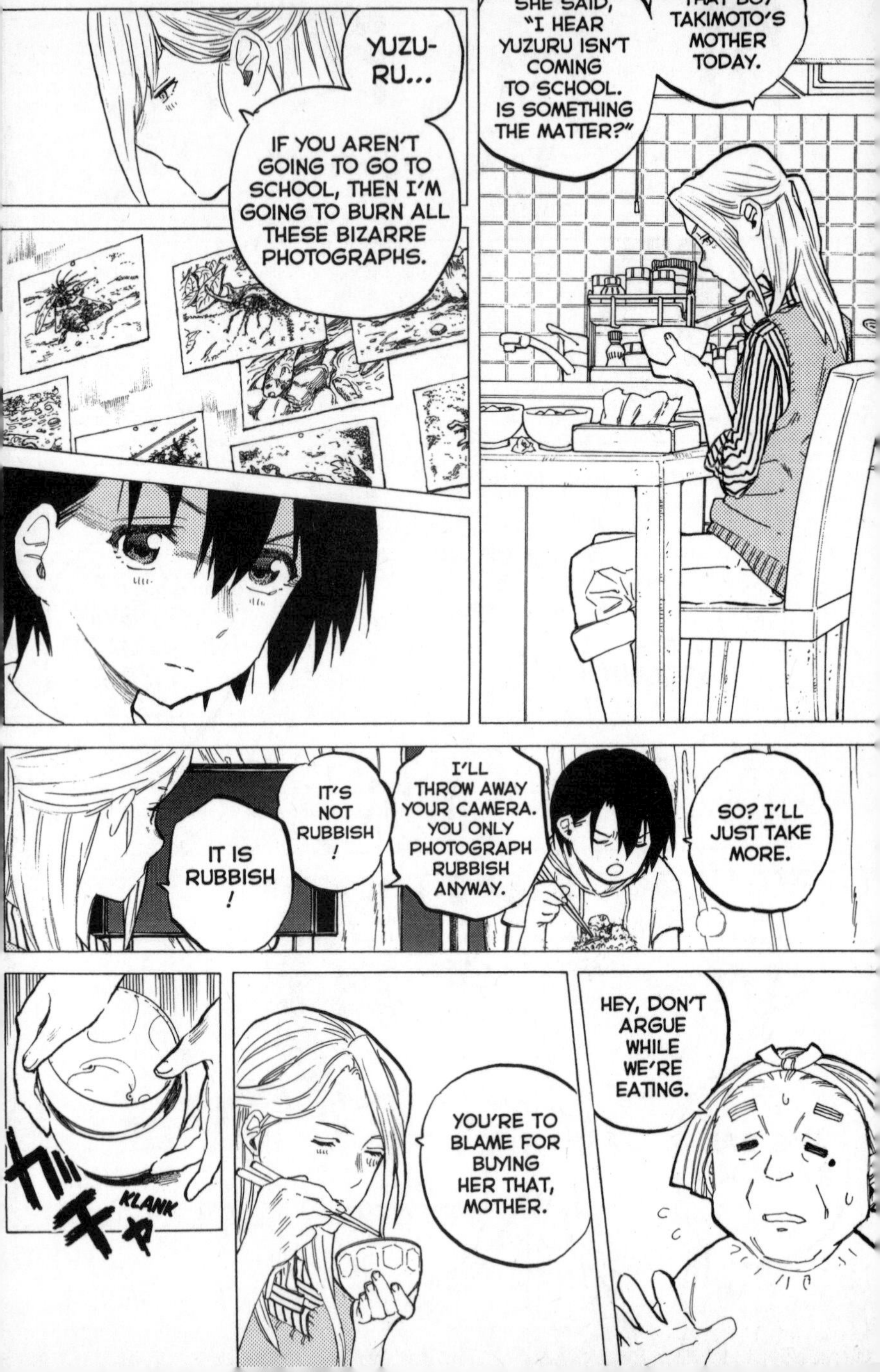
I RAN INTO THAT BOY TAKIMOTO'S MOTHER TODAY.
SHE SAID, "I HEAR YUZURU ISN'T COMING TO SCHOOL. IS SOMETHING THE MATTER?"
YUZU-RU...
IF YOU AREN'T GOING TO GO TO SCHOOL, THEN I'M GOING TO BURN ALL THESE BIZARRE PHOTOGRAPHS.
SO? I'LL JUST TAKE MORE.
I'LL THROW AWAY YOUR CAMERA. YOU ONLY PHOTOGRAPH RUBBISH ANYWAY.
IT'S NOT RUBBISH!
IT IS RUBBISH!
HEY, DON'T ARGUE WHILE WE'RE EATING.
YOU'RE TO BLAME FOR BUYING HER THAT, MOTHER.
KLANK

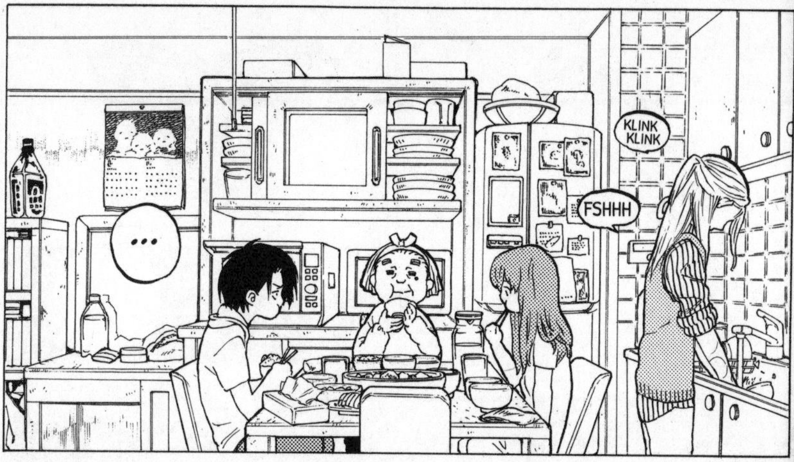
KLINK KLINK
FSHHH
...

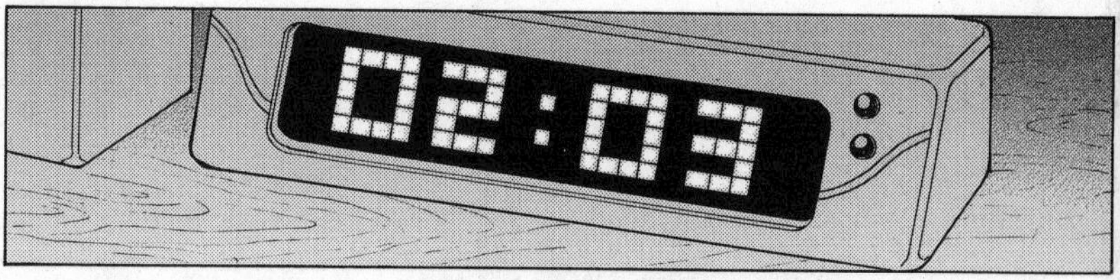
02:03

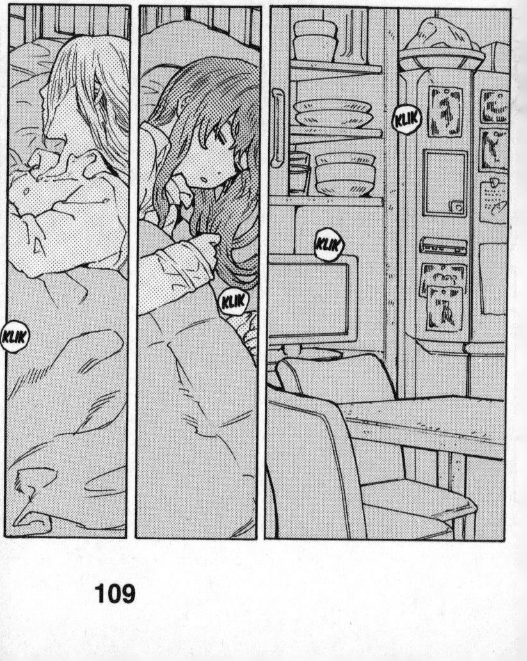
KLIK
KLIK
KLIK
KLIK

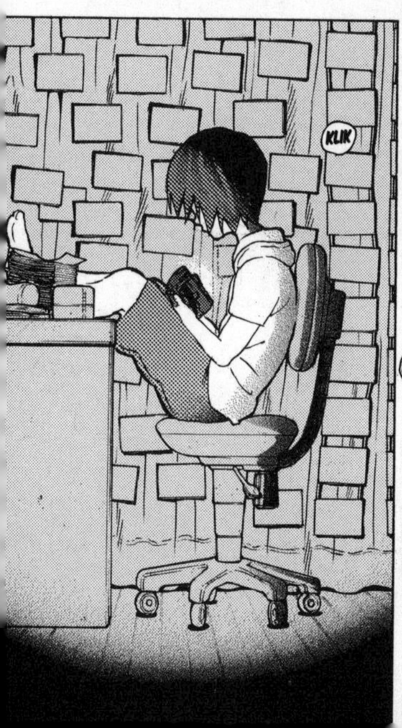
KLIK

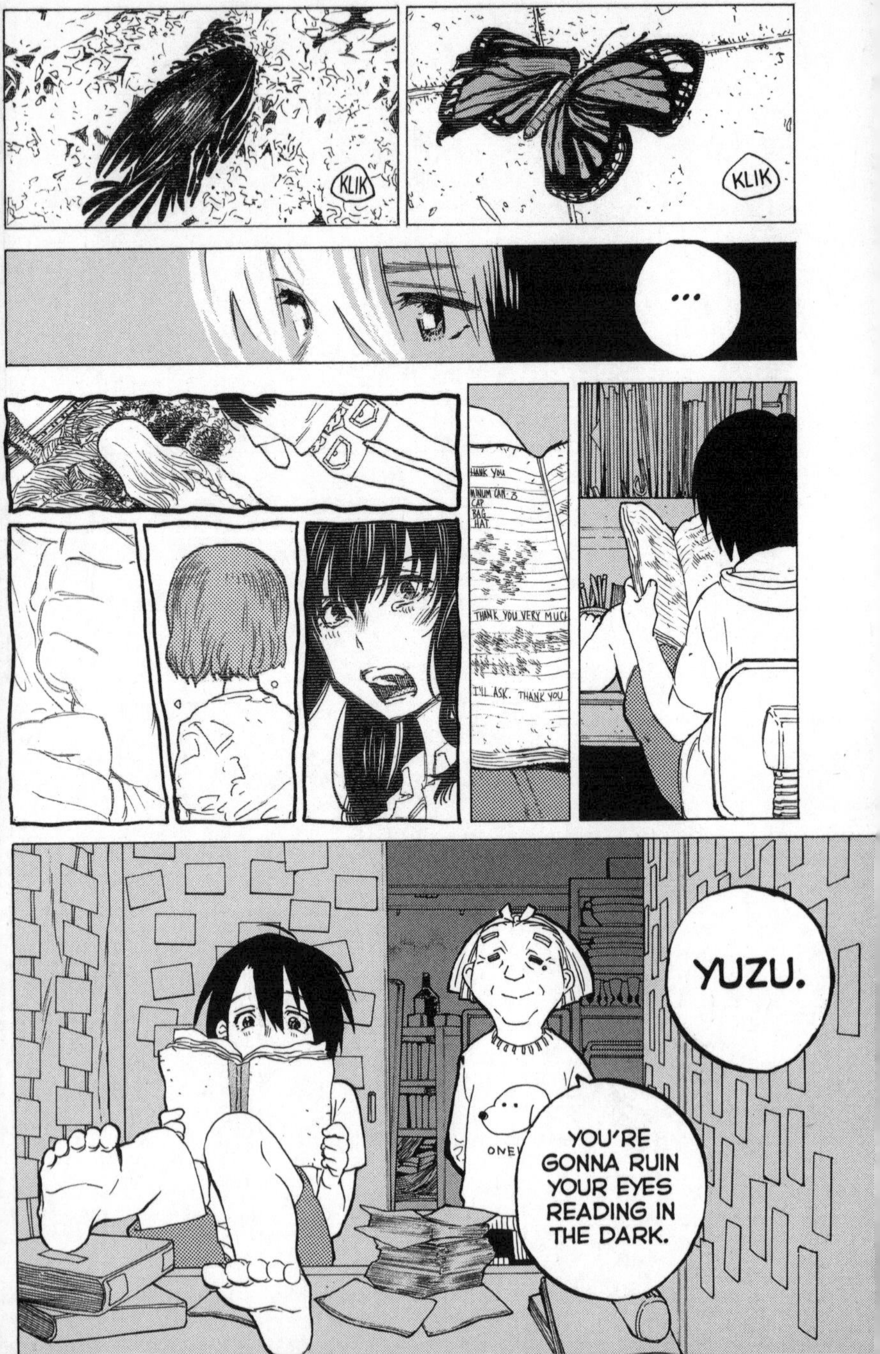
KLIK
KLIK
...
HANK YOU
MINUM CAN 3
CAP
BAG
HAT
THANK YOU VERY MUC
I'LL ASK. THANK YOU
YUZU.
YOU'RE GONNA RUIN YOUR EYES READING IN THE DARK.
ONE

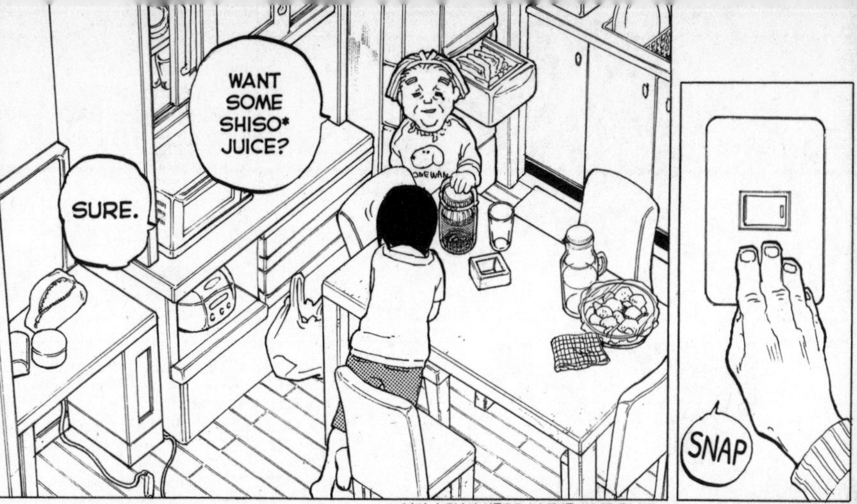
SNAP
WANT SOME SHISO* JUICE?
SURE.

*AN ASIAN HERB IN THE MINT FAMILY

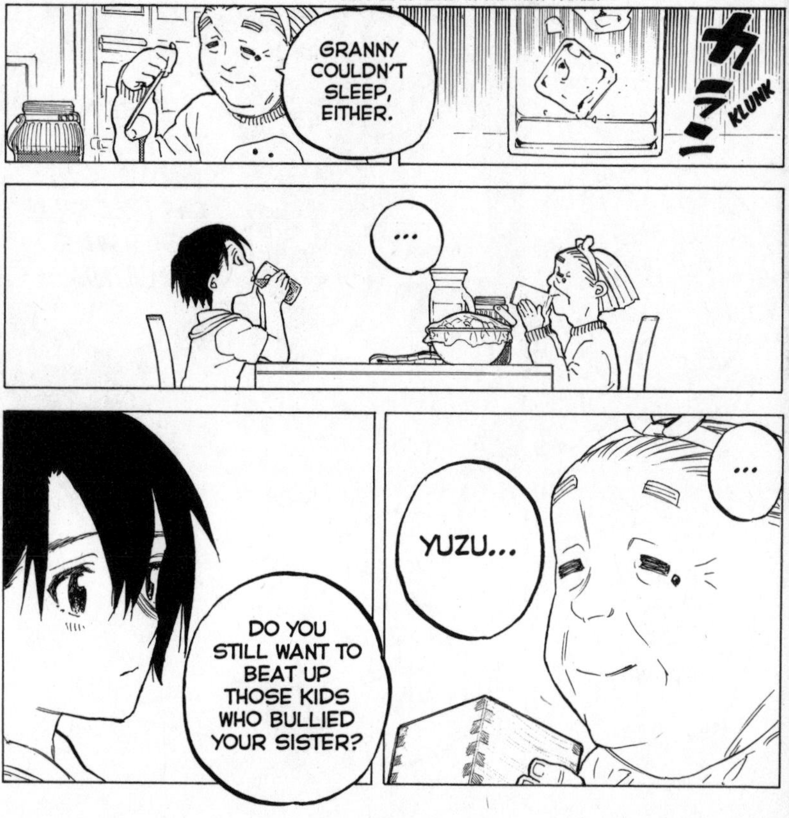
カラン
KLUNK
GRANNY COULDN'T SLEEP, EITHER.
...
...
YUZU...
DO YOU STILL WANT TO BEAT UP THOSE KIDS WHO BULLIED YOUR SISTER?

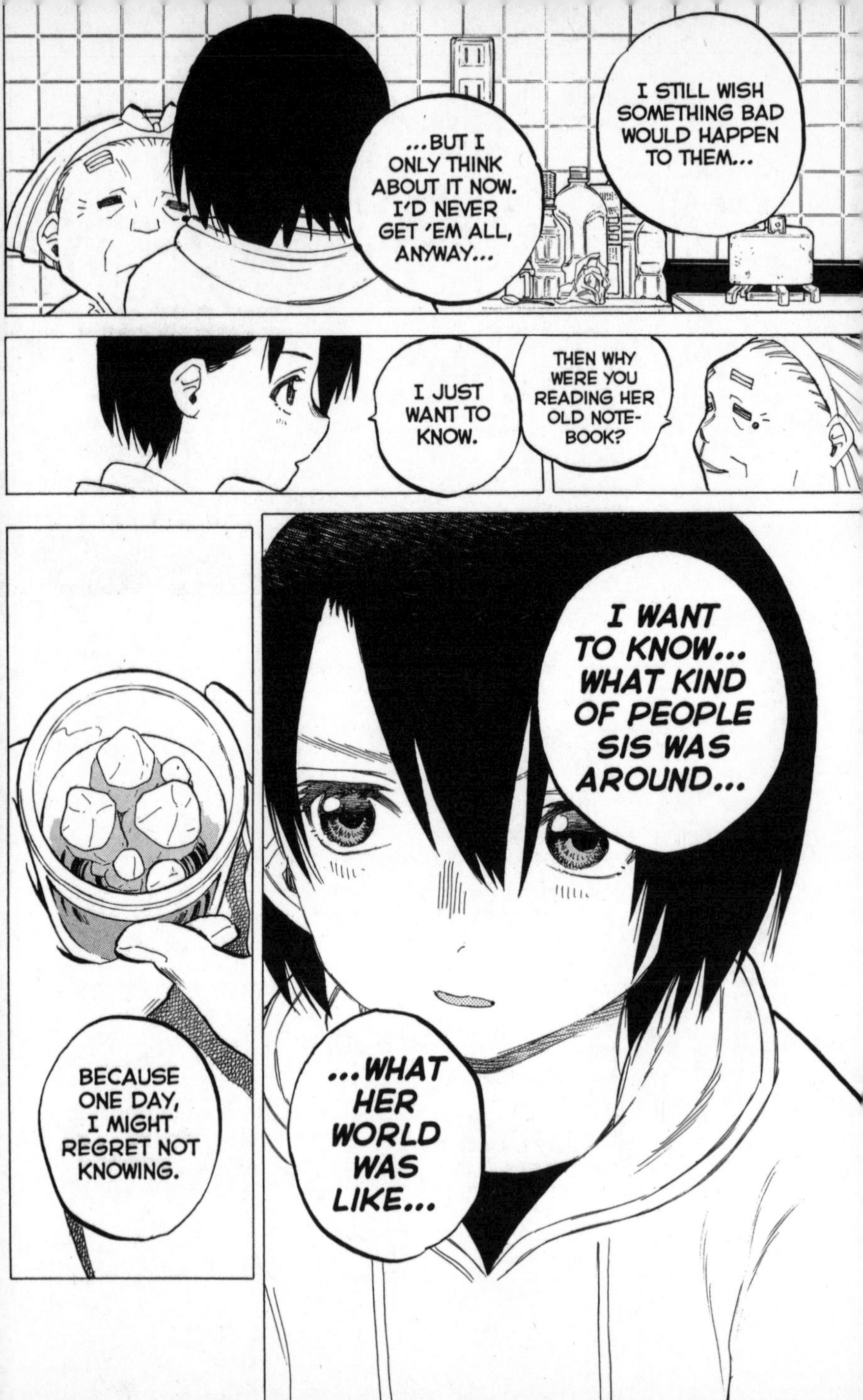
I STILL WISH SOMETHING BAD WOULD HAPPEN TO THEM...
...BUT I ONLY THINK ABOUT IT NOW. I'D NEVER GET 'EM ALL, ANYWAY...
THEN WHY WERE YOU READING HER OLD NOTE-BOOK?
I JUST WANT TO KNOW.
I WANT TO KNOW... WHAT KIND OF PEOPLE SIS WAS AROUND...
...WHAT HER WORLD WAS LIKE...
BECAUSE ONE DAY, I MIGHT REGRET NOT KNOWING.

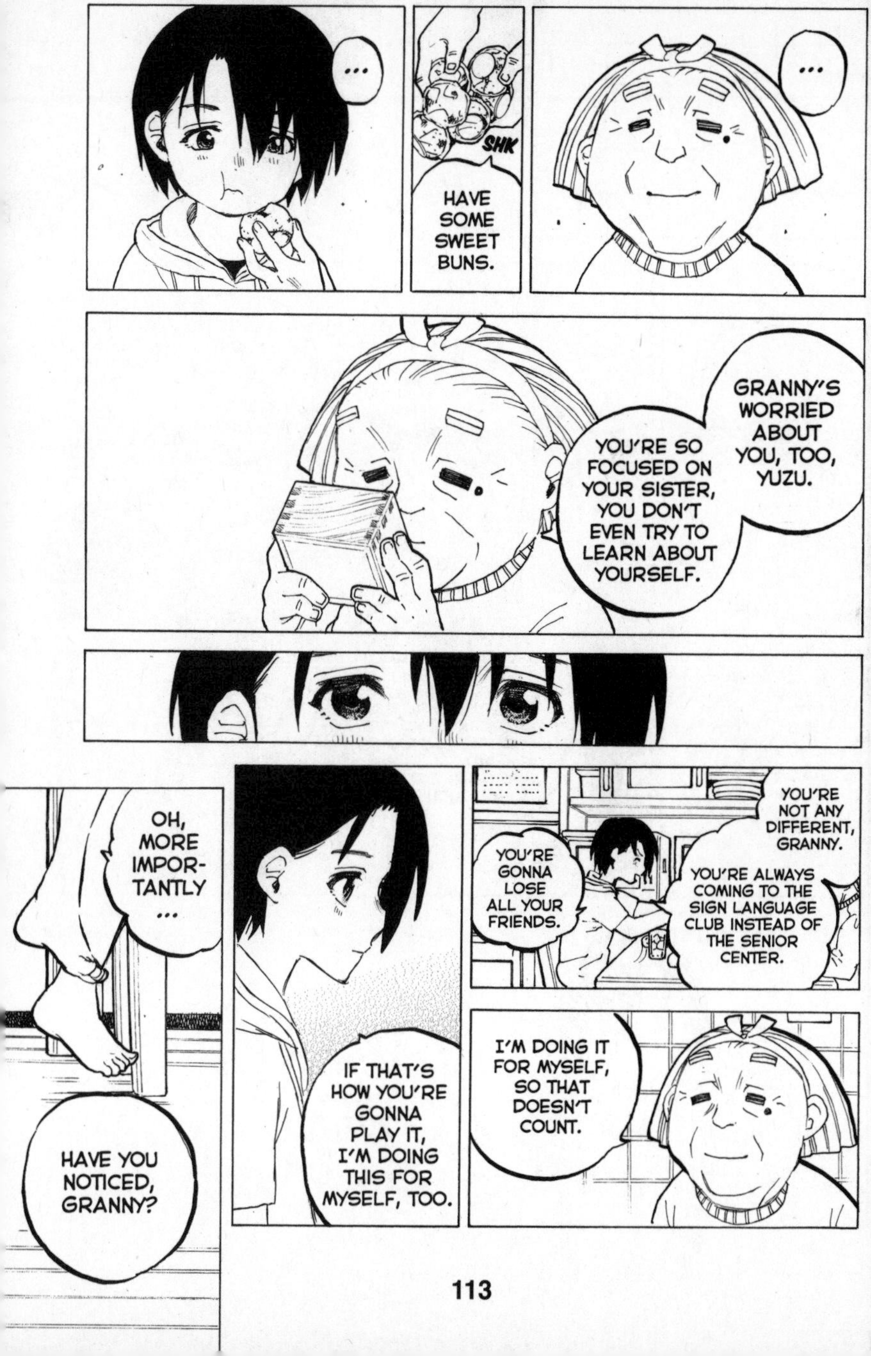
...
SHK
HAVE SOME SWEET BUNS.
...
GRANNY'S WORRIED ABOUT YOU, TOO, YUZU.
YOU'RE SO FOCUSED ON YOUR SISTER, YOU DON'T EVEN TRY TO LEARN ABOUT YOURSELF.
YOU'RE NOT ANY DIFFERENT, GRANNY.
YOU'RE ALWAYS COMING TO THE SIGN LANGUAGE CLUB INSTEAD OF THE SENIOR CENTER.
YOU'RE GONNA LOSE ALL YOUR FRIENDS.
I'M DOING IT FOR MYSELF, SO THAT DOESN'T COUNT.
IF THAT'S HOW YOU'RE GONNA PLAY IT, I'M DOING THIS FOR MYSELF, TOO.
OH, MORE IMPOR-TANTLY ...
HAVE YOU NOTICED, GRANNY?

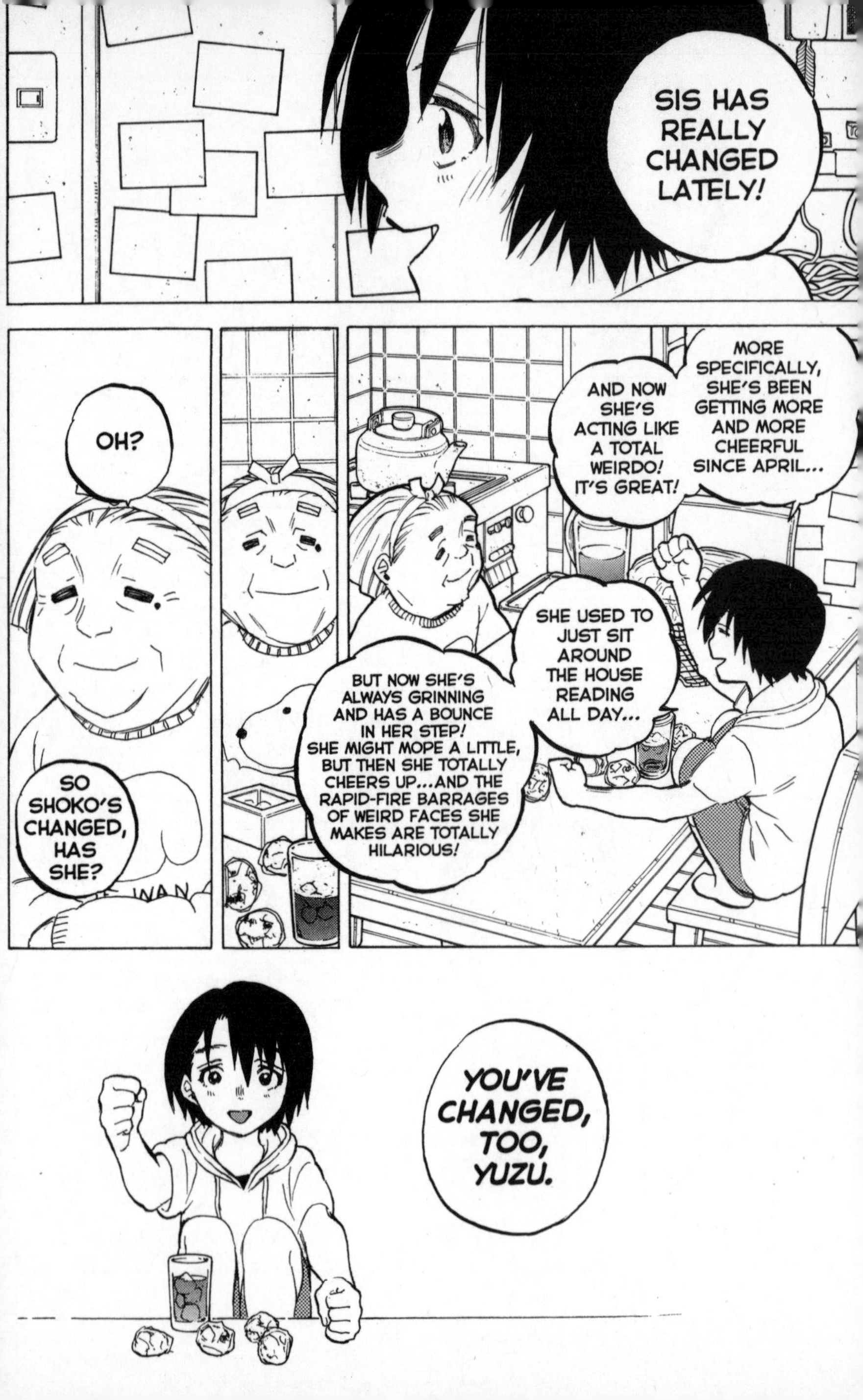
SIS HAS REALLY CHANGED LATELY!
MORE SPECIFICALLY, SHE'S BEEN GETTING MORE AND MORE CHEERFUL SINCE APRIL...
AND NOW SHE'S ACTING LIKE A TOTAL WEIRDO! IT'S GREAT!
SHE USED TO JUST SIT AROUND THE HOUSE READING ALL DAY...
BUT NOW SHE'S ALWAYS GRINNING AND HAS A BOUNCE IN HER STEP! SHE MIGHT MOPE A LITTLE, BUT THEN SHE TOTALLY CHEERS UP...AND THE RAPID-FIRE BARRAGES OF WEIRD FACES SHE MAKES ARE TOTALLY HILARIOUS!
OH?
SO SHOKO'S CHANGED, HAS SHE?
YOU'VE CHANGED, TOO, YUZU.

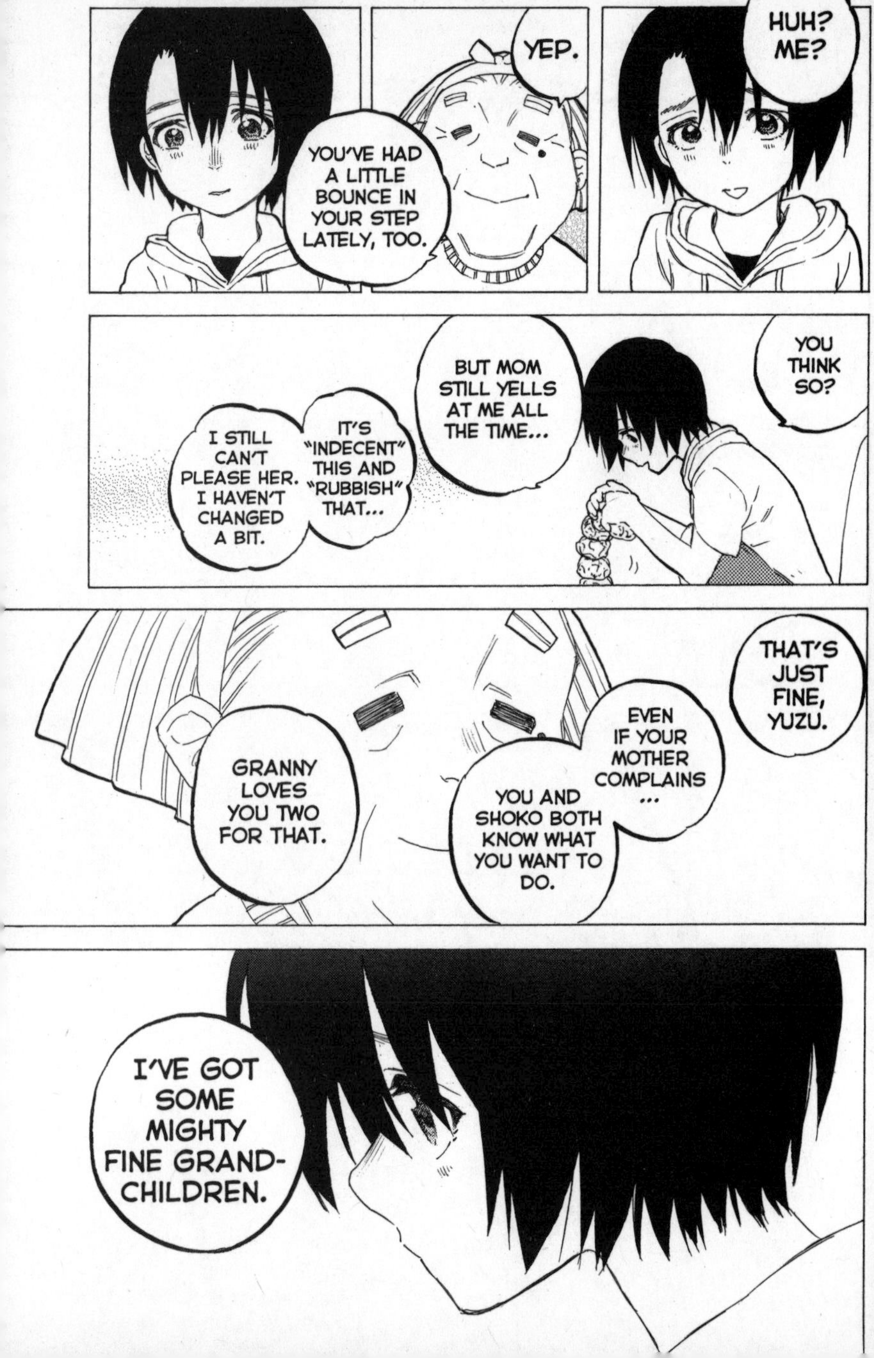
HUH? ME?
YEP.
YOU'VE HAD A LITTLE BOUNCE IN YOUR STEP LATELY, TOO.
YOU THINK SO?
BUT MOM STILL YELLS AT ME ALL THE TIME...
IT'S "INDECENT" THIS AND "RUBBISH" THAT...
I STILL CAN'T PLEASE HER. I HAVEN'T CHANGED A BIT.
THAT'S JUST FINE, YUZU.
EVEN IF YOUR MOTHER COMPLAINS...
YOU AND SHOKO BOTH KNOW WHAT YOU WANT TO DO.
GRANNY LOVES YOU TWO FOR THAT.
I'VE GOT SOME MIGHTY FINE GRANDCHILDREN.

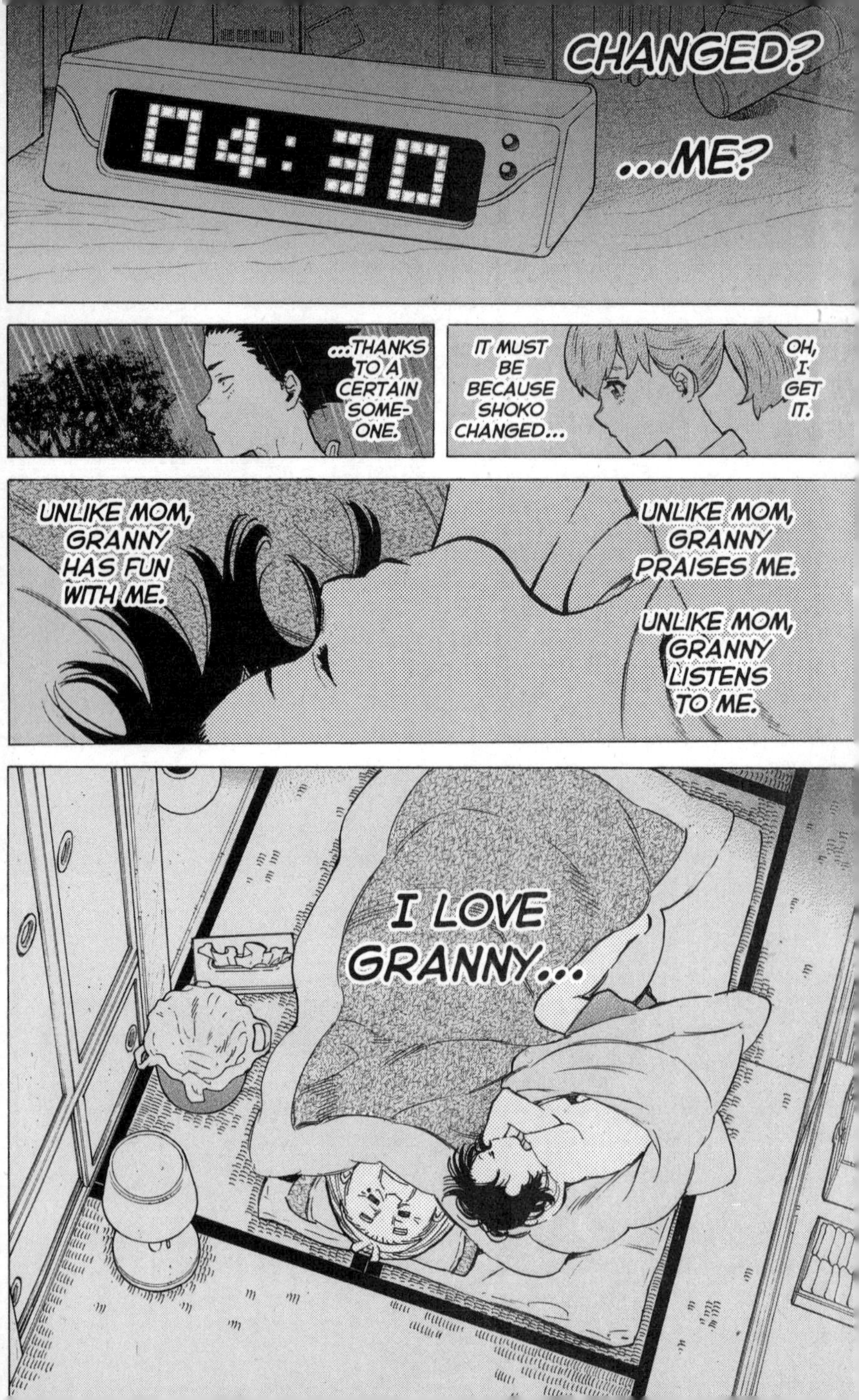
04:30
CHANGED?
...ME?
OH, I GET IT.
IT MUST BE BECAUSE SHOKO CHANGED...
...THANKS TO A CERTAIN SOME-ONE.
UNLIKE MOM, GRANNY PRAISES ME.
UNLIKE MOM, GRANNY LISTENS TO ME.
UNLIKE MOM, GRANNY HAS FUN WITH ME.
I LOVE GRANNY...

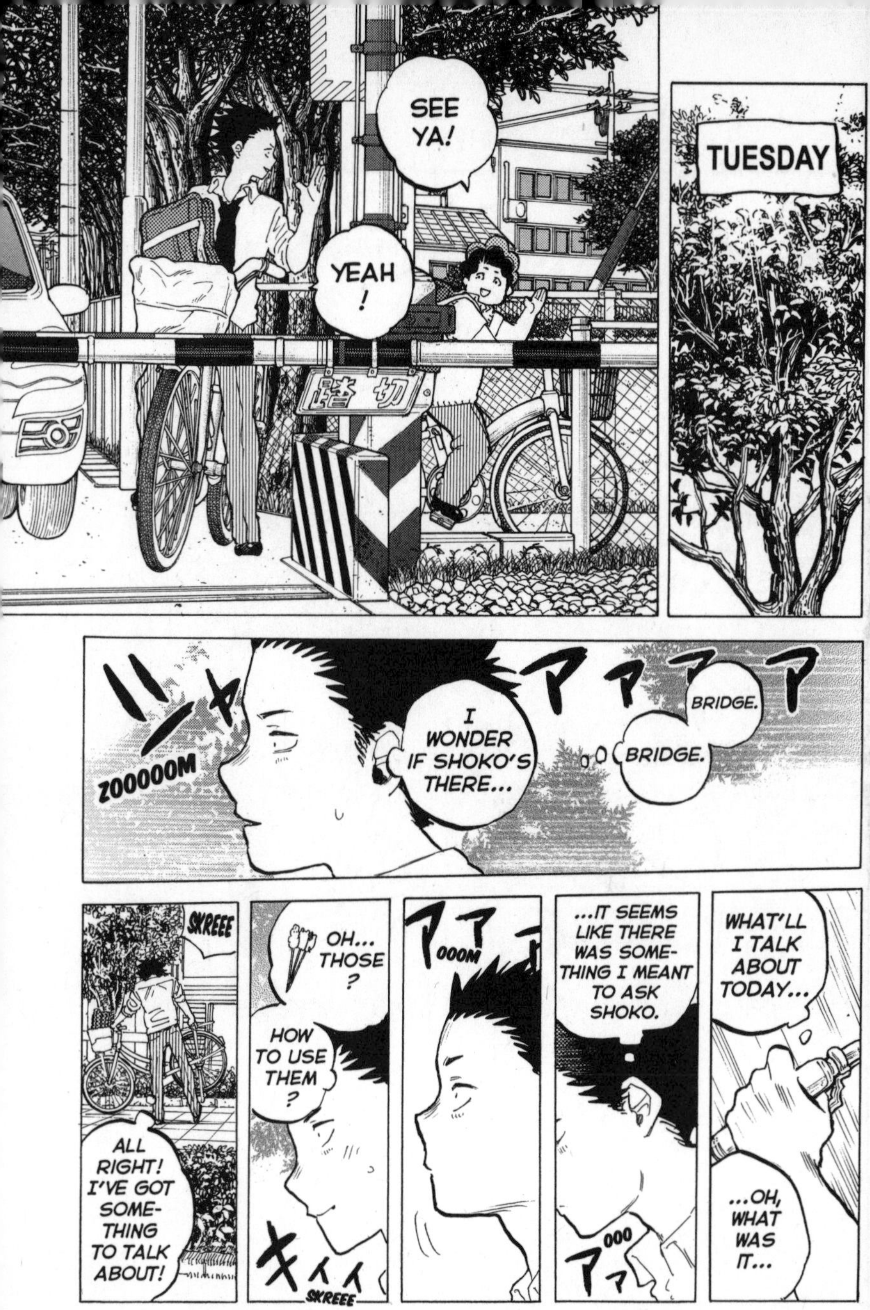
TUESDAY
SEE YA!
YEAH!
BRIDGE.
BRIDGE.
I WONDER IF SHOKO'S THERE...
ZOOOOOM
WHAT'LL I TALK ABOUT TODAY...
...OH, WHAT WAS IT...
...IT SEEMS LIKE THERE WAS SOMETHING I MEANT TO ASK SHOKO.
OOO
OOOM
OH... THOSE?
HOW TO USE THEM?
SKREEE
SKREEE
ALL RIGHT! I'VE GOT SOMETHING TO TALK ABOUT!

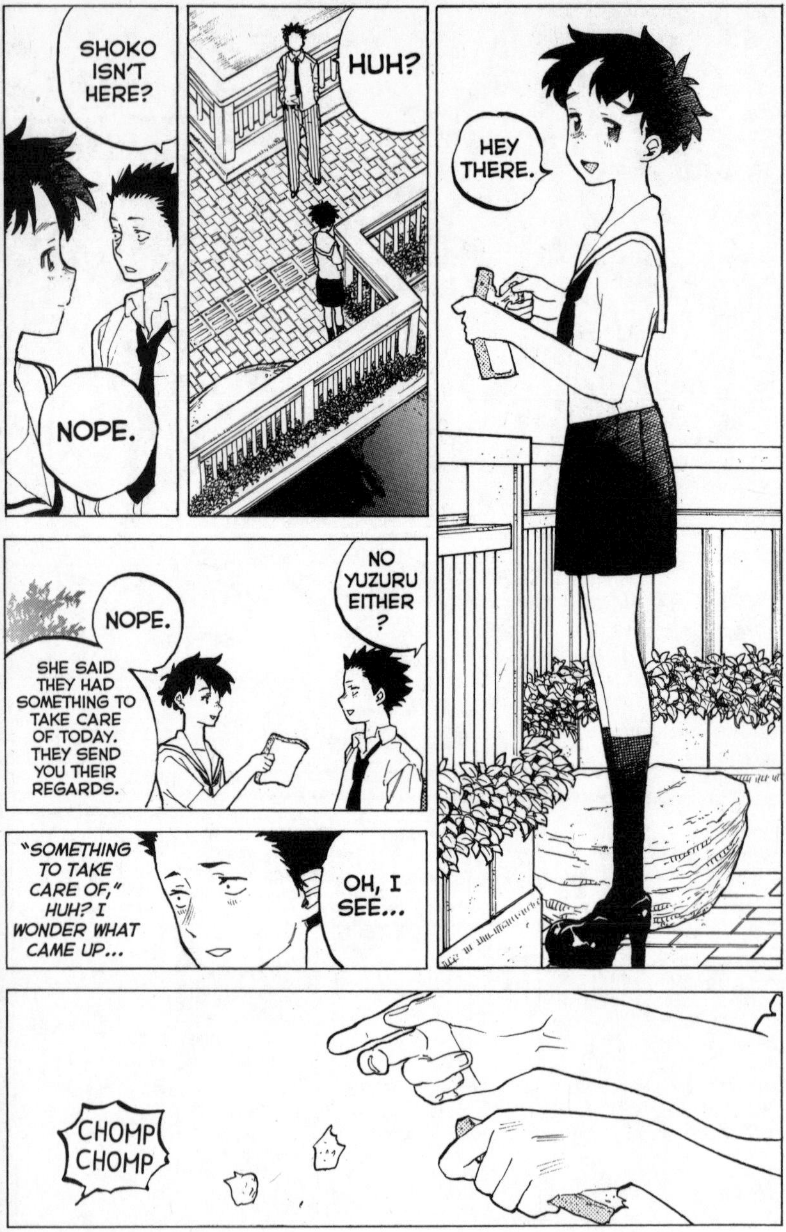
HEY THERE.
HUH?
SHOKO ISN'T HERE?
NOPE.
NO YUZURU EITHER ?
NOPE.
SHE SAID THEY HAD SOMETHING TO TAKE CARE OF TODAY. THEY SEND YOU THEIR REGARDS.
OH, I SEE...
"SOMETHING TO TAKE CARE OF," HUH? I WONDER WHAT CAME UP...
CHOMP CHOMP

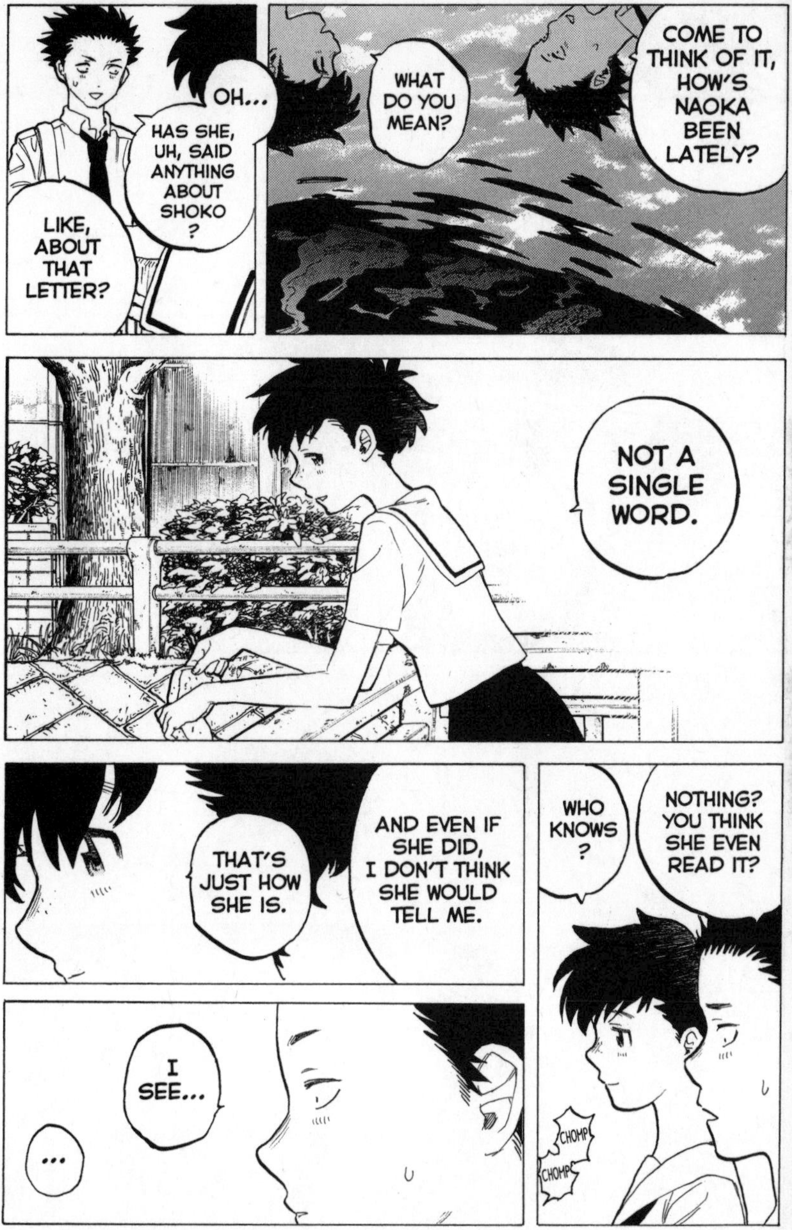
COME TO THINK OF IT, HOW'S NAOKA BEEN LATELY?
WHAT DO YOU MEAN?
OH...
HAS SHE, UH, SAID ANYTHING ABOUT SHOKO?
LIKE, ABOUT THAT LETTER?
NOT A SINGLE WORD.
NOTHING? YOU THINK SHE EVEN READ IT?
WHO KNOWS?
CHOMP
CHOMP
AND EVEN IF SHE DID, I DON'T THINK SHE WOULD TELL ME.
THAT'S JUST HOW SHE IS.
I SEE...
...

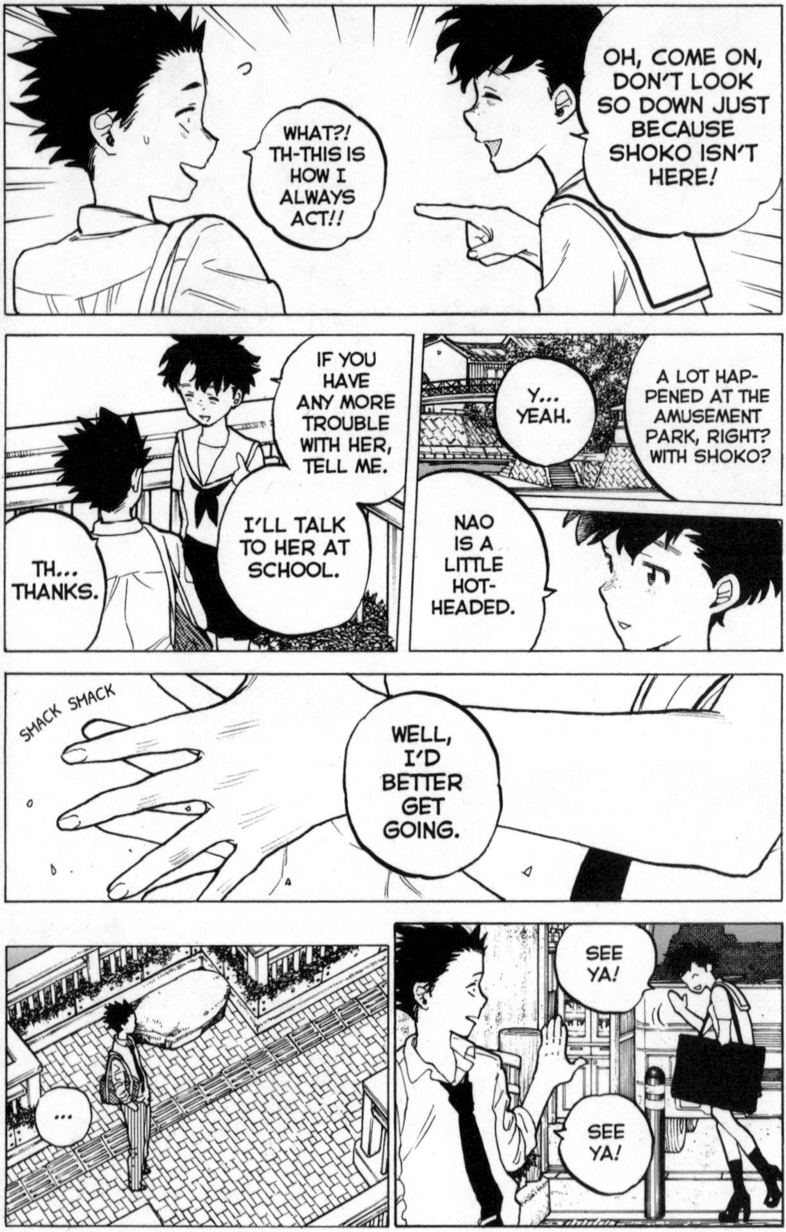
OH, COME ON, DON'T LOOK SO DOWN JUST BECAUSE SHOKO ISN'T HERE!
WHAT?! TH-THIS IS HOW I ALWAYS ACT!!
A LOT HAPPENED AT THE AMUSEMENT PARK, RIGHT? WITH SHOKO?
Y... YEAH.
NAO IS A LITTLE HOT-HEADED.
IF YOU HAVE ANY MORE TROUBLE WITH HER, TELL ME.
I'LL TALK TO HER AT SCHOOL.
TH... THANKS.
WELL, I'D BETTER GET GOING.
SMACK SMACK
SEE YA!
SEE YA!
...

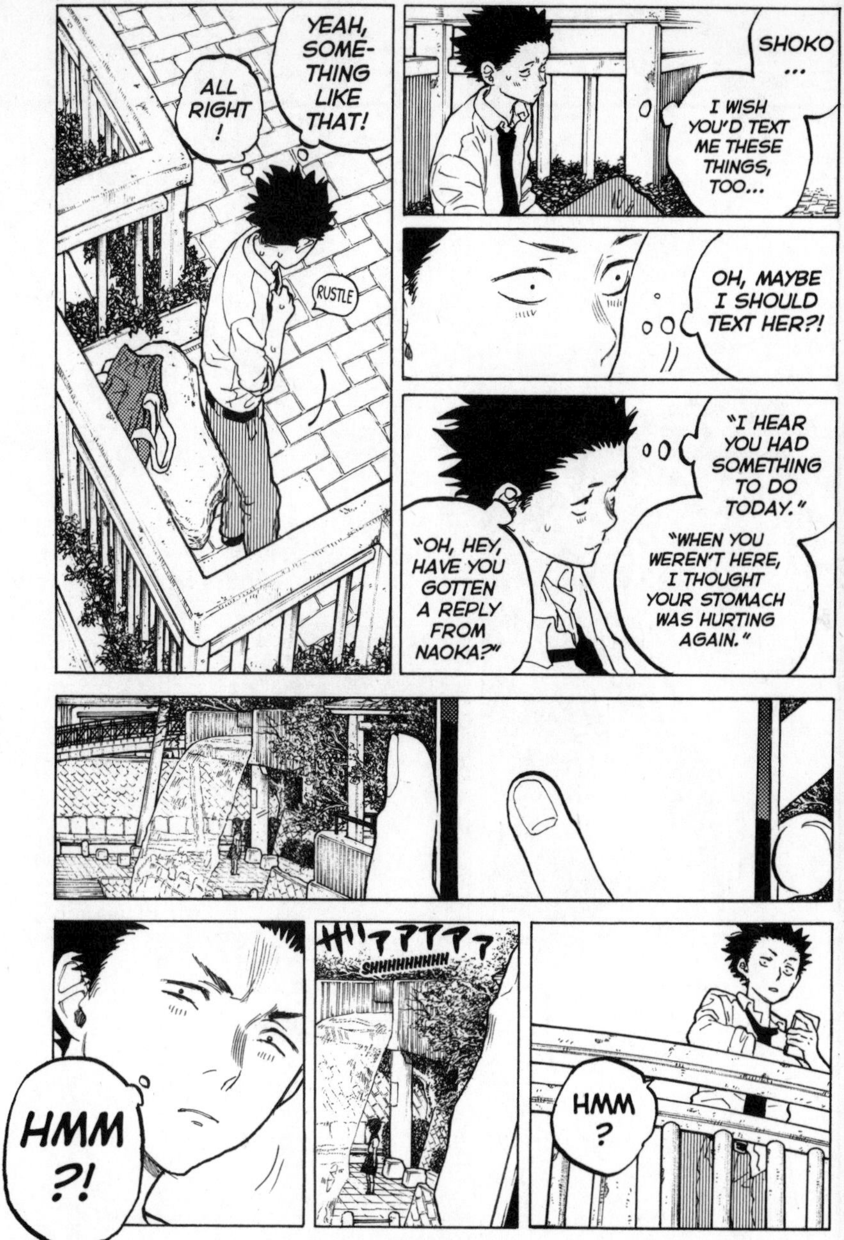
SHOKO ...
I WISH YOU'D TEXT ME THESE THINGS, TOO...
OH, MAYBE I SHOULD TEXT HER?!
"I HEAR YOU HAD SOMETHING TO DO TODAY."
"WHEN YOU WEREN'T HERE, I THOUGHT YOUR STOMACH WAS HURTING AGAIN."
"OH, HEY, HAVE YOU GOTTEN A REPLY FROM NAOKA?"
YEAH, SOMETHING LIKE THAT!
ALL RIGHT !
RUSTLE
HMM ?
SHHHHHHHHHH
HMM ?!

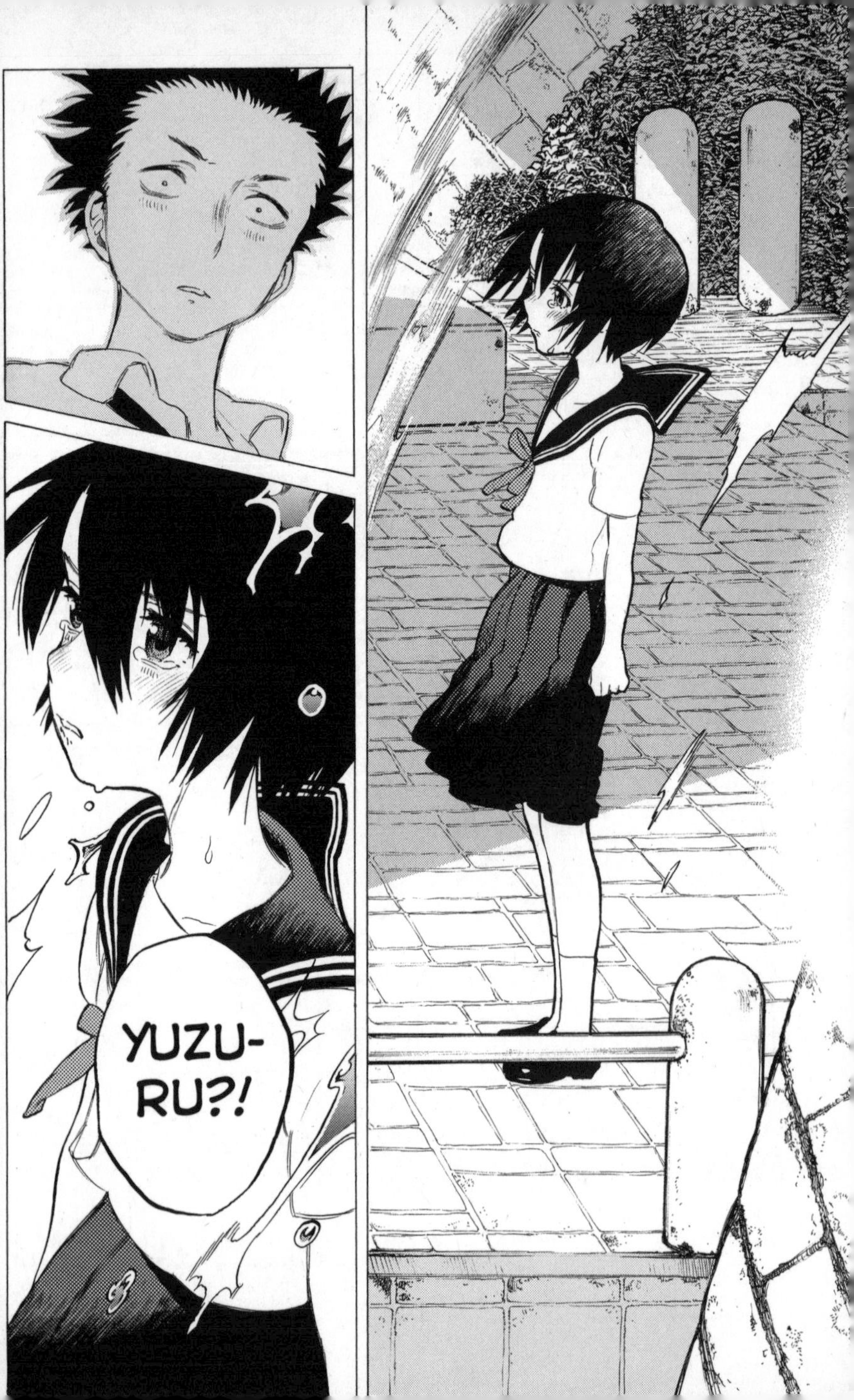
YUZU-
RU?!

a Silent Voice

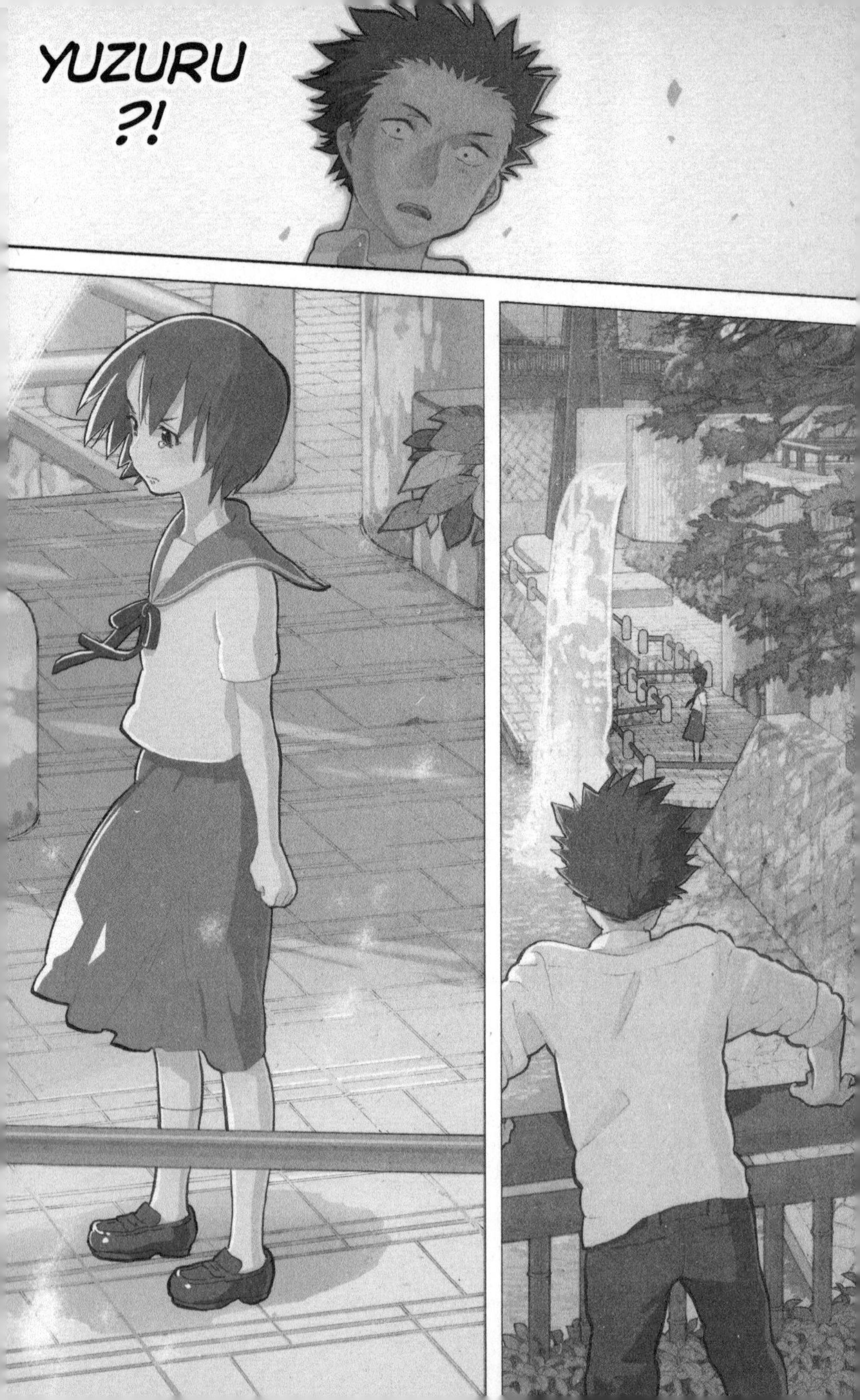
YUZURU ?!

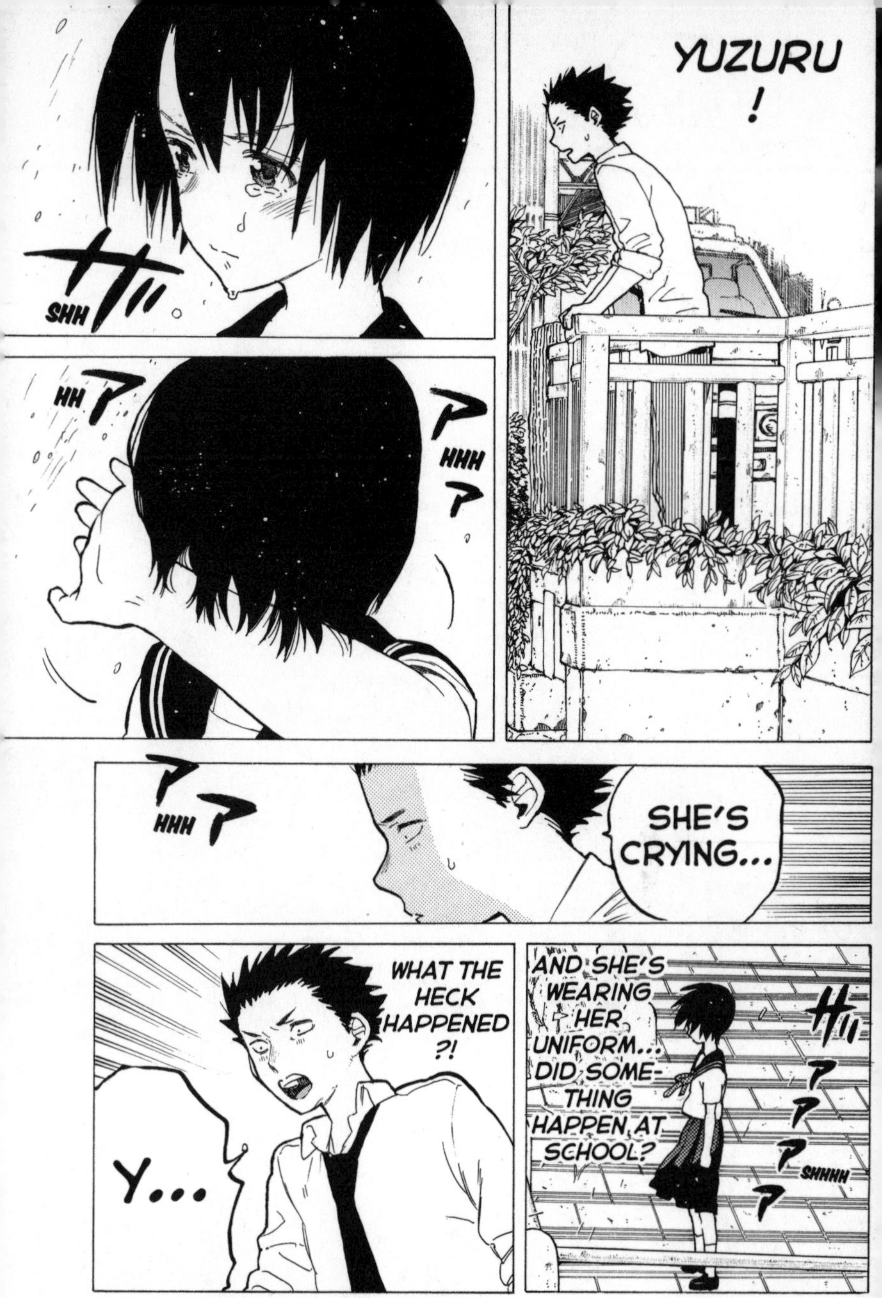
YUZURU
!
SHH
HH
HHH
HHH
SHE'S CRYING...
AND SHE'S WEARING HER UNIFORM... DID SOMETHING HAPPEN AT SCHOOL?
SHHHH
WHAT THE HECK HAPPENED ?!
Y...

CHAPTER 30: SUPPORT

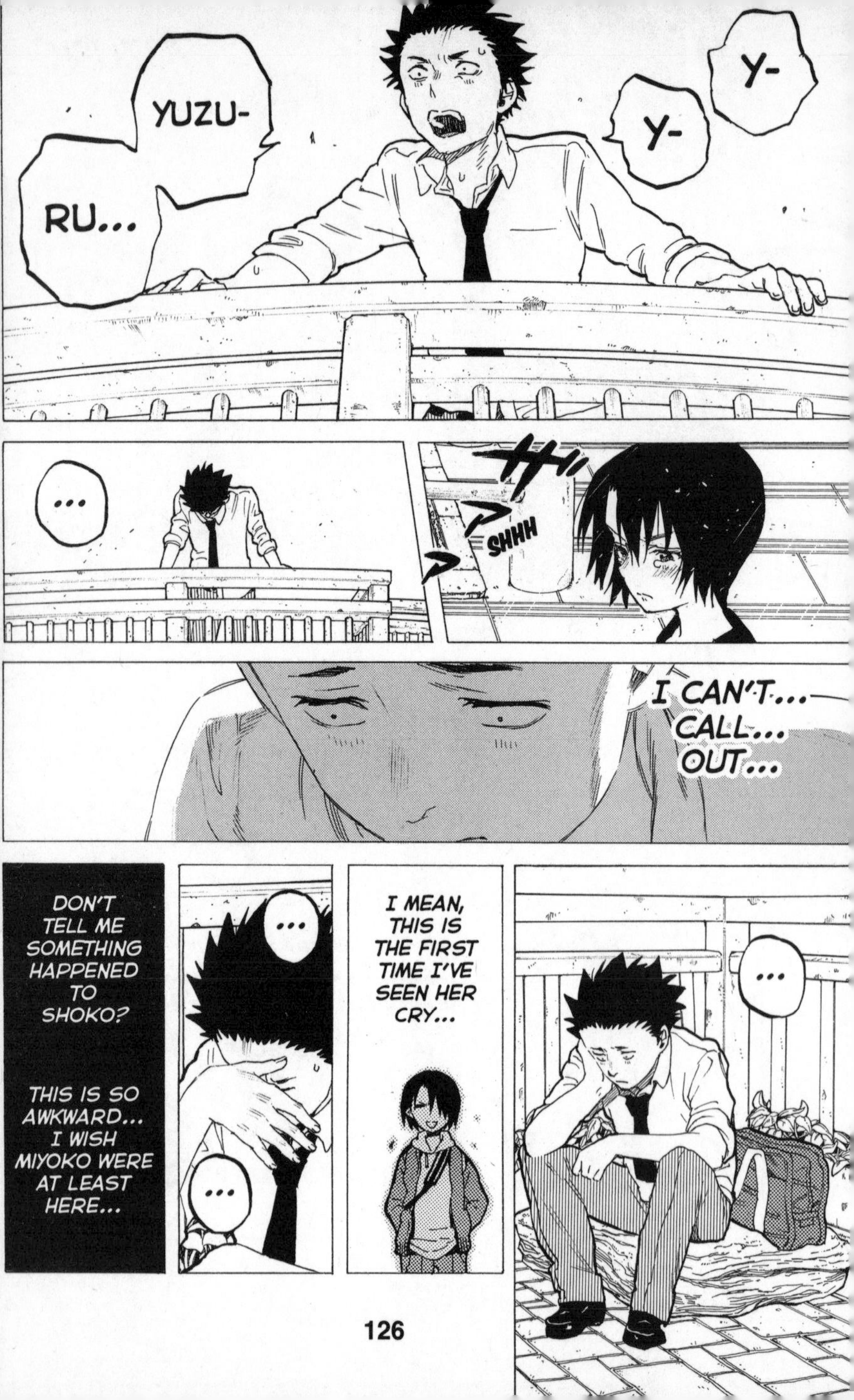
Y-
Y-
YUZU-
RU...
SHHH
...
I CAN'T... CALL... OUT...
...
I MEAN, THIS IS THE FIRST TIME I'VE SEEN HER CRY...
...
...
DON'T TELL ME SOMETHING HAPPENED TO SHOKO?
THIS IS SO AWKWARD... I WISH MIYOKO WERE AT LEAST HERE...

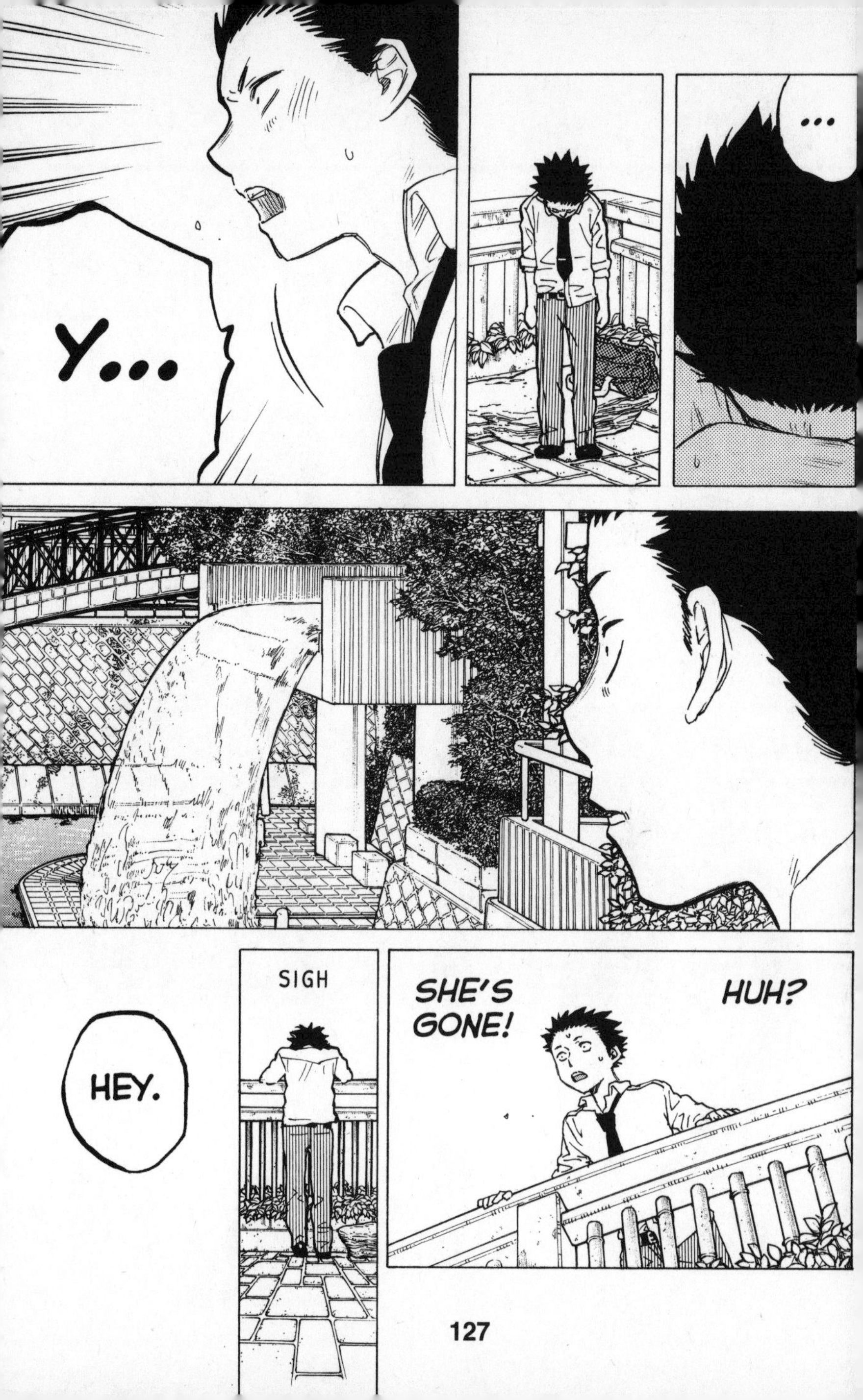
...
Y...
HUH?
SHE'S GONE!
SIGH
HEY.

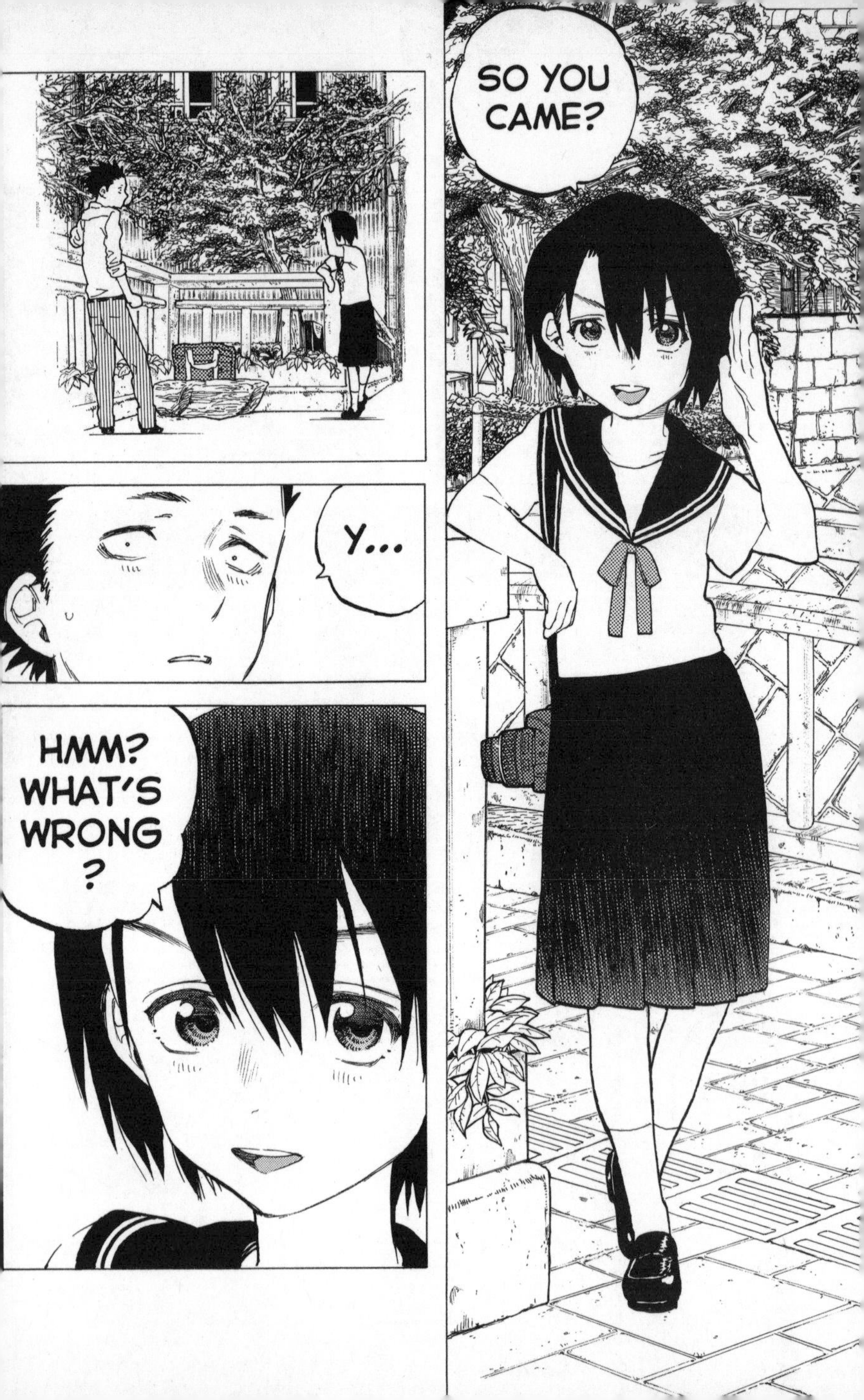
SO YOU CAME?
Y...
HMM? WHAT'S WRONG?

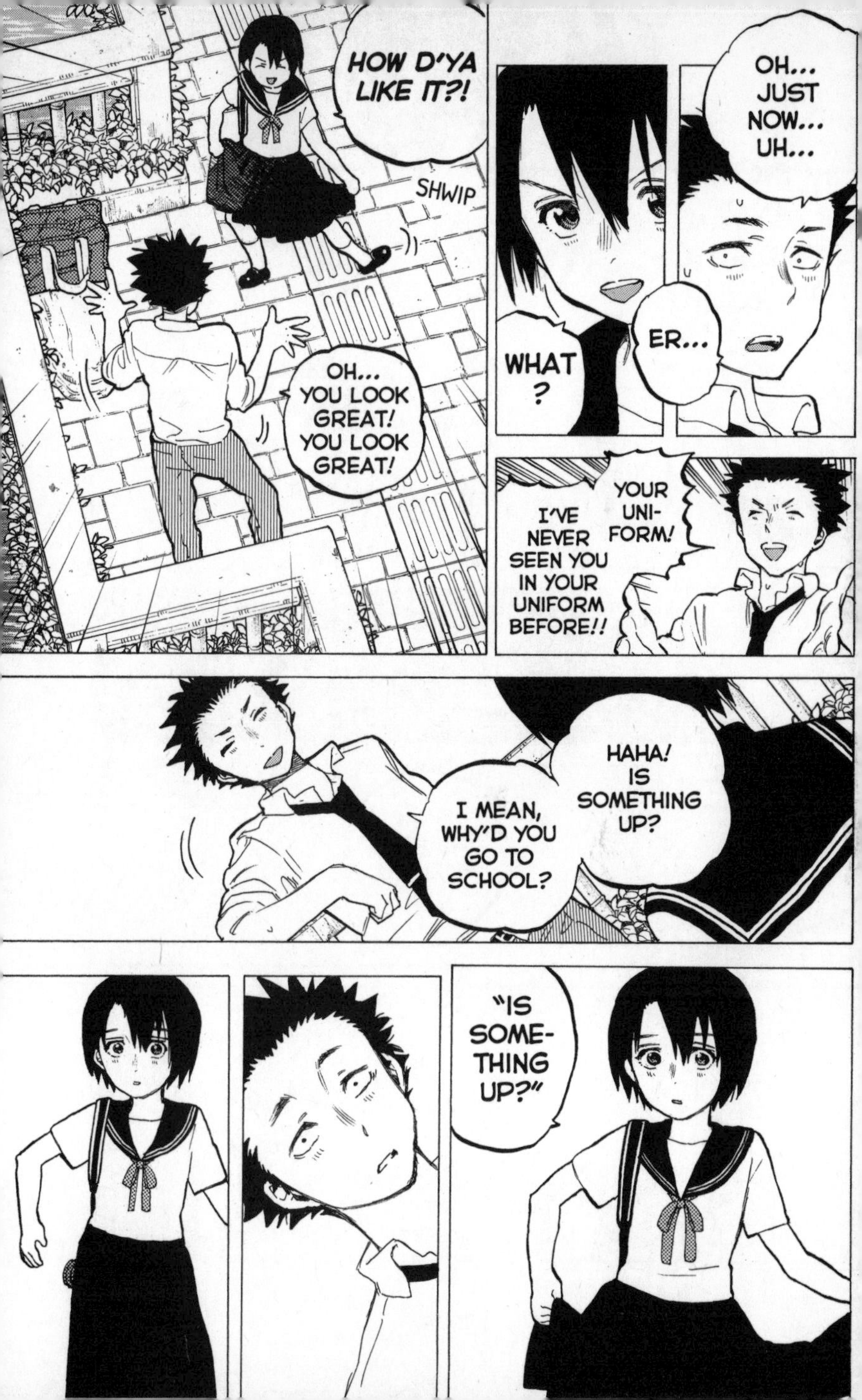
OH... JUST NOW... UH...
ER...
WHAT?
YOUR UNI- FORM!
I'VE NEVER SEEN YOU IN YOUR UNIFORM BEFORE!!
HOW D'YA LIKE IT?!
SHWIP
OH... YOU LOOK GREAT! YOU LOOK GREAT!
HAHA! IS SOMETHING UP?
I MEAN, WHY'D YOU GO TO SCHOOL?
"IS SOME- THING UP?"

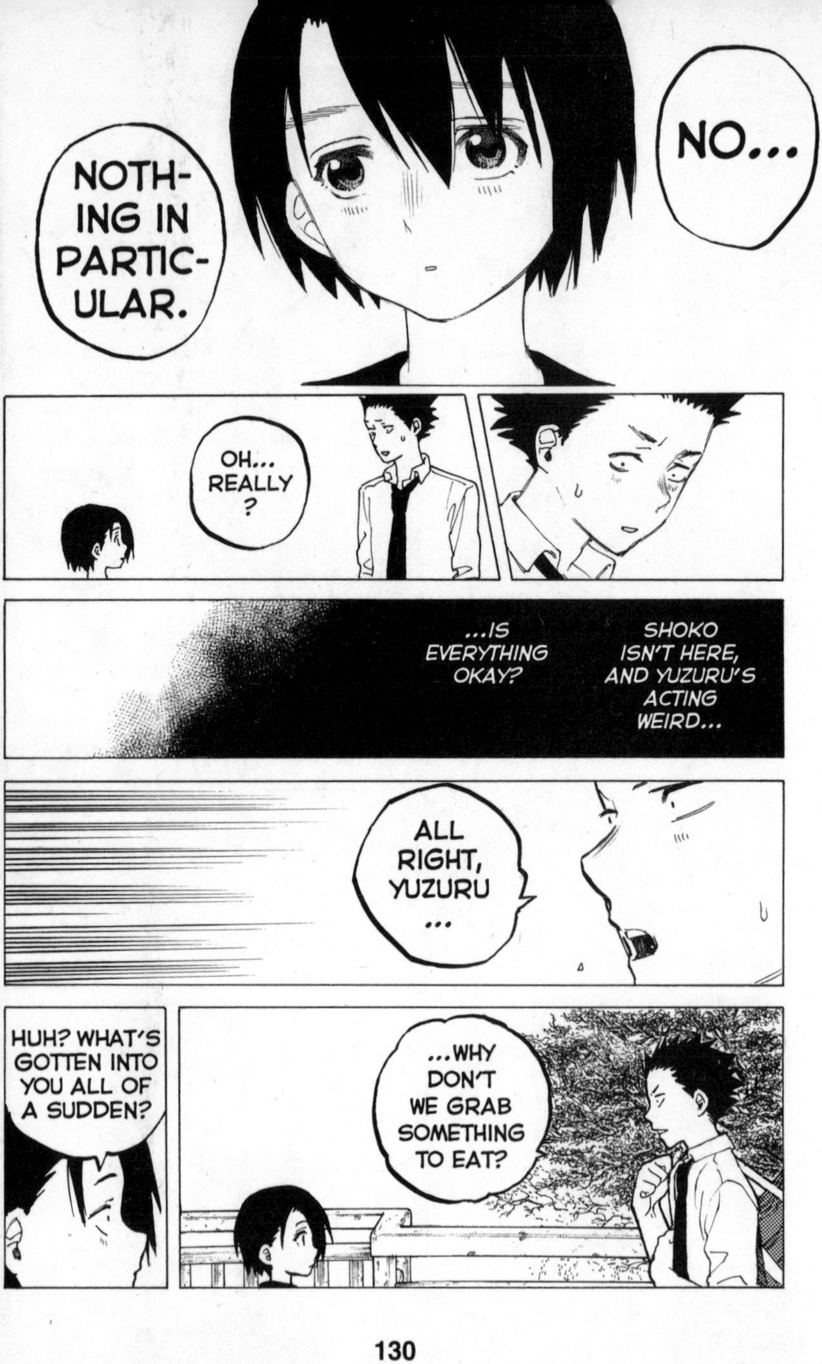
NO...
NOTHING IN PARTICULAR.
OH... REALLY?
SHOKO ISN'T HERE, AND YUZURU'S ACTING WEIRD...
...IS EVERYTHING OKAY?
ALL RIGHT, YUZURU...
...WHY DON'T WE GRAB SOMETHING TO EAT?
HUH? WHAT'S GOTTEN INTO YOU ALL OF A SUDDEN?

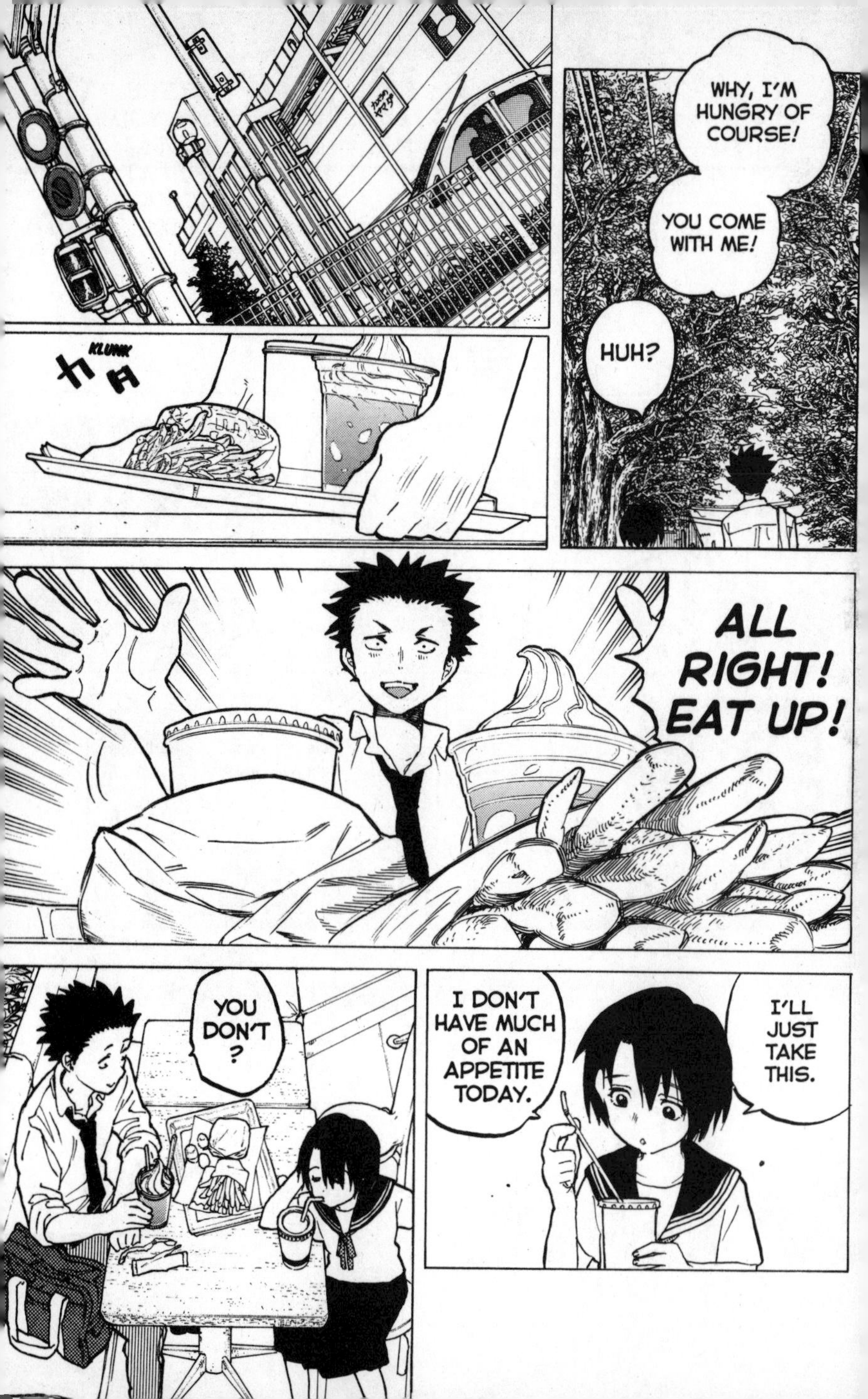
WHY, I'M HUNGRY OF COURSE!
YOU COME WITH ME!
HUH?
KLUNK
ALL RIGHT! EAT UP!
I'LL JUST TAKE THIS.
I DON'T HAVE MUCH OF AN APPETITE TODAY.
YOU DON'T?

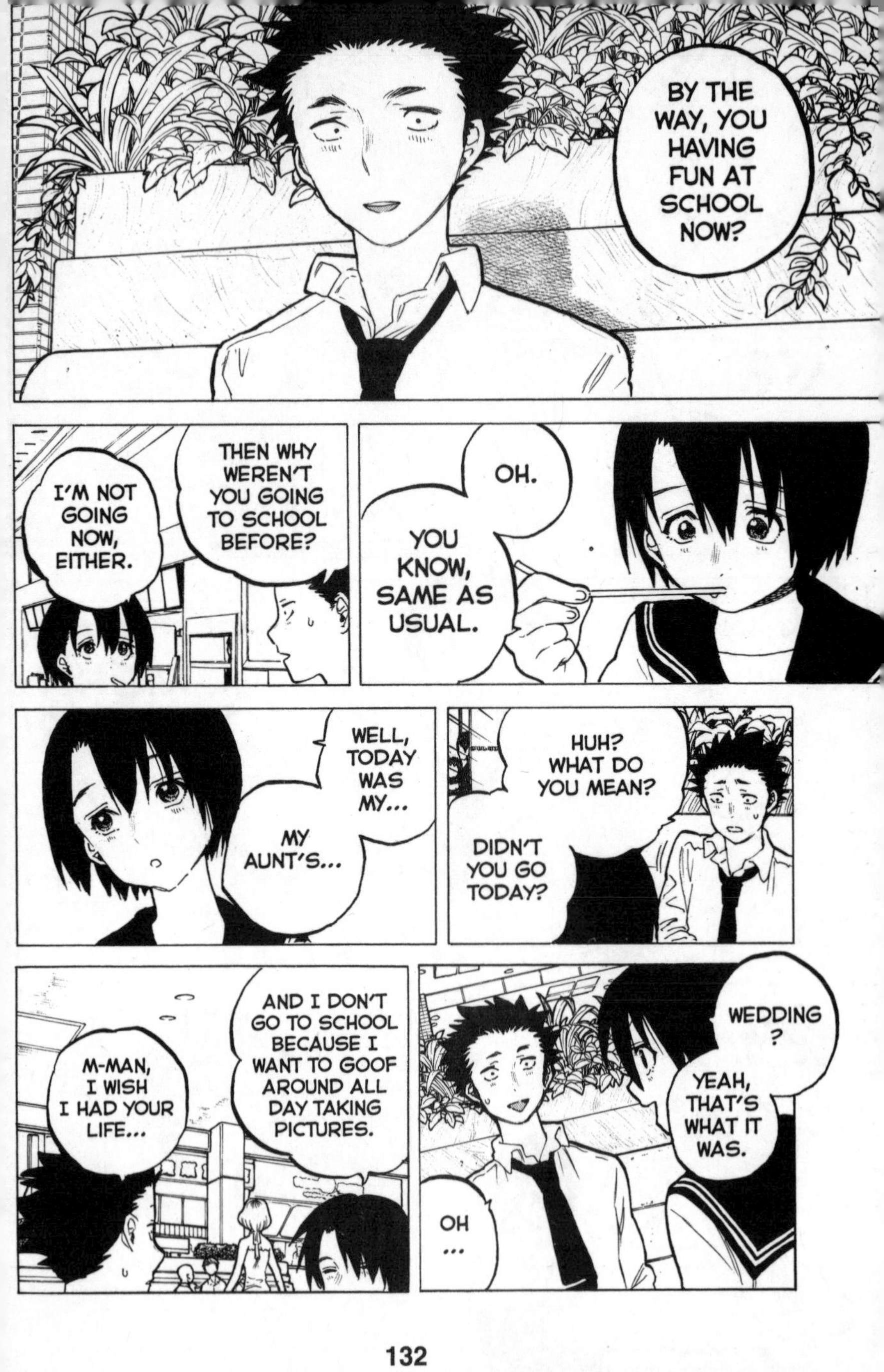
BY THE WAY, YOU HAVING FUN AT SCHOOL NOW?
OH.
YOU KNOW, SAME AS USUAL.
THEN WHY WEREN'T YOU GOING TO SCHOOL BEFORE?
I'M NOT GOING NOW, EITHER.
HUH? WHAT DO YOU MEAN?
DIDN'T YOU GO TODAY?
WELL, TODAY WAS MY...
MY AUNT'S...
WEDDING?
YEAH, THAT'S WHAT IT WAS.
OH ...
AND I DON'T GO TO SCHOOL BECAUSE I WANT TO GOOF AROUND ALL DAY TAKING PICTURES.
M-MAN, I WISH I HAD YOUR LIFE...

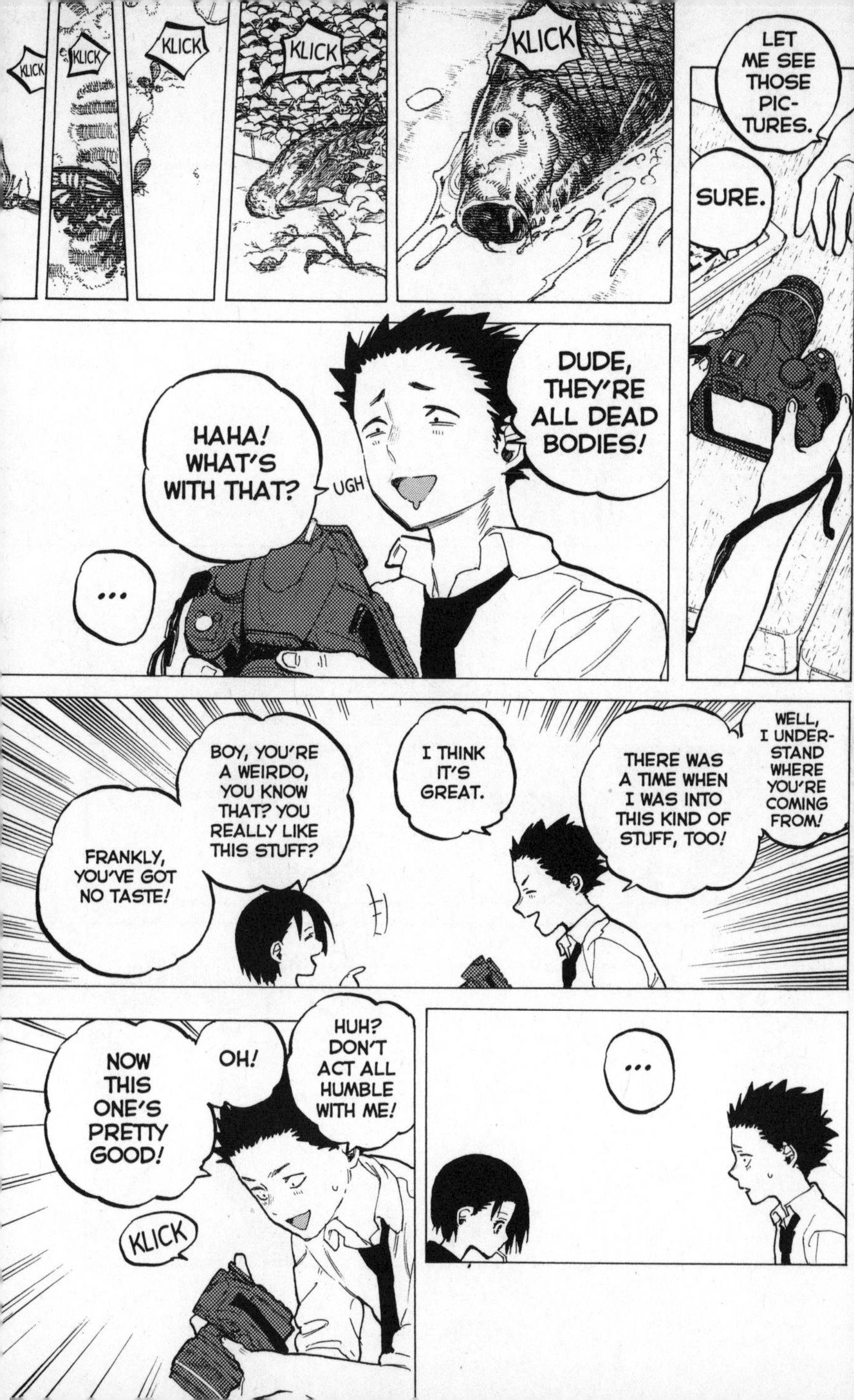

LET ME SEE THOSE PIC-TURES.
SURE.
KLICK
KLICK
KLICK
KLICK
KLICK
DUDE, THEY'RE ALL DEAD BODIES!
UGH
HAHA! WHAT'S WITH THAT?
...
WELL, I UNDER-STAND WHERE YOU'RE COMING FROM!
THERE WAS A TIME WHEN I WAS INTO THIS KIND OF STUFF, TOO!
I THINK IT'S GREAT.
BOY, YOU'RE A WEIRDO, YOU KNOW THAT? YOU REALLY LIKE THIS STUFF?
FRANKLY, YOU'VE GOT NO TASTE!
...
HUH? DON'T ACT ALL HUMBLE WITH ME!
OH!
NOW THIS ONE'S PRETTY GOOD!
KLICK

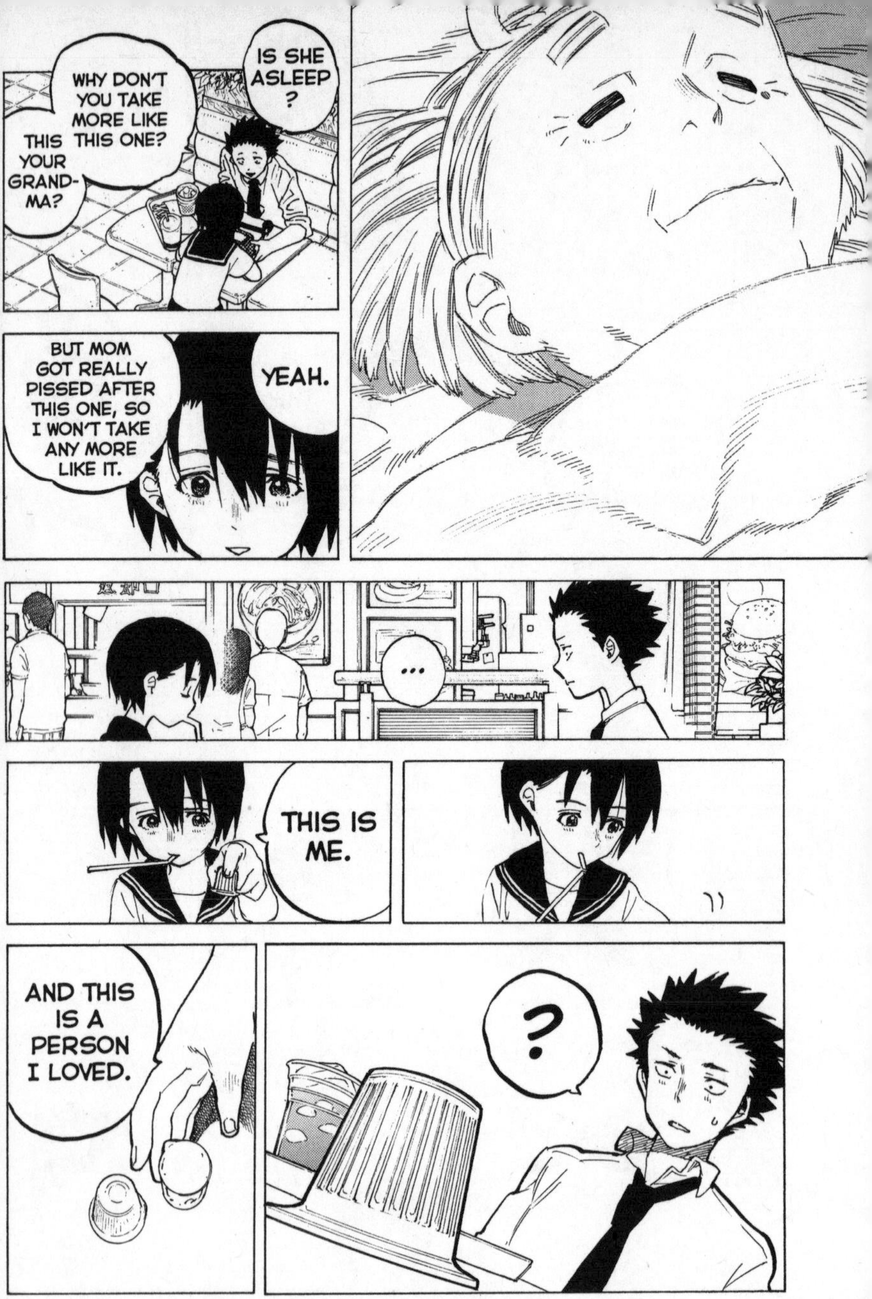
IS SHE ASLEEP?
WHY DON'T YOU TAKE MORE LIKE THIS ONE?
THIS YOUR GRANDMA?
YEAH.
BUT MOM GOT REALLY PISSED AFTER THIS ONE, SO I WON'T TAKE ANY MORE LIKE IT.
...
THIS IS ME.
?
AND THIS IS A PERSON I LOVED.

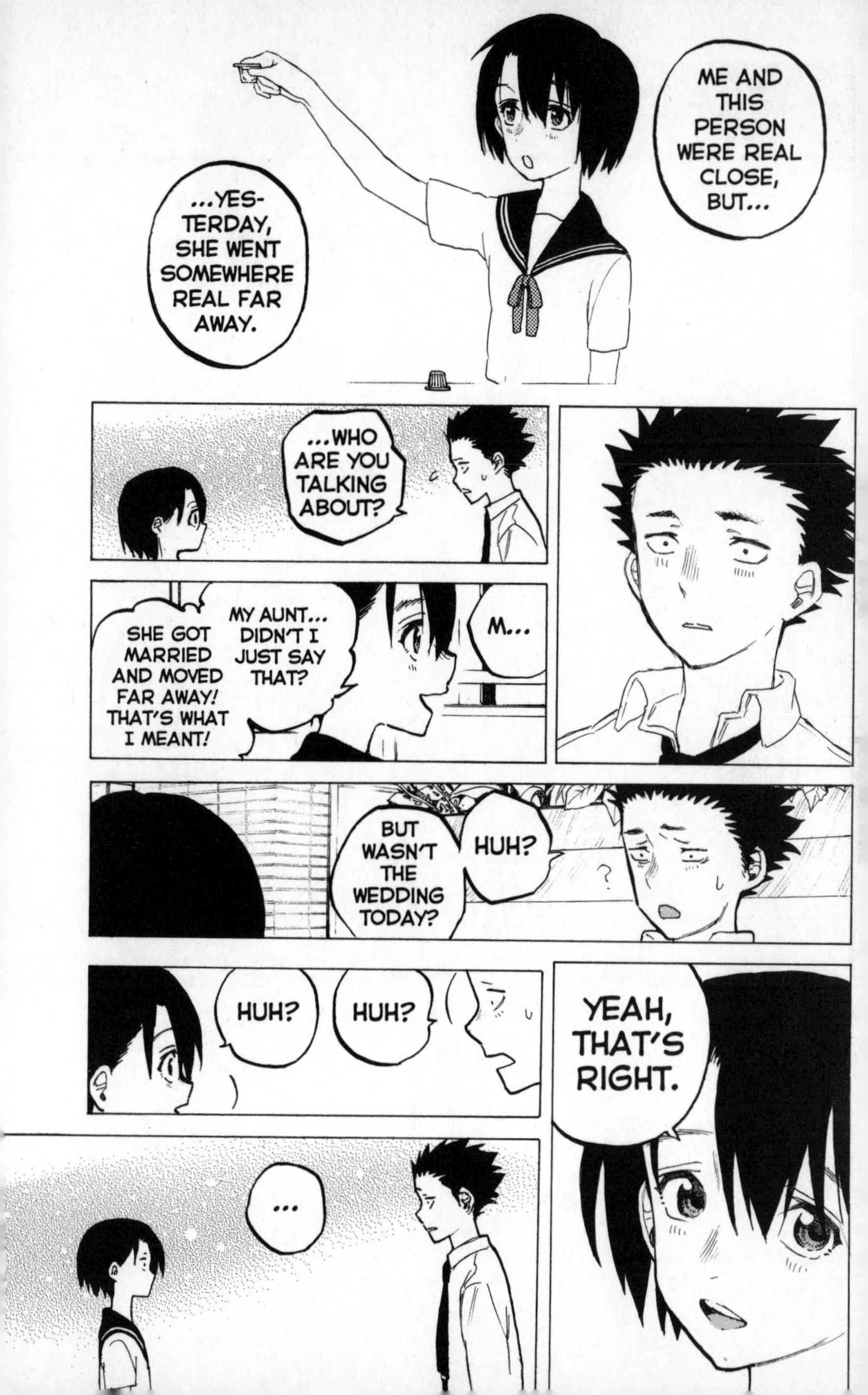
ME AND THIS PERSON WERE REAL CLOSE, BUT...
...YES-TERDAY, SHE WENT SOMEWHERE REAL FAR AWAY.
...WHO ARE YOU TALKING ABOUT?
M...
MY AUNT... DIDN'T I JUST SAY THAT?
SHE GOT MARRIED AND MOVED FAR AWAY! THAT'S WHAT I MEANT!
HUH?
BUT WASN'T THE WEDDING TODAY?
YEAH, THAT'S RIGHT.
HUH?
HUH?
...

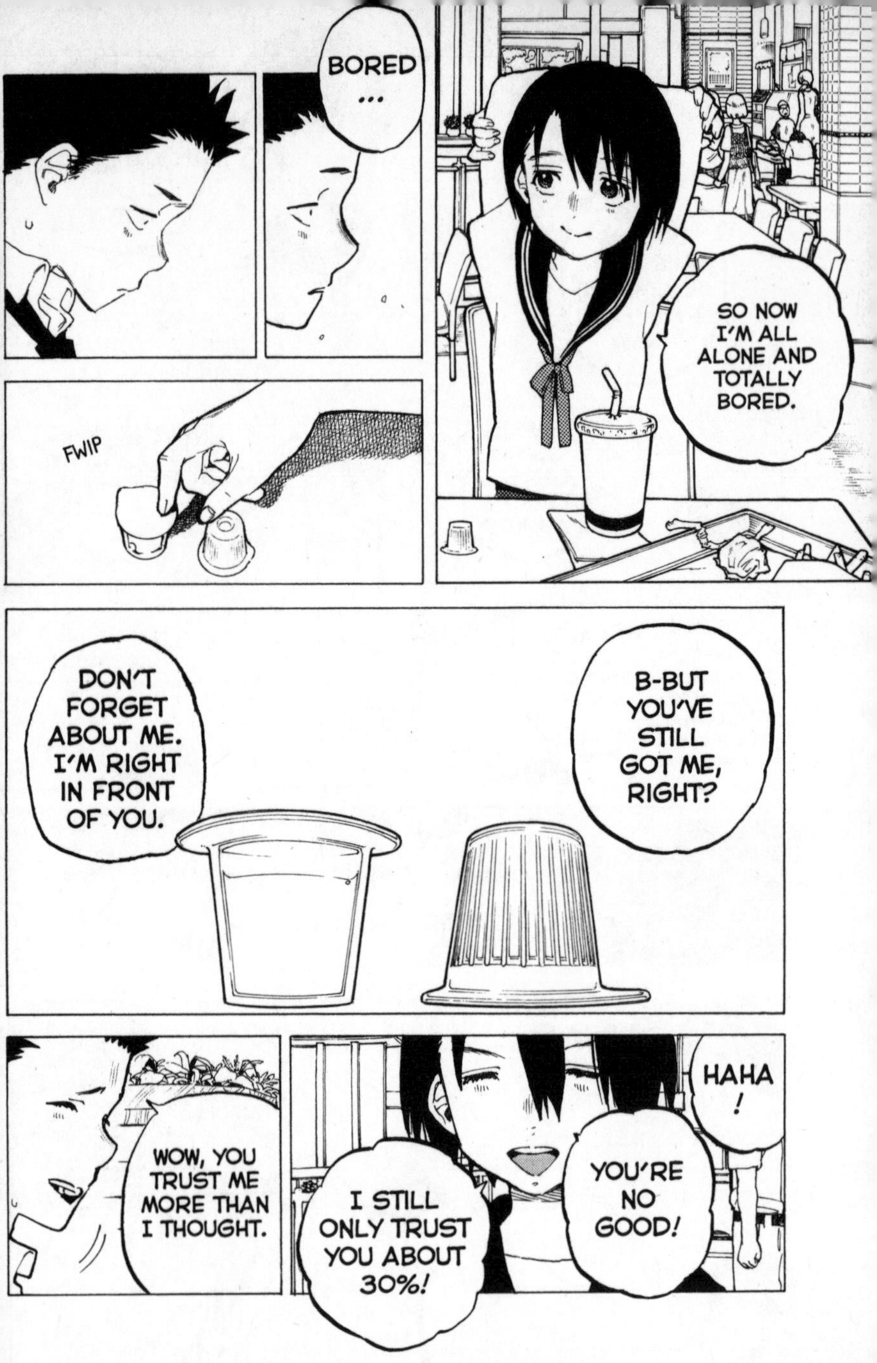
SO NOW I'M ALL ALONE AND TOTALLY BORED.
BORED ...
FWIP
B-BUT YOU'VE STILL GOT ME, RIGHT?
DON'T FORGET ABOUT ME. I'M RIGHT IN FRONT OF YOU.
HAHA!
YOU'RE NO GOOD!
I STILL ONLY TRUST YOU ABOUT 30%!
WOW, YOU TRUST ME MORE THAN I THOUGHT.

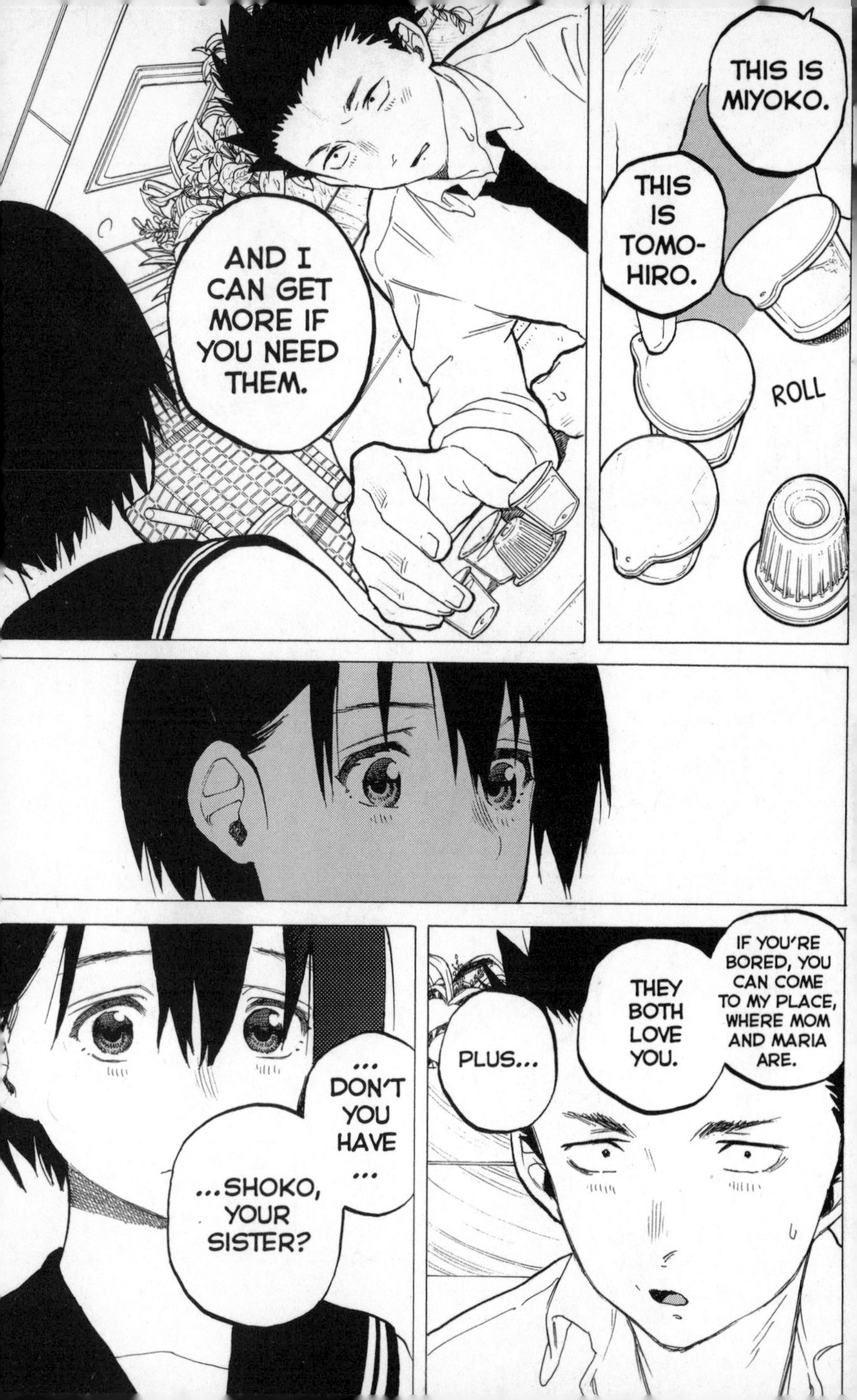
THIS IS MIYOKO.
THIS IS TOMO-HIRO.
ROLL
AND I CAN GET MORE IF YOU NEED THEM.
IF YOU'RE BORED, YOU CAN COME TO MY PLACE, WHERE MOM AND MARIA ARE.
THEY BOTH LOVE YOU.
PLUS...
... DON'T YOU HAVE ...
...SHOKO, YOUR SISTER?

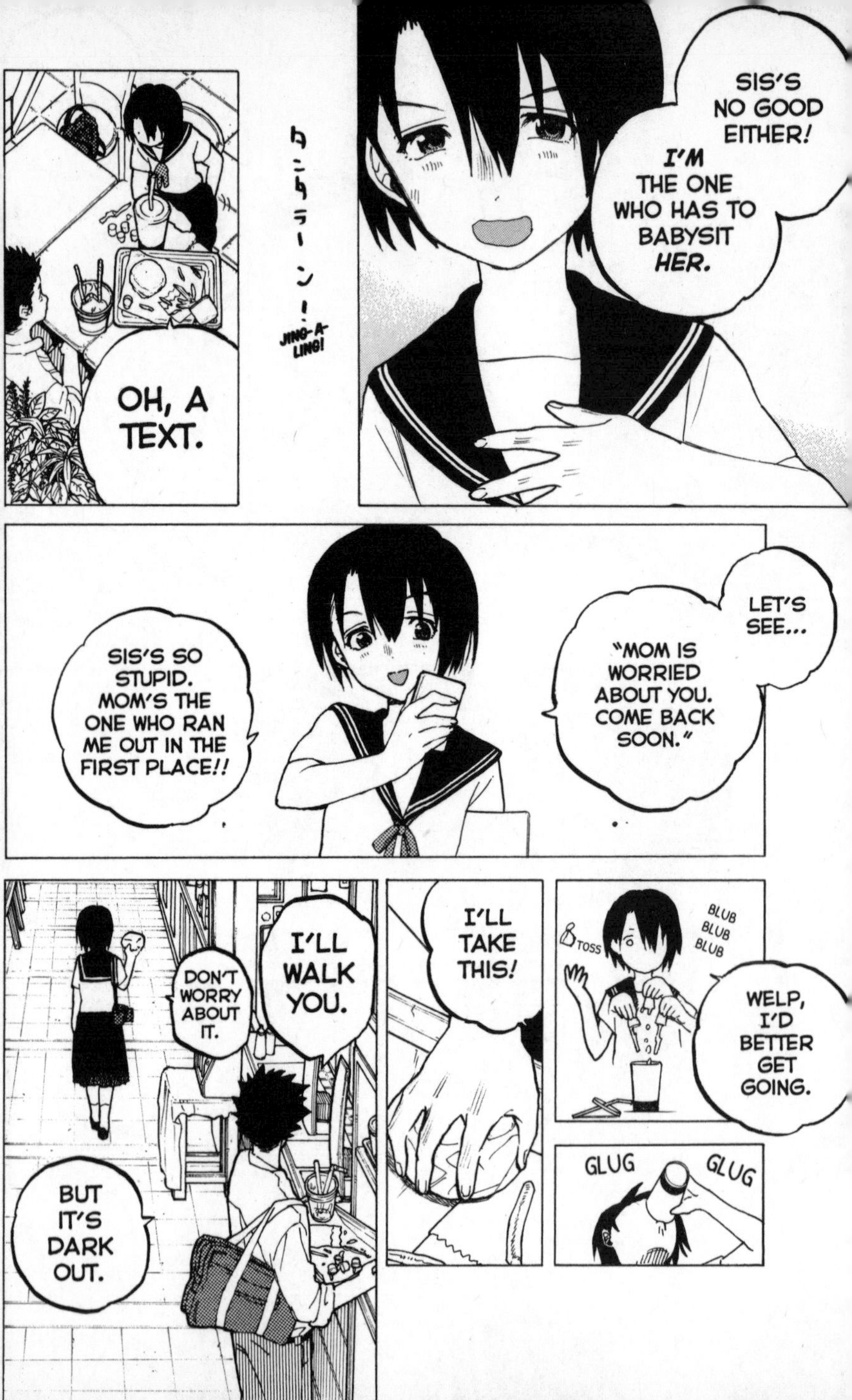
SIS'S NO GOOD EITHER! I'M THE ONE WHO HAS TO BABYSIT HER.
JING-A-LING!
OH, A TEXT.
LET'S SEE...
"MOM IS WORRIED ABOUT YOU. COME BACK SOON."
SIS'S SO STUPID. MOM'S THE ONE WHO RAN ME OUT IN THE FIRST PLACE!!
BLUB BLUB BLUB
WELP, I'D BETTER GET GOING.
TOSS
GLUG GLUG
I'LL TAKE THIS!
I'LL WALK YOU.
DON'T WORRY ABOUT IT.
BUT IT'S DARK OUT.

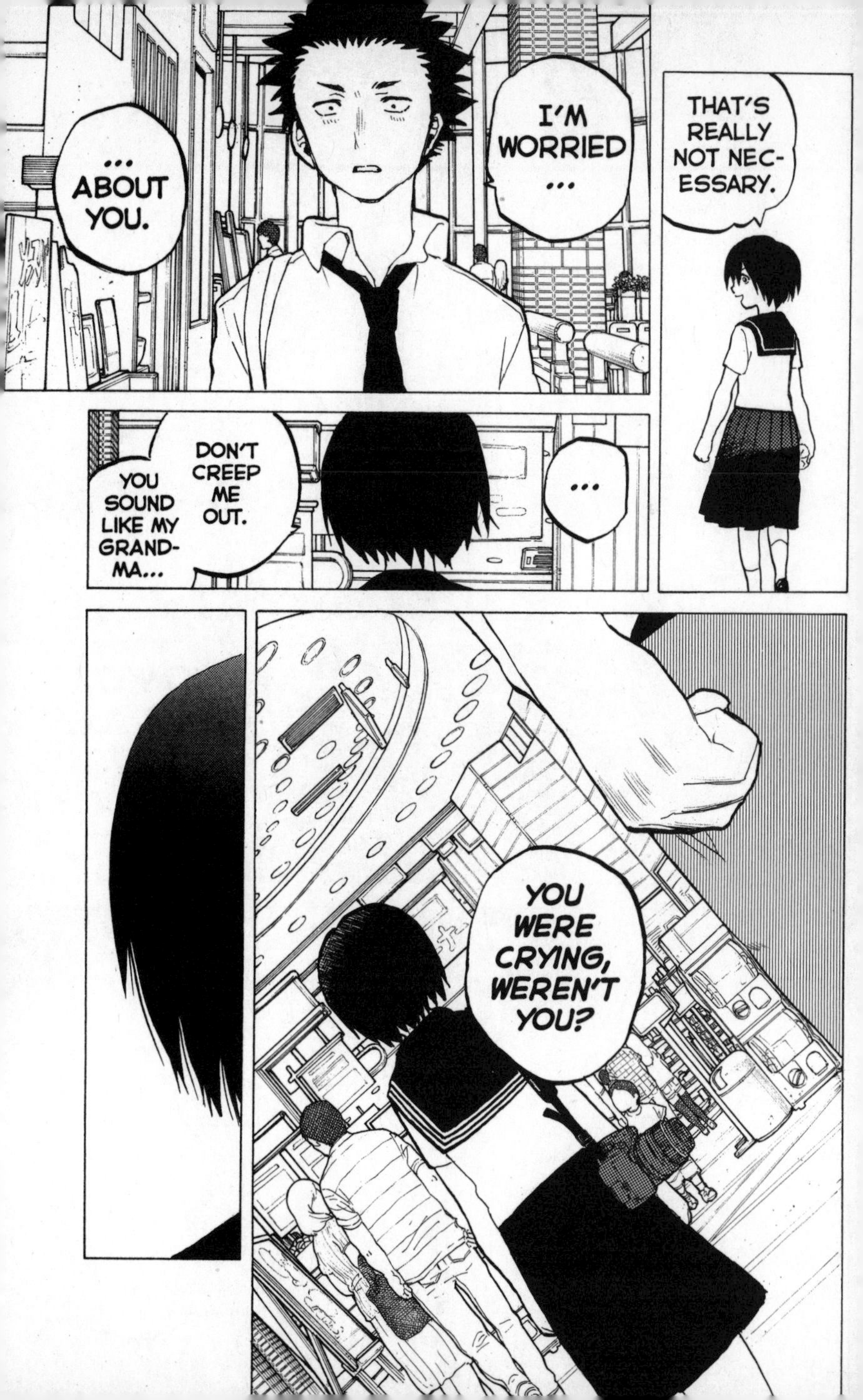
THAT'S REALLY NOT NEC-ESSARY.
I'M WORRIED ...
... ABOUT YOU.
...
DON'T CREEP ME OUT.
YOU SOUND LIKE MY GRAND-MA...
YOU WERE CRYING, WEREN'T YOU?

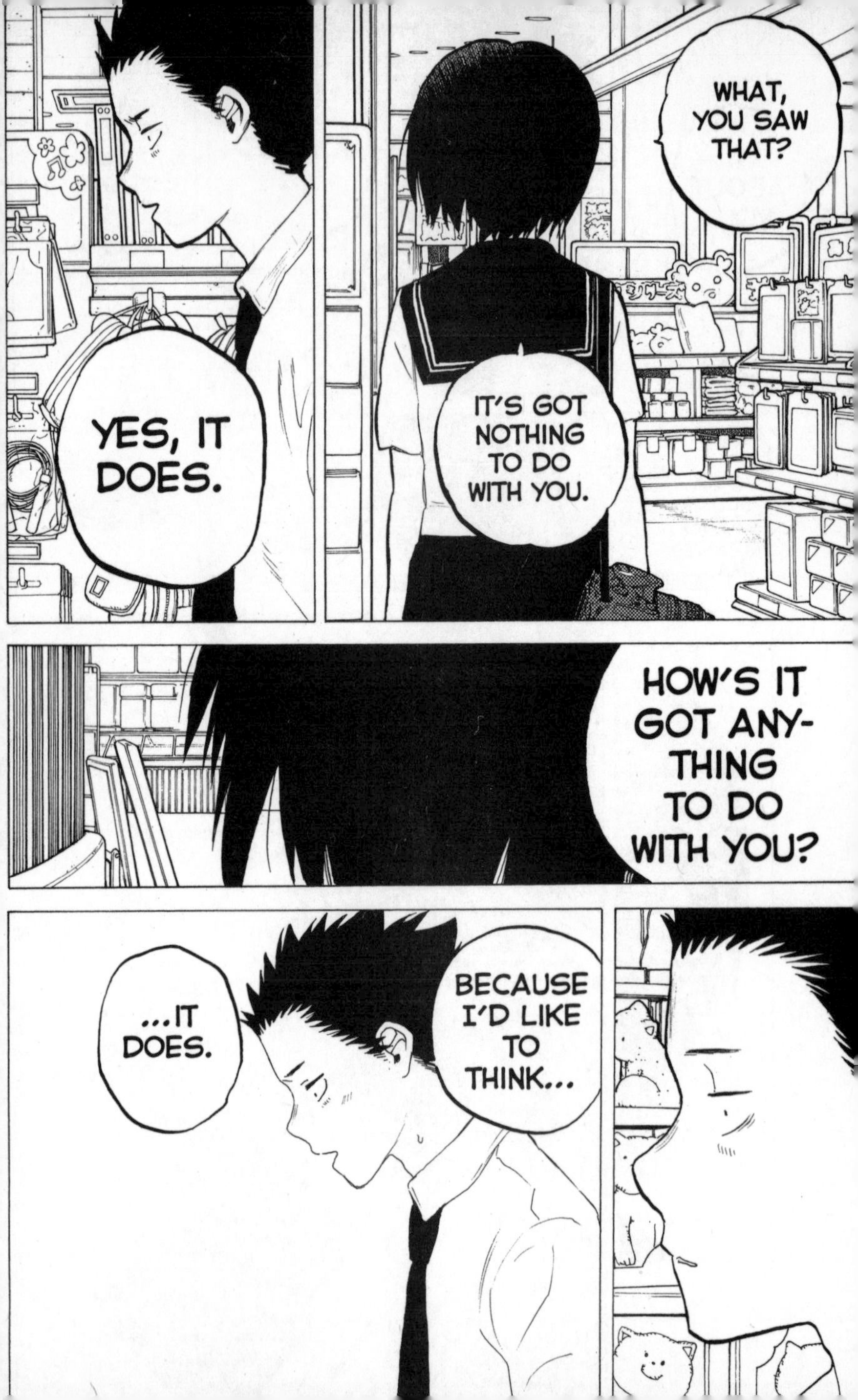
WHAT, YOU SAW THAT?
IT'S GOT NOTHING TO DO WITH YOU.
YES, IT DOES.
HOW'S IT GOT ANY-THING TO DO WITH YOU?
BECAUSE I'D LIKE TO THINK...
...IT DOES.

... BECAUSE I DON'T WANT TO HAVE ANY REGRETS.

THEN TAG ALONG FOR ALL I CARE.

THANKS.

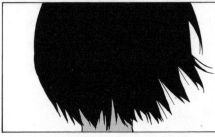

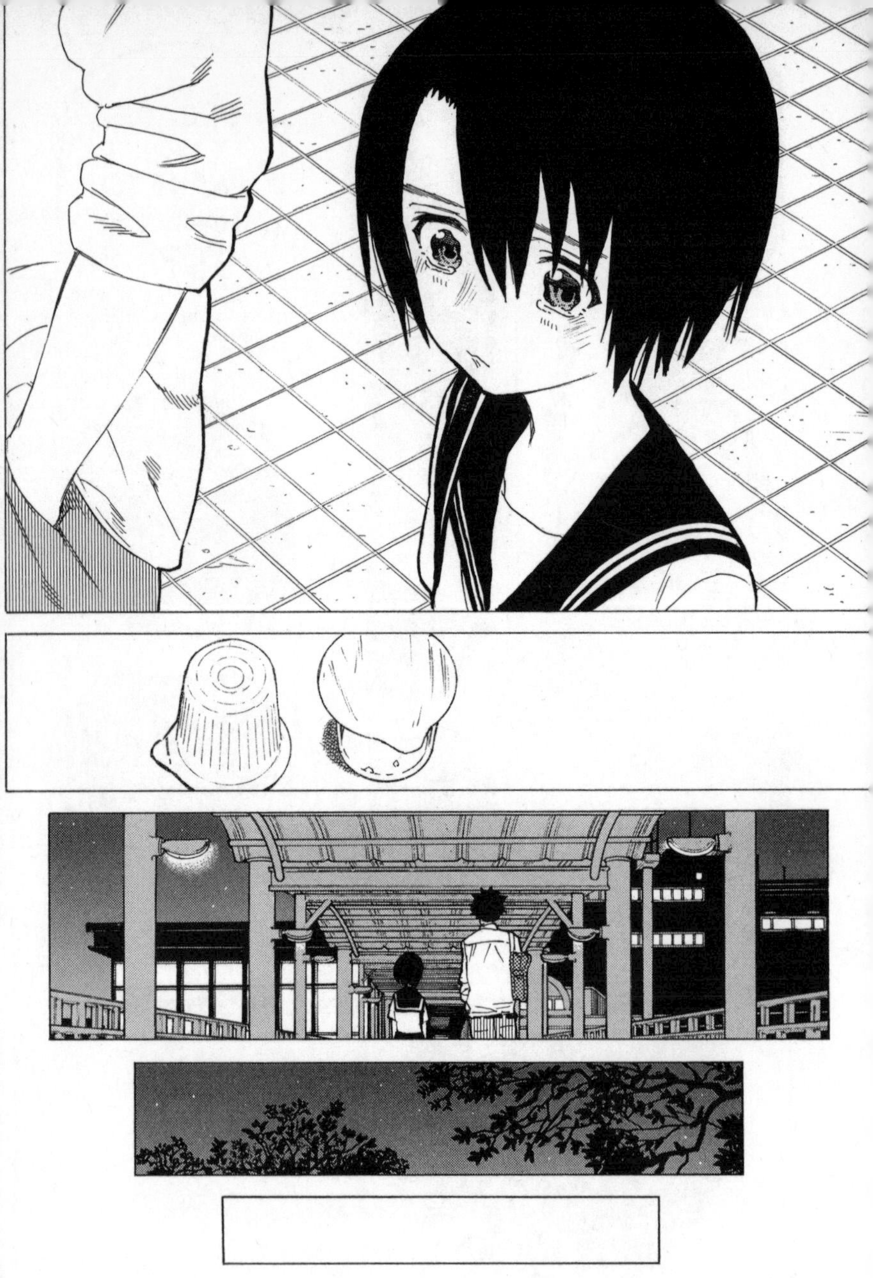

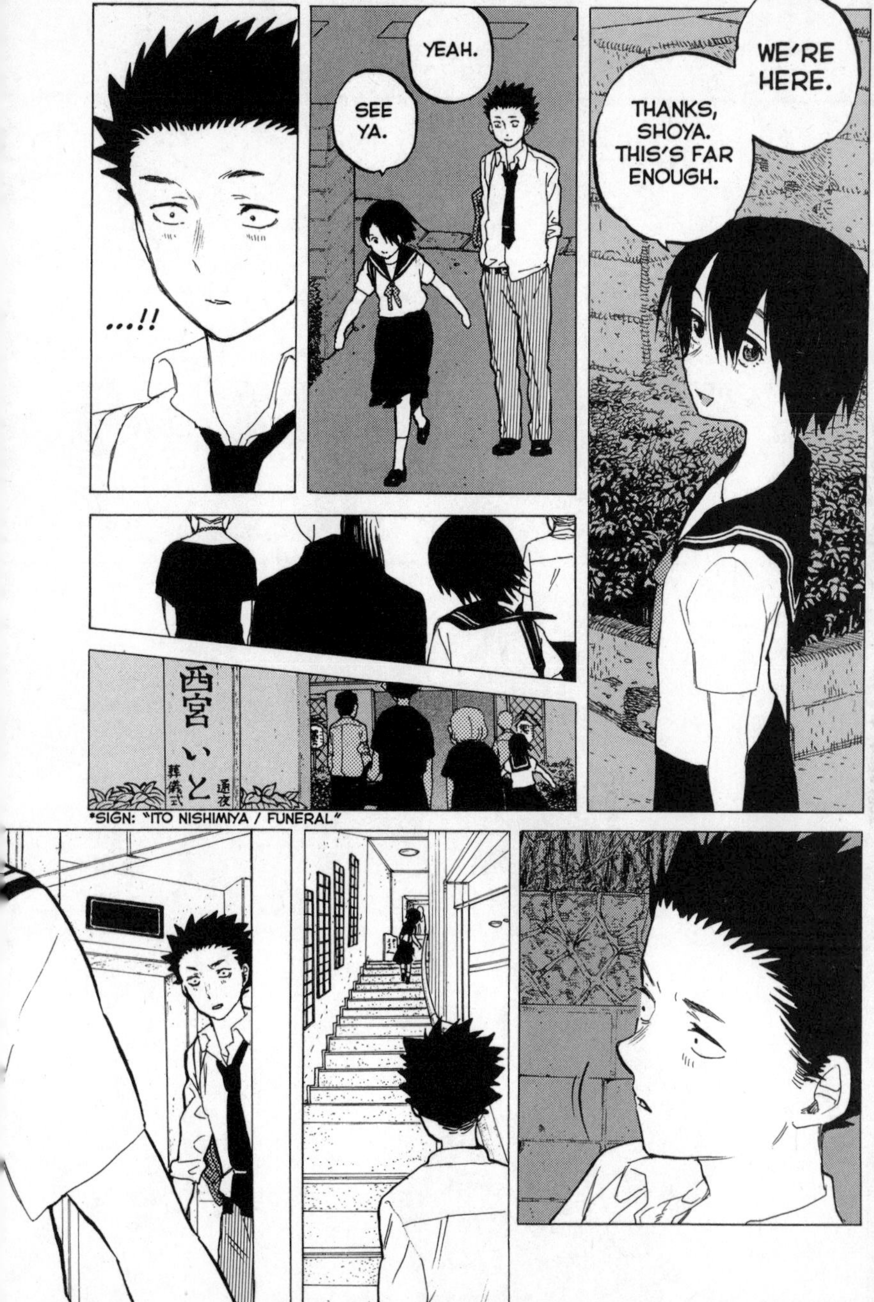
WE'RE HERE.
THANKS, SHOYA. THIS'S FAR ENOUGH.
YEAH.
SEE YA.
...!!
西宮 いと 通夜 葬儀式
*SIGN: "ITO NISHIMIYA / FUNERAL"

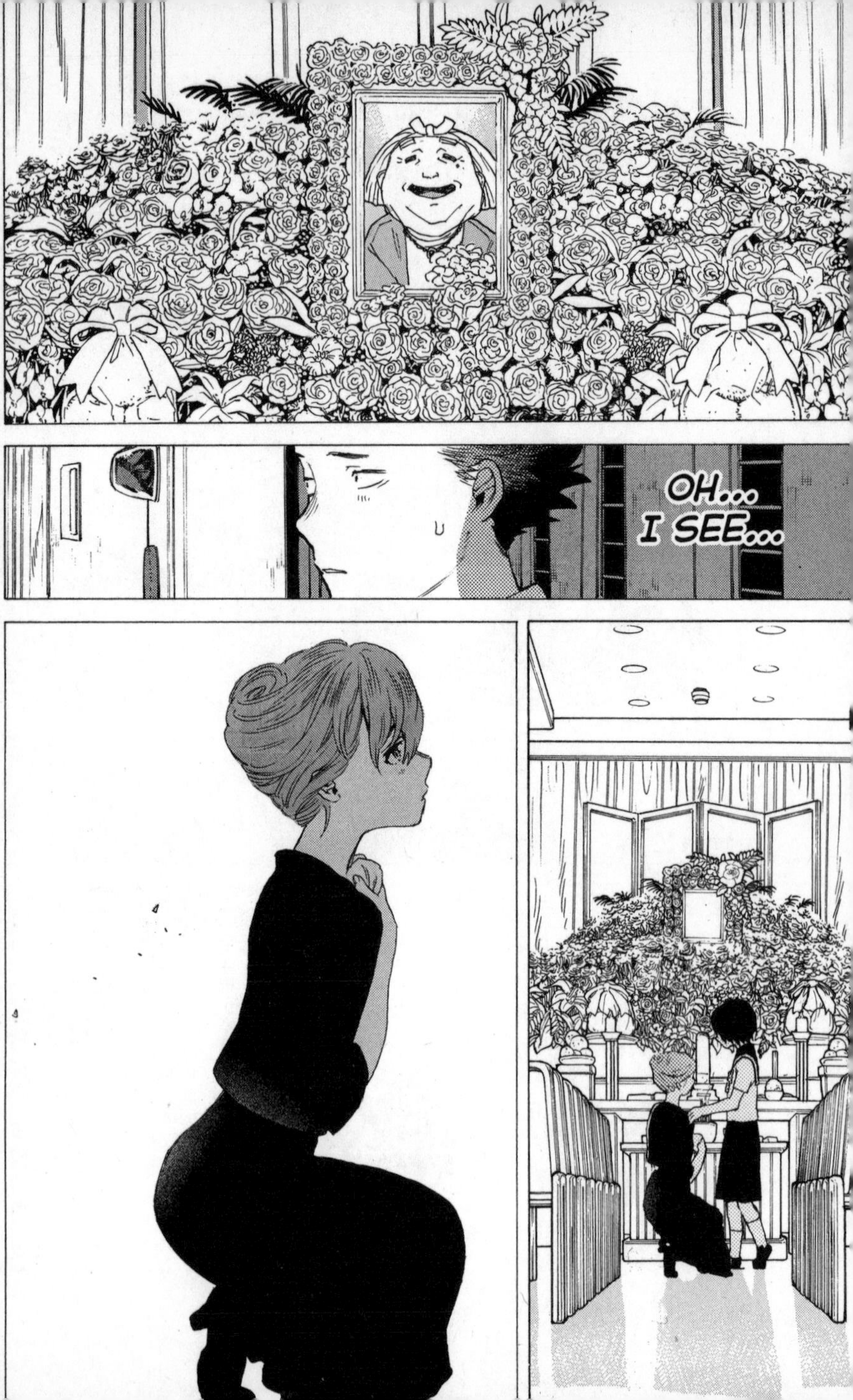
OH... I SEE...

CHAPTER 31: LETTER

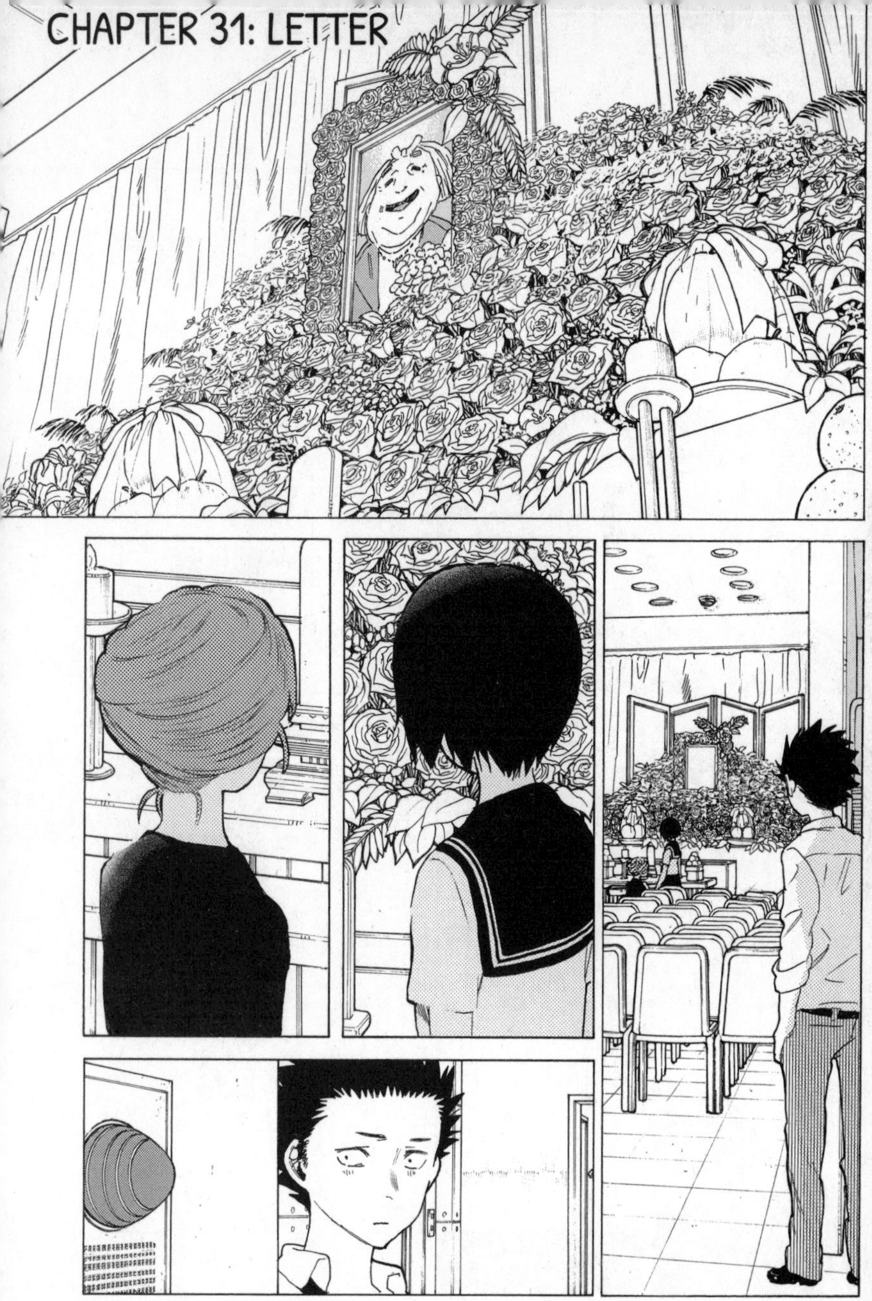

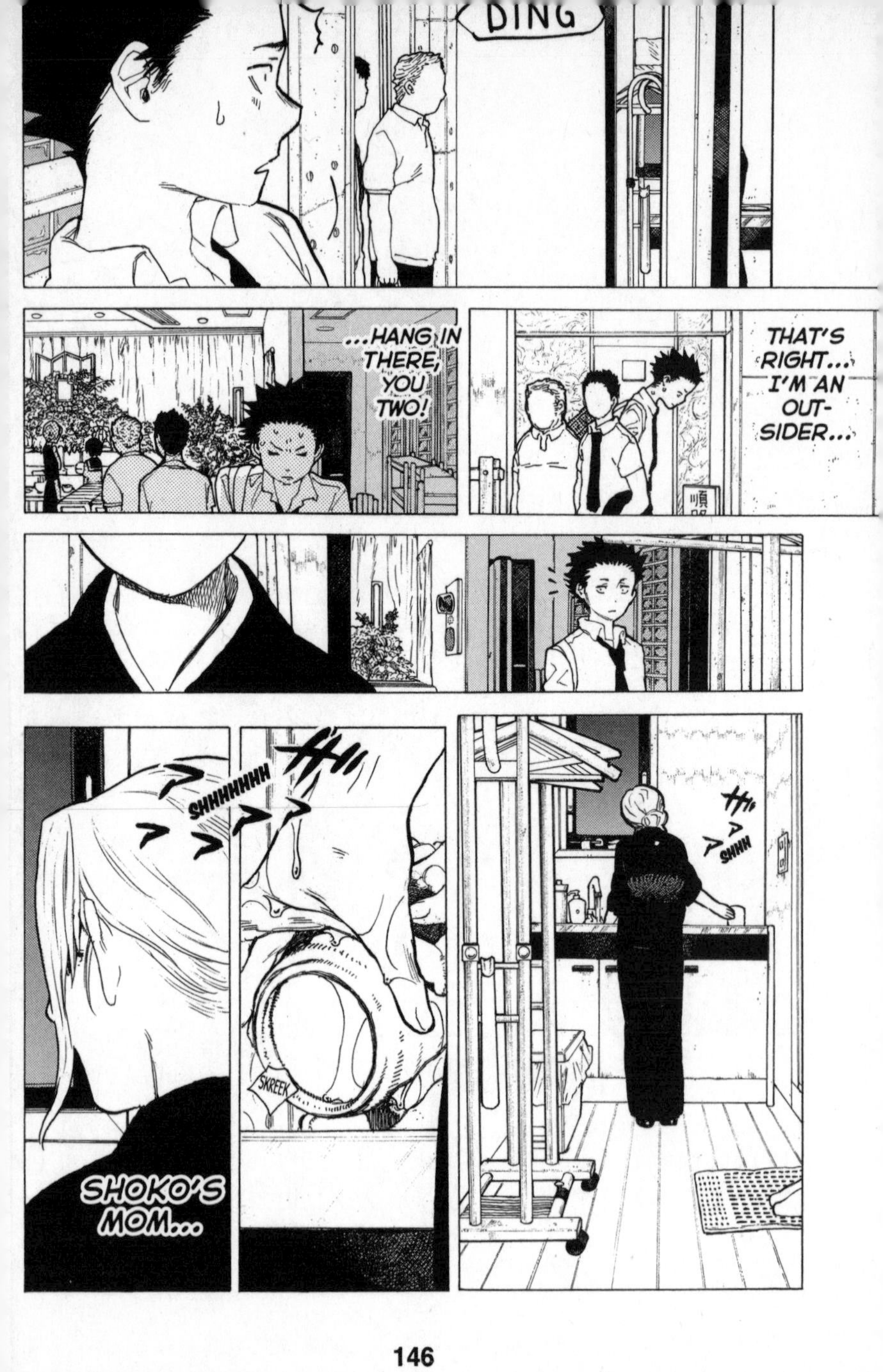
DING
THAT'S RIGHT... I'M AN OUTSIDER...
...HANG IN THERE, YOU TWO!
SHHH
SHHHHHHH
SKREEK
SHOKO'S MOM...

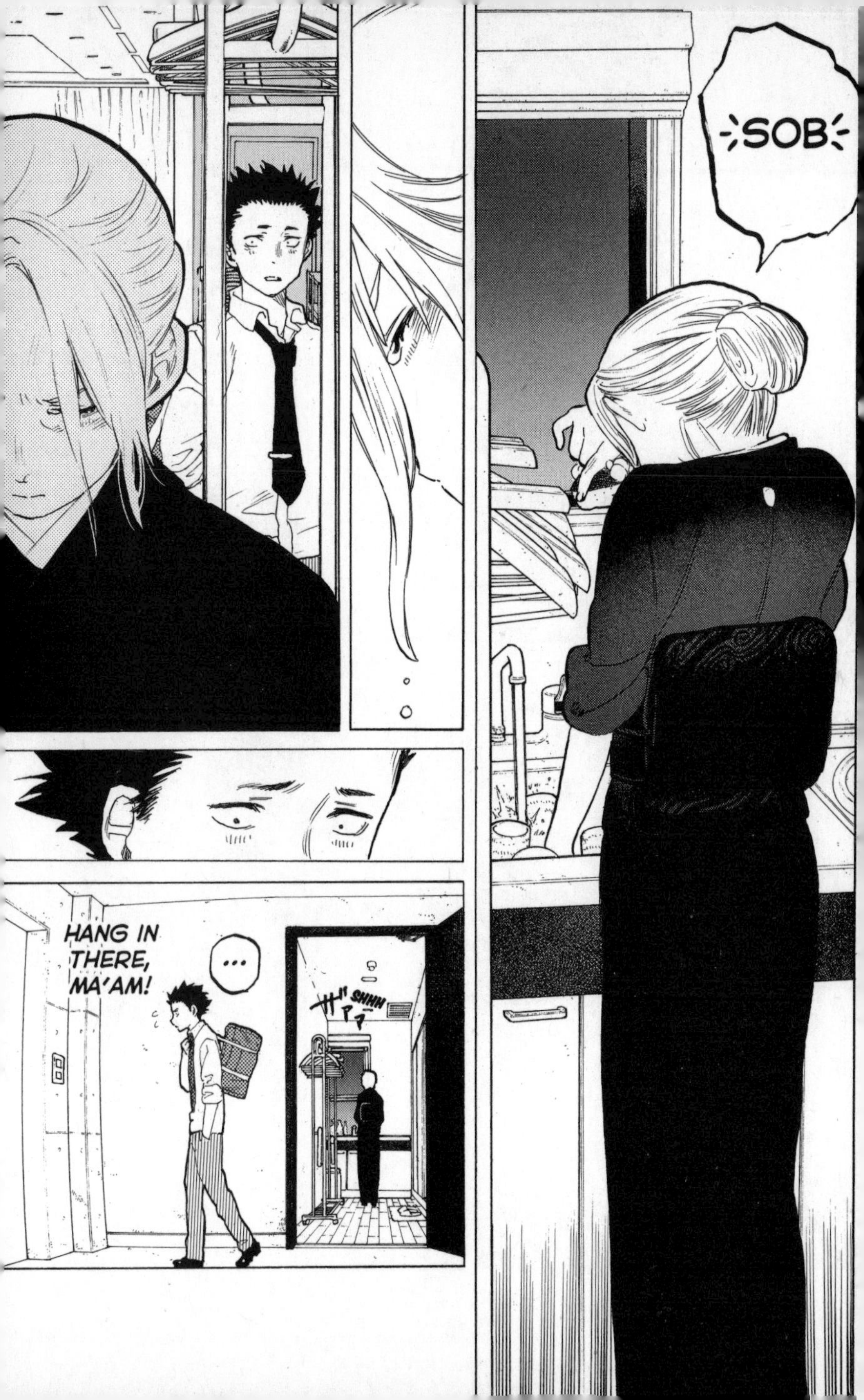
SOB
...
HANG IN THERE, MA'AM!
SHHH

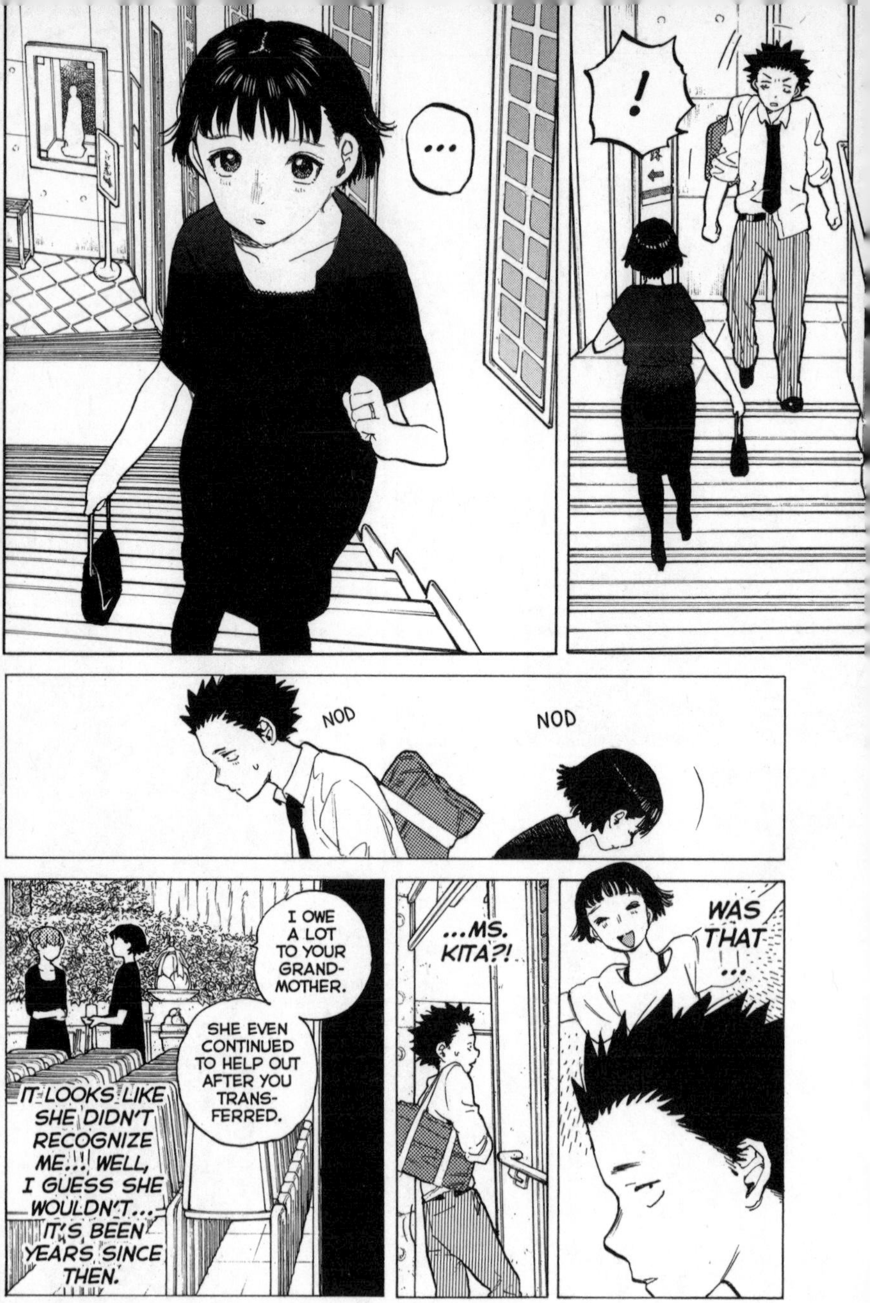
!
...
NOD
NOD
WAS THAT !...
...MS. KITA?!
I OWE A LOT TO YOUR GRAND-MOTHER.
SHE EVEN CONTINUED TO HELP OUT AFTER YOU TRANS-FERRED.
IT LOOKS LIKE SHE DIDN'T RECOGNIZE ME... WELL, I GUESS SHE WOULDN'T... IT'S BEEN YEARS SINCE THEN.

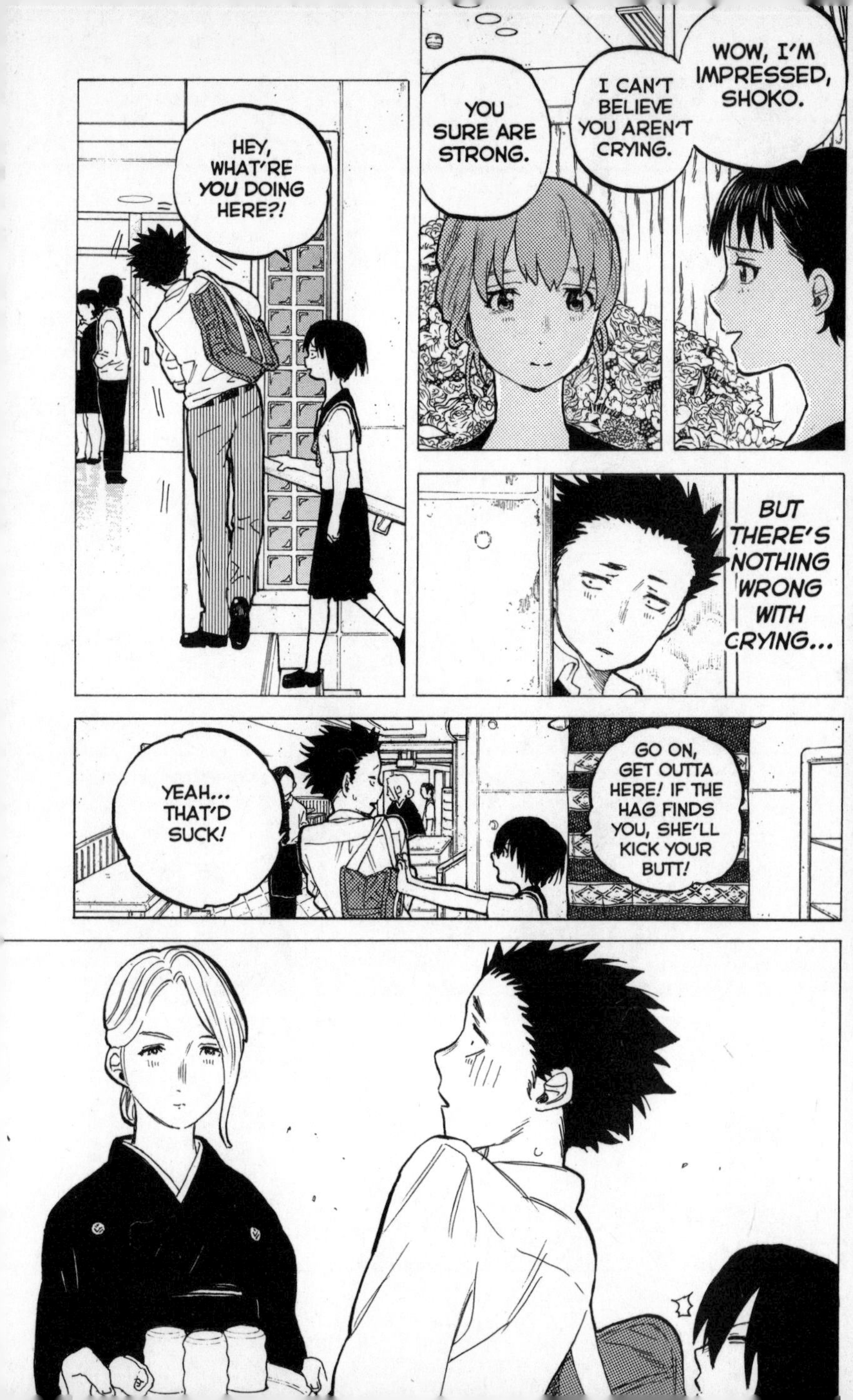
WOW, I'M IMPRESSED, SHOKO.
I CAN'T BELIEVE YOU AREN'T CRYING.
YOU SURE ARE STRONG.
BUT THERE'S NOTHING WRONG WITH CRYING...
HEY, WHAT'RE *YOU* DOING HERE?!
GO ON, GET OUTTA HERE! IF THE HAG FINDS YOU, SHE'LL KICK YOUR BUTT!
YEAH... THAT'D SUCK!

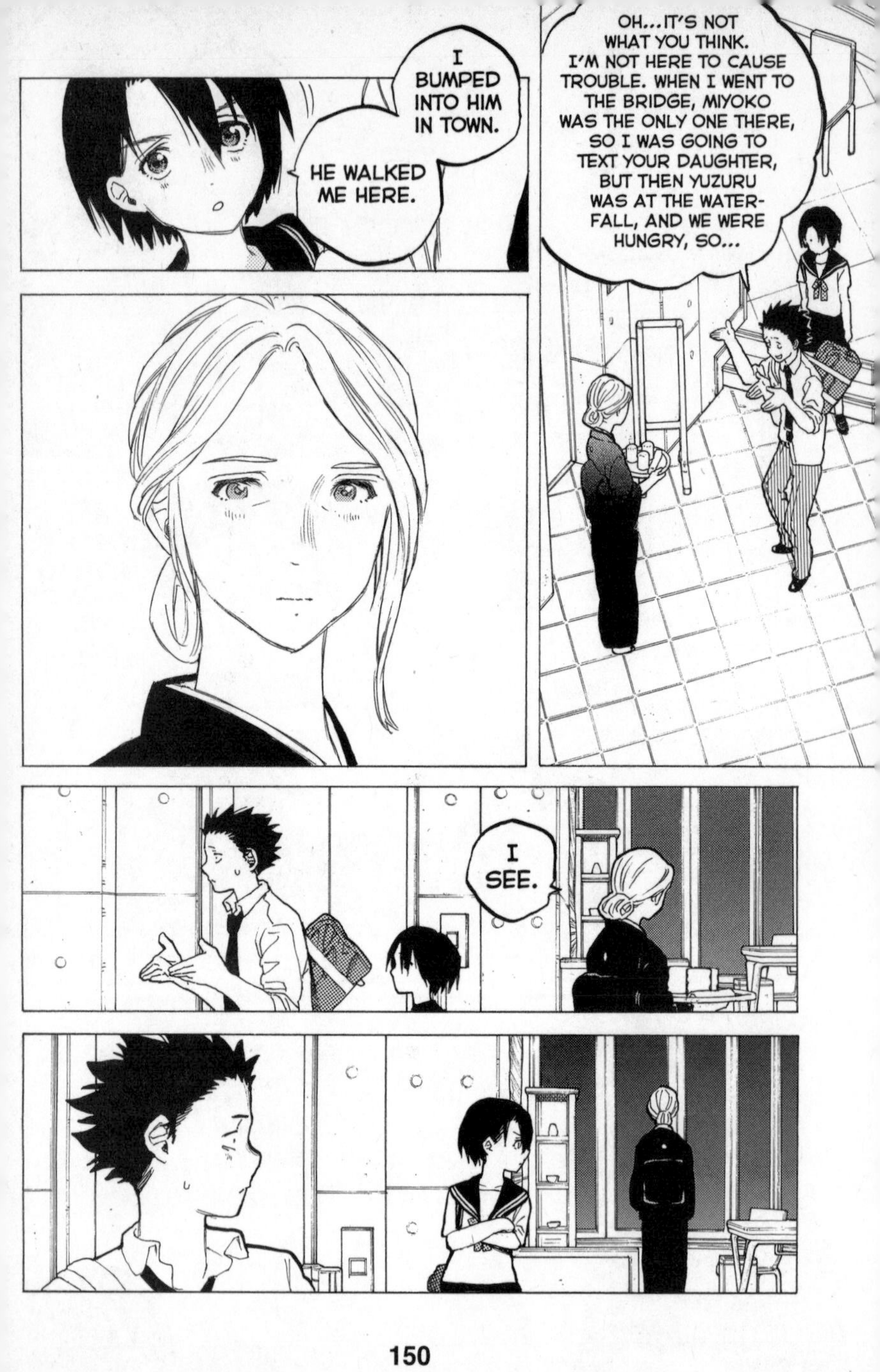
OH... IT'S NOT WHAT YOU THINK. I'M NOT HERE TO CAUSE TROUBLE. WHEN I WENT TO THE BRIDGE, MIYOKO WAS THE ONLY ONE THERE, SO I WAS GOING TO TEXT YOUR DAUGHTER, BUT THEN YUZURU WAS AT THE WATER-FALL, AND WE WERE HUNGRY, SO...
I BUMPED INTO HIM IN TOWN.
HE WALKED ME HERE.
I SEE.

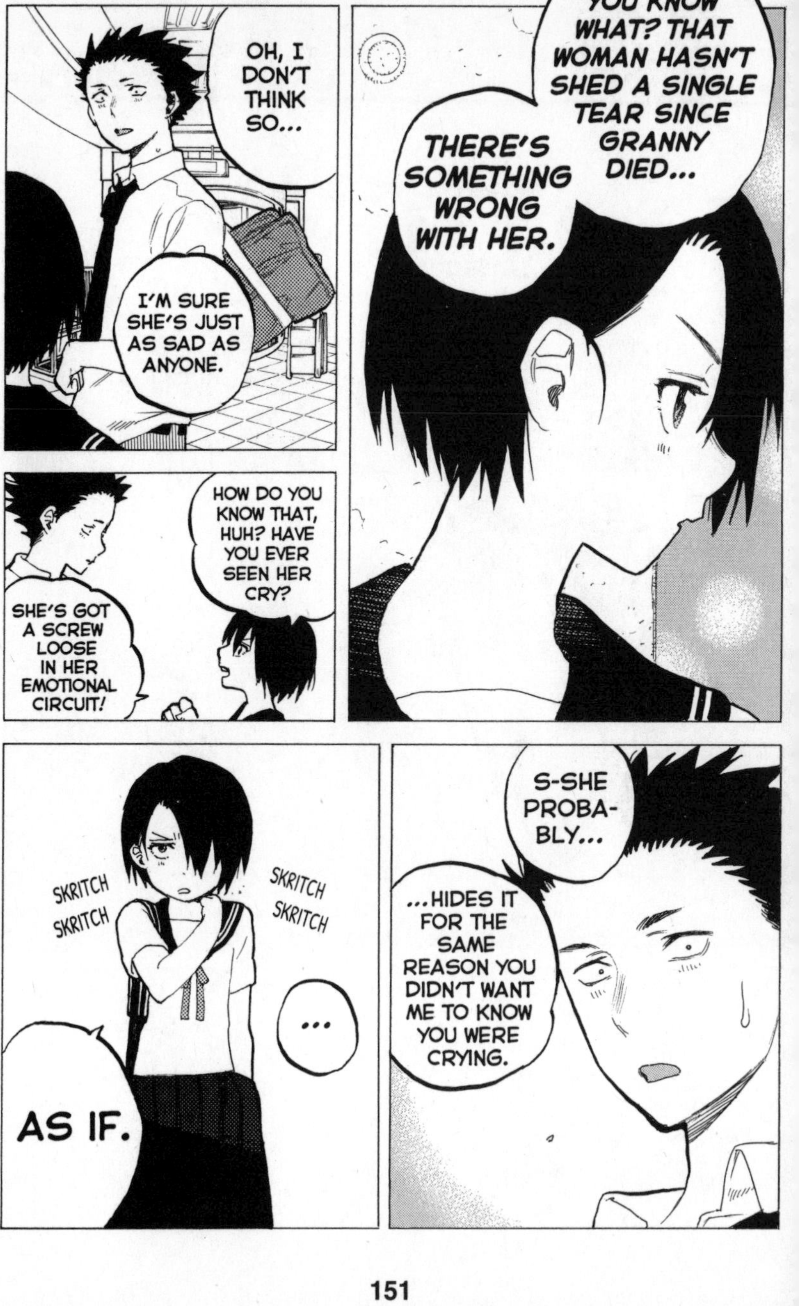
YOU KNOW WHAT? THAT WOMAN HASN'T SHED A SINGLE TEAR SINCE GRANNY DIED...
THERE'S SOMETHING WRONG WITH HER.
OH, I DON'T THINK SO...
I'M SURE SHE'S JUST AS SAD AS ANYONE.
HOW DO YOU KNOW THAT, HUH? HAVE YOU EVER SEEN HER CRY?
SHE'S GOT A SCREW LOOSE IN HER EMOTIONAL CIRCUIT!
S-SHE PROBA-BLY...
...HIDES IT FOR THE SAME REASON YOU DIDN'T WANT ME TO KNOW YOU WERE CRYING.
SKRITCH SKRITCH
SKRITCH SKRITCH
...
AS IF.

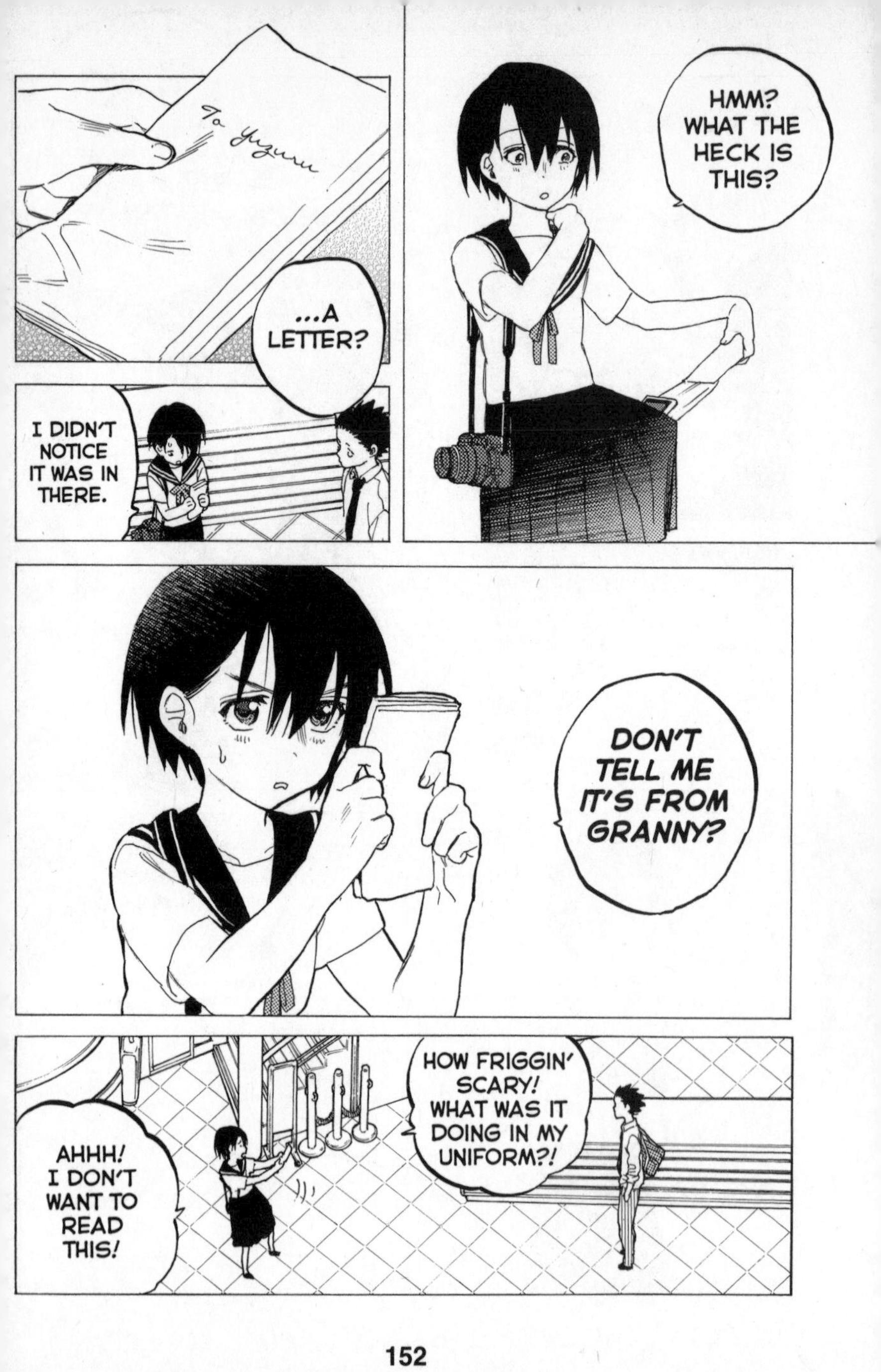
HMM? WHAT THE HECK IS THIS?
To Yuzuru
...A LETTER?
I DIDN'T NOTICE IT WAS IN THERE.
DON'T TELL ME IT'S FROM GRANNY?
HOW FRIGGIN' SCARY! WHAT WAS IT DOING IN MY UNIFORM?!
AHHH! I DON'T WANT TO READ THIS!

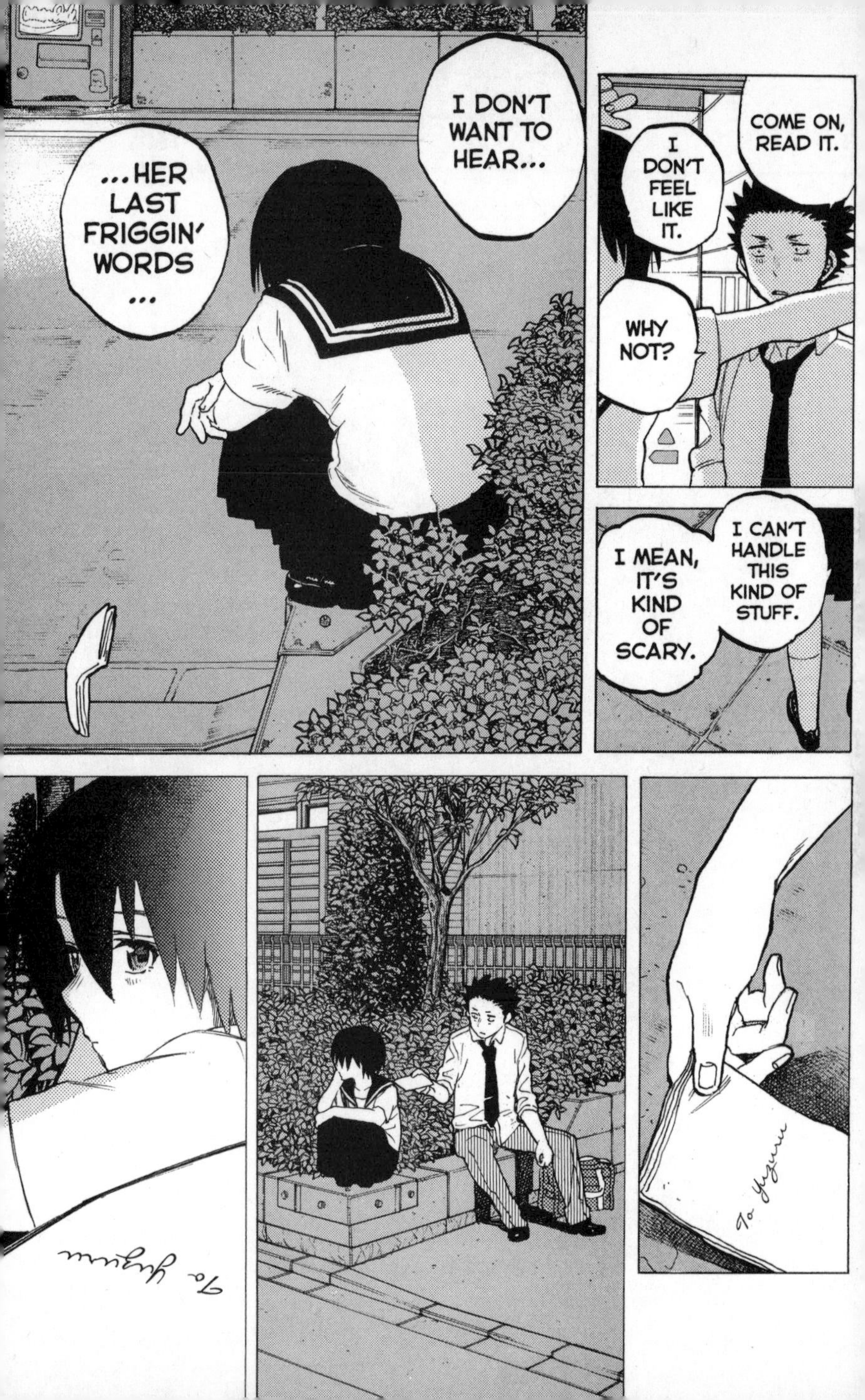
COME ON, READ IT.
I DON'T FEEL LIKE IT.
WHY NOT?
I CAN'T HANDLE THIS KIND OF STUFF.
I MEAN, IT'S KIND OF SCARY.
I DON'T WANT TO HEAR...
...HER LAST FRIGGIN' WORDS ...
To Yuzuru

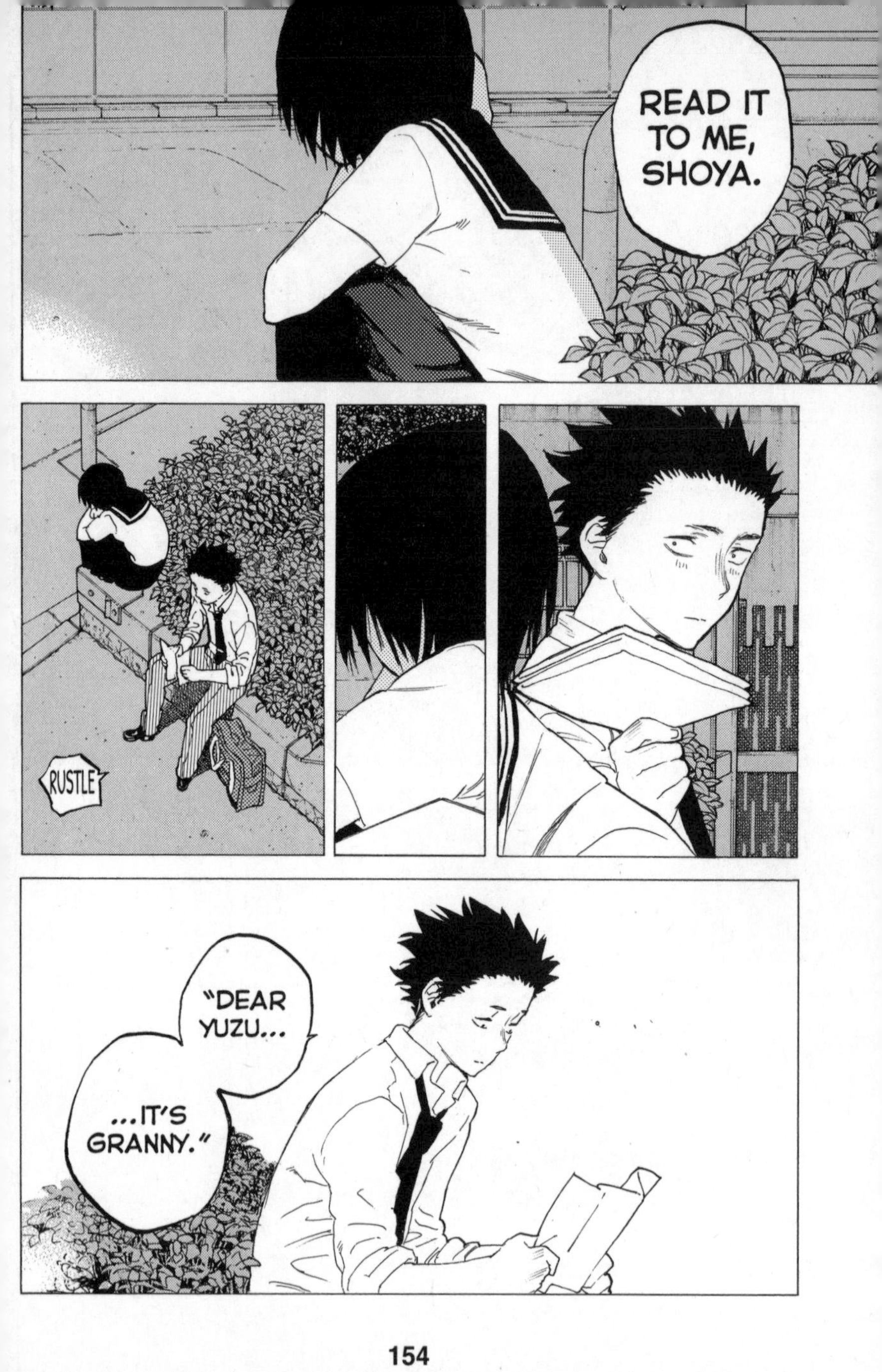
READ IT TO ME, SHOYA.
RUSTLE
"DEAR YUZU...
...IT'S GRANNY."

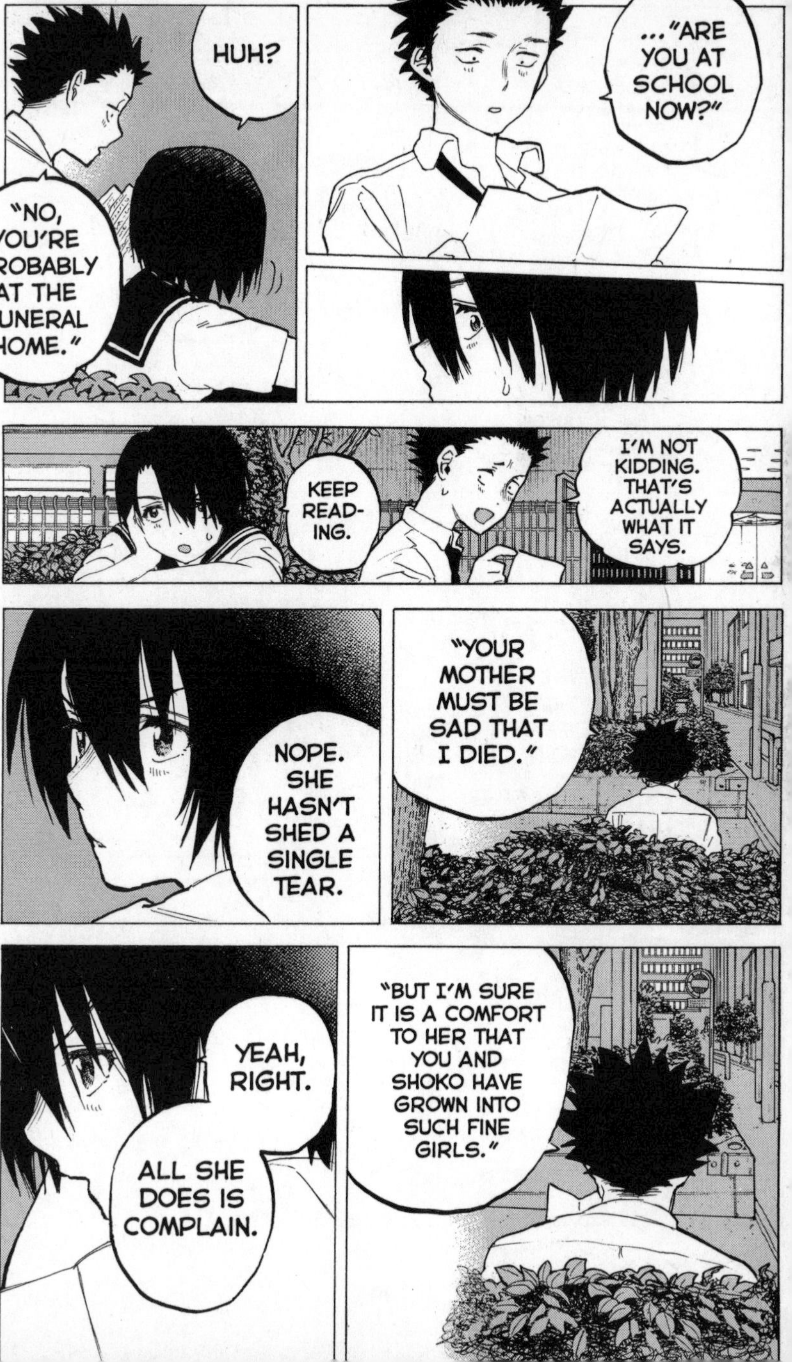
..."ARE YOU AT SCHOOL NOW?"
HUH?
"NO, YOU'RE PROBABLY AT THE FUNERAL HOME."
I'M NOT KIDDING. THAT'S ACTUALLY WHAT IT SAYS.
KEEP READ-ING.
"YOUR MOTHER MUST BE SAD THAT I DIED."
NOPE. SHE HASN'T SHED A SINGLE TEAR.
"BUT I'M SURE IT IS A COMFORT TO HER THAT YOU AND SHOKO HAVE GROWN INTO SUCH FINE GIRLS."
YEAH, RIGHT.
ALL SHE DOES IS COMPLAIN.

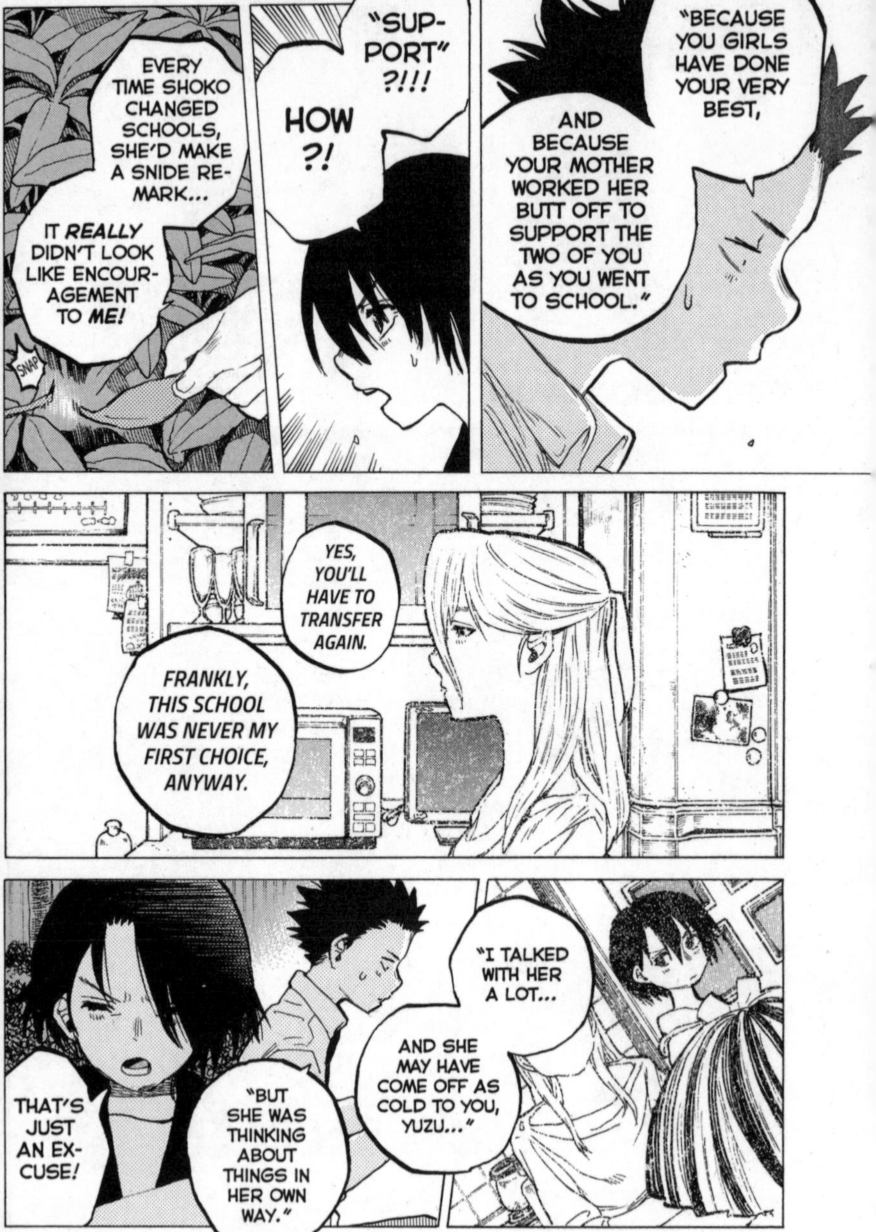
"BECAUSE YOU GIRLS HAVE DONE YOUR VERY BEST,
AND BECAUSE YOUR MOTHER WORKED HER BUTT OFF TO SUPPORT THE TWO OF YOU AS YOU WENT TO SCHOOL."
"SUP-PORT" ?!!!
HOW ?!
EVERY TIME SHOKO CHANGED SCHOOLS, SHE'D MAKE A SNIDE RE-MARK...
IT *REALLY* DIDN'T LOOK LIKE ENCOUR-AGEMENT TO *ME!*
SNAP
YES, YOU'LL HAVE TO TRANSFER AGAIN.
FRANKLY, THIS SCHOOL WAS NEVER MY FIRST CHOICE, ANYWAY.
"I TALKED WITH HER A LOT...
AND SHE MAY HAVE COME OFF AS COLD TO YOU, YUZU..."
"BUT SHE WAS THINKING ABOUT THINGS IN HER OWN WAY."
THAT'S JUST AN EX-CUSE!

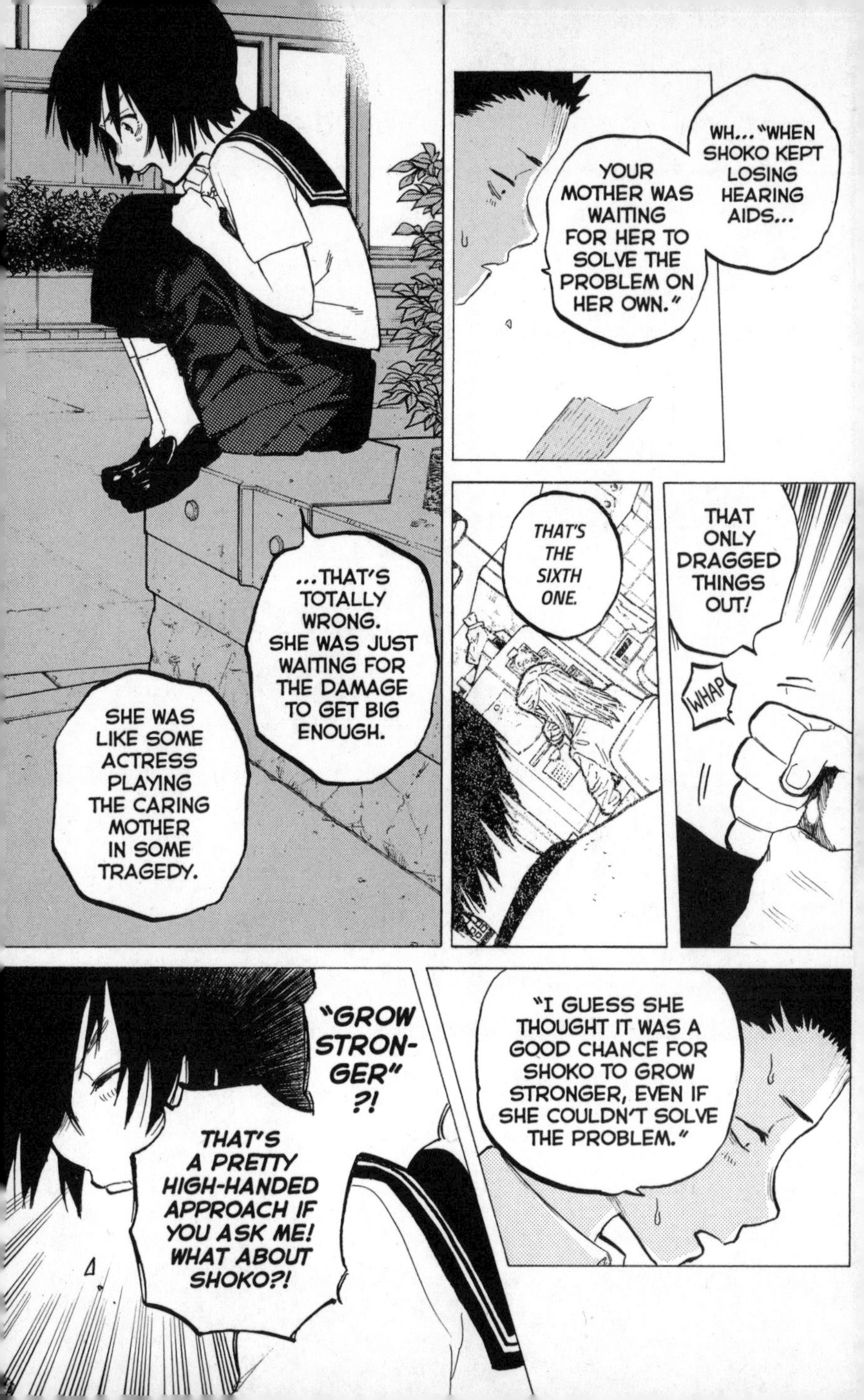
WH... "WHEN SHOKO KEPT LOSING HEARING AIDS...
YOUR MOTHER WAS WAITING FOR HER TO SOLVE THE PROBLEM ON HER OWN."
THAT ONLY DRAGGED THINGS OUT!
WHAP
THAT'S THE SIXTH ONE.
...THAT'S TOTALLY WRONG. SHE WAS JUST WAITING FOR THE DAMAGE TO GET BIG ENOUGH.
SHE WAS LIKE SOME ACTRESS PLAYING THE CARING MOTHER IN SOME TRAGEDY.
"I GUESS SHE THOUGHT IT WAS A GOOD CHANCE FOR SHOKO TO GROW STRONGER, EVEN IF SHE COULDN'T SOLVE THE PROBLEM."
"GROW STRON-GER" ?!
THAT'S A PRETTY HIGH-HANDED APPROACH IF YOU ASK ME! WHAT ABOUT SHOKO?!

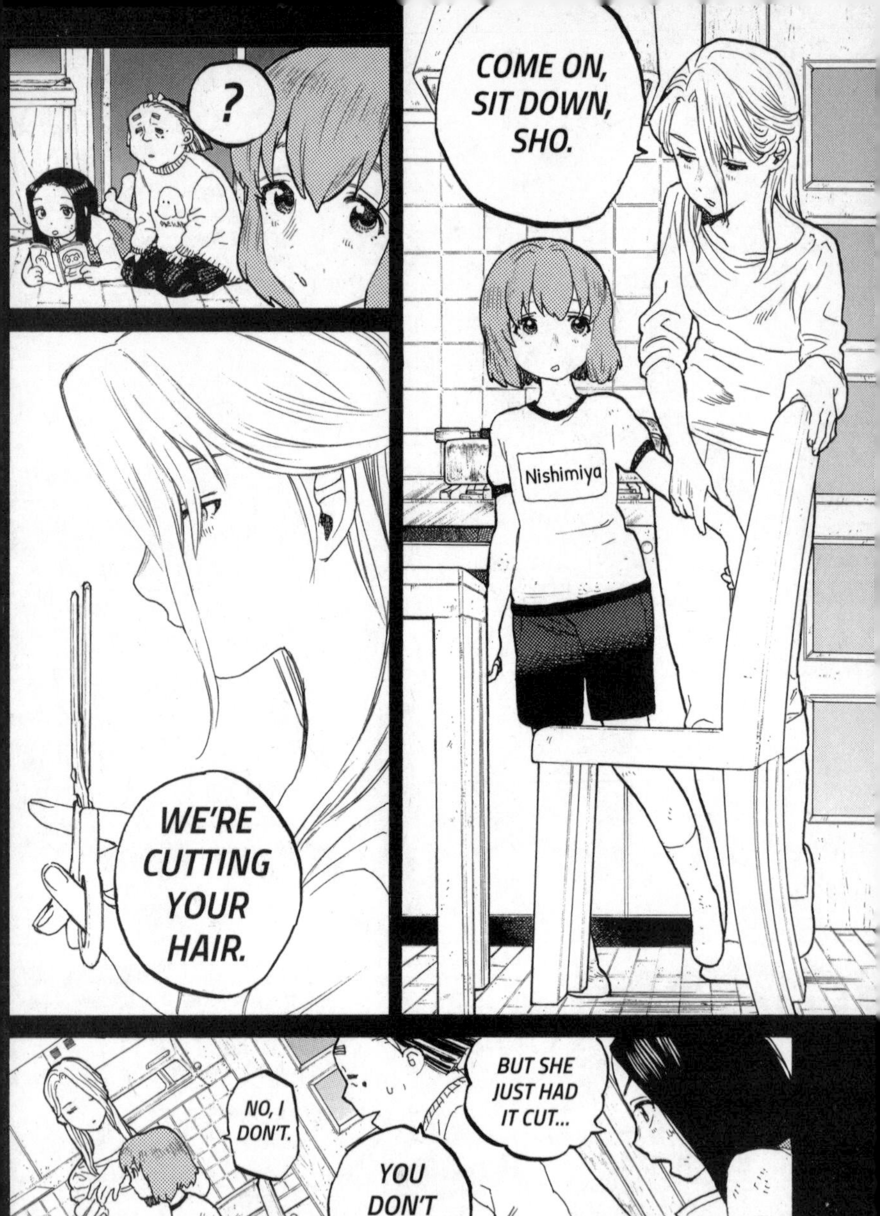
COME ON, SIT DOWN, SHO.
Nishimiya
?
WE'RE CUTTING YOUR HAIR.
BUT SHE JUST HAD IT CUT...
YOU DON'T LIKE IT?
NO, I DON'T.

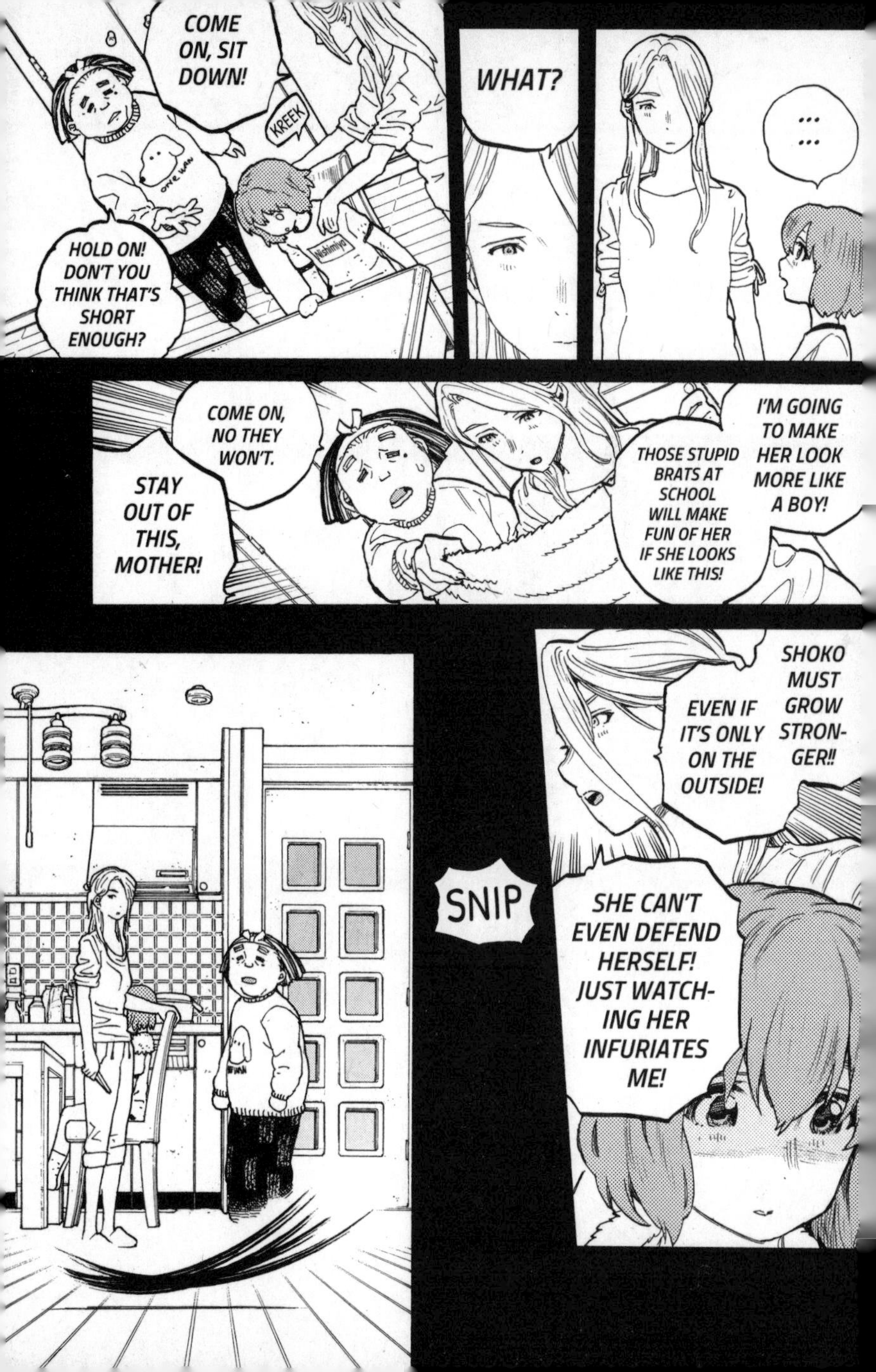
......
WHAT?
COME ON, SIT DOWN!
KREEK
HOLD ON! DON'T YOU THINK THAT'S SHORT ENOUGH?
I'M GOING TO MAKE HER LOOK MORE LIKE A BOY!
THOSE STUPID BRATS AT SCHOOL WILL MAKE FUN OF HER IF SHE LOOKS LIKE THIS!
COME ON, NO THEY WON'T.
STAY OUT OF THIS, MOTHER!
SHOKO MUST GROW STRON-GER!!
EVEN IF IT'S ONLY ON THE OUTSIDE!
SHE CAN'T EVEN DEFEND HERSELF! JUST WATCH-ING HER INFURIATES ME!
SNIP

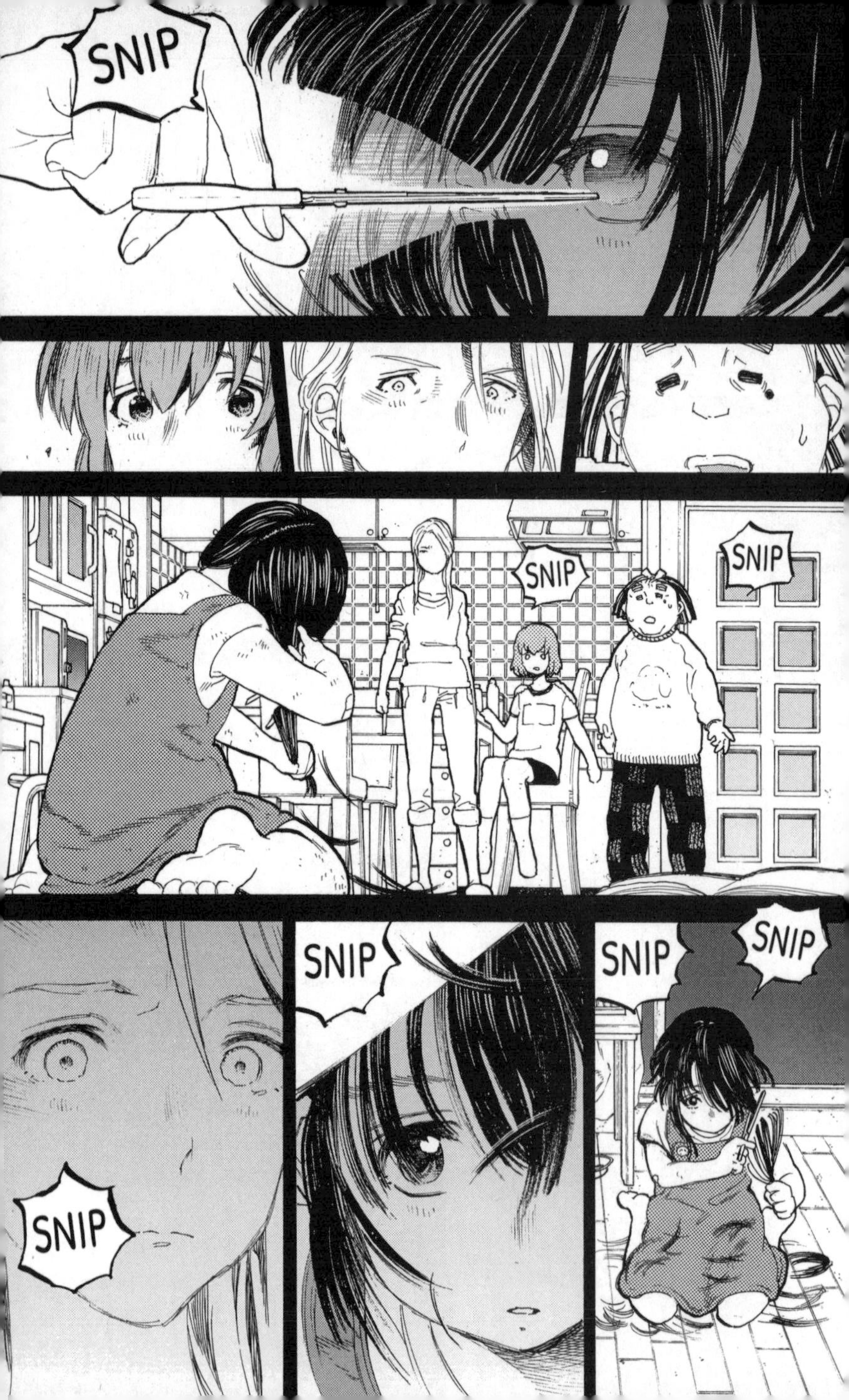
SNIP
SNIP
SNIP
SNIP
SNIP
SNIP
SNIP

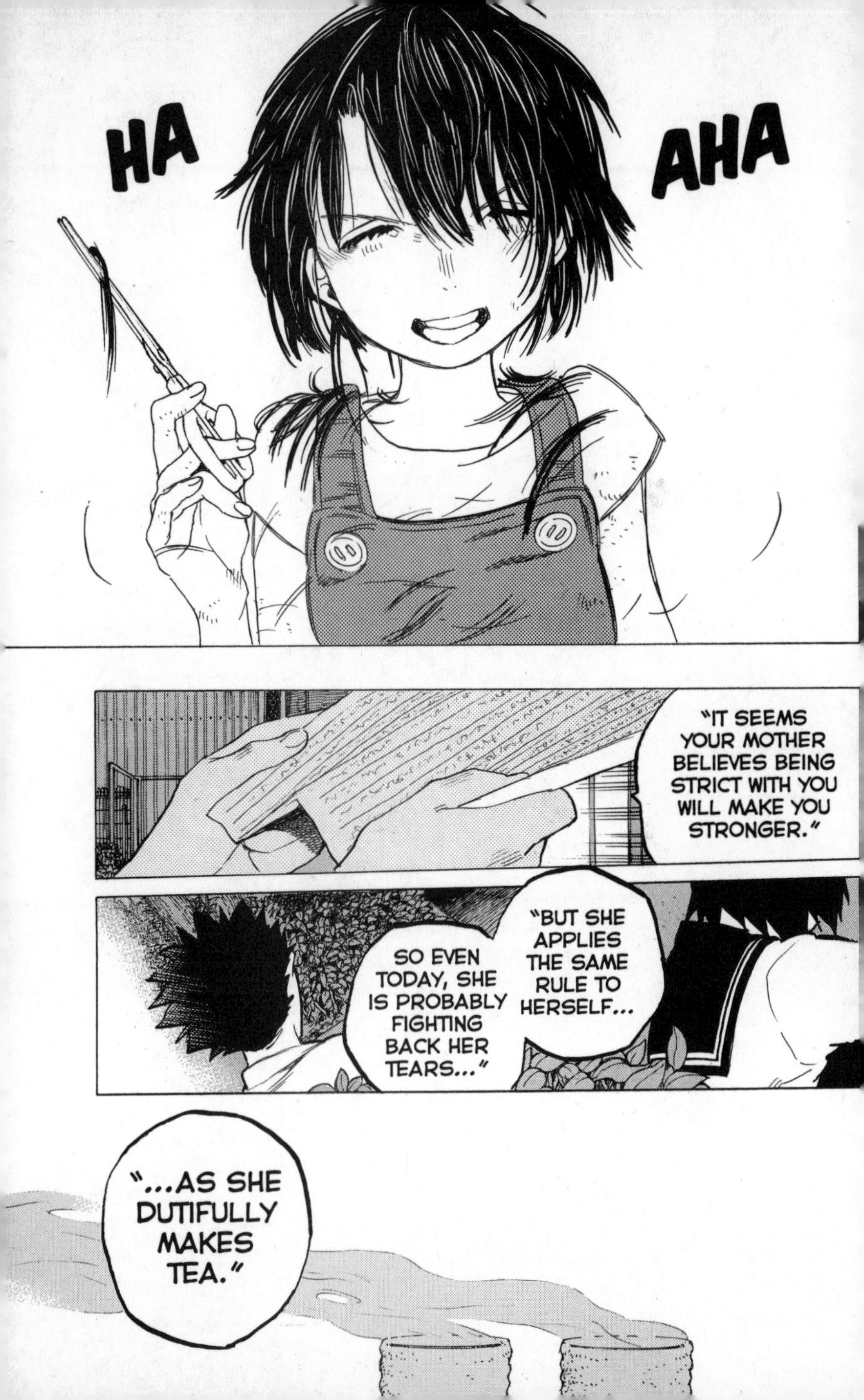
HA AHA
"IT SEEMS YOUR MOTHER BELIEVES BEING STRICT WITH YOU WILL MAKE YOU STRONGER."
"BUT SHE APPLIES THE SAME RULE TO HERSELF...
SO EVEN TODAY, SHE IS PROBABLY FIGHTING BACK HER TEARS..."
"...AS SHE DUTIFULLY MAKES TEA."

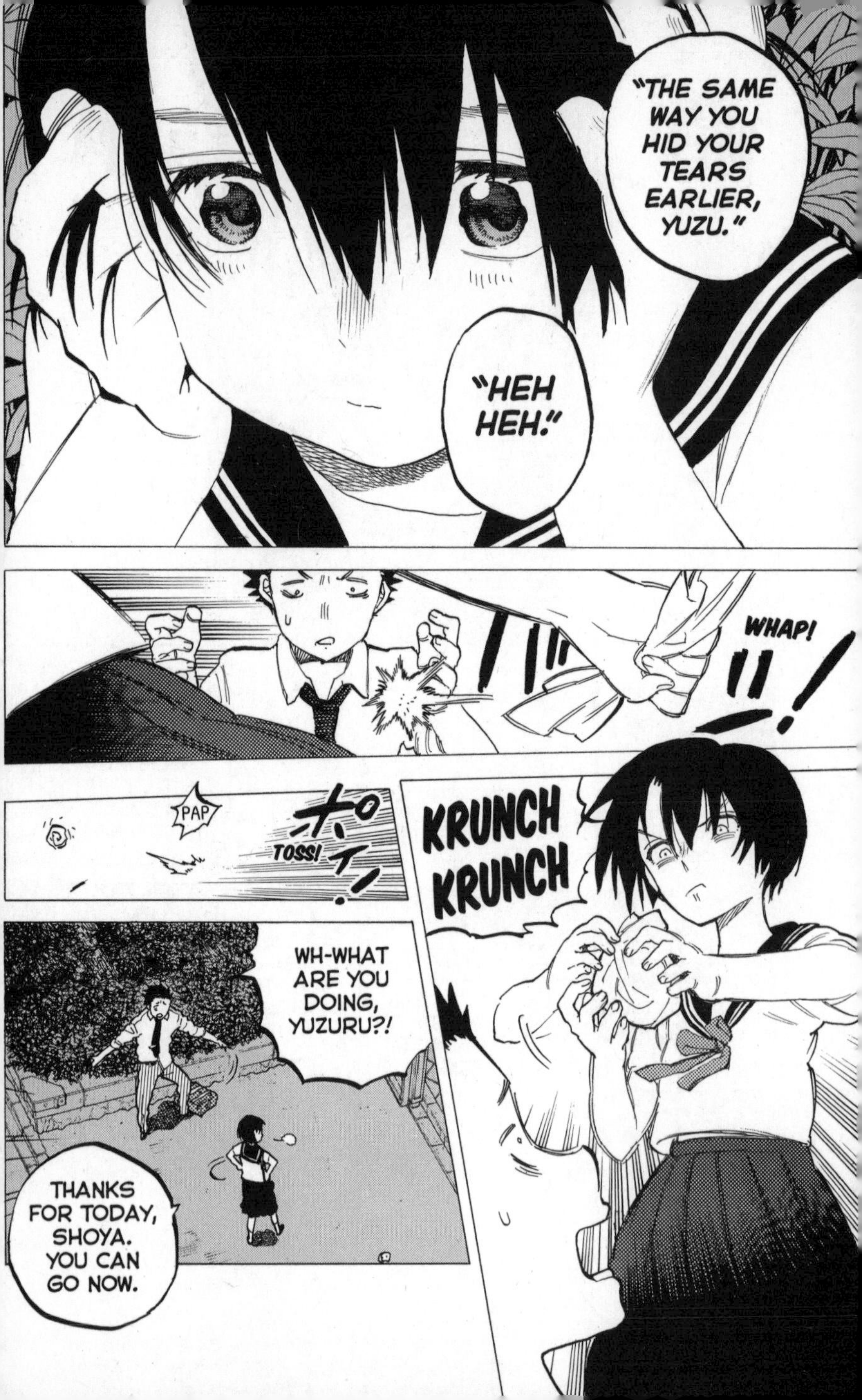
"THE SAME WAY YOU HID YOUR TEARS EARLIER, YUZU."
"HEH HEH."
WHAP!
KRUNCH KRUNCH
PAP
TOSS!
WH-WHAT ARE YOU DOING, YUZURU?!
THANKS FOR TODAY, SHOYA. YOU CAN GO NOW.

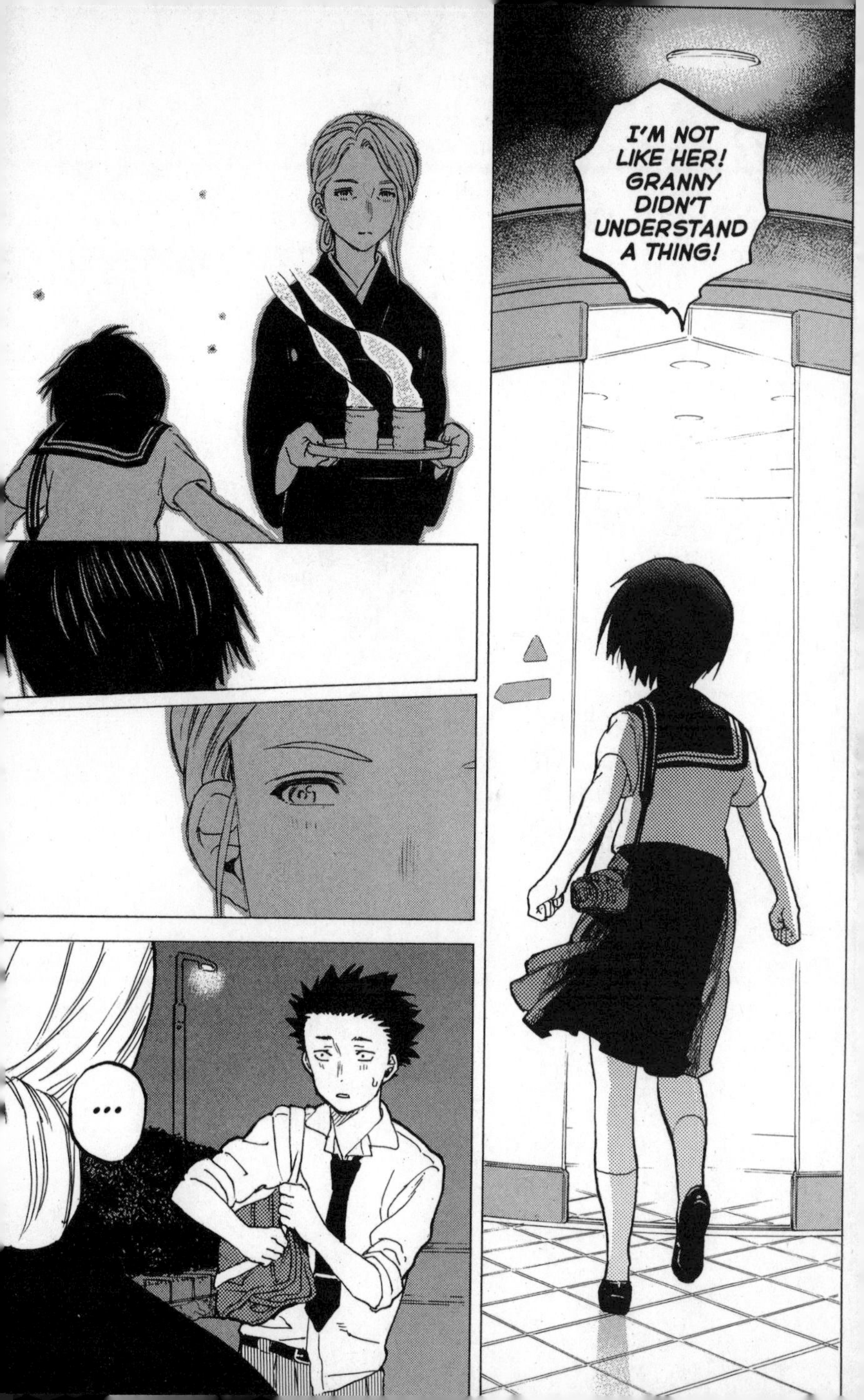
I'M NOT LIKE HER! GRANNY DIDN'T UNDERSTAND A THING!
...

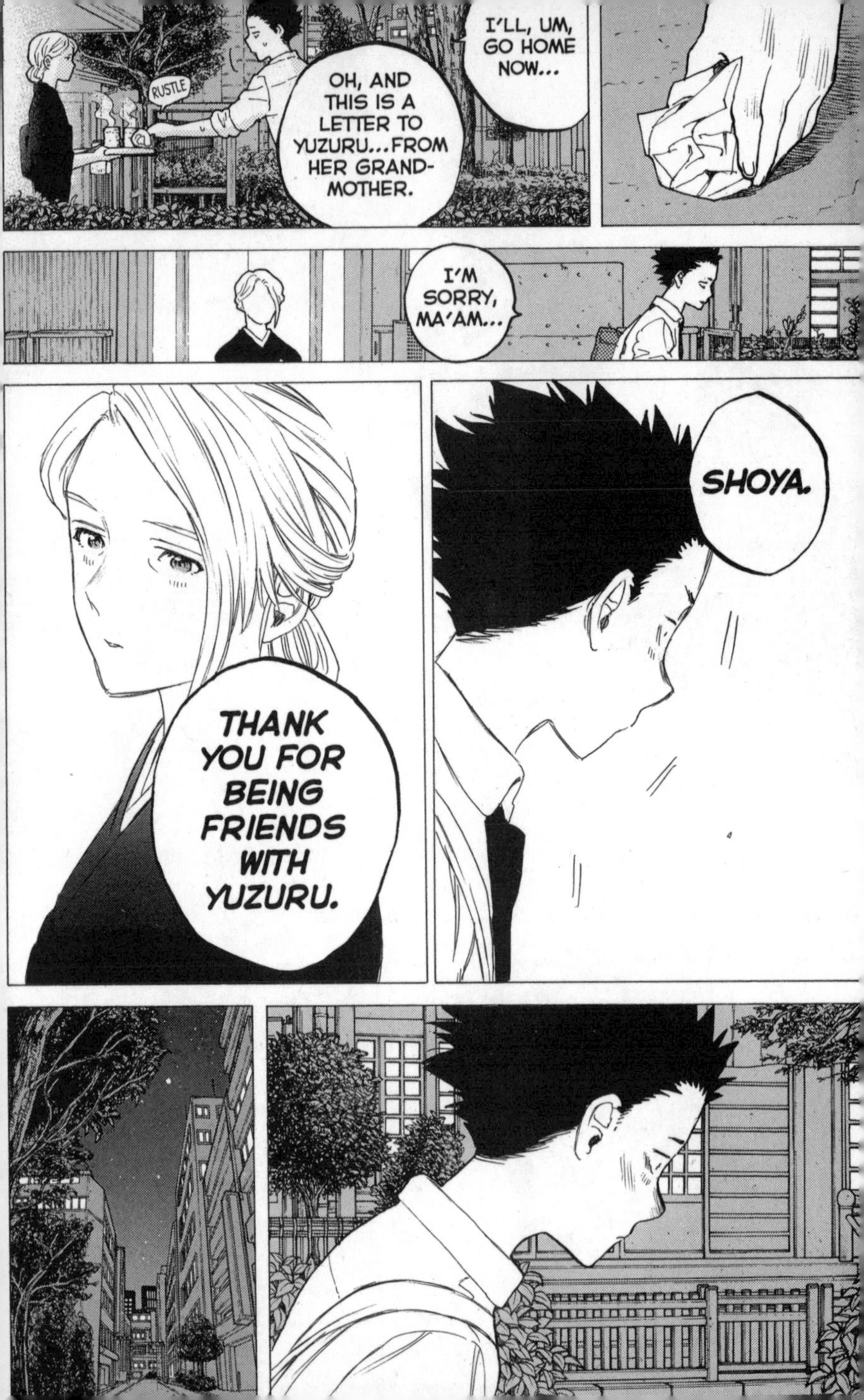
I'LL, UM, GO HOME NOW...
OH, AND THIS IS A LETTER TO YUZURU...FROM HER GRAND-MOTHER.
RUSTLE
I'M SORRY, MA'AM...
SHOYA.
THANK YOU FOR BEING FRIENDS WITH YUZURU.

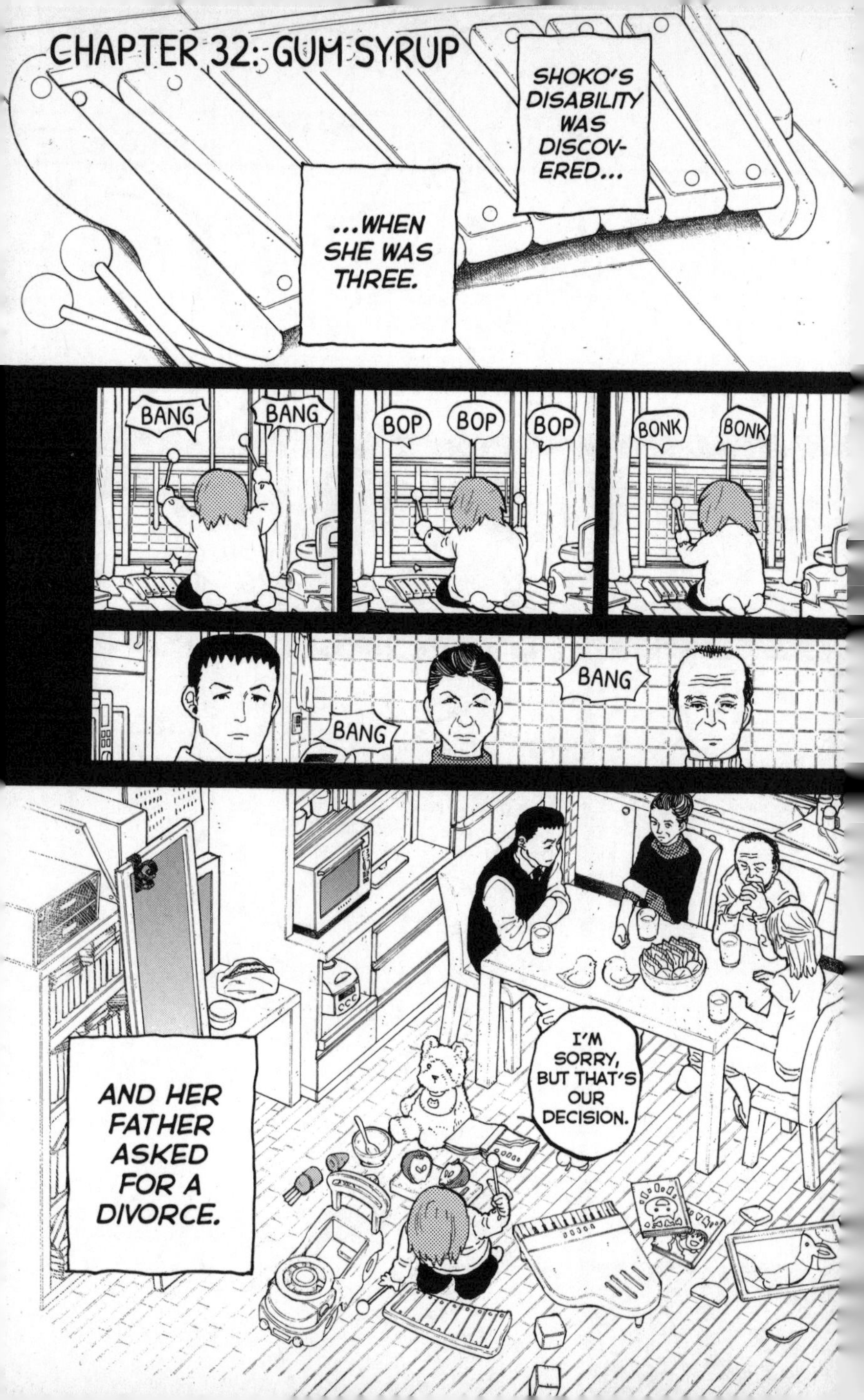
CHAPTER 32: GUM SYRUP
SHOKO'S DISABILITY WAS DISCOVERED...
...WHEN SHE WAS THREE.
BONK
BONK
BOP
BOP
BOP
BANG
BANG
BANG
BANG
I'M SORRY, BUT THAT'S OUR DECISION.
AND HER FATHER ASKED FOR A DIVORCE.

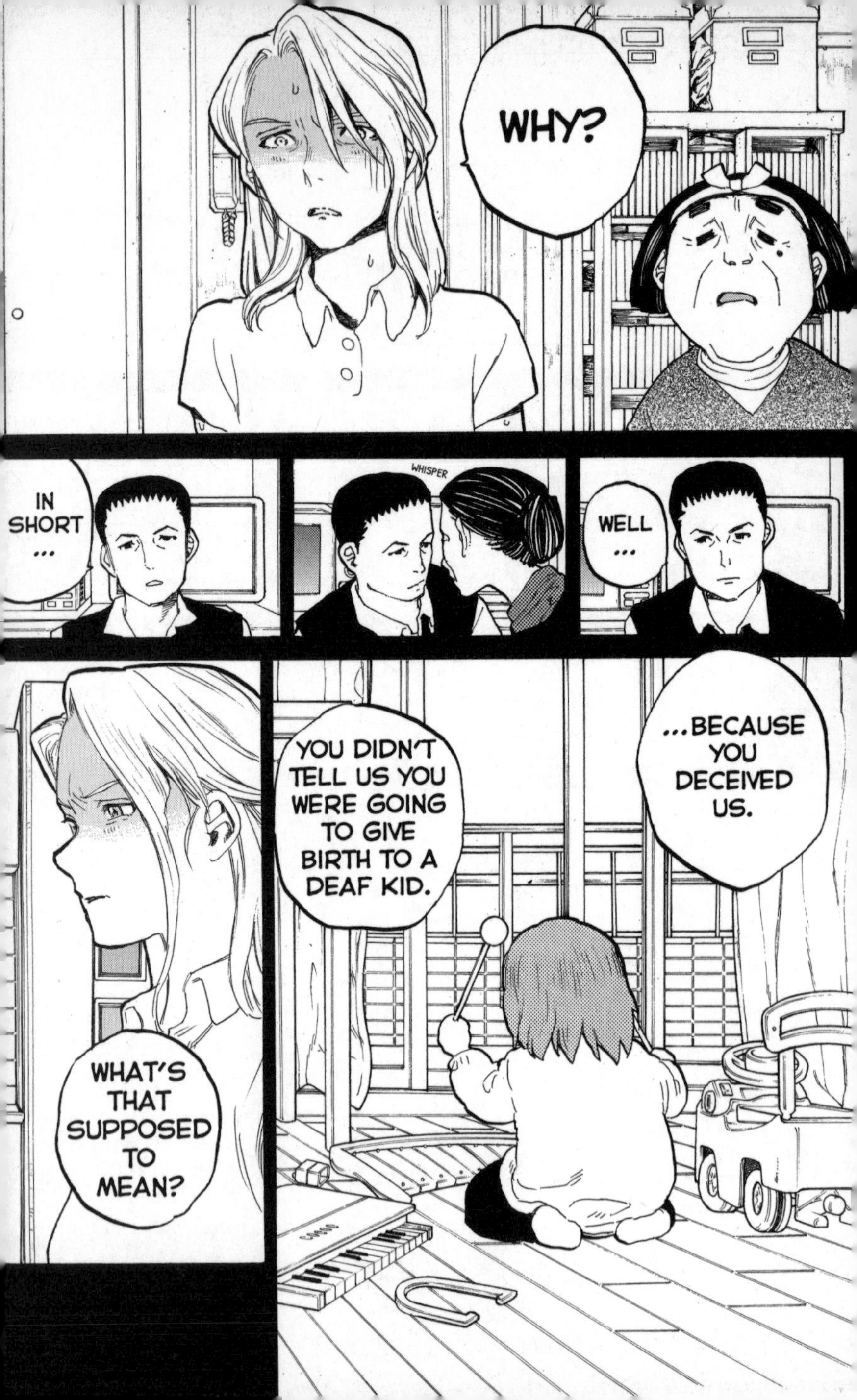
WHY?
WELL ...
WHISPER
IN SHORT ...
...BECAUSE YOU DECEIVED US.
YOU DIDN'T TELL US YOU WERE GOING TO GIVE BIRTH TO A DEAF KID.
WHAT'S THAT SUPPOSED TO MEAN?

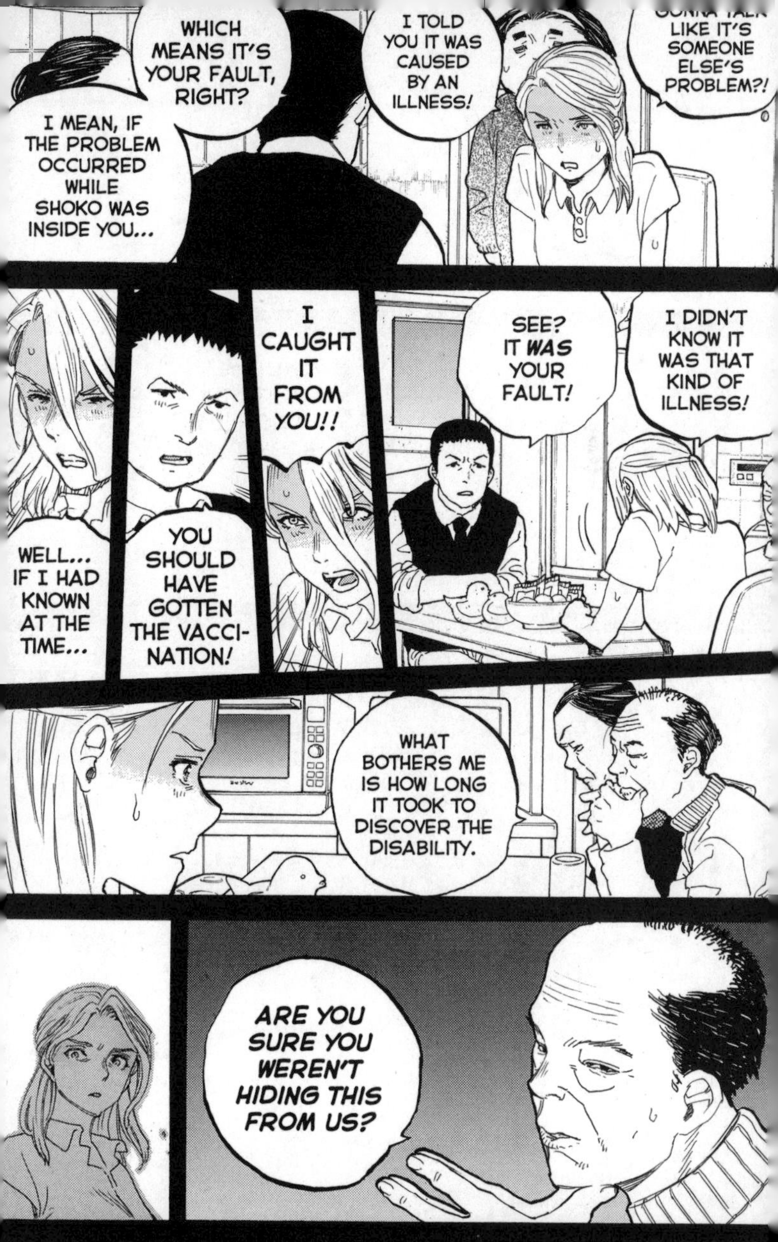
LIKE IT'S SOMEONE ELSE'S PROBLEM?!
I TOLD YOU IT WAS CAUSED BY AN ILLNESS!
WHICH MEANS IT'S YOUR FAULT, RIGHT?
I MEAN, IF THE PROBLEM OCCURRED WHILE SHOKO WAS INSIDE YOU...
I DIDN'T KNOW IT WAS THAT KIND OF ILLNESS!
SEE? IT *WAS* YOUR FAULT!
I CAUGHT IT FROM *YOU*!!
YOU SHOULD HAVE GOTTEN THE VACCINATION!
WELL... IF I HAD KNOWN AT THE TIME...
WHAT BOTHERS ME IS HOW LONG IT TOOK TO DISCOVER THE DISABILITY.
ARE YOU SURE YOU WEREN'T HIDING THIS FROM US?

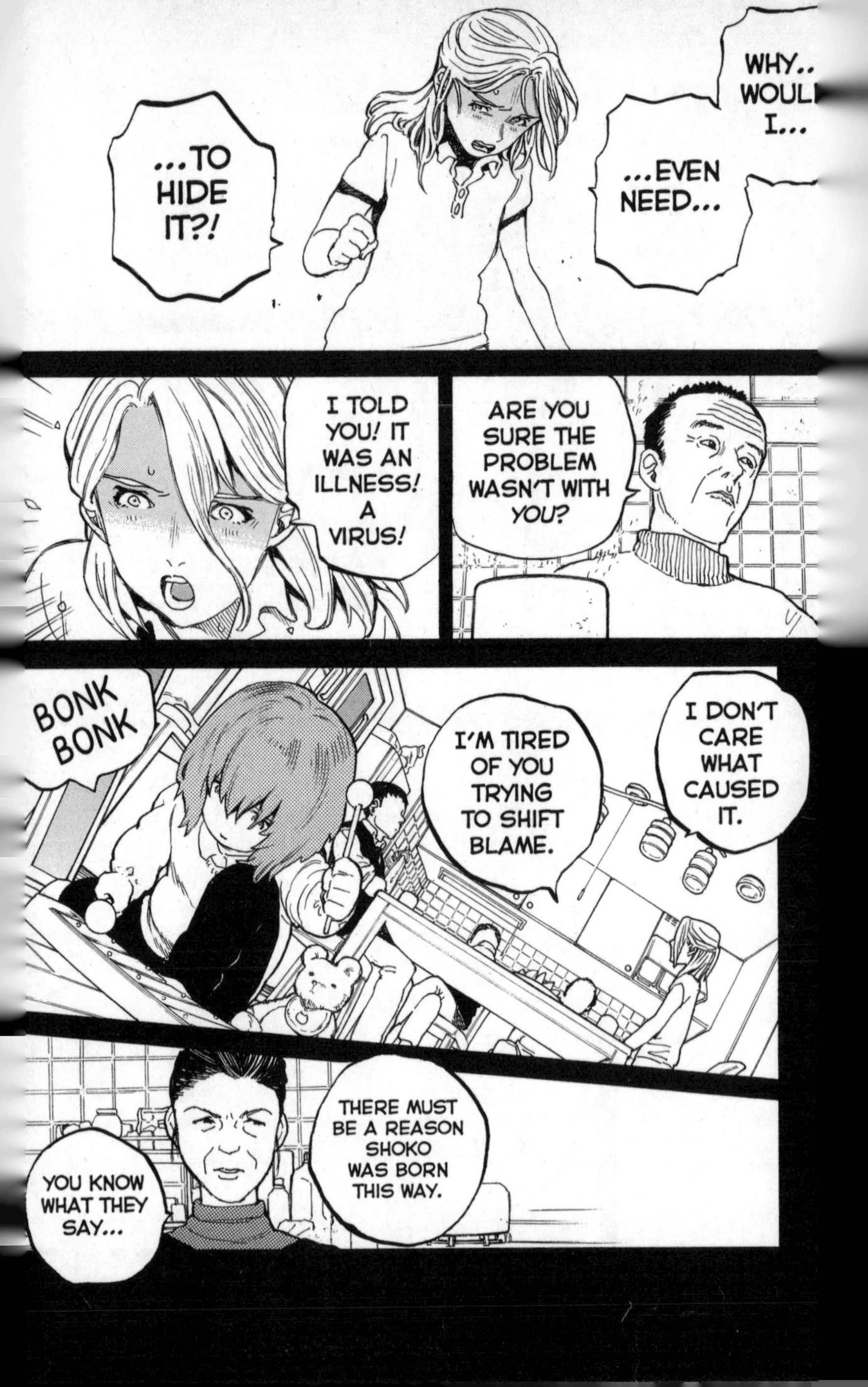
WHY.. WOUL I...
...EVEN NEED...
...TO HIDE IT?!
ARE YOU SURE THE PROBLEM WASN'T WITH *YOU*?
I TOLD YOU! IT WAS AN ILLNESS! A VIRUS!
I DON'T CARE WHAT CAUSED IT.
I'M TIRED OF YOU TRYING TO SHIFT BLAME.
BONK BONK
THERE MUST BE A REASON SHOKO WAS BORN THIS WAY.
YOU KNOW WHAT THEY SAY...

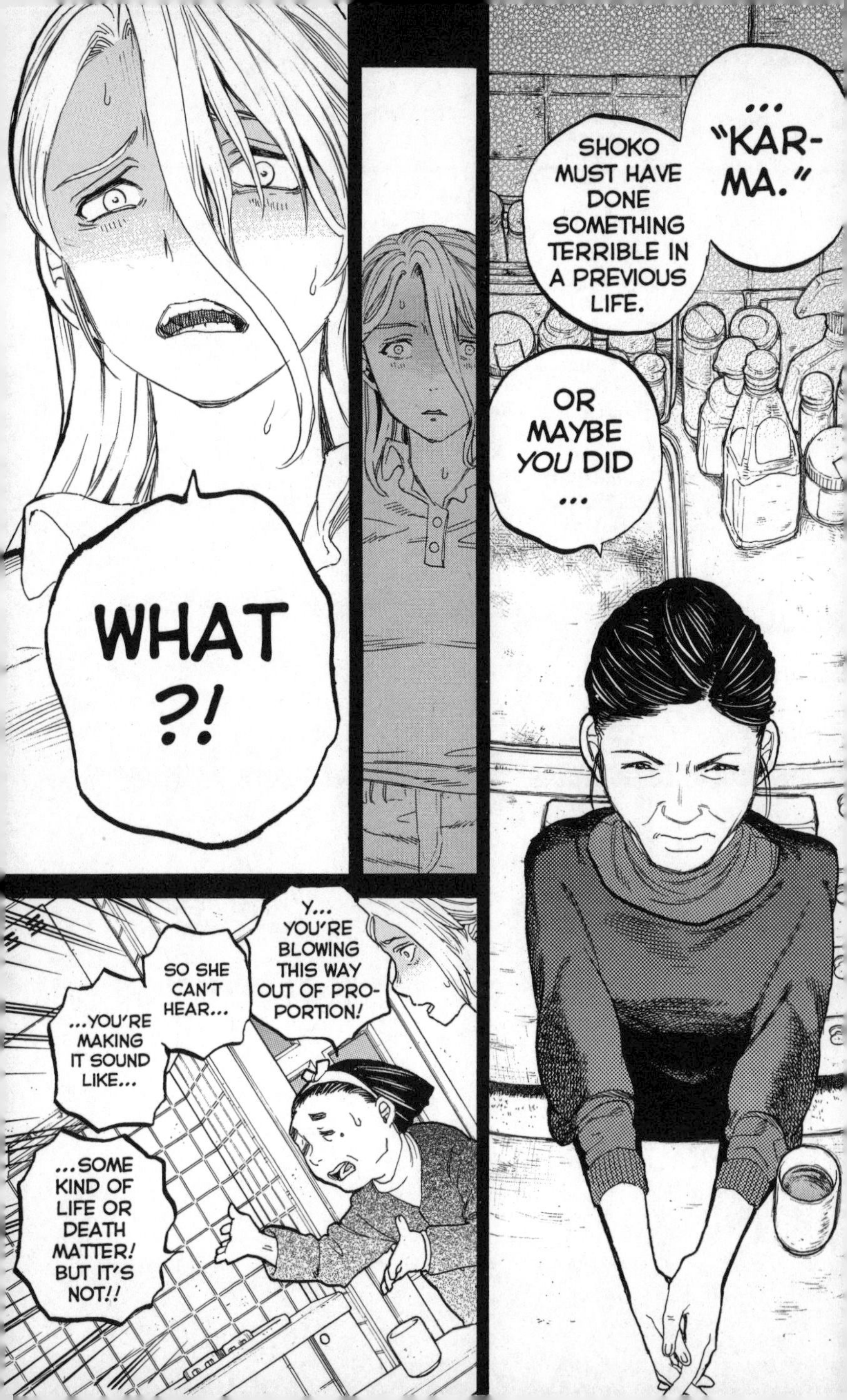
... "KAR-MA."
SHOKO MUST HAVE DONE SOMETHING TERRIBLE IN A PREVIOUS LIFE.
OR MAYBE *YOU* DID ...
WHAT ?!
Y... YOU'RE BLOWING THIS WAY OUT OF PRO-PORTION!
SO SHE CAN'T HEAR...
...YOU'RE MAKING IT SOUND LIKE...
...SOME KIND OF LIFE OR DEATH MATTER! BUT IT'S NOT!!

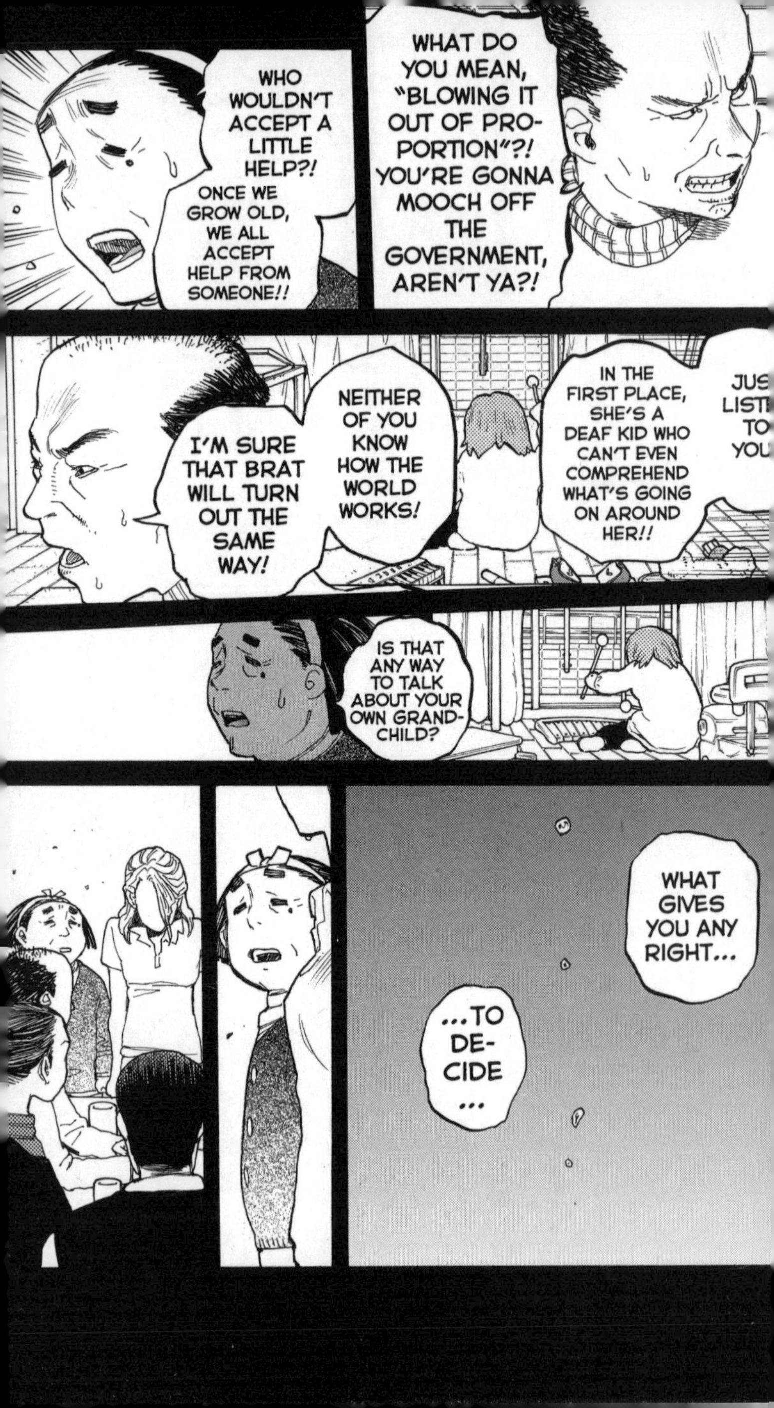
WHAT DO YOU MEAN, "BLOWING IT OUT OF PRO-PORTION"?! YOU'RE GONNA MOOCH OFF THE GOVERNMENT, AREN'T YA?!
WHO WOULDN'T ACCEPT A LITTLE HELP?!
ONCE WE GROW OLD, WE ALL ACCEPT HELP FROM SOMEONE!!
JUS LISTE TO YOU
IN THE FIRST PLACE, SHE'S A DEAF KID WHO CAN'T EVEN COMPREHEND WHAT'S GOING ON AROUND HER!!
NEITHER OF YOU KNOW HOW THE WORLD WORKS!
I'M SURE THAT BRAT WILL TURN OUT THE SAME WAY!
IS THAT ANY WAY TO TALK ABOUT YOUR OWN GRAND-CHILD?
WHAT GIVES YOU ANY RIGHT...
...TO DECIDE...

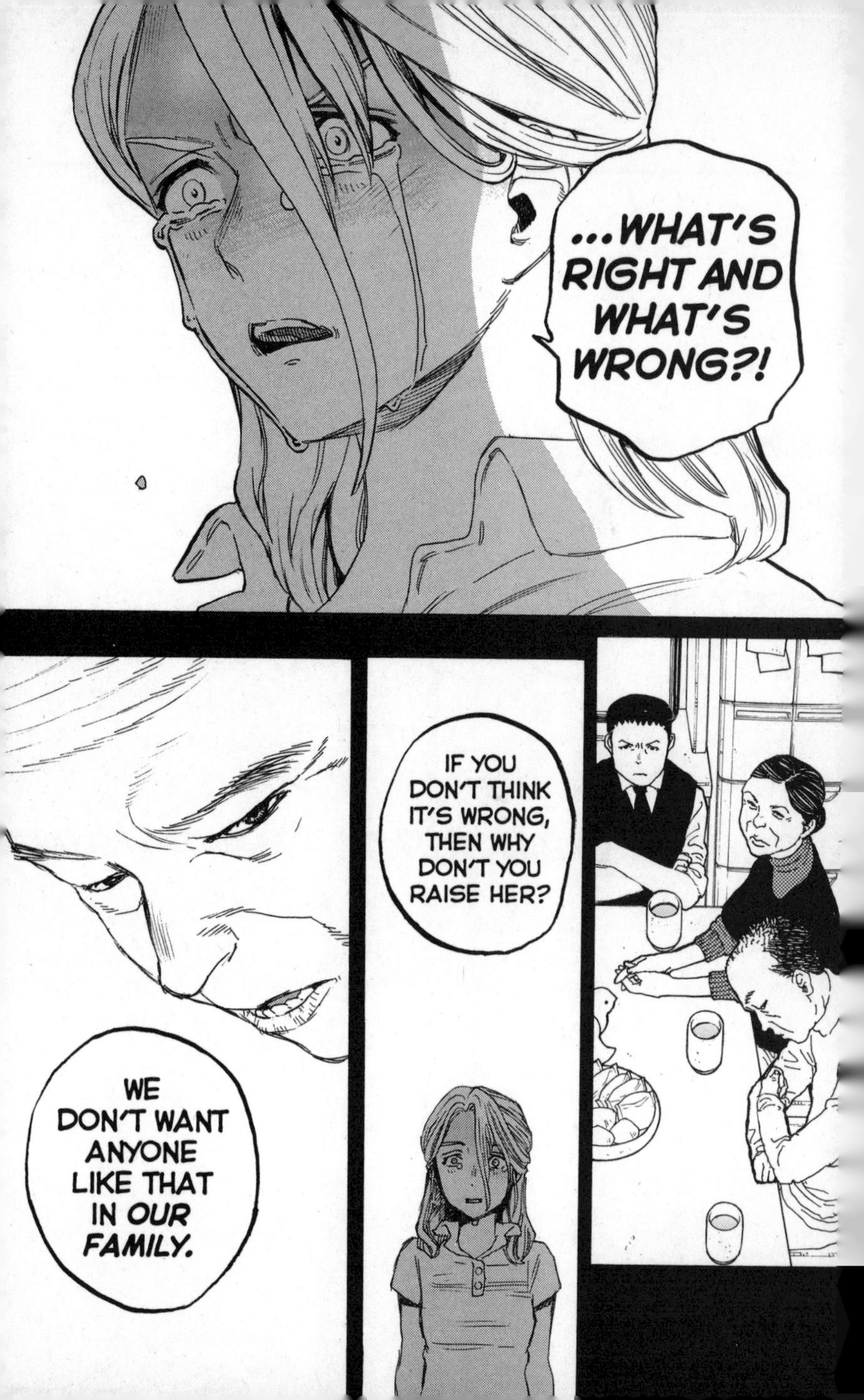
...WHAT'S RIGHT AND WHAT'S WRONG?!
IF YOU DON'T THINK IT'S WRONG, THEN WHY DON'T YOU RAISE HER?
WE DON'T WANT ANYONE LIKE THAT IN *OUR FAMILY.*

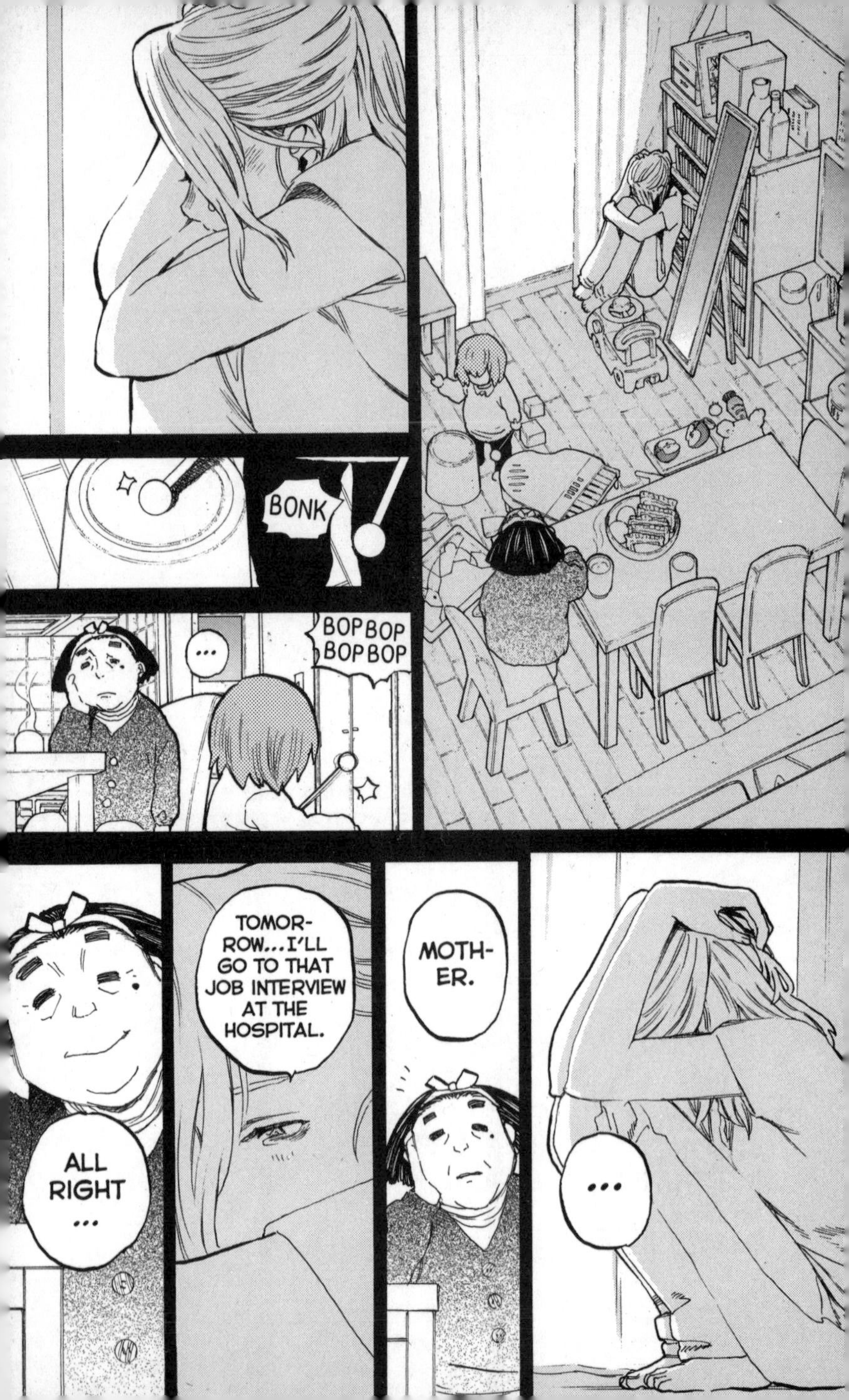
BONK
BOP BOP BOP BOP
...
...
MOTH-ER.
TOMOR-ROW...I'LL GO TO THAT JOB INTERVIEW AT THE HOSPITAL.
ALL RIGHT ...

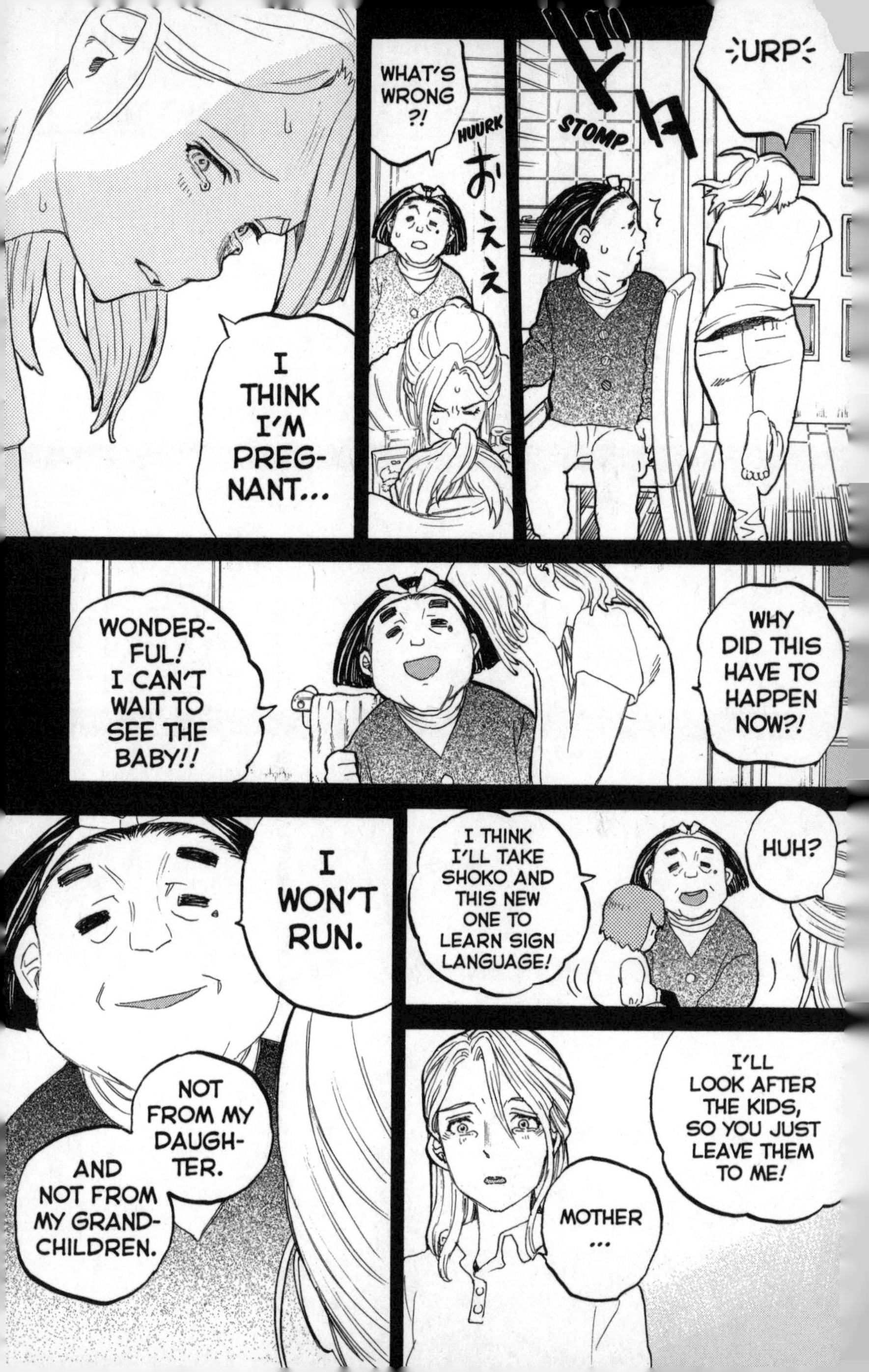

URP
ドタ
STOMP
WHAT'S WRONG?!
HUURK
おえぇ
I THINK I'M PREGNANT...
WHY DID THIS HAVE TO HAPPEN NOW?!
WONDERFUL! I CAN'T WAIT TO SEE THE BABY!!
HUH?
I THINK I'LL TAKE SHOKO AND THIS NEW ONE TO LEARN SIGN LANGUAGE!
I'LL LOOK AFTER THE KIDS, SO YOU JUST LEAVE THEM TO ME!
MOTHER...
I WON'T RUN.
NOT FROM MY DAUGHTER.
AND NOT FROM MY GRANDCHILDREN.

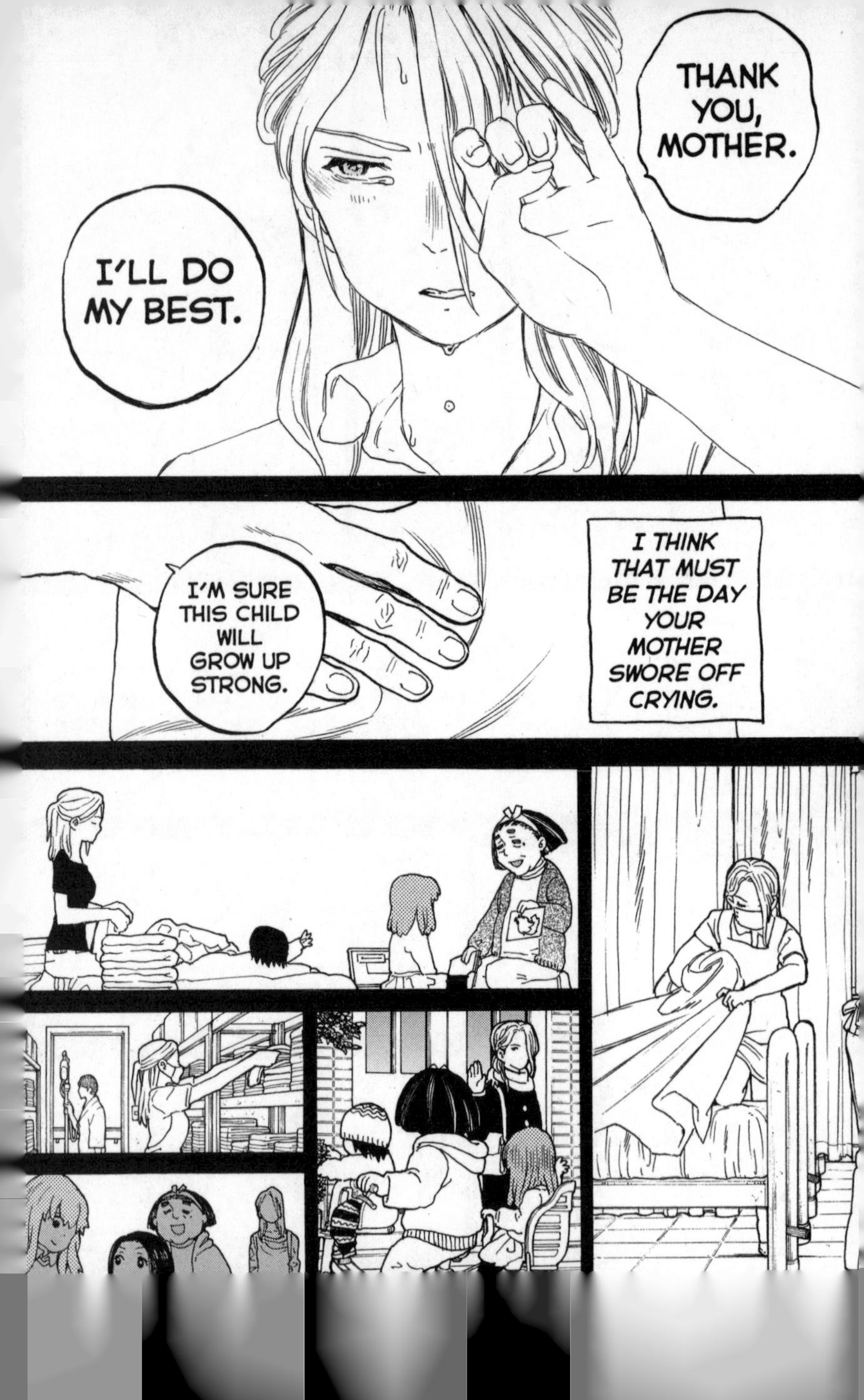
THANK YOU, MOTHER.
I'LL DO MY BEST.
I THINK THAT MUST BE THE DAY YOUR MOTHER SWORE OFF CRYING.
I'M SURE THIS CHILD WILL GROW UP STRONG.

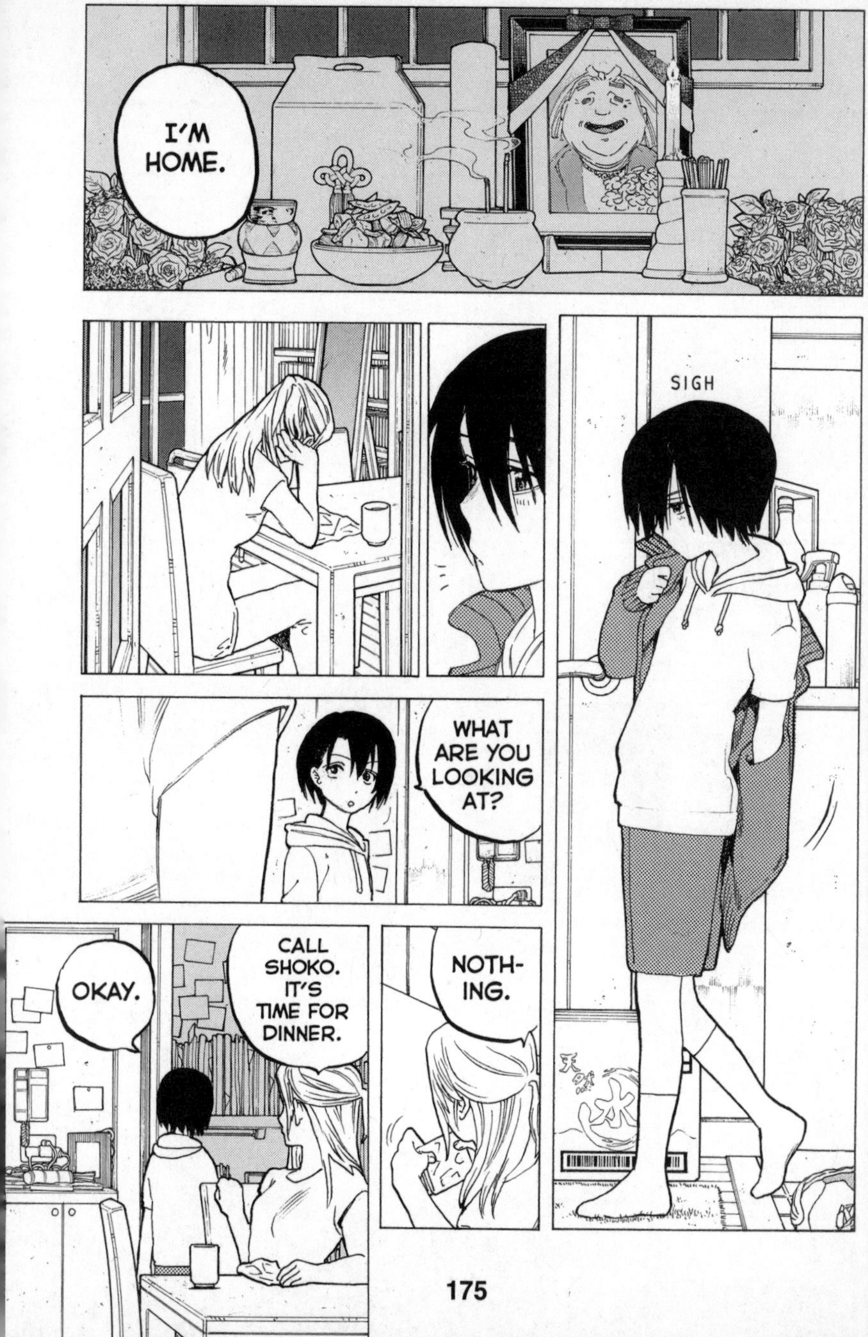
I'M HOME.
SIGH
WHAT ARE YOU LOOKING AT?
NOTH-ING.
CALL SHOKO. IT'S TIME FOR DINNER.
OKAY.

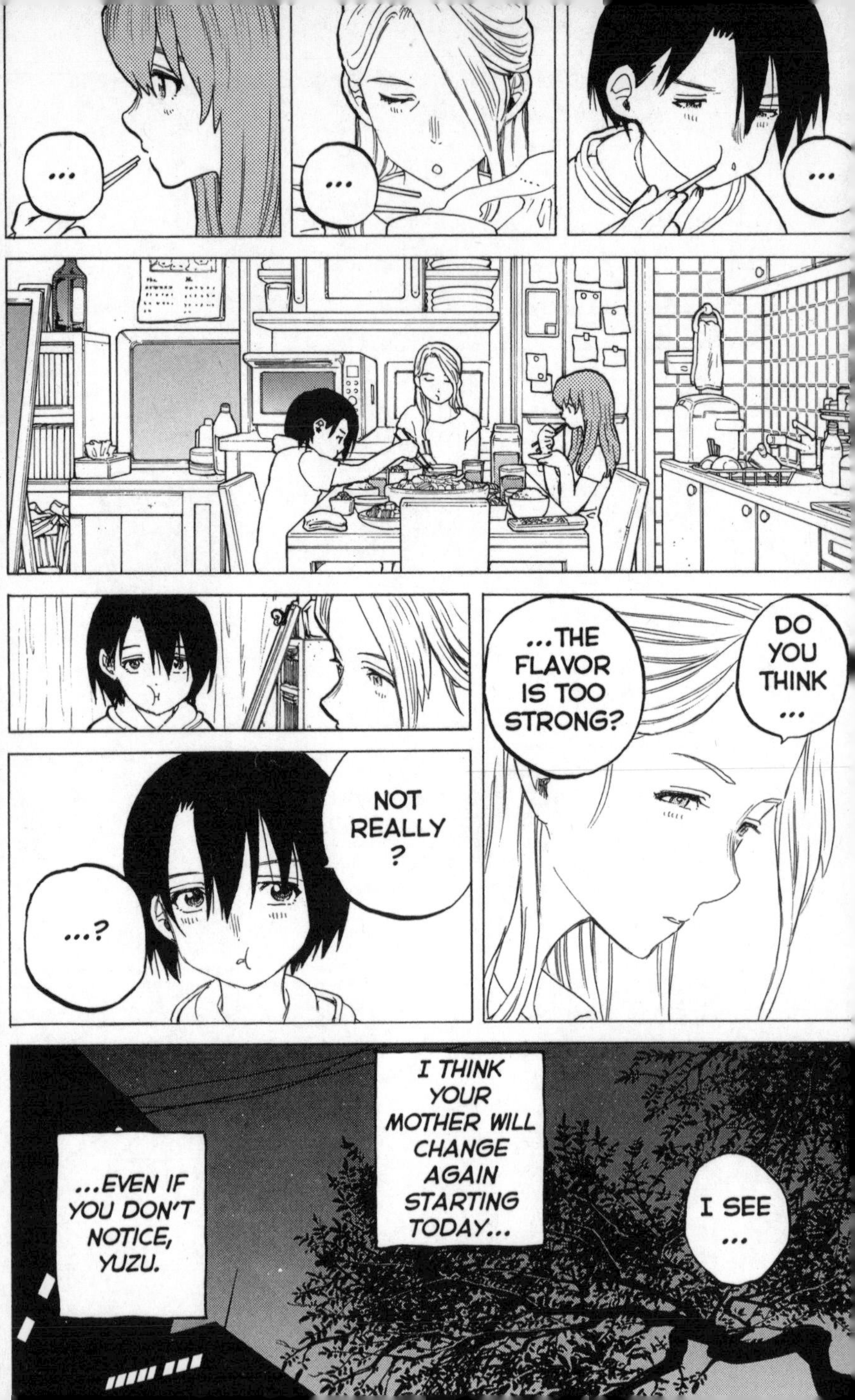
...
...
...
DO YOU THINK ...
...THE FLAVOR IS TOO STRONG?
NOT REALLY ?
...?
I SEE ...
I THINK YOUR MOTHER WILL CHANGE AGAIN STARTING TODAY...
...EVEN IF YOU DON'T NOTICE, YUZU.

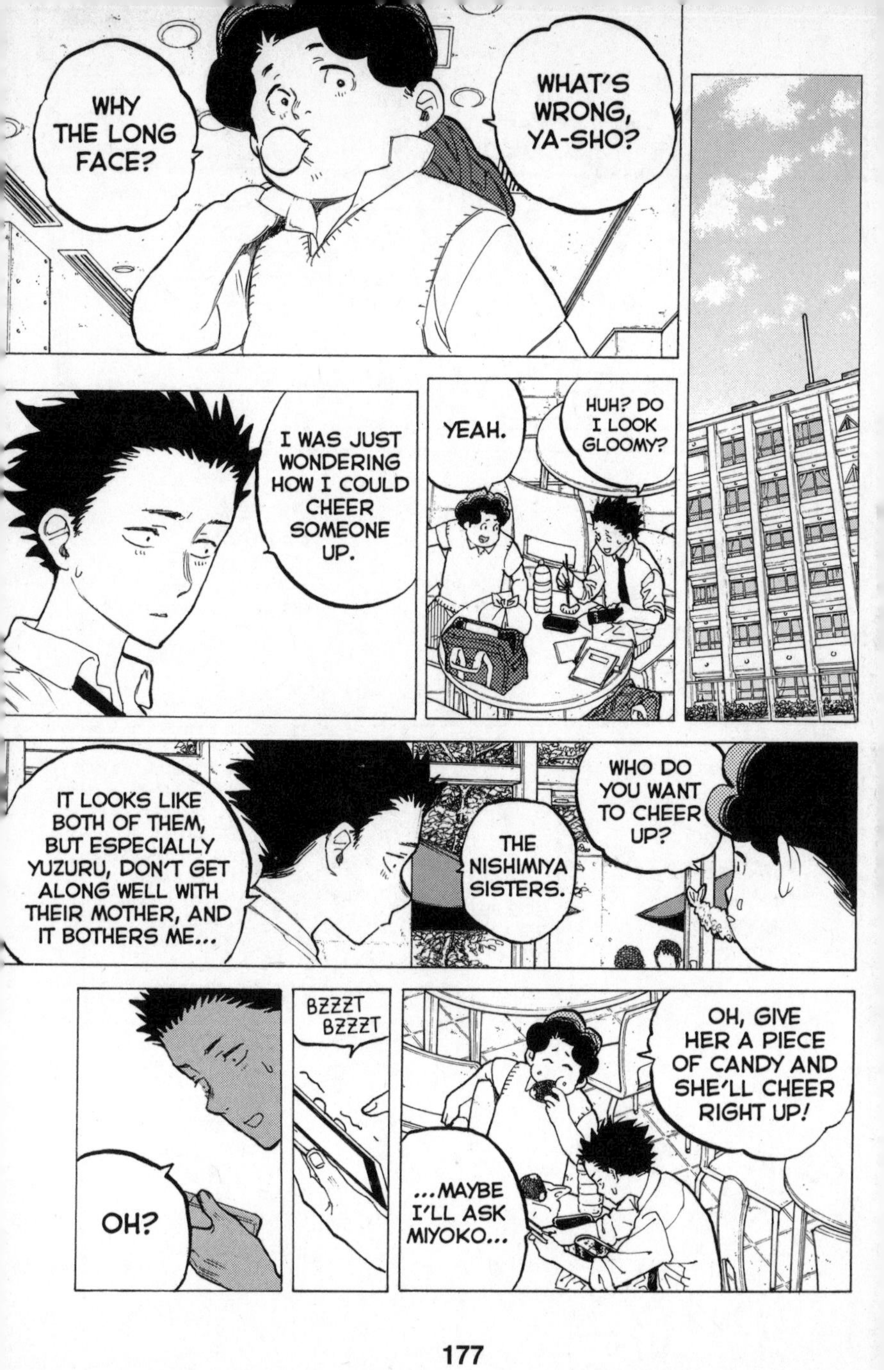
WHAT'S WRONG, YA-SHO?
WHY THE LONG FACE?
HUH? DO I LOOK GLOOMY?
YEAH.
I WAS JUST WONDERING HOW I COULD CHEER SOMEONE UP.
WHO DO YOU WANT TO CHEER UP?
THE NISHIMIYA SISTERS.
IT LOOKS LIKE BOTH OF THEM, BUT ESPECIALLY YUZURU, DON'T GET ALONG WELL WITH THEIR MOTHER, AND IT BOTHERS ME...
OH, GIVE HER A PIECE OF CANDY AND SHE'LL CHEER RIGHT UP!
...MAYBE I'LL ASK MIYOKO...
BZZZT BZZZT
OH?

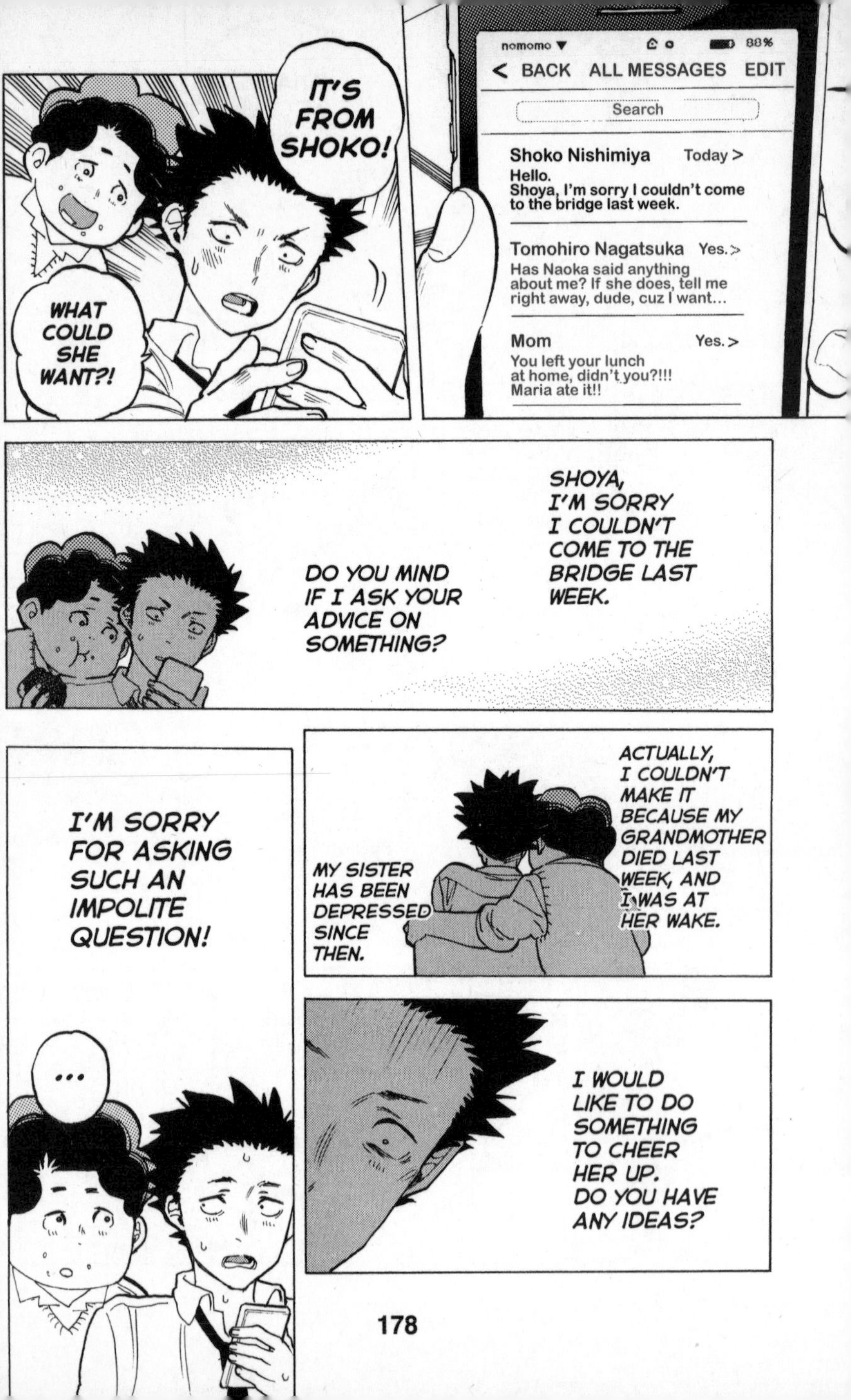
nomomo ▼ 88%
< BACK ALL MESSAGES EDIT
Search
Shoko Nishimiya Today >
Hello.
Shoya, I'm sorry I couldn't come to the bridge last week.
Tomohiro Nagatsuka Yes. >
Has Naoka said anything about me? If she does, tell me right away, dude, cuz I want…
Mom Yes. >
You left your lunch at home, didn't you?!!! Maria ate it!!
IT'S FROM SHOKO!
WHAT COULD SHE WANT?!
SHOYA, I'M SORRY I COULDN'T COME TO THE BRIDGE LAST WEEK.
DO YOU MIND IF I ASK YOUR ADVICE ON SOMETHING?
ACTUALLY, I COULDN'T MAKE IT BECAUSE MY GRANDMOTHER DIED LAST WEEK, AND I WAS AT HER WAKE.
MY SISTER HAS BEEN DEPRESSED SINCE THEN.
I WOULD LIKE TO DO SOMETHING TO CHEER HER UP. DO YOU HAVE ANY IDEAS?
I'M SORRY FOR ASKING SUCH AN IMPOLITE QUESTION!
...

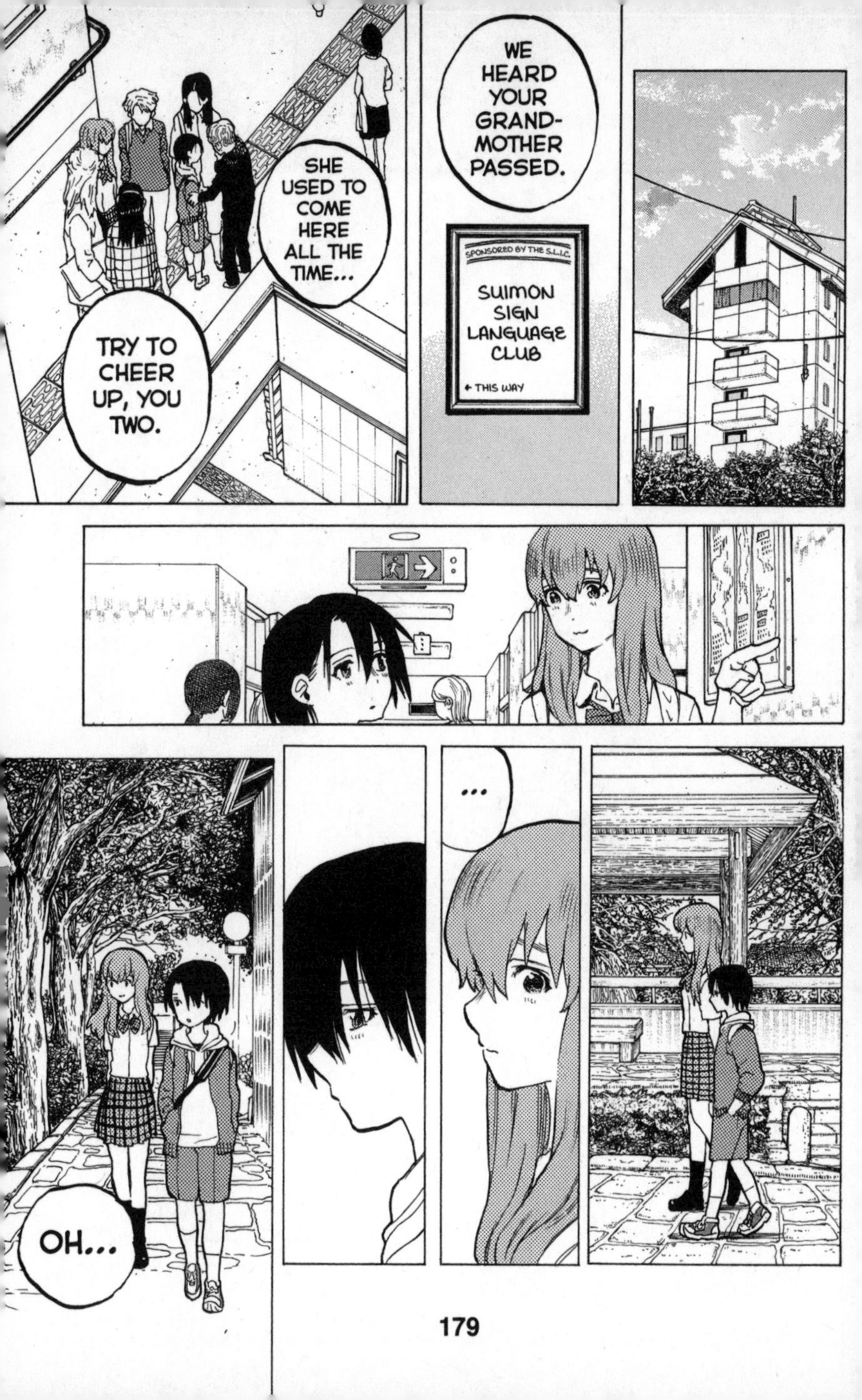
WE HEARD YOUR GRAND-MOTHER PASSED.
SPONSORED BY THE S.L.I.C.
SUIMON SIGN LANGUAGE CLUB
← THIS WAY
SHE USED TO COME HERE ALL THE TIME...
TRY TO CHEER UP, YOU TWO.
...
OH...

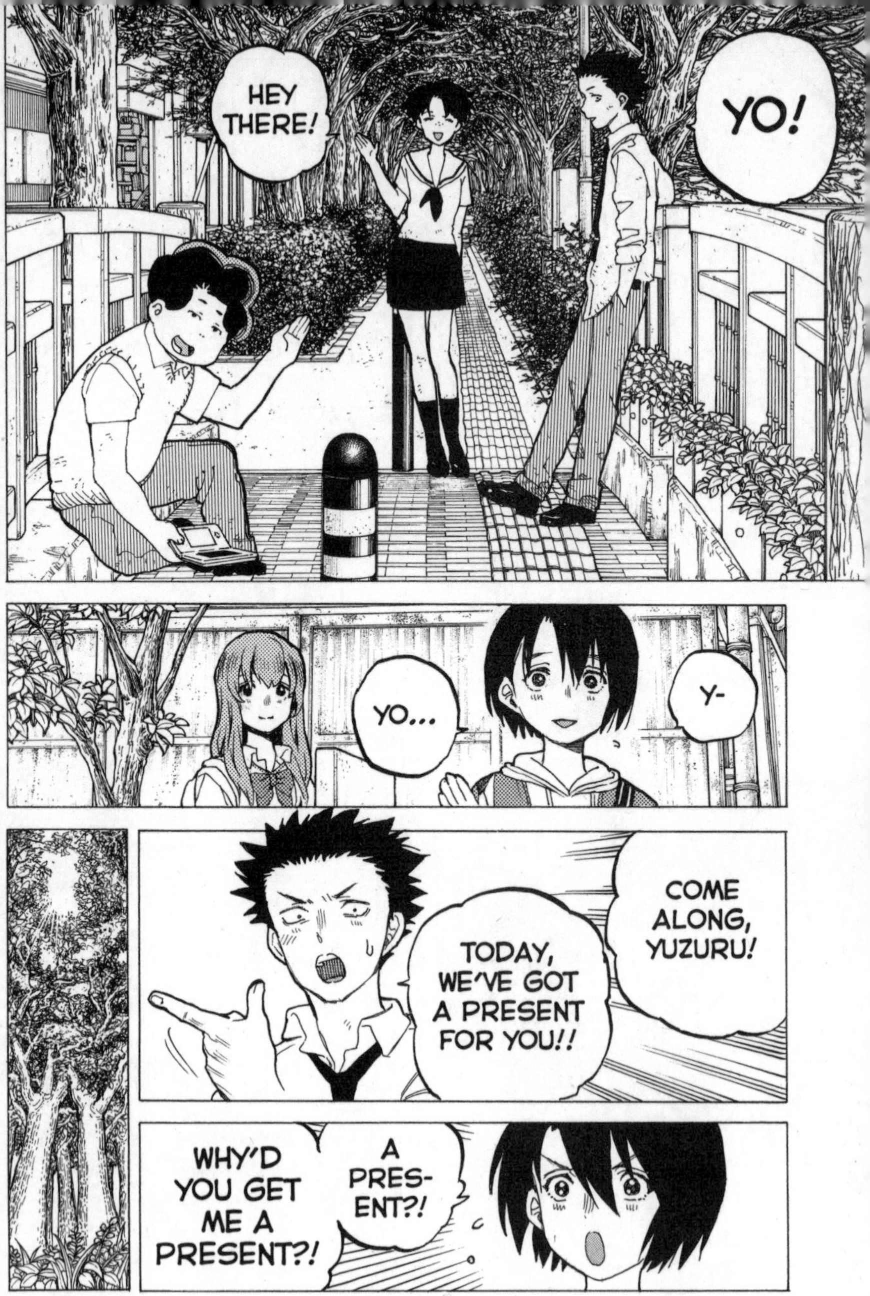
YO!
HEY THERE!
Y-
YO...
COME ALONG, YUZURU!
TODAY, WE'VE GOT A PRESENT FOR YOU!!
A PRES-ENT?!
WHY'D YOU GET ME A PRESENT?!

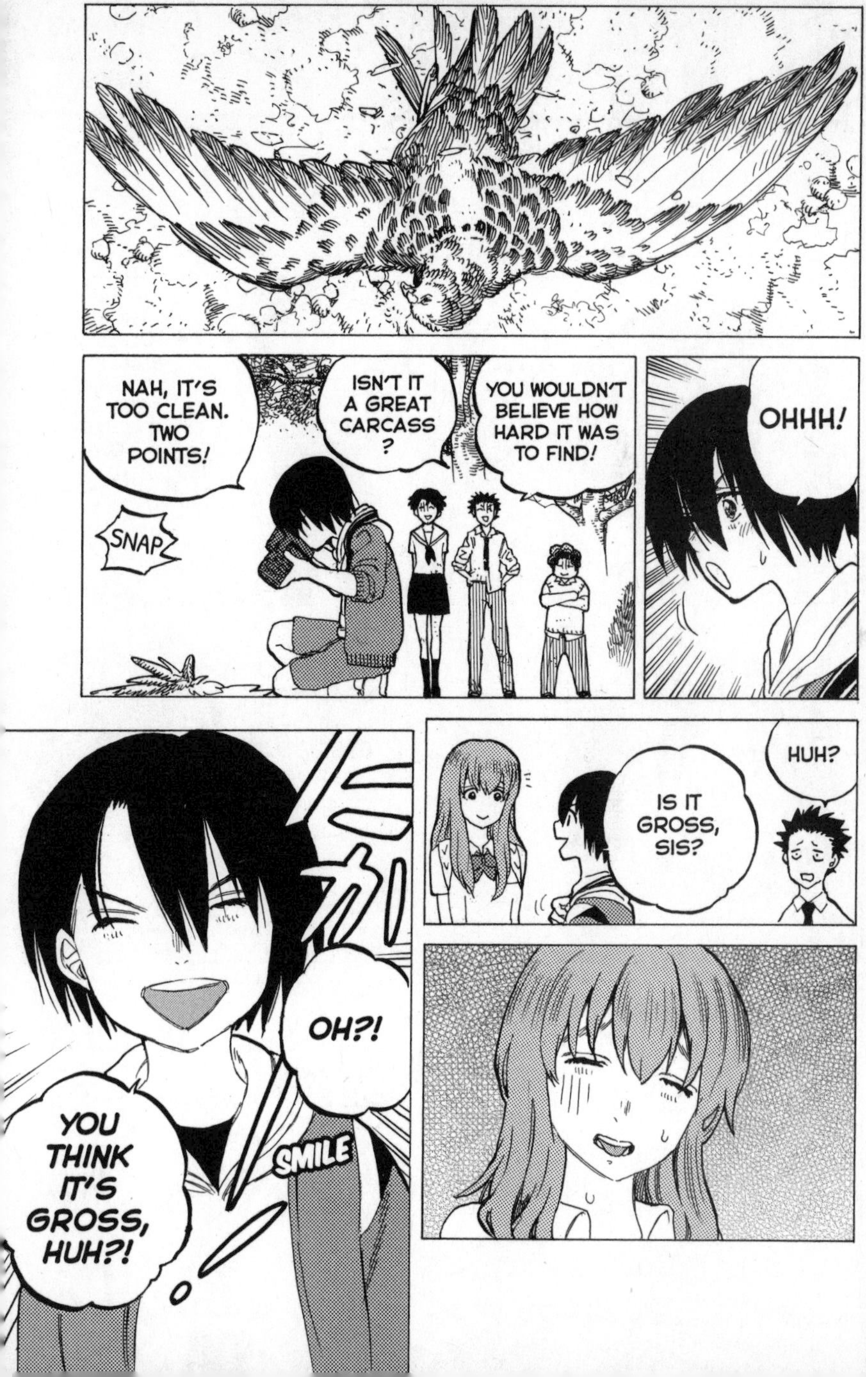
OHHH!
YOU WOULDN'T BELIEVE HOW HARD IT WAS TO FIND!
ISN'T IT A GREAT CARCASS?
NAH, IT'S TOO CLEAN. TWO POINTS!
SNAP
HUH?
IS IT GROSS, SIS?
OH?!
SMILE
YOU THINK IT'S GROSS, HUH?!

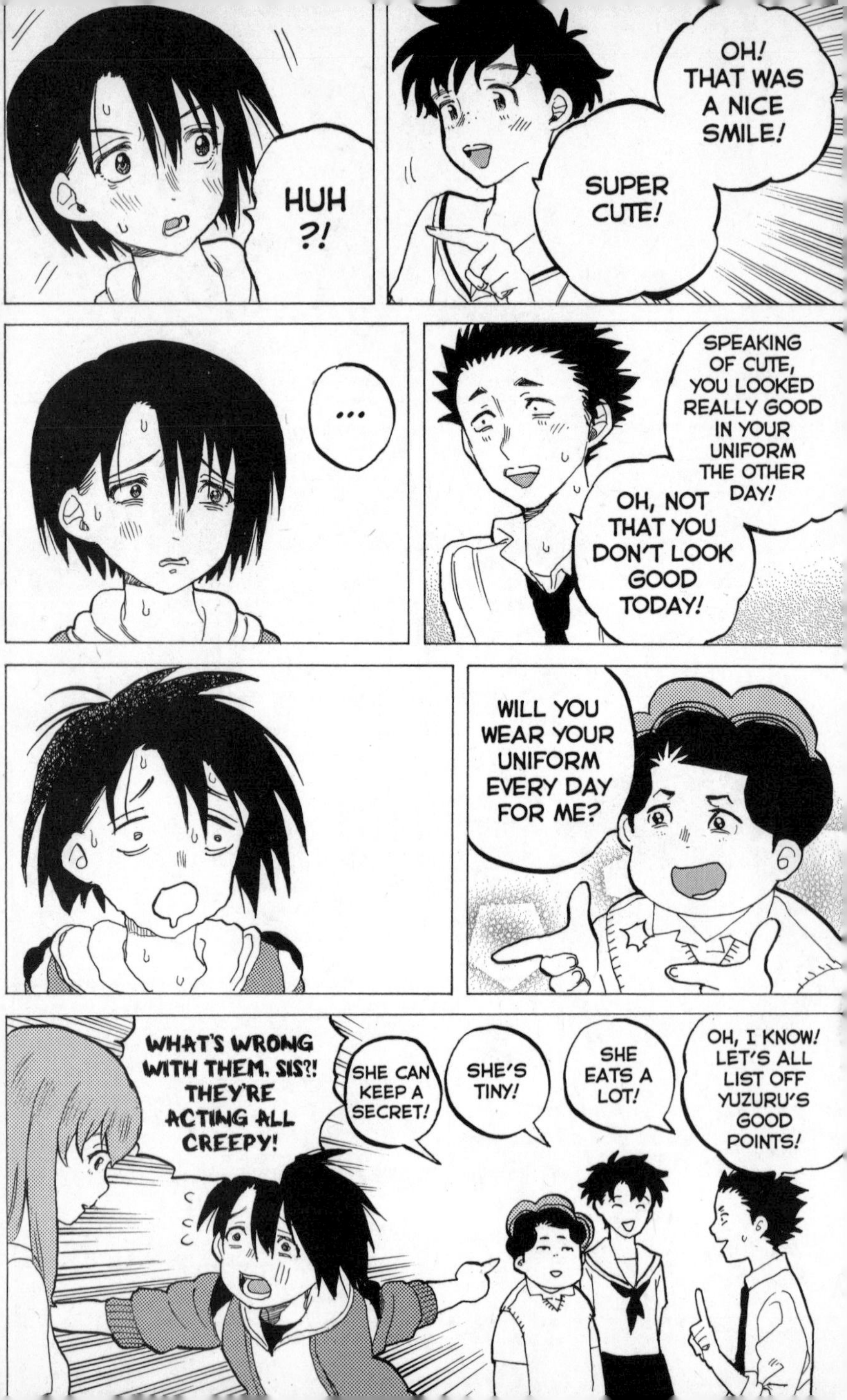
OH! THAT WAS A NICE SMILE!
SUPER CUTE!
HUH ?!
SPEAKING OF CUTE, YOU LOOKED REALLY GOOD IN YOUR UNIFORM THE OTHER DAY!
OH, NOT THAT YOU DON'T LOOK GOOD TODAY!
...
WILL YOU WEAR YOUR UNIFORM EVERY DAY FOR ME?
OH, I KNOW! LET'S ALL LIST OFF YUZURU'S GOOD POINTS!
SHE EATS A LOT!
SHE'S TINY!
SHE CAN KEEP A SECRET!
WHAT'S WRONG WITH THEM, SIS?! THEY'RE ACTING ALL CREEPY!

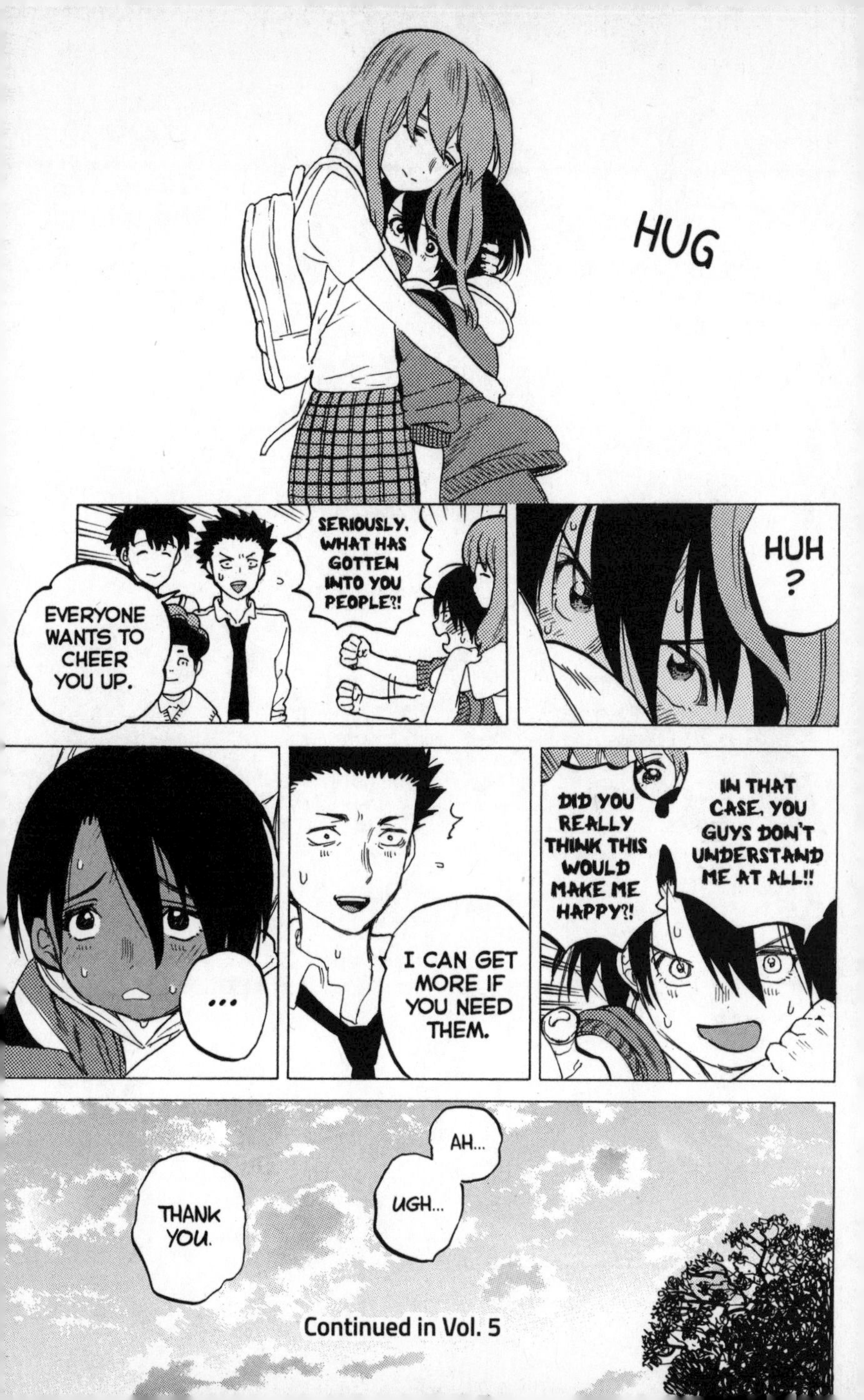
HUG
HUH ?
SERIOUSLY, WHAT HAS GOTTEN INTO YOU PEOPLE?!
EVERYONE WANTS TO CHEER YOU UP.
IN THAT CASE, YOU GUYS DON'T UNDERSTAND ME AT ALL!!
DID YOU REALLY THINK THIS WOULD MAKE ME HAPPY?!
I CAN GET MORE IF YOU NEED THEM.
...
AH...
UGH...
THANK YOU.
Continued in Vol. 5

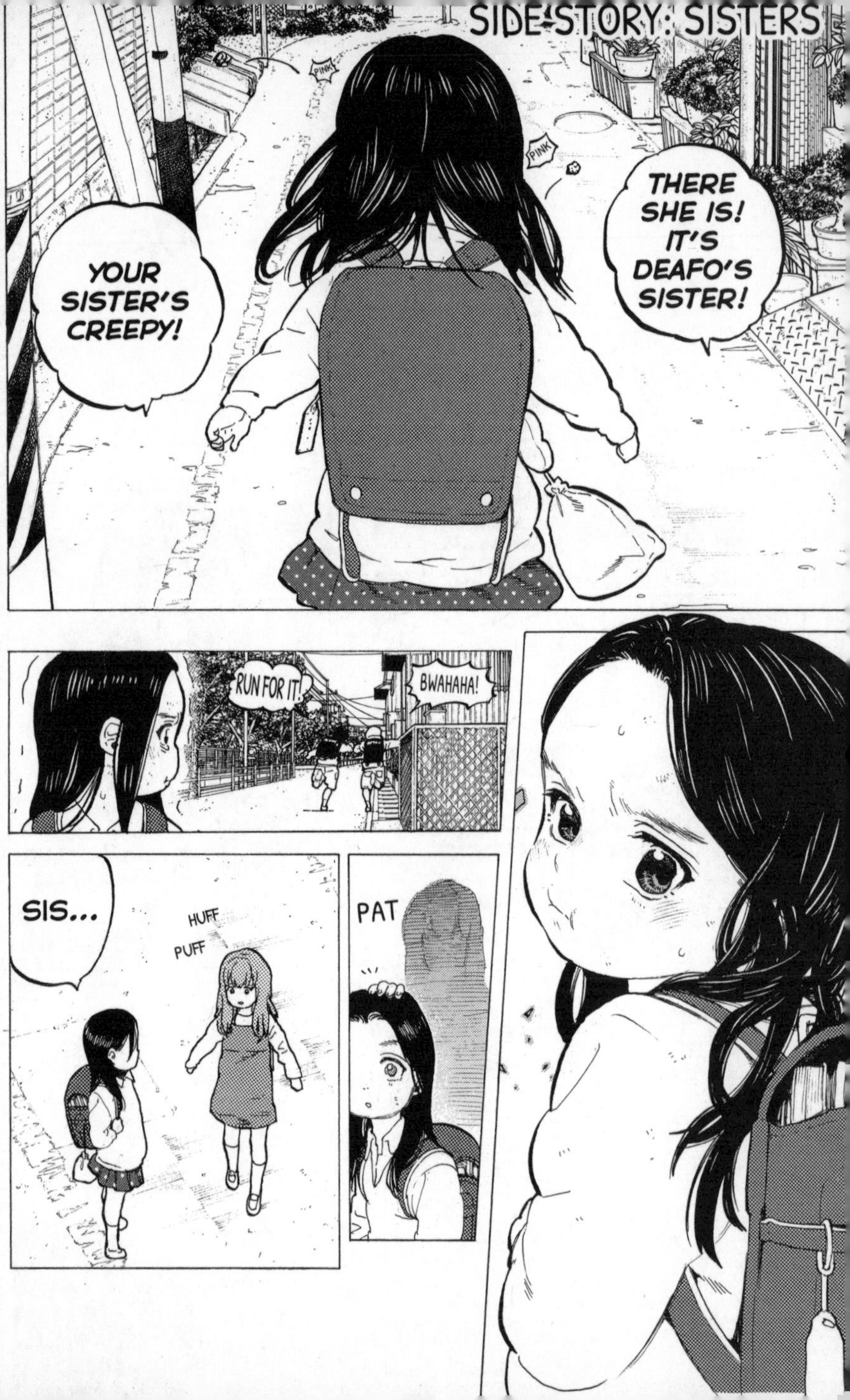
SIDE STORY: SISTERS
PINK
PINK
THERE SHE IS! IT'S DEAFO'S SISTER!
YOUR SISTER'S CREEPY!
BWAHAHA!
RUN FOR IT!
PAT
SIS...
HUFF
PUFF

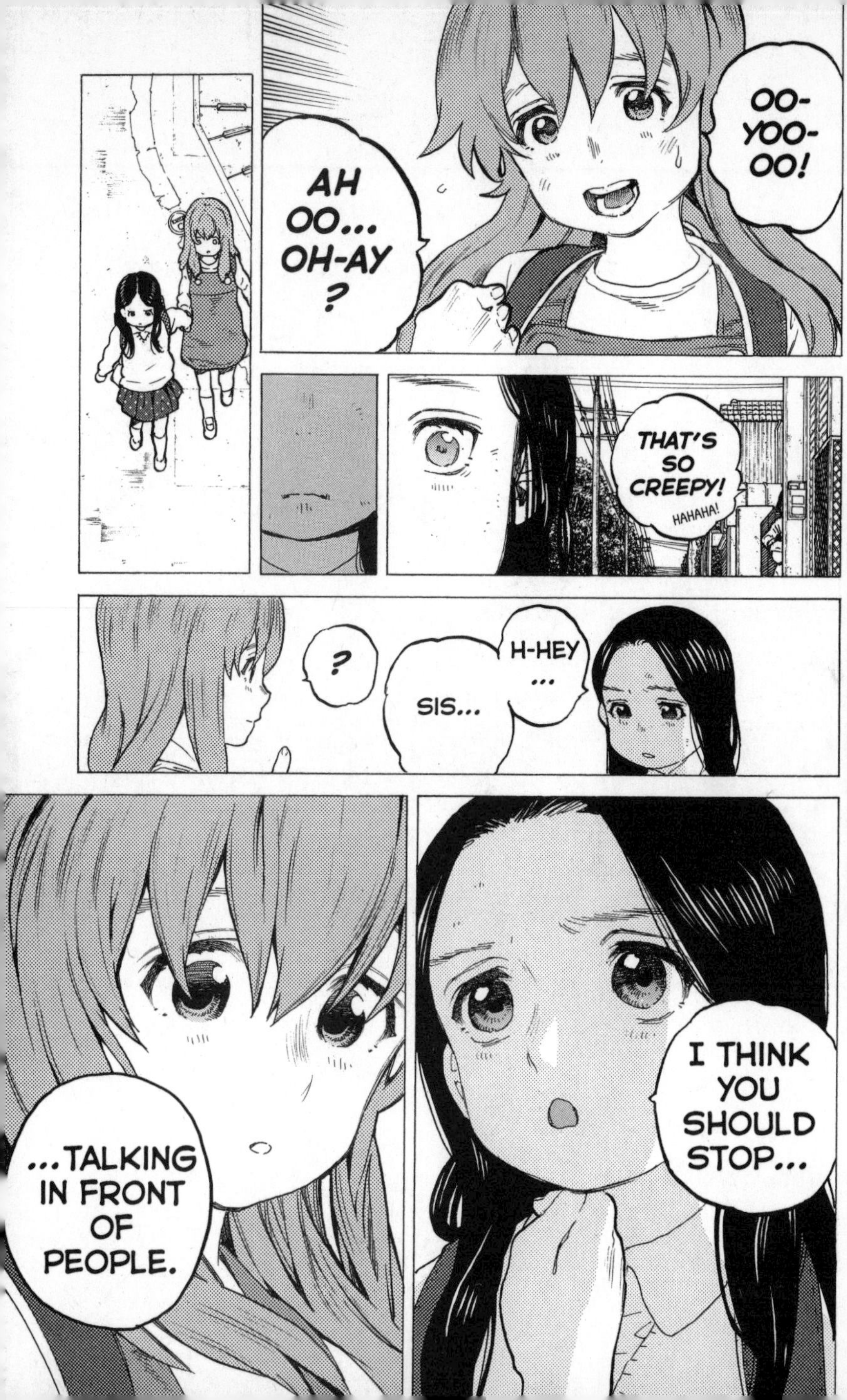
OO-YOO-OO!
AH OO... OH-AY?
THAT'S SO CREEPY!
HAHAHA!
H-HEY...
SIS...
?
I THINK YOU SHOULD STOP...
...TALKING IN FRONT OF PEOPLE.

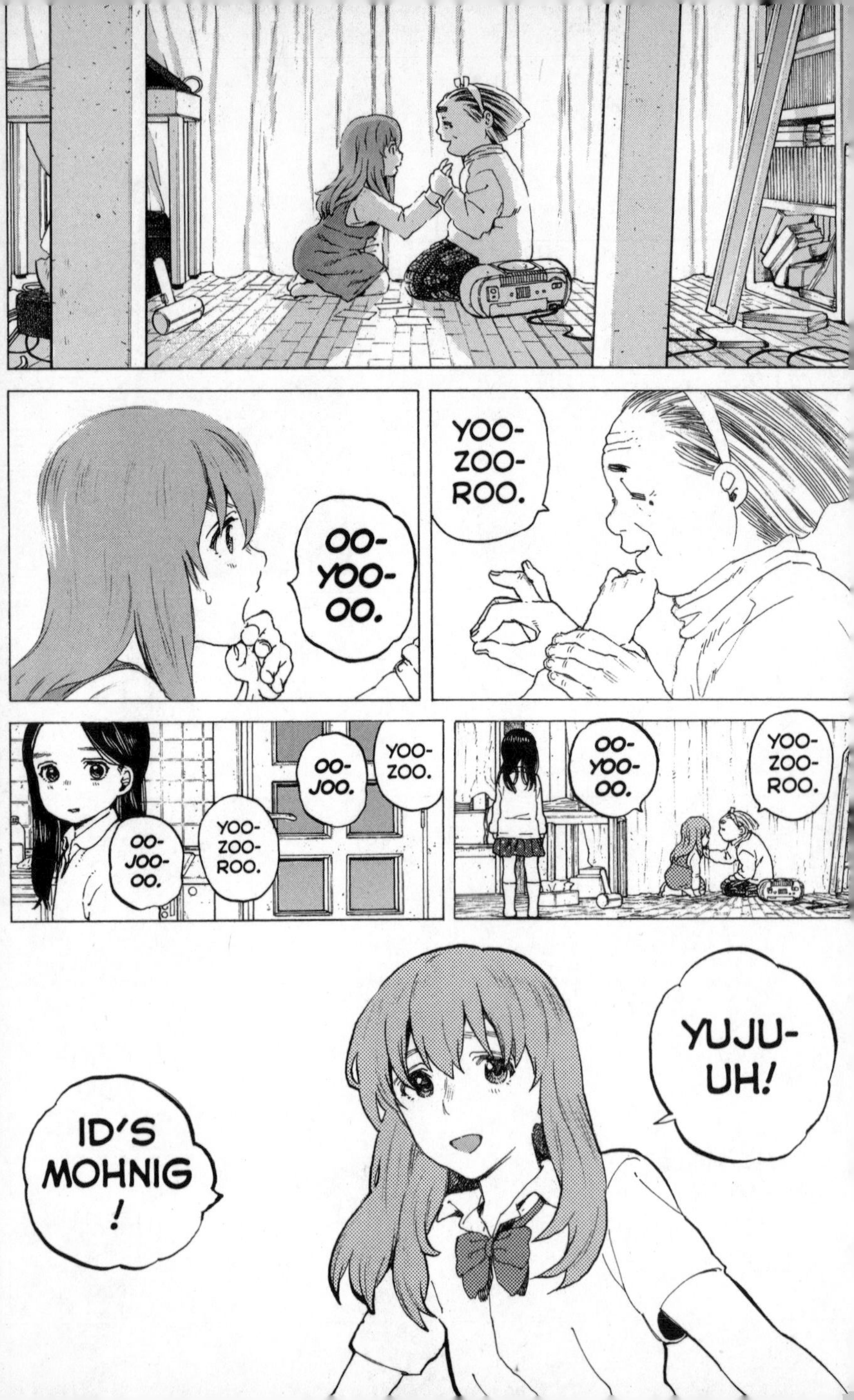
YOO-ZOO-ROO.
OO-YOO-OO.
YOO-ZOO-ROO.
OO-YOO-OO.
YOO-ZOO.
OO-JOO.
YOO-ZOO-ROO.
OO-JOO-OO.
YUJU-UH!
ID'S MOHNIG!

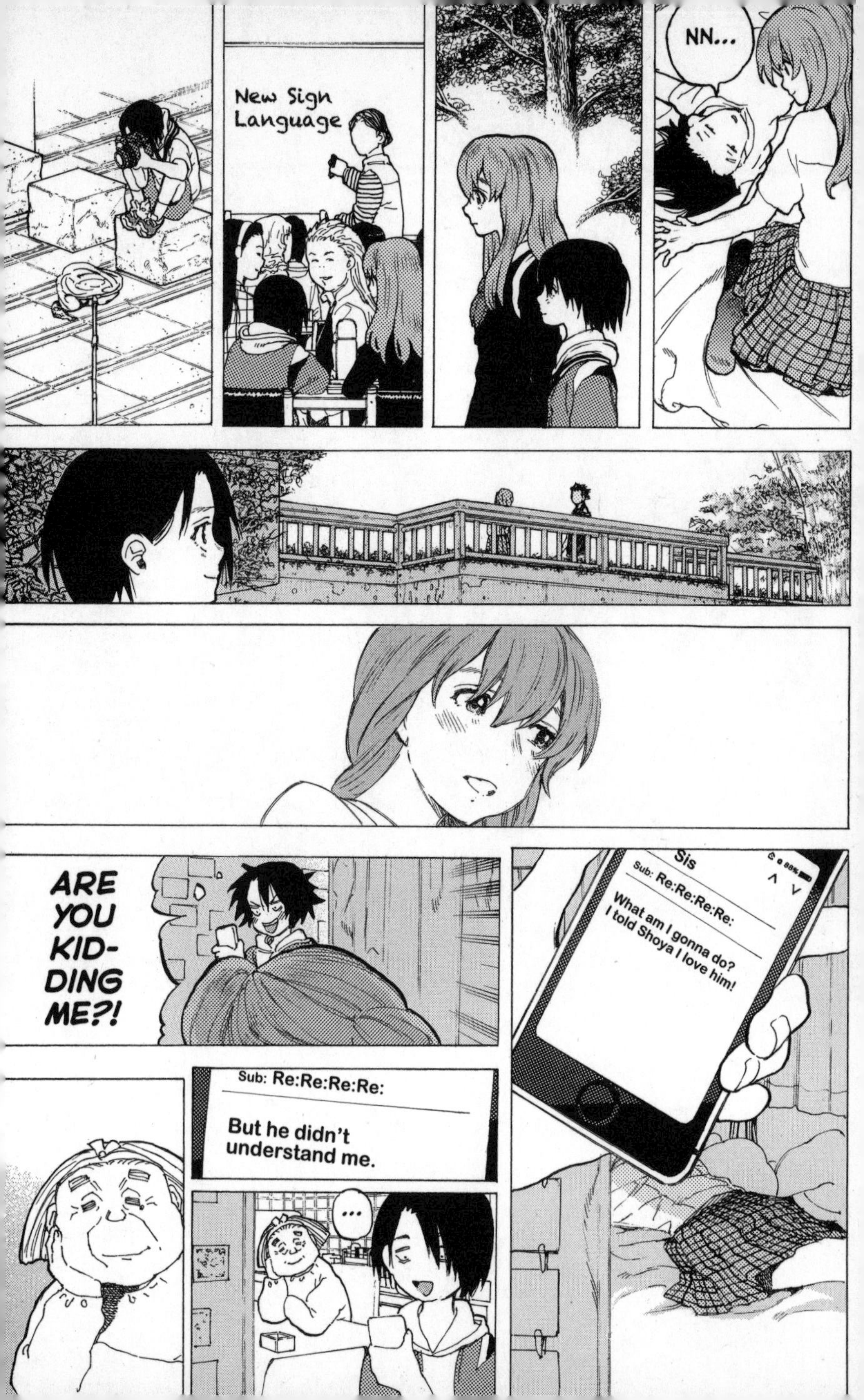
NN...
New Sign Language
Sis
Sub: Re:Re:Re:Re:
What am I gonna do? I told Shoya I love him!
ARE YOU KID-DING ME?!
Sub: Re:Re:Re:Re:
But he didn't understand me.
...

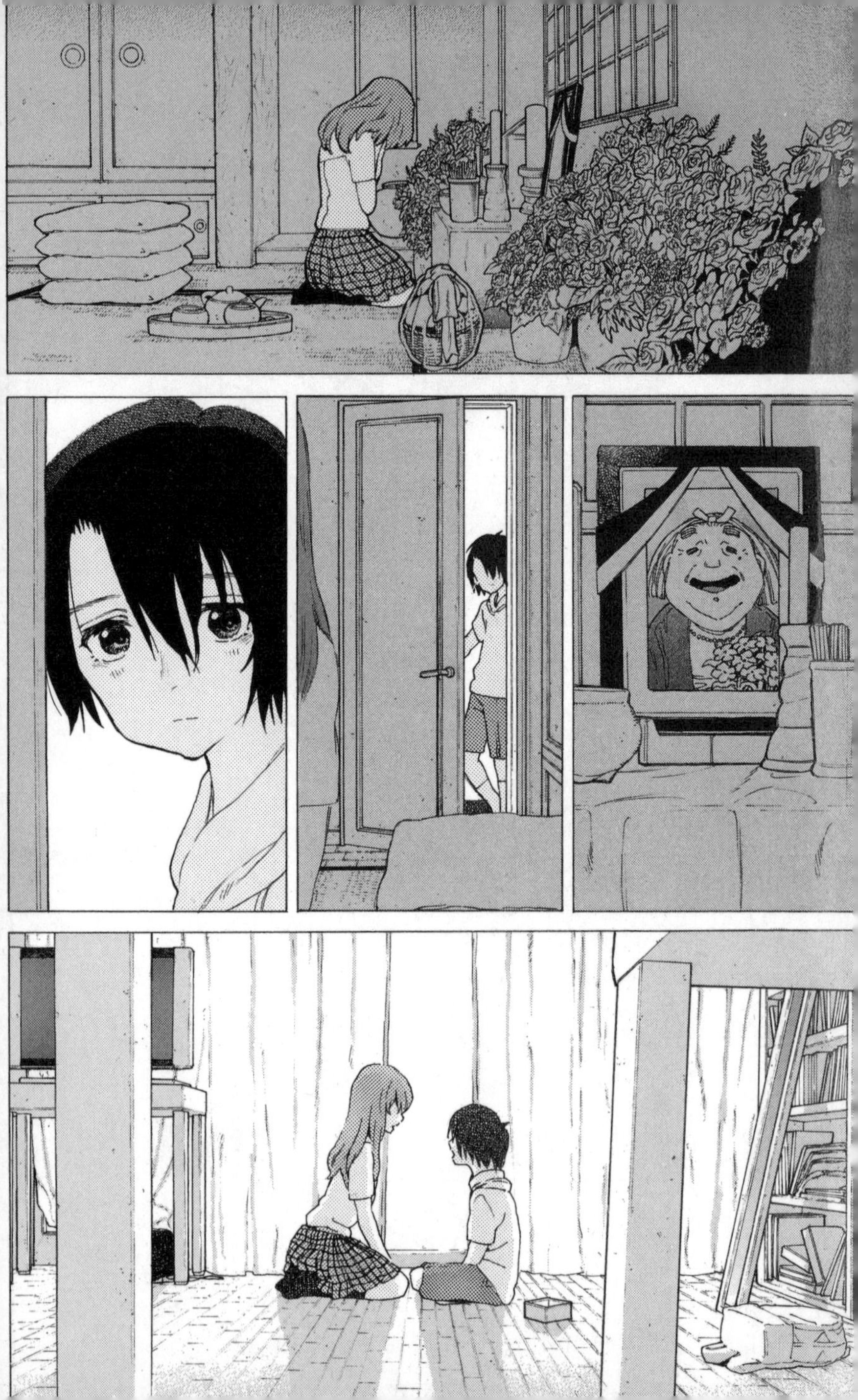

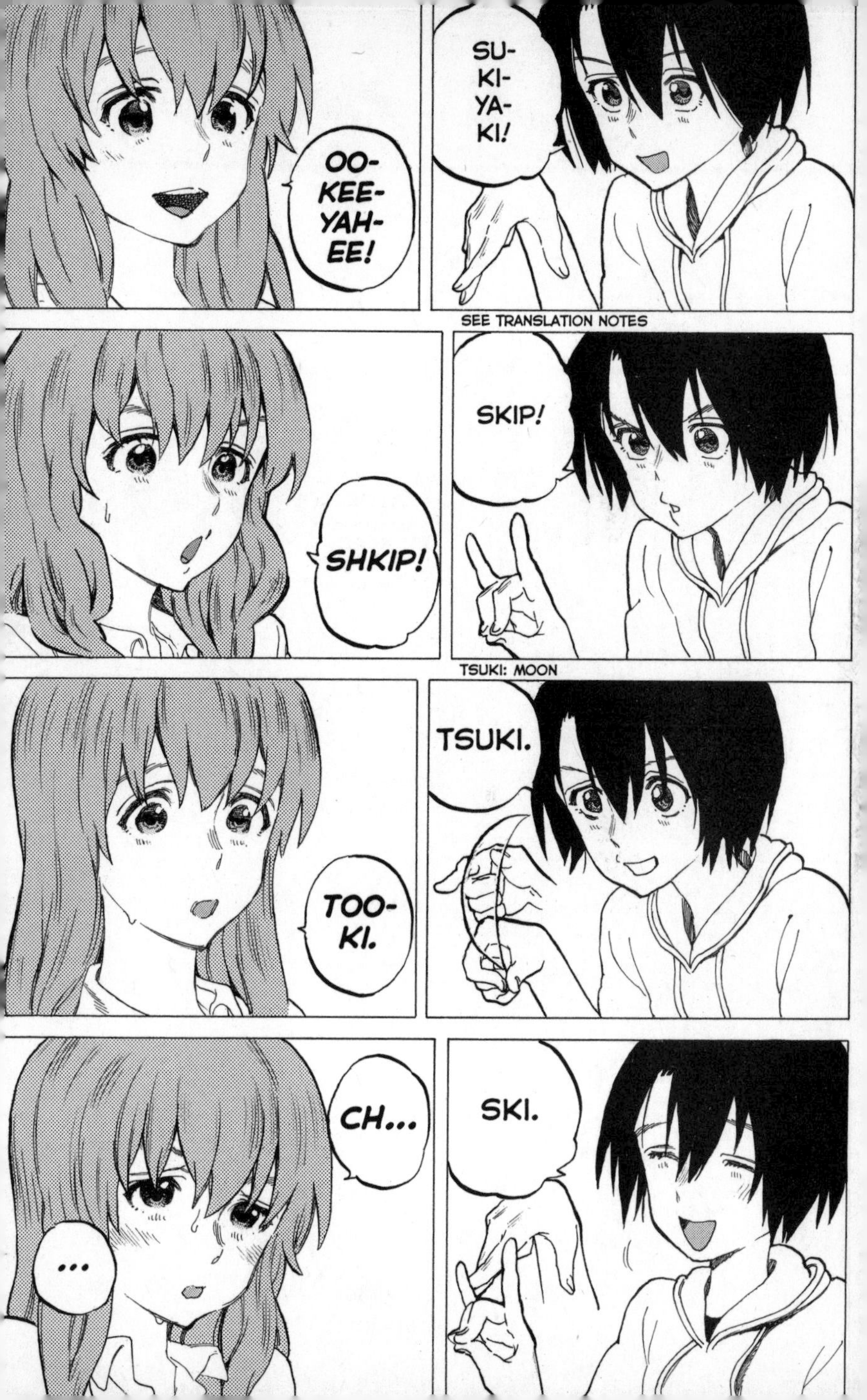
SU-KI-YA-KI!
OO-KEE-YAH-EE!
SEE TRANSLATION NOTES
SKIP!
SHKIP!
TSUKI: MOON
TSUKI.
TOO-KI.
SKI.
CH...
...

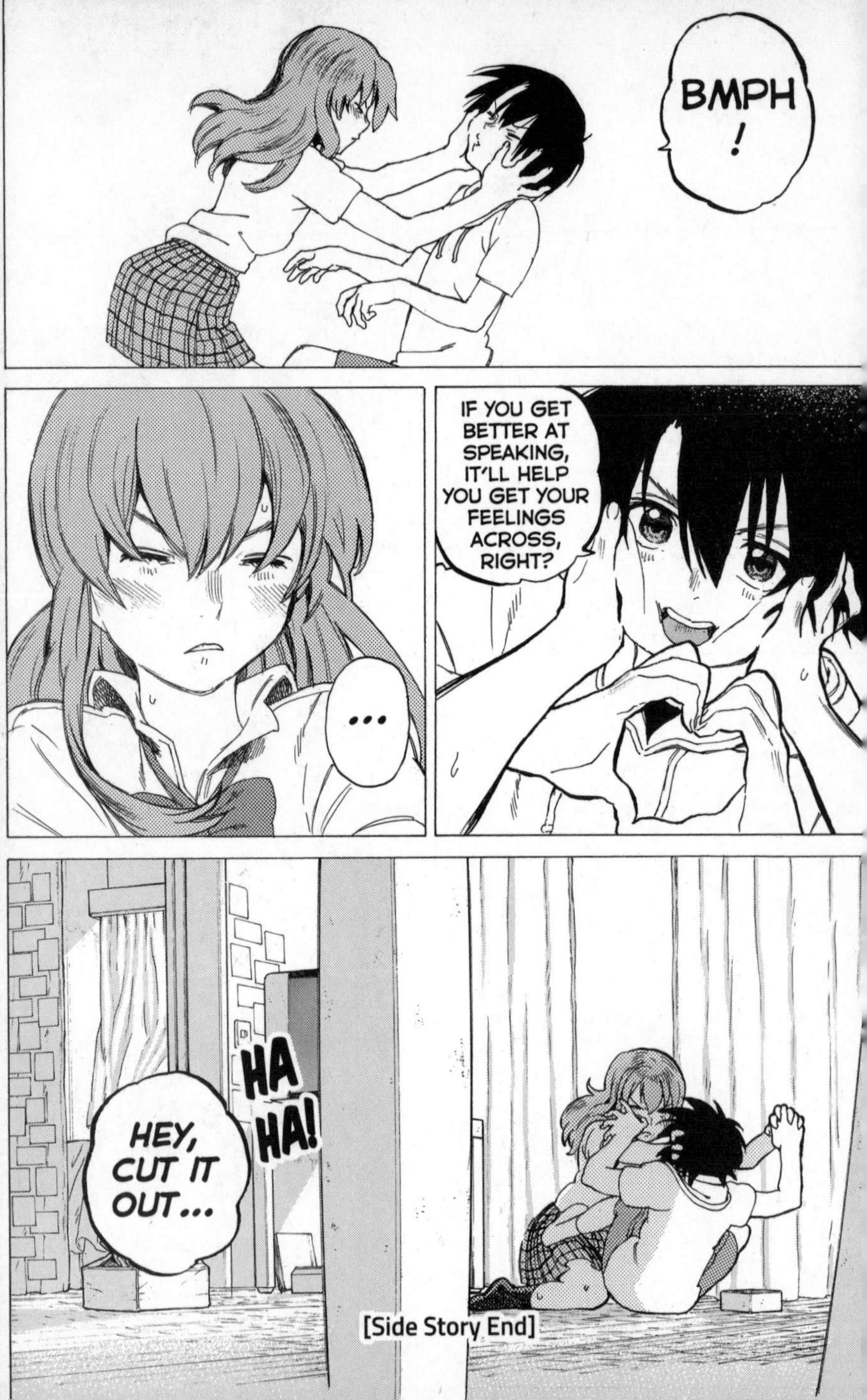
BMPH!
IF YOU GET BETTER AT SPEAKING, IT'LL HELP YOU GET YOUR FEELINGS ACROSS, RIGHT?
...
HA HA!
HEY, CUT IT OUT...
[Side Story End]

a Silent Voice

Translation Notes

Japanese can be a difficult language for some readers, and translation is often more art than science. For your edification and reading pleasure, here are notes on some of the places where we could have gone in a different direction with our translation, or where a Japanese cultural reference is used.

Takoyaki, p.40

Takoyaki is a popular Japanese festival food and street food; *tako* is the Japanese word for "octopus" and *yaki* means "grilled." It is a savory, bite-sized ball of batter that is cooked with a piece of octopus in the middle. It has many variations of seasonings and flavors, but is traditionally served with a special sauce, bonito flakes, and *aonori* seaweed flakes. Since they are bite-sized snacks, each order has multiple pieces, making it easy to share. In volume three of *A Silent Voice* (p.93), you can see Kazuki and Keisuke in the background, eating takoyaki at a festival.

Yuzuru teaches Shoko how to pronounce words, p.189

To say, "I love you" in Japanese, you would say, "*suki.*"
Here, Yuzuru teaches Shoko how to pronounce other Japanese words that sound like *suki*, so that Shoya can understand her message. In Japanese, Yuzuru's choice of words sound like: *suki*yaki (a Japanese dish), *su-kippu* (skip), *tsuki* (moon), and *su-kee* (ski). At the end of volume three, as recalled on p.19 in this volume, Shoya mistakes Shoko's confession of "lub moo" as "the moon," because *tsuki* and *suki* sound very similar.